MANAGING EMOTIONS

CREATE, ENHANCE, AND MAINTAIN HARMONY

Joseph A. Bailey II MD, FACS

Member of the clinical faculty at the UCR/UCLA Division of Biomedical Sciences at the University of California, Riverside

Managing Emotions

Printed in the United States of America

Published by WingSpan Press, Livermore, CA

www.wingspanpress.com

ISBN: 978-1-59594-223-4

First edition 2007

Library of Congress Control Number: 2007941244

CONTENTS

ABOUT THE COVER x

PREFACE xi

Chapter I OVERVIEW OF EMOTIONS 1
- The Evolution Of Emotions 3
- The Emotional Experience 6
- The Mind's Castle Committee 7
- Emotional Reactions 11
- Emotional Triggers 14
- "Trigger" Emotions and 'Target" Emotions 16

Chapter II EMOTIONAL SOURCES AND MATRIXES 22
- Selfishness 24
  - Destructive Selfishness 26
  - Constructive Selfishness 29
- The Brain/Mind 30

Chapter III THE DEVELOPMENT OF EMOTIONS 39
- Good Emotions 41
- Bad Emotions 45
  - Attacks 51
  - Child Abuse 52
  - Disrespect 54
  - Loneliness 60
  - Rejection 61

Chapter IV THE FIVE BASIC NATURAL EMOTIONS 68
- Rage/Anger 71
- Fear 90
- Depression 103
- Emotional Pain 120
- Pleasure 132

Chapter V COMPLEX "NORMAL" EMOTIONS 147
- Anxiety 151
- Belonging 164
- Disappointment 165
- Embarrassment 165

Grief 168
Hurt Feelings 169
Mourning 169
Non-Hateful Envy 170
Greed 173
Guilt 178
Humiliation 183
Jealousy 184
Pride 189
Shame 191

Chapter VI EMOTIONS INSIDE MINDSETS 196
Defense Mechanisms 198
Emotions inside Addictions 199
Emotions inside Apathy 202
Emotions inside Arrogance 205
Emotions inside Complexes 207
Inferiority Complex: 208
Superiority Complex 210
Emotions inside Delusions 211
Emotions inside Frustrations 214
Emotions inside an Overwhelmed Mindset 226
Emotions inside Suffering 231
Emotions inside Worry 232

Chapter VII ESCAPE EMOTIONS 237
Denial 239
Dissociations 241
Distortion 242
Fantasy 244
"Fright" Emotions 246
Insulation of Emotions 247
Repression 249
Wishes 252

Chapter VIII MASQUERADE EMOTIONS 253
Blame 255
Civility Emotions 259
Disguise 261
Hypocrisy 261
Naggers 262
Projection 262

Reaction Formation 263
Suppression 263
Withdrawal 265

Chapter IX EVIL EMOTIONS 268
Hate 269
Cause of Hate 272
Ignorance 272
Revenge 273
Categories of Hate 278
Indifference 278
Aversion 278
Adversion 278
Hateful Envy 281
Masochism 284
Sadism 287
General Management of Hate 289

Chapter X SELFHOOD TOOLS FOR HANDLING EMOTIONS 292
General Orientation for Managing Emotions 294
Philosophy of Life 294
Emotional Maturity 303
General Methods for Managing Emotions 307
Congenial Mindset 307
Courage 307
Methods for Tool Usage 311
The "SOBMER" Process 312
Bridge Method 316
Check Method 317
The Court Room Method 318
Desensitization 321
Cognitive Psychology 322
The Philosophical Psychology Method 326

Chapter XI MANAGING EMOTIONAL FLAWS 329
Management Overview of Emotions 330
Flaws in Good Emotions 332
Flaws Leading To Bad Emotions 334
People Types Who Cause Flaws 336
Problems with Being Liked 339
Switching To Good Emotions 341
Replace Flawed Mindsets 343

Helplessness Mindsets 345
Hopelessness Mindsets 347
Stubbornness Mindset 349
Vulnerable Mindsets 356
Moving On With Your Life 358
Letting Go 358
Forgiveness 358
Self-Forgiveness 361
Self-Love 363
Spiritual Pain 364
Love Your Enemies 366

CONCLUSIONS 367

REFERENCES 369

ILLUSTRATIONS

Figure 1	The Three Brains of Humans, 33
Figure 2	The Stress Curve, 73
Figure 3	Thinker's Scale, 77
Figure 4	Good Character Wheel, 103
Figure 5	Comb Concept, 148
Figure 6	Life Triangle Arenas, 153
Figure 7	Skyscraper Building Concept, 295
Figure 8	One's Acquired Nature, 297
Figure 9	Spiritual Feelings Connections, 299
Figure 10	Check Method, 311
Figure 11	Bridge Method, 311

Table I	Planes of Existence, 6
Table II	Frequency Scale, 70
Table III	A Classification of Offensive Language, 75
Table VI	Self-Confidence Cultivation, 95
Table V	Rational Thinking Steps, 97
Table VI	Classification of Pleasure, 136
Table VII	Formation of Complex Emotions, 149
Table VIII	Defense Mechanisms, 199
Table IX	Emotional Planes of Existence, 269
Table X	Five "S" Human Fundamentals, 305
Table XI	An Experience, 312

ABOUT THE COVER

This book's cover consists of caricatures of special façade appearances seen in many emotional people. One idea for its cover design came from spending many early morning hours watching seagulls at the marina fishing dock. Their day's work consists of pursuing fishing boats arriving into harbor (in hopes of catching food scraps from filleted fish thrown overboard by fishermen). When full, they perch on rails and wires around the "Bait" sign to rest and to observe the ocean.

Between feeding times they show emotional reactions similar to those that characterize emotional people. Most engage in emotional noisy play— as when one gull holds the wing of another to prevent that other from going into water. A few of these long-winged swimming birds are isolated from the others and one or two seem to be alone in the crowd. Some are quarrelsome and often threaten and scream at other birds who invade their space. So as to maintain peace and order among them all, my self-assigned job is to supervise these seagulls.

A second idea for the cover has derived from the histrionic presentations (see text discussion) in each of three groups of my orthopaedic surgical patients: (1) the Honest and Straight Forward (who may display histrionics but only because it reflects cultural socialization); (2) the Self-Deceivers (those with Somatoform Disorders who believe they have an organic problem but do not—or at least it is not as bad as they present); and (3) the Conscious Deceivers (liars for the purpose of obtaining some secondary gain).

Self-Deceivers and Conscious Deceivers are specialist in verbal and behavioral histrionics as, for example, a "ceremonial gait." Their objective is to impress by means of histrionics rather than to "connect" with the physican. Behind their façade is tremendous emotional pain and suffering—both of which display as every conceivable negative or bad emotion and like-kind behavior.

Examples of their histrionic display are illustrated by different pictures on the cover—e.g. those whose low self-esteem can be symbolized by the chicken (because that is how they feel); or the arrogant male who acts as if he is a lion; or the emotionally disturbed female who wears too much make-up.

Interacting with emotionally disturbed patients and others has taught me several things. By increasing my understanding (via listening and through empathy) of them as unique individuals and as a group, my tolerance and compassion capacities expanded. For example, deliberate liars formerly angered me until the realization that, instead of judging, the physician's job is to merely diagnosis and treat. Because Self-Deceivers and Conscious Deceivers do have significant problems—albeit it emotional—I no longer judge them or others— and, instead, just accept people "as I find them."

PREFACE

Son, I want you to be dignified, cultured, and refined!" Although Mother never elaborated on these words and although as a boy I was never sure what she meant, writing this book on "Managing Emotions" has given me an idea about how to take the first step toward this masterpiece achievement.

Dignified is powered by the loving spirit within ones character and displays in a compassionate and forceful manner. *Cultured*, a lofty elevation of ones Mind and Soul, results from a Poetic interweave of Intellect and Pure Feelings. *Refined* is sincere mannerly, courteous, and principled behavior.

The development of these three starts with the prevention, the stoppage, the masterful control, the modification, and/or the shedding of ones self-defeating emotions and passions. This book's general purpose is to give suggestions for designing such self-improvement. Its Foundational Priniciples are from Ancient African Philosophy because those principles have benefitted me and, during a 40 year orthopaedic surgical practice, my patients.

A specifically focused purpose is to give management approaches and methods that can be customized for the struggling poor. From having been one of them and from direct dealings with them socially and as a physician, I believe the causes of and ingredients inside their emotions are quite different from those in other members of society. If so, mis-diagnoses and inappropriate treatment by unaware mental health specialists are quite likely.

Besides my exposure-based orientation to the struggling poor, other factors have fashioned a management approach quite different from Western approaches. It started by my limited formal exposure to Western psychiatry or psychology. That exposure consisted of only a semester at the University of Michgan (Psychology in Industry) and a semester of "An Introduction to Psychiatry" at Meharry Medical School (Nashville, Tennessee).

The gap further widened by the way I formed ideas about Managing Emotions: by trial-and-error socially and in medical practice; by enlarging upon what worked for me; and by studying Ancient African Philosophy. Out of those three spring my suggestions for the self-improvement of the struggling poor; for bettering their interactions with "difficult" people; and for their proper mindset in handling "tough problems."

Much of what I learned before being aware of Ancient African Philosophy came from experiential approaches as a U. S. Air Force general practioner in the Philippines. Here, I developed the habit of doing the simplest things first.

As a private practice orthopaedic surgeon, specializing in treating injuried workers, I learned a great deal about emotions from three groups. The *Honest and Straight Forward* Group—i.e. "normal" patients —taught me about "normal" emotions associated with pain. The organically healthy *Self-Deceiver* patients devise quite creative emotional presentations in trying to prove their false belief in being organically sick. The organically healthy *Conscious Deceiver* patients show great anger or other emotional displays to convince physicians of their knowingly false disabilities.

Perhaps in sufficient numbers to fill up a professional baseball stadium, I evaluated each patient—e.g. taking a thorough history, doing a thorough physical examination, and reviewing pertinent laboratory and radiographic records. In at least half of those evaluated, I reviewed thick medical records related (among others) to their emotional problems.

Each individual in the Self-Deceiver Group and the Conscious Deceiver Group requires unique management approaches and methods for his/her unique problems. Thus, it has been essential for me to remain "open" to any management program that does no harm and yet might work—like recommending to receptive patients a "full moon and a sweet potato." Such openness began in medical school upon hearding an amazing statistic. Western physicians' cure rate of patients is 81.3% and for ritual specialist of Africa (whom Westerners derogatorily call "Voodoo doctors") it is 87.9%.

A great expansion of my understanding about emotions occurred after an early retirement from practice. One realm derived from the practical experience gained in living among and mentoring struggling Black and Hispanic youth—individually and in organized programs (e.g. The Los Angeles Conservation Core, in Boys and Girls Club workshops, youth in "special" schools, Church Youth Groups, and the Cub and Boy Scouts).

Another was from intense research into African American slavery, Black American history, and Ancient African history. A surprising research finding was that "Reality" for Ancient Africans embraced the Subjective, the Spiritual, and the Objective as part of Wholism (spiritual interrelatedness of all God's creations). They believed the Objective arose out of the Subjective and the Spiritual—and all three serve as foundations of Truth.

Whereas African Tradition is oriented to understanding Truth and Reality by means of Wholistic synthesis on and of all planes of existence, Western authorities prefer a linear analysis limited to the Tangible (the Objective) as the only thing "Real" enough to be used as evidence or proof. An analogy is in dealing with the entire hub and spokes of a wheel (the African approach) as opposed to dealing with one spoke, or part of one spoke (the Western approach). The differences in making choices, decisions, and solutions lead the Afrocentric and Eurocentric in opposite lifestyle directions.

The subject of Emotions is so huge as to be impossible to cover completely. Since Anger is the dominant emotion of the struggling poor, it has been dealt with separately in my book: Anger In Black Americans. In that book are special sections (e.g. Chapter X— "Philosophical Management") pertinent to managing the 116 Emotions discussed herein.

My suggestions inside "Managing Emotions" are offered only for people whose emotional problems are not bad enough to seek the care of mental health specialist. Even then, professional advice is recommended first— if it is available, affordable, and suitable.

Chapter I is an Overview of Emotions— the Emotional Experience and it keystone factors.

Chapter II discusses the Sources (e.g. Selfishness) and Matrixes (the Brain/ Mind) of emotions.

Chapter III is about the Causes of Good and Bad Emotions

Chapter IV elaborates on the Five Basic Emotions—Rage, Fear, Depression, Emotional Pain, and Pleasure.

Chapter V pertains to the Complex Emotions that are normal in human beings. They are an inter-weave of thoughts and emotions.

Chapter VI delves into the special world of specific emotions inside different types of mindsets.

Chapter VII, the Escape Emotions, are those used to run away from reality by way of mental masquerades.

Chapter VIII is Masquerade Emotions—those with double meanings (usually the opposite of the emotion expressed) and causing false realities.

Chapter IX deals with the various types of Evil Emotions

Chapter X goes into the selfhood tools needed for dealing with emotions. It starts with a general orientation and then expounds on the methods.

Chapter XI concerns how to manage Emotional Flaws in both Good and Bad Emotions. Emphasis is placed of Ancient African principles, which I believe to be the very best in existence for bringing peace and harmony throughout the world.

This book is dedicated to the truly needy and the struggling poor people.

Sincere appreciation goes to Julan Jau for her technical assistance.

Joseph A. Bailey II MD, FACS

1

OVERVIEW OF EMOTIONS

Ones Mindset
*Of **Peace** or **Conflict***
Depends upon
Ones Choice of
Thoughts** and **Feeling Tone

Two Stories-in-one of Emotions: "Emotion" ("an eddy, similar to the eddy occurring in a whirlpool) is an Aryan word for migration. It originated among Aryan nomadic tribes who lived in the grasslands of Eastern Europe, north of the Black and Caspian Seas. Although inter-tribal warfare was an everyday occurrence, fighting would stop temporarily in order to form alliances with fellow tribesmen whenever threats by "out-siders" arose.

These horse-riding bands of tribes were not a genetic race but rather they spoke a common language. As part of a larger group now known as Indo-Europeans, their great migratory movements began in successive waves from central Asia, South Russia, and Turkestan during the 2nd millennium B.C. and spread throughout such places as Iran, Mesopotamia (Sumeria, Iraq), Persia, the Balkan Peninsula, and Asia Minor (an expanded Turkey). As each civilized city fell, these warring barbarians destroyed every bit of culture and civilization they encountered and could not use.

The Aryans' superiority in the development of weapons; in the use of tools for war; and in the ability to conquer—or subdue—peaceful people led to their possession of a "sinful pride." They invaded India around 1700 B.C. and colonized the Punjab region of Northwest India; plundered the rich cities of the Indus valley civilizations; absorbed much of the culture; and considered themselves superior and noble compared to the slaves they captured. While setting up caste systems (e.g. in India), they assumed positions of kings, priest, warriors, artisans, and traders.

Besides assigning victims to be farmers, laborers, and servants as well as forbidding them to mix with the higher castes, the Aryans and their invasions profoundly affected the normally calm minds and peaceful living conditions of their victims. These invasions, characterized by a "vehemence of passion," generated in the civilized slave victims a stirred-up mental agitation. Because those victims were forever moved out of their peaceful states of mind, this dynamic was known as a "shaking of the heads."

Meanwhile and also starting in ancient times, an analogus "stirring" situation occurred when earthquakes caused ocean tidal waves. Since its turbulence rumbled within caverns, people believed that whereas the calm ocean simply vibrated, the rumbling tidal waves inside caverns meant stirred up vibrations—a stirring accounting for the eddying of the water.

By them defining "Feelings" as "vibrations, it was an easy next step to link the calm ocean (with its vibrations) to "Feelings." By extension, the tidal waves' stirred up vibrations rumbling in caverns were equated to stirred-up "Feelings" (eventually termed "Emotions"). Hence, to have a "rumbling" in ones head was to have stirred up vibratory motor energy headed away from its center and toward the outside.

So how did "rumbling vibrations" and "shaking of the heads" combine to contribute to ideas inside the word "Emotion"? Recall that the 16th century BC physical migratory movement of the Aryan invaders caused conquered civilized people to be mentally stirred-up. This mental stirring was metaphorically applied to "strongly affecting the Feelings"—equivalent to "rumbling vibrations." In a religious sense "agitated feelings" literally referred to "movement of the spirit" brought about by "shaking of the heads."

During the Renaissance support for these ideas was the rediscovery of Aristotle's (384-322 B.C.) works—works influential in extending "physical migrations of people" into the mental realm of emotions. This as well as the concepts of "rumbling vibrations" associated with eddying of water and the "movement of the spirit" gave rise to the 16th century European word "**Emotion**" ("moving out with agitation"). Since different types of eddies with different types of effects could be seen in the tidal waves inside the caverns, this served as the basis for subdividing emotions.

For example, if an eddy current was stirring clockwise, it was called a **Positive Emotion**; if the eddy current was stirring counter-clockwise it was deemed to be a **Negative Emotion** (not the same as "Bad" or "Destructive, which were said to be from evil spirits).

Gradually, there were concept branches. Anything causing Feelings to move into

Emotions became known as EMOTIVE. Whereas both Emotion and Motives refer to the motor that moves things, MOTIVES were said to move one *within* oneself while Emotions move one *out of* oneself. Thus, when people "emote," they literally move out of their minds. Clear emotive (i.e. expressive) language is offensive language—the swearing or spewing of obscenities used by people under stress to get rid of nervous energy (Table III).

However, an unspoken context for the connotation of this meaning of "moving out of ones mind" derived from the distain Europeans—as prominently displayed by the ancient Greeks—had for "female" dominated mental features. Hence, after the European Renaissance (of the 15th-16th centuries), "Emotion," like "Depression," became a lenient term for the human weakness of showing stirred up feelings under stress—e.g. agitation, excitement, fear, anger, surprise, or grief.

Thereafter, more "Emotion" branches occurred: e.g. specific emotive utterances as involuntary responses to beautiful art or scenery (like "Ahhh"); expressions of fear or affection; and the outpourings found in a great deal of poetry. Those outpourings were often elevated sufficiently to reverse the process of "Feelings giving rise to Emotion" to that of Lofty Emotions now generating a higher state of "Feelings"—i.e. "Feelings of the Sublime."

THE EVOLUTION OF EMOTIONS

One of the great birth systems animals and humans have in common is that of Feelings associated with behavior. Even the lowest form of animal life —the one cell creatures called Monera —shows behavior based on feeling with their senses. BEHAVIOR, in its broadest sense, is an action or a reaction done by living things and generated by the three main subdivisions of the System of Feelings.

Spiritual or Pure Feelings are those which connect ones Real Self with the Sublime (as discussed later).

Physical feelings are behaviors affecting the physical body, as in touching a hot stove.

Psychical Feelings have a purely mental source and arise from some idea or mental state; they cause pleasure or pain of a non-physical nature. Like a cross, stirred up psychical feelings can go in a positive (pleasure) or negative (self-preservation) or destructive (harmful) or constructive (improvement) direction. Or, psychical emotions may go off on an angle to involve combinations — like finding pleasure in hard work that is designed to make something better; or the over-use of negative and destructive emotions—as in unrealistic situations which lead to harm of oneself and/or others. Out of these three have come a **Classification of Feelings**:

Affections— Loving feelings that go out toward a person(s), a place, an animal, a plant, a thing, or oneself for the purpose of creating, maintaining, or enhancing harmony. A true display is affection for a person is shown by patience and tolerance of whatever is non-hateful and non-evil.

Desires—Concentrated feelings related to cravings in order to acquire something one lacks.

Emotions, as mentioned, are stirred up feelings whose purpose is to create, enhance, or maintain pleasure; call attention to something significance; or defend self-preservation. Stirred up feelings may be about one emotion alone or more than one becoming interwoven. Or, stirred up feelings— for good or bad— can go round and round in a circle, as in self-fulfilling prophecies.

Distorted or fantasy emotions go through something similar to **airplane acrobatic maneuvering** — outside and inverted spins, outside loops, pushovers, inverted flight and any other intended and controlled variation from a straight and level flight.

Emotions may stay in one place or be shifted (as in empathy) or become rippled (as in "win-win" situations whereby everyone concerned benefits) or be an influence on the emotions of others.

Emotions may be expressed inwardly and/or outwardly—as overt, tempered, masked, or concealed. Predator animals do attack or deception (e.g. camouflage, mimicry) to grab prey and prey do the same in order to survive.

Emotional expressions may relate to what is real, distorted, or fantasy. Either of these three may come from a place that is familiar and comforting, familiar and uncomforting, unfamiliar and comforting, unfamiliar and uncomforting, or uncomforting and exciting.

Pleasant or unpleasant emotions may spring from thoughts of harmony or disharmony. For example, unpleasant harmonious thoughts are associated with cutting out a cancer so as to improve the patient's quality of life. Pleasant thoughts of disharmony characterize revenge.

It may be that several emotions, each represented by a different colored piece of clay, are all "mashed" together to form a **glob emotion**. An example is present at birth. At this time the first visible sign of emotion is a general excitement inside of which are different "seed" emotions. This is like the genetic material inside a fertilized egg which is about to undergo meiosis into a cell which has two rounds of nuclear division.

Then, emotions evolve out of that general excitement glob. At about three months of age arise two definite emotions —pleasure and displeasure. Soon afterward, the emotions of anger, disgust, and fear appear—usually in that order. Between 6 and 12 months of age, elation and affection show in a child; and jealousy at the 18th month. Then the general emotion of distress differentiates into the more specific feelings of shame, envy, and disappointment. Youth do not fully have an emotional reaction to or appreciate the significance of death until they reach adolescence.

Meanwhile, at its best, *Emotional control begins in the 24th month.* However, but much of this depends, if it occurs at all, on the nature and tone of ones thoughts and feelings/emotions. Those of a Sublime nature and tone are unified; those in Tangible realms are not. The worst emotions are thoughts of disharmony and feeling tones that are unpleasant. The best emotions are harmonious thoughts combined with pleasant feeling tones.

The **COSMIC LADDER**: If you can imagine an "A" FRAME STEP-LADDER of the Feelings/Emotional Awareness of human beings extending from the earth to the Sublime (Table I), this illustrates the relationship of Emotions (on the lower rungs) to Feelings (on the top rungs). At the top of the ladder are Sublime Feelings and as they extend down the ladder they become increasingly stirred into Emotions. The point is that things look separate and individualist at an earth world (i.e. Tangible) level and yet become harmonious and unified at a Sublime level—an experience common people of such awareness.

To elaborate, as a 13 year old boy my Mother, a high school English teacher, confused me each time she said: *"Beauty is in the eye of the beholder"* and then followed this with: *"a thing of beauty is a joy forever."* Since two of my outdoor jobs were tending to the flower and vegetable gardens and painting the house, the latter caused me to think of my flower garden (though the flowers did not last forever).

Her first saying led to a mental picture of my "A" frame step-ladder—with its two ladders hinged at the top and its opposite end resting on the ground, as if each leg represented four humans. In other words, her two phrases seemed to be at opposite ends of the cosmos. So great was my mental conflict over these two phrases that one day I rode my bicycle to a downtown book store in Greensboro, North Carolina to look up "beauty" in a "big fat" dictionary.

Item 13 under "beauty" sort of correlated "a thing of beauty is a joy forever" with the top step of the step-ladder. However, at the bottom, each leg was like an individual "beholder" living a unique life, having a unique philosophy, and being uniquely individualist. But as people climb each step, their lives, their philosophies, and their individualism become more and more alike until, at the top, they have a "Group Mind" and a "Group Spirit"—a unity.

However, unsophisticated individuals see beauty—not as a unity—but based upon what satisfies their unique taste. For them, "beauty is in the eye of the beholder." As they reach higher planes of existence, they will begin to see that **"All is in One and One is in All**." To realize this perspective leads to an awe-inspiring inner atmosphere—an atmosphere checkered with reverence–an atmosphere causing one to be forever overwhelmed with pleasure in its highest realm.

Table I -- **Planes of Existence**

A. The **Immaterial** and unknowable Plane (i.e. Spiritual) of the heavens has no boundaries; no beginning, middle, or end; no definition.

B. The **Sublime** Plane (**Intangible**), made of pre-matter, is above time and space; has boundaries but they are beyond human perception. It contains the world's highest concentration of love, goodness, truth, and beauty—and is located just below the heavens.

C. The **Tangible** (made of matter) is subdivided into three parts.

1. Unbounded Tangible. It contains the earliest matter, like a thought energy (limited only by time and space unless of a Sublime nature present in thought clouds).
2. Partially Bounded Tangible. Its items have hazy boundaries -- heat, cold, electricity, radiation, sound, and emotions -- and can sort of be defined. Can be experienced but not seen or touched.
3. Concrete Tangible (completely bounded) is specifically defined by size, weight, number, mass, volume, height, extent, and/or capacity. People agree on definitions because the objects can be seen, touched, and measured.

In descending this Cosmic ladder from the Sublime to the Earth (Table 1), the offspring of each Lofty thing takes on more and more matter and therefore acquires more and more boundaries so that mental pictures can appear. Individual "beholders" interpret mental pictures uniquely.

THE EMOTIONAL EXPERIENCE

The emotional experience (Table XI) has three aspects—the experience itself in the outside world; the experience in the brain; and the interpretation the outside experience is given by an individual's mind committee. Both of these relate to what actually happened or to what is now happening. Factors involved include:

(1) What the person believed happened—which may be somewhat accurate (yet, honest men differ), quite distorted, or a complete fantasy;

(2) How the person interpreted what he/she believed happened;

(3) The purpose of the experience on the interpretation and

(4) What the person plans to do about what he/she concluded.

To illustrate these four aspects, Ancient Africans knew the great importance of the heart, although they did not understand its true importance or its true function. The feelings they had about things were real. However, since they did not know where psychological feelings were located, they placed them inside the heart. From that belief has come such interpretations and conclusions that "*warm hearted*" means friendly or "*broken-hearted*" means crushed by sorrow.

These beliefs have slowly been replaced by the modern knowledge of what the heart really does in the body but even now all is not known. Here is a concept of these four aspects are handled in the mind.

THE MIND'S CASTLE COMMITTEE

During the European Middle Ages "*everybody*" was fighting everybody else. To have a place of residence as well as a place of defense, the rich built "castles" — a word meaning fort. A castle was often built on a route, perhaps overlooking a pass or a river crossing, where the garrison (the warriors) could stop the advancing enemy or at least cut off their supplies if they did get by. Inside the castle walls the usual residents were the lord and his household and the men who defended it. Those garrisons protected their own possessions at the castle; took by force things belonging to their neighbors; and were constantly trying to get control of more land. Their success depended upon the strength and numbers of the garrisons, the war weapons, and the location of the castle.

Some castles were built upon steep, rocky hills almost impossible to climb or reach because of cliffs on two or three sides. On the unprotected side (or sides) deep ditches, called **moats**, usually filled with water, were built outside the castle walls. If the castle was not on a hill, the moat would completely surround it. Crossing the moat was a drawbridge, which could be raised or lowered at will. Between the moat and castle was a high and thick wall called a "bailey." The "bailey" surrounded the castle and was crowned with battlements (indentations for shooting weapons). Along the wall were towers with loopholes through which arrows, spears and rocks could be hurled. Round towers were set at intervals along the wall.

Between two of the towers was the entrance to the castle enclosure. The main entrance was protected by an armored gate called a portcullis, the last barrier in the castle gate. Since the gate was the weakest point in the defense, a small outer walled enclosure; or barbican, was often built to screen it and give extra protection. If the enemy could pry up the portcullis, they found themselves in an open courtyard, called the outer ward. If the enemy could fight off the defenders from the outer ward, they had to take another low wall before reaching the inner ward.

The strongest part of the castle was the donjon, or keep — a tower-like structure designed to be easily defended, even if an enemy had captured or destroyed the rest of the castle. Its lower part was the dungeon for prisoners. If attackers entered the donjon, they still had to fight fiercely in the dark halls. Still there were escape routes where the lord and his garrison could hide in the woods.

Our minds, with its defense and coping mechanisms—both representing forms of self-protection— are very much like the fortified castle in that the same types of battles often occur in the front, in the middle, and in the recesses of our minds. **Coping Mechanisms** are actions taken to make it easier to get along in ones environment. **Defense Mechanisms** (Table VIII) are ways of handling philosophical and/or psychological concerns that are happening within oneself (Bailey, Anger p25). Just as the lord and his family lived in the donjon and made defensive and offensive decisions together, so is there a committee our minds.

Members of a person's mind who are engaged in making defensive and offensive decisions about dealing with activities of daily living are named love, right, wrong, proper, improper, legal, illegal, imagination, reason, memory, feelings, emotions, instruct, capacity, ability, talent, and others. Members that are destructive in their desires stay in the far away recesses of the mind's castle and keep their ignorance and sense of inferiority prisoners in the dungeon. They utilize all of the defenses and warring aggression similar to those present in the medieval castles. By contrast, members that are constructive live in a separate residence inside the castle. Their orientation is to seek truth, beauty, and goodness.

Within the walls of the mind's castle are also workrooms, store houses, and supplies for making whatever the constructive group or the destructive group decide it needs to reach the goal. The goal is outlined by the mind's *philosophy of life*—i.e. a prioritized system of values which consist of a Standard, of cherished Values, and a Power Approach to maneuver through the maze of life. For example, Ancient Africans' Standard was God; the cherished Values, Ma'at (love in action); and the Power Approach of Non-aggression (i.e having good relations with and good behaviors toward fellow humans). From ones philosophy of life arise intentions or leanings of the mind, desires, character, self-esteem, choices, decisions, and solutions.

Whether the constructive or the destructive group wins out in decision-making depends on which one is the stronger. Each time a choice, decision, or solution is to be made the presence or absence of Love at the committee table makes the difference. If Love is present, the constructive group wins. What happens from that point on depends on the type and effectiveness of thinking the mind uses and/or the strength of desire and willpower.

The constructive mind committee can never know everything there is to know about a real experience but mature individuals with a high level of sensitivity to all the factors involved (e.g the environment) are capable of keen appreciations of beauty and refinements of emotions.

Immature people are full of opinions from guesses but their lack of self-discipline and having minds filled with mental conflicts prevent sharp distinctions. Self-discipline, a clear mind, and pursuing one's child-like curiosity into varied interest (e.g. sports, hobbies, community activities) all lead to increasing the riches of emotional experiences.

Another reason for the wide gap between what actually happened and what we believed happened is that the experience we are in or were in was not a simple, isolated experience. No experience and no part of an experience (Table XI) can be separated from what is on all sides of it—front/back, right/left, top/bottom, and anything in between.

Whatever affects one experience affects the entire net of what is around it. For example, when a child lives in poverty, that child's health, cheerfulness, ambitions, and values are likely to be compromised. Then a compromised life-style develops in separate areas and forms a pattern which makes poverty a vicious cycle (Bailey, Rational Thinking).

Socialization—also called "*second nature*"— plays a tremendous role in the type of experiences we have and in how we intreprete those experiences. A mother reared in China but who has a son reared in the USA will have vastly different views on the same experience. The mother's view will be from the perspective of the "old school" tradition (which emphasizes peace and harmony) whereas the son will have a mix of "old school" tradition and opposing Western views (which emphasizes the material). Second nature differs from human nature (what everybody possesses) and from tertiary nature ("I'll do it my way").

The VICARIOUS Experiences about romance or superior fighting strength gained from reading, movies, television, and folktales involve feelings. Those stirred up feelings are the result of interpretating "*second-hand*" material coming from sources that may or may not have ever been real. Thus, many youth are greatly deceived into believing that the "*rich and famous*" live a wonderful life (which most do not—especially since rich nor famous are nothing special once the novelty wears off).

It is also "make-believe" or fantasy that the television hero sees, knows, hears, and does "*everything*" perfectly and is always successful and gets the best of the rewards. Once a naïve youth's attention is hooked on that purpose, each feels a hunger, an urge, a craving, a restlessness wrapped in excitement that sways them in a good (e.g. generating a thirst for knowledge) but far, far more often, in a bad (e.g. gang violence) way.

What youth plan to do is based upon their interpretations and conclusions about what they believed happened. These youth are strongly influenced by their *Emotional Vocabulary* and the kinds of pleasant or unpleasant experiences they prefer. A big part of their emotional vocabulary includes the figurative expressions they choose to describe the emotion, and which distinctions they draw between shades of an emotion. Since most have a limited vocabulary, the inability to adequately express what they are specifically feeling or experiencing is so frustrating that they usually go into an ever-ready fighting mode or become chronically hostile.

The *label degree* applied to the emotion one selects is extremely important. To say you were "terrified" when you were merely frightened; or that you were "enraged" when you were angry; or that you were happy when you were ecstatic greatly influences how you react; how you interpret what is going on; and what you do about your conclusions.

EMOTIONAL DOUBLE-EDGED SWORDS refer to the fact that a given emotion can be useful under certain circumstances and bad under other circumstances. It is proper to get angry over someone being mistreated but it is improper to be angry over things you can do nothing about. In another instance, an emotion may be beneficial at a certain intensity but not when too little or too much. To be a little anxious may help sharpen your thinking skills and concentration but if that intensity is increased, it has the opposite effect (fig. 2).

These examples are what is meant by the expression: "*double-edged sword*"— a sword that cuts both ways — that is, having opposite effects either at different times or at the same time. Its story starts in Africa about 1.5 million years ago when some bright man-like creature invented a stone knife for butchering prey. It did not take long for him and the members of his group to realize they could use that same knife to cut an enemy's throat — whether animal or human — and thereby reduce their fear or anger.

When humans came along and discovered metal, they made metal knives, lengthened them, and fashioned a cutting edge on each side — what was now called a **sword**. This sword was usually wielded with both hands. The reason is that warriors learned from experience that swinging the sword with great force not only cut off the enemy's head but sometimes, with the same stroke, cut the warrior himself. It was from this combination of a desirable as well as an undesirable action from the same instrument that gave rise to the term "*double-edged*" sword.

This concept spread into other usages. For example, the most famous of all the ancient shrines outside of Africa was the temple of Apollo at Delphi. Following the pattern laid out by Ancient Egyptians, the ancient Greeks believed that the god Apollo visited the temple to speak with its priestess about the affairs of men. People came from far and wide to seek advice from the god-inspired priestess. This was called consulting the **Oracle**. Her pronouncements were usually so ambiguous that they could be taken two different ways — one good and the other bad. Because these double-edged statements cut on either side, they were called a DELPHIC SWORD.

Modem psychologists carried this mental concept into the realm of emotions. They said, for example, that FEAR is something having an opposite effect depending upon how it is used. Examples of its good ways include preventing actions that people should not be doing (i.e. commissions). Also, fear can cause people to avoid or to escape from situations that threaten their well-being, as in life or limb; stimulate people to plan better for the future or do more reasonable actions in the present, as in driving their cars with greater alertness; and, if mild, people focus better, become sharper mentally, and are more efficient.

By contrast, too much (e.g. moderate or extreme) stress, anger, or fear causes people to feel as if their minds, bodies, and spirits have been so violently shaken as to be in a chaotic state, similar to that of a scrambled television picture. When that happens we are "out of our senses" and so upset that we have trouble trying to figure out what to do. At this point there is a tendency to Project on to others those disliked emotions within oneself as being the same emotions the other person is experiencing — perhaps stressed, angry, revengeful, hateful, or fearful—and then punish their scapegoat(s) for having those projected emotions.

The accumulation of multiple slight fears make us vulnerable to advertisers who play on our insecurities and bad emotions so that we will be more dissatisfied with the way we are. For example, they may spotlight the fears we have of offending others through bad breath or perspiration odor. If these concepts are internalized, the result is the sense that we "*are not good enough*" and that can result in ineffective behavior and sensitive emotions. From this point, some people's insecurities from inadequate self-acceptance cause them to strive for destructive or constructive goals.

Clues to this complex mind turmoil include extraneous negative SELF-TALK — "*I'm stupid*" — and the interference with healthy recall needed for good solutions. The point is to clearly beware of all your significant emotions and extract meaningful lessons from them. Sharpen the good edges and break off the bad edges of your emotional sword.

EMOTIONAL REACTIONS

From the discussion to follow regarding the sources related to and the meanings of Matrix, Selfishness, Selflessness, the "Trigger Person," the "Trigger Event," and the brain/mind, what brings this altogether is ones reactions to things inside ones selfhood and to things coming in from the outside world.

These will consist of hurt feelings, a tragedy, emergency, or crisis—one or more of which will have occurred in each of our lives at some point before we die. We or someone we love may be the victim of violent crime, a disabling accident, a serious, sometimes terminal, illness, or verbal abuse.

TRAGEDIES are unhappy events about the villain winning which cause calamity or disaster. One's reaction to a tragedy is either of an emergency or crisis nature.

An EMERGENCY is a sudden, serious, and unforeseen circumstance that calls for immediate action, as with earthquakes or the in-flight fire on an airplane engine. Without a doubt, there can be crises inside an emergency.

A CRISIS is a turning point because of a decisive moment, an unsettled time, or a chaotic state of affairs. In other words, a crisis represents a defining moment and how one reacts will determine the direction of ones life thereafter.

Hurt feelings about certain things and at certain ages, tragedies, emergencies, and crises are about high level distress and may precipitate serious emotional disturbances unless handled immediately and properly, One's reaction depends upon ones ability to think rationally and in common sense patterns; prior preparation; present emotional control; insightful thought; and speed of response. What the effects of these will be like is determined by ones philosophy of life, self-esteem, and creativity to immediately handle the unexpected and the novel and the complex.

For teens, the "gut response" part of the animal (or lower) brain — the amygdala — rules. This almond-shaped tiny bundle of nerves mediates emotions like anger, anxiety, and fear. During maturity, the frontal lobes of teens (the home of reason and judgment) gradually wrestle control over the amygdala and thereby temper the emotional swings of teen life.

For teens whose emotions are more sensitive, ordinary life stresses in school or social life — poor grades, embarrassments, romantic breakups — can trigger emotional pain and despondency headed in the direction of suicide. Their serotonin levels are low and some may benefit from the proper anti-depressants.

It is now an outdated belief that once one reaches middle adult years the brain undergoes rapid deterioration. Instead, the brain throughout life is in constant flux, with cells both born and dying all the time. It is well known that the human brain undergoes extensive shaping and pruning in the first few years of life. Added to this is another brain remodeling spurt occurring around puberty and extending into the 20s.

It would be wise to start teaching children in beginning grade school about themselves (emotionally, philosophically, physically, and spiritually) and about social relationships and dealing with difficult people. The anti-teaching forces say there is not enough time in the schedule. My answer: "What is more important than learning to have better relationships with and behaviors towards people?" This is far more important than focusing only on academic prowess. What damage can be done from donating five minutes of every classroom session—starting in the first grade—to ways of males improving relationships with females and each other—and vice versa?

Emotional Reactions to Crises: Whatever causes a bad emotion is a crisis. To repeat, a CRISIS is a turning point because of a decisive moment, an unsettled time, or a chaotic state of affairs. In other words, a crisis represents a defining moment and how one reacts will determine the direction of ones life thereafter.

Tragedies, emergencies, and crises are about high level distress and may precipitate serious emotional disturbances unless handled immediately and properly, One's reaction depends upon ones ability to think rationally and in common sense patterns; prior preparation; present emotional control; insightful thought; and speed of response.

Clinics, hospitals, half-way houses, and crisis hot-lines are ways of meeting the needs of troubled people. The suicide-prevention centers established during the 1960's were the forerunners of the crisis-intervention centers and hot lines. Hot lines are immediate, economical, and effective for rape or crime victims, alcoholics, drug addicts, child-abusing parents, runaway children, and people under all kinds of distress. However, most distressed people do not seek mental health specialists but instead turn to family or friends, self-help books, or self-help groups.

Whereas a crisis is a sudden, severely upsetting situation that forces you to mobilize resources, a TRANSITION is a change in your roles, routines, or relationship — lonely elderly men who see no future for themselves; or recent widows who have depended upon their husbands; or students who feel the world holds no meaning for them. These situations cause crises and the methods of coping may result in emergencies and/or tragedies and/or a commitment to a system of beliefs and/or investments that have far reaching implications.

There are ways to get ready for emergencies and crises, but all call on desire and willpower. In general, this involves planning, preparation, and practice — first to learn the right things to do and then to become aware of possibilities off the beaten path which might occur.

Next, the process starts by knowing your own weaknesses. What types of situations disturbs, threatens, or destroys your sense of well-being? Create and practice plans for management (the ongoing handling of all aspects of the problem) by both preventing harm to yourself and others and then maintaining a steady state, if not a cure.

Begin with easy problems of ordinary stress — the sort you have learned to handle through the use of rational thinking, education, training, and experience. Do the research to discover the socially acceptable problem-solving techniques for increasingly harder problems. Ask yourself a series of pertinent questions — is the change planned/unplanned? Is it predictable/unpredictable? Does the change involve one event or many? What emotional skills will I need when the crises occurs? Plan scenarios that include different combinations — e.g. one unpredictable planned event; many unpredictable unplanned events.

Part of the emotional preparation process includes learning relaxation techniques and part of thought preparation perfects the step-by-step rational thinking and troubleshooting processes that separate fact from distortion or fantasy. From prior thought be very clear as to what crises you should face head on, which ones to do nothing about, and those from which to flee.

Know when to go for help — some problems cannot be solved alone but they must not be allowed to get out of hand. A clue to a loss of control is when you have trouble sleeping. Find people you trust and that can help before you need them in a crisis. Now, when suddenly overwhelmed by an unfamiliar problem, step back to the problem most similar to the way you have handled one before in practice or in real life. Let us turn our attention to some of the cornerstones of the emotional experience which trigger things.

EMOTIONAL TRIGGERS

The word "gun," a name generally given to all firearms, comes from the forename of the Scandinavian female, Gunnhildr (which means war). As a result of three events — the development of gun powder by Ancient Egyptian priests, the development of the gun the Arabs in 1304, and the perfection of the gun by Europeans in the 14th century — "guns" have done as much to change history as any other single invention.

Firearms have subsequently ranged in size from cannons to small pistols. Nevertheless, the basic principle of the gun has remained the same — a machine for shooting bullets. The bullet is propelled and directed by the force of an explosion. In order for the explosive to be set off, a lever to do the pushing — called a TRIGGER — was invented in 1475. Once the shooter squeezed the trigger to set the bullet in motion, usually some type of damage was done — like something being injured or killed. Much less often the gun was put to good use.

TRIGGER PERSONS AND TRIGGER EVENTS: In the life of every human being there comes a time where some event is set in motion—a TRIGGER EVENT — or a person does something — THE TRIGGER PERSON — that alters the course of our life. Sometimes our lives are changed for the better by the trigger event or the trigger person; sometimes for the worse. The change may come all of a sudden (e.g. getting shot) or it may occur over a period of time (e.g. continuing abuse).

A personal "Big Bang" trigger event caused by a trigger person was the night my mother suddenly died while I, an Orthopaedic Surgeon, was across the country operating on a patient. Her death affected me to the point that I never operated again.

An example of a "Continuing Trauma" (or cumulative micro-trauma) trigger event carried on by my parents — the trigger persons — pertained to the actions leading up to their divorce. The divorce was painful enough for me to decide the reason why it happened and what I could do to correct it. In my 4-year-old mind I thought the cause was a lack of money and therefore I vowed to make enough money to bring them back together. From that point on, my life was very different in that my energies and thoughts were directed to the goal of becoming a physician.

There is nothing more terrible than the every day evil things happening to children all over the world — regardless of race, creed, color, or class. Examples of trigger events affecting them include beatings; sexual abuse; babies born with diseases from the mother's use of drugs, alcohol, or sexually transmitted infections; the pushing of children into isolation or into enslavement; making them feel shamed, guilty, or embarrassed for doing things natural to them; or being torn away from one or both parents, as occurred during African American slavery.

Examples of trigger persons can be anyone doing an evil act — one or both parents, a brother or a sister, a neighbor or a friend or stranger or rapist or robber or religious leader or teacher or baby sitter. Or, it may be systems such as the educational, the legal, the government, the media, and any other system not run by honorable people.

Children too young to reasonably deal with their troubled emotions usually interpret trigger persons or trigger events in a distorted or fantasy bad way. They lack the vocabulary to put what they feel into words and that causes such frustration that they will "act ugly." Correctly or incorrectly, they will either take the blame or blame the other person. Possible results from their emotional scars could be the feelings of insecurity, a life long sense of danger, the development of an inferiority complex, becoming angry "at the world," depression, and self-pity.

Older youth may take on the attitude of: "*I'll show you*" and thereby become troublemakers. Those youth stay in a state of rage, seek revenge, take on the cause of hate, have an arrogant and controlling attitude, and welcome leaders engaging in illegal or immoral behaviors. Most become addicted, follow destructive doctrines, show great defensiveness, and/or cheat and steal. Equally as bad, all people controlled by bad trigger events or persons repress their natural affections, pleasures, and enjoyments of living.

"TRIGGER" EMOTIONS and 'TARGET" EMOTIONS:

"Trigger Emotions" are those which have such an impact on an individual as to be a defining moment. An example of a "Big Bang" trigger emotion occurred, when to get across a shallow ditch, I put a board over it to keep from always having to jump over it. Titan, my Pekingese dog, slipped off the board and I had to pull him out of the ditch. Thereafter, his fear prevented him from ever crossing the board again.

An example of a "trigger emotion" from cumulative micro-psychic traumas is the result of my having been around so many people who judge me—and invariably improperly— that I now try to avoid them. Together, they have made me hypersensitive to being judged wrongly and then acting on those wrong guesses.

Since Titan's fear and my irritation were sufficient enough to cause us to alter how or what we do, then they qualify for a "trigger emotion." Now if I was trying to discover why I avoid certain people, I would be looking for a "target emotion." By thinking about it a great deal and noticing what is common to the people I avoid, one day I would stumble on the fact that each judges me without justification. Thus, the "target emotion" is the same as the "trigger emotion."

"How do I know when I am *getting close to the main emotion*—the "trigger emotion"— the "target emotion" or comparable main thought? The more each clue is explored, the more the most significant ones will cause you to experience *increasing tensions and vague anxieties.*

Another clue pops up by what you do not do or by what significant things you procrastinate about or even fail to respond to. This is because *repressions*, which are linked to unpleasant emotions like guilt, shame, fear, or anger, keep the significant from being recognized.

Still another clue is your refusal to discuss a topic. There are many other ways repressed material is expressed — like atypical behaviors and personality quirks. Such is indicated when you say: "*I don't know why I did (or said) that.*"

All of these clues are like the tip of an iceberg. As you start exploring beneath the surface you will be surprised at the incorrectness of your memory in both recall and recognition. The date and time of a trigger event may be seriously wrong; or some essential details are in error; and/or there may be general confusion, as in thinking you did or saw something which only occurred in your mind. Each of these occasionally happen to me—and that is why I try not to react until all available evidence is collected.

What you are looking for is fears, hurts, losses, lacks, or obstruction that caused emotional and/or spiritual pain. They may be in *Lettuce-type layers* — like the original traumatic event at the core and others added on top. These repressed materials can only be spot-lighted and brought back to your awareness when some of the target emotions covering them are removed.

Since stirring up bad emotions may be too overwhelming for you to handle, repressions of an extreme or moderate nature require the help of mental health specialists. For repressed material of a slight or mild degree, progress can come from the writing that explores the bad emotional "*iceberg.*" Being intensely unpleasant, you will want to not do this process at all and if you do, the experience is like a mother delivering a baby who improperly wants to "*stop and rest.*" It is best to "*keep pushing*" rather than stopping to rest.

Understand that it is difficult to deal with dangers that come from within — especially those dealing with self-depreciation. Keep in mind that bad emotions also create bad habits and both need to be corrected at the same time.

TRIGGER FLAWS: A feature common to each of the categories in which managing of emotions is indicated is to find the trigger flaw—the one flaw from which others are generated and manifested. We are acquainted with the opposite of this point from the discussion on Cherished Values springing out of the trigger perfection of Love.

Something more like the "top dog flaw"—the trigger flaw— is seen in individuals with an Inferiority Complex. In these individuals the trigger flaw word is "FAILURE," defined as "emptied of power." It is the judgment of having given up.

Since this is a *"complex"* situation, let us attempt to get to a *"common ground"* understanding of an inferiority complex by imagining four strings of different colors. Each string corresponds to the four components making up self-esteem—self-meaning, self-identity, self-image, and self-concept (extensively discussed in my book on Self-Esteem).

Also imagine that each of the four string contains different colored beads—one string being all red; another, all blue, etc. Whereas a string represents one of the four foundational components of self-esteem, a bead on any given string represents a subcategory of that component (e.g. a body image bead on the string of self-image). If one declares oneself a *"failure"* on one *"bead"*—say the body image bead— of the self-image string, this believed *"failure"* can be of the nature of:

Type I—Remain confined to that one body image *"bead"* (as might occur in a person with *"normal"* self-esteem);

Type II—Or it may affect adjacent beads on the same self-image string (as might occur in patients with low self-esteem);

Type III—Or it may affect *"beads"* on the same self-image string as well as on adjacent self-meaning, self-identity, and/or self-concept strings (as might occur in an inferiority complex).

A trigger flaw in any of the four self-esteem components can create profound changes along the scale that ranges from one bead to all four strings. For example, a trigger flaw in one's self-meaning can create a profound sense of insecurity, inadequacy, and unstableness that sets off a chain reaction within the self-esteem complex. Two of the very first self-destructive reactions are a lack of self-trust and a loss of self-confidence. From those two there can be burst ripples of Bad Emotions and bad behavioral manifestations.

An organic illustrator of a trigger flaw is _Sickle Cell Anemia_. Here, the patient's defective hemoglobin differs from normal hemoglobin by only one single and normal amino acid — that is, the presence of valine substituted for glutamic acid. Yet, this one tiny defect out of 146 in the beta hemoglobin chain can cause bone changes, hemolytic anemia, splenomegaly, vascular infarcts, and leg ulcers.

In other words, the trigger flaw is about: (1) a rearrangement of what is normal rather than (2) a defective amino acid. But trigger flaws may also be about (3) a new combination or (4) a new form of something.

Emotions inside the violation of trust have the violation of trust as its trigger flaw. Although situations, say between men and women, may seem vastly different, there may be a common theme. To elaborate, apart from a violation of trust, for a women to get raped by a friend causes in her a variety of emotional pains which leave emotional scars. The same occurs when a good male friend acts dishonorably toward another male friend.

The question is: how do you deal with that violation of trust? The obvious answer is to re-establish trust. But can that be done? In the story of the egg called Humpty Dumpty—who was pushed off a wall and shattered—all the king's horses and all the king's men could not put Humpty Dumpty back together again.

If the trigger flaw can not be corrected, then the focus turns to dealing with the emotions springing out of the trigger flaw.There are several parts.

One is whether to maintain a relationship—especially if the violator acts as if he/she did nothing wrong.

If there is a reason to maintain at least some degree of a relationship, then do you, on a deep level, tell that person how you feel and risk losing control— which in turn creates an even worse enemy? Do you question the violator as to why he/she did it? Do you avoid the deep part and instead talk superficially about things you and/or the violator are interested in? If you and the violator do not have anything in common to talk superficially about, what do you do then—especially if you need the violator's help?

You recognize that the violator is weak—from a character flaw or from meanness or from envy. You know it is best, based on your Higher Self, to maintain compassion. However, that compassion is interfered with by your painful emotions.

You can not get access to your painful emotions until the shock wears off. It is best to wait until that has worn off before making a decision. If possible, write out your emotions until you have absolutely nothing else to say. Then allow your compassion to dictate your next move.

If you are holding your tongue because you want what the violator has to offer, then you are trying to force the Helping Hand to act—and that will not happen. If what you want is to have a chance at happening, it will happen with or without the violator's help.

But it is important to have good evidence of what you are accusing the violator of having done and a good way to handle somewhat questionable evidence is to talk it out with the violator. If you are convinced of the violator's guilt, then let him/her go—or at least keep the relationship at a distance.

If there is a deep conversation, then keep it about how you feel rather than accusing—because the violator is too weak to admit his/her part and to put the truth of is wrong doings in his/her face will cause a denial and will not bring about any change.

Only you can change if you decide to do so. You might try asking the violator what he/she thinks you should do with respect to the relationship. Yet, do not believe any promises the violator makes.

*People are who they are and they are not going to change***.** If they wanted to change they would already be in the process of changing. There is nothing you can do to make them change—not with guilt, pity, or threats. Before making a final decision, read the "Love Your Enemy" section.

SELF AS TRIGGER: Up to the beginning of modern times people believed as a fact that the earth was flat and that the sun swept across the sky from morning to night. However, modern facts have shown the earth to be round and that it is the earth's movement, not the sun's movement, which designs the sunrise and sunset.

Similarly, we are fooling ourselves when we think that all we do and say is right and that those who do not agree are wrong. We are engaging in an illusion or are operating inside a delusion when we think we have what it takes to direct other people's lives; when we expect them to know how to deal with us properly; and when we think people should do what we ask them to do and then do it the way we think it should be done.

We are under a misperception when we reject everything our enemies say about us because some of what they say may be true. It is not in our best interest to blame other people, even if they are at fault. Nor is it worth it—because, afterall, what difference will it make next year?

Thus, the fundamental question is: **WHAT PART DID I PLAY IN THIS PROBLEM?** The answer represents the very beginning for getting ones selfhood on the right road. First, look at the part one plays in those losses, lacks, or obstructions which keep one from getting what one wants or causing one to get what one does not want.

One problem may be in paying too much attention to what others are doing or to what others are telling you to do. Another may be failing to deal with reality in favor of resorting to denials, distortions, fantasies, and other escape defense mechanisms. Still another may be in not assuming responsibility for your problems.

A typical method is the *Deceptive Mental Self-Purifying* of something bad that was said or done. Mental self-purifying is very much like an EXCUSE (i.e. any thing but what happened). It is made possible by a person taking only a little piece of what he/she did wrong and changing the words, tone, or setting so that it seems okay outside of the big picture of what really happened.

Example: Atlas invites only Titan to his home but Titan brings a little kid who proceeds to break up things. Titan, without asking permission, goes into Atlas' refrigerator and takes Atlas' food. Atlas becomes very upset. Then, six months later, in an attempt to mentally transform his bad behavior so as to look "clean," Titan explains to Atlas that he had asked permission to bring the little kid and to get the food. Of course, neither of these statements was true.

Two major factors involved in our not wanting to look at the part we played in a problem is a need to "safe face" and the failure to recognize our own prejudices and biases.

Saving face is doing whatever is necessary to slow, stop, or reverse the loss of one's sense of worth and sense of value to neself and/or to others.

Prejudice is pre-judging people objects, or situations in terms of stereotypes ("they all look alike") or over-generalizations ("you always do . ." or "you never do. . .").

A **Bias** is simply a tendency, usually below your awareness, to see facts in a certain way because of your habits, wishes, desires, interests, values, or need to "save face." Whereas prejudice occurs when you do not know the facts or have not examined the facts and do not want to be confused by the facts, bias is developed by viewing the facts and then selecting only those facts which support your point of view.

It may also be that you can only grab out of a bag of facts those which you are familiar with and/or expect. One reason for staying with biases and prejudices of which you are aware is your *fear of exploring the unknown.* This fear comes from not having developed the tools of Rational Thinking to know how to handle new problems as they pop up in the unknown.

This fear is also about *not honoring the truth.* A feature of mine is to pursue the truth and follow it wherever it leads, regardless of what damage it does to my feelings.

One of the things which Rational Thinking teaches is to start at the origin or source and then proceed down each step as you get to it. Suppose Titan tells Atlas that he is coming over to Atlas' house to pick up a packaged chicken to take home and cook. Then, when Titan arrives he decides to stay and cook the chicken there. Atlas gets upset and Titan says bad things about Atlas and looks to others for sympathy.

In this situation, titan is wrong because he said one thing and wanted to do another. Titan was disrespectful of other things Atlas had to do. Titan was wrong in assuming that being involved in cooking a chicken would not interfere with Atlas' plans.

Titan does not deserve sympathy for being so undisciplined as to not keep his agreement. Rather, he needs to go through whatever it takes to get his attention as to what proper behavior is all about — even if that involves facing the truth of what he did wrong; of being selfish; and of experiencing hurt feelings from it.

Your obligation to **KEEP YOUR PROMISE TO YOURSELF** is the tool that puts things in order; maintains a constant direction; and keeps you motivated to continue going straight ahead. It also forces you into a self-correcting process that comes from Rational Thinking. General suggestions are to practice making well-thought-out decisions, putting those decisions into action, sticking with your with plan and actions to the end (unless they are bringing great harm), and doing post-action judgments (i.e. troubleshooting) to find out where you went wrong. The better you get at deciding what is most important and then planning, preparing, and practicing to get it, the more you will be able to take advantage of opportunities.

Apply these lessons to your next problem and figure out how to measure your improvement. If you fail to solve your small problems from lack of interest or sloppy work, you cannot solve bigger problems. As a result, all your problems and Bad Emotions will grow.

11

EMOTIONAL SOURCES AND MATRIXES

EMOTIONS **either**

PERFUME *or* STINK UP

LIFE

The Source of any thing is that which first produces a range of essentials and then ensures a free flowing continuous supply of whatever the thing is about. For example, the brain/mind is the source of emotions.

The Matrix is the womb in which the essentials develop. The Matrix is determined by how one uses ones brain/mind. Whether for selfish and/or selfless purposes, the brain/mind will produce corresponding emotions.

But this brings us to a "chicken and egg" question as to which came first. Does ones degree of selfish and/or selfless orientation shape the brain/mind or does ones brain/mind shape ones selfish and/or selfless orientation? Since both occur at the same time, they represent "Central Head-Quarters."

"Central Head-Quarters" is fed by what is going on emotionally within the remainder of ones selfhood and what is going on in the outside world that generates emotions. Things in the outside world that stimulate emotions are called the "Trigger Person" or the "Trigger Event." Bad things inside ones selfhood that stimulate emotions are "Trigger flaws." For better understanding, let us now look more closely at the meanings of Matrix, Selfishness, Selflessness, and the brain/mind.

The Matrix: The source of a creation (e.g. an emotion) is the creator (i.e. the individual). The womb sustaining the life of the creation is the matrix. When the creation meets the matrix, a PROCESS begins. For example, when a hen and a rooster create a fertilized egg, the result is a zygote (*"joining together"*)—the creation— destined to become a baby chick. The zygote then settles in the womb—the Matrix (*"womb," "mother"*) so that the newly created zygote can develop. Since this is so fundamental for managing emotions, let us pause to explore the meaning of "*matrix.*"

Originally, "*matrix*" referred to a female animal kept for breeding purposes; then the female's "*womb*" or uterus; then the membrane of or the formative cells in the uterus contributing to the creation's growth; then whatever gives form to something enclosed within it. A major problem these "*Terminologists*" had in giving these partly right but incomplete definitions was *failing to see the entire big picture.* Incidentally, this is usually the same reason why one is unable to solve any very difficult problem.

The big picture here is that everything about the egg allowing the zygote's growth constitutes the matrix. Since the zygote and matrix are together an interacting *Organism,* development and degradation are occurring in various places all at once in a Yin/Yang type fashion. On the yolk the zygote beds down. Surrounding the yolk is the egg white. The egg's *hard shell* ("*the surrogate mother*") surrounds the egg white, the yolk, and the zygote.

Once in the yolk bed, the "*speck*" sized zygote and the matrix, despite being separate entities, become woven together. Because the matrix is between parts of the zygote and has aspects in direct contact with the cells of the zygote, they constitute a Context. *"Context"* means weaving ("*text*") together ("*con*"), as when the texture of a woven fabric consists of threads so intertwined as to create a single, coherent fabric held together on its own. As a result of this interweave, the zygote receives nourishment from the "*mother*" by way of "the womb."

The first obvious sign of the zygote's development is the spreading outward of its tiny blood vessels on the yolk as they "*eat up*" the food of the yolk and later "*eat up*" the egg white. Once development is complete, the chick delivers itself by pecking through the inside of the hard shell.

Notice how this beautiful total structural integration for producing a chick, shaped from within the womb, resembles the matrix for good works of art, speaking, and literature. Its beauty comes from the composite of the parental union of the genetic packages and the matrix—all of which are harmonized into a unity which produces the chick.

In rational thinking, including critical thinking, the matrix is the form for the causation, the origin, and the progressive development of thought created by the thinking source. It also serves as the womb to provide a meaning to a term. In short, a Matrix Mothers a Given Creation—regardless of whether the thought is a creation which in turn produces an emotion or whether the emotion is a creation which in turn produces a thought.

SELFISHNESS

The Story of Selfish: The concepts contained in selfishness, individuality, and self-preservation originally sprang out of each other and the practices resulting from these concepts have been present since life began in the universe. Perhaps the original meaning in *"selfishness"* occurred in the universal "*genes*" derived from God's mind. Those "*genes*" acted according to the laws of its own individual nature. Such laws gave it, as an essential part of the universe, the best chance for coming into being and surviving. In other words, its selfish, individual, and self-preservation parts possessed no regard for anything outside itself and thereby constituted laws concerning its own welfare and interest. This archetype (i.e. the ultimate original "seed" pattern) of selfishness started the "*first law of nature*" concept of self-preservation.

If the original action of these "*genes*" is considered as the first time cosmic genetic material came into being, all cells involved were selfishly struggling to preserve themselves as individuals. To illustrate, when millions of sperms from a male were on their journey to locate and fertilize the egg of the female, there was selfishness, individuality, competitiveness, and self-preservation for the winning sperm.

In early African society an "*indivisible individual*" meant a necessary relatedness of a person with the group by means of spiritual unity. In other words, at a spiritual level, all of God's creatures and creations were unified. Such inter-relatedness was continued by genetics and by the natural rhythmic cycle of social and environmental experiences shared by everyone within the culture. There were certain implications for those who lived by the concept of "*all for one and one for all.*" One was that, by being part of one humanity organism, selfishness was proper because it was about the preservation of every individual part.

But as people became more numerous there was a descending down the Cosmic Ladder where more and more differences were emphasized. As a result, ideas contained in selfishness, individuality, and self-preservation changed considerably. For example, to the ancients, the word "*selfish*" implied a "*closed heart.*" Then there was an even greater change during the Presbyterian upswelling of the mid-1600s. They coined the word "*selfish*" from the components of "*self*" and "*ended*" and "*self*" and "*full*" — the idea being that one is full of one's own self-interest and is oriented to pursue that interest as an end for one's life.

Put another way, "*Self-ended*" implied one's own interest was the objective one sought and thereby one became "*self-full.*" From that arose a number of rough synonyms: self-centered, self-seeking, self-aggrandizing, self-serving, and narcissistic.

However, for precision in self-assessmcnt, it is better to stay with the concepts within selfishness and analyze their meanings. The reason for being so specific is that true thoughts about where you stand right now will allow the committee of your mind to properly discover and assess the seed thought for your selfishness. That thought has expanded to give birth to your seed emotions and selfish behaviors as, for example, self-preservation.

SELF-PRESERVATION is an umbrella term for any thoughts of human nature, behaviors, or practices which function to increase one's chances for survival. By originating in one's mind "*genes,*" the objective of this innate urge is to do whatever it takes to satisfy basic needs — things like thirst, hunger, temperature control, elimination of waste, and offspring reproduction as well as avoiding pain, pursuing pleasure, and maintaining sanity and self-esteem.

SELF-PROTECTION, a subcategory of self-preservation, embraces both inborn and acquired needs. Acquired needs can be too much, too little, or just right. "*Too much*" self-preservation causes one to be overly defensive; "*too little*" causes one to be naïve and gullible; "*just right*" allows one to both self-protect and "*step outside oneself*" so as to consider the feelings of others. In this way, kindness, warmth, tenderness, compassion, and friendships evolve.

The World of Selfishness: Imagine what it was like to be the very first human on earth. When you looked around and saw nothing but yourself, at some point you would probably say "*I am it.*" Could this "*I*" centeredness be the first thought of a newborn baby? If so, the first human and every newborn thereafter have had the unfocused and self-serving energies similar to a wild pony.

A society depends for its existence on the presence of its members to break this wild free spirit and reformat him/herself into conformity with the needs which work best for all the members. Otherwise, members chronically engaged in individual selfishness generate sorrow, needless struggle, and weaknesses in the entire group.

"*Selfish*" is a life-shaping word of a complex nature because of its good and bad aspects. An approach to bringing some order is to subdivide both the constructive and destructive forms of selfishness into mild, slight, moderate, and extreme degrees. Next is to start untangling these eight subdivisions by focusing on their very beginnings. But first, consider the subject in perspective.

Although children were cautioned to avoid being selfish, seldom was the meaning of selfish ever explained at all to them, or completely explained or correctly explained. So, from a child's perspective, the ideas formed about what it is to be selfish took him/her far away from the truth and this subsequently created needless problems along the wrong path.

Imagine drawing the number "*8*," putting yourself in the bottom circle, and placing people in the top circle. The type, amount, frequency, and intensity of thoughts you put into each circle will determine the size of each circle. If you are very selfish, the size of the "*people*" circle will be tiny; if you are a "*people person*" the size of the "*people*" circle will be quite large; if you are balanced, the size of both circles will be equal.

From this we can fashion a "*People Scale*" to formulate how each of us thinks about human beings. On one end of the scale there is "*ME*"; in the middle, "*WE*"; and on the far end, "*YOU*." Let us say that on the top of the scale is good or constructive aspects of "*ME*," "*WE*," and "*YOU*" and whatever is below the scale are bad or destructive aspects.

The "*ME*" end is boxed by self-centered, self-preservation, individual's seeking pleasure, avoiding pain, and striving to remain alive forever — either by not dying or through one's children.

When these focuses are properly "People balanced", the mature work to create, enhance, and maintain mental, spiritual, physical, and social health. Social health is special because it develops by expanding beyond the "*ME*" to include the "*WE*."

Extraordinary development is shown by HEROES and HEROINES — those who reverse self-preservation by disregarding personal safety during crisis in order to bring about a "you" survival. Closely related are the mature who give up an advantage or take on a disadvantage in order to do the right thing. Such unselfish individuals are located on the "*good*" position of the "*People Scale*."

Whether constructive or destructive, selfishness has mild, slight, moderate, and extreme degrees. However, since most people have an incomplete idea about selfishness, let us look more closely at this.

Destructive Selfishness

Mention has been made that constructive selfishness is natural within one's selfhood. It contains not only self-preservation but also achievement self-interest, and the desire of immortality. When one perceives one's "*5S*" values (Table X) — safety, security, sureness, stability, and strength — are present, one allows one's natural social "being" to flow freely within human interactions.

But if one or more of these fives is threatened, disturbed, or destroyed, one engages in *"fight, fright, or flight"* as a form of reaction or action. These are normal as long as they remain appropriate for the situation or circumstances. However, an assessment of the situation or circumstances as being exaggerated (i.e. *"too much"*) or overwhelming and thereby causing a *"too little"* (i.e. apathy response leads into a disordered and unbalanced mindset associated with destructiveness). When prolonged, "too little" can cause one to withdraw into a world focused exclusively on oneself—a "self-centered" selfishness. They are driven to do what it takes to get what they want and thereby become "spoiled."

"*Spoiled brats*," by lacking a perception of possessing the "5S," try to compensate by controlling others, over-powering others, resorting to a "*poor me*" helpless victim approach, or assuming a superiority complex. In the process, their selfishness keeps them from developing—or causes them to lose what they had already developed—compassion or empathy for others. The denial of the rights, interest, and welfare of others is perfectly acceptable to them if any of those three interfere with their self-interest. This destructive arrogant mind-set, called "***BRUTE***" SELFISHNESS, is the worse form of selfishness.

Brutes are envious, jealous, boasters, prideful, unappreciative, disobedient, mean, stubborn, false accusers, untrustworthy, and power hungry. Despising good people, they are fiercely vindictive; haters of those who are not like them; aggressive toward those who challenge them; suspicious and distrustful of fellow brutes; and intensely seek money and material pleasures. Devoid of a sense of fair play and moral "*rightness*," they are perpetrators of hate and evil. Hitler, Stalin, and Hussein are extreme examples.

Reversing brute selfishness starts with separating one's realistic self-interest from whatever harms others. Focusing on things of value (e.g. money, power, possession) must be switched to things of worth (e.g. peace, harmony, unity, love) in order to gain the "5S." In other words, *the "5S"* is about things of worth one cannot see and cannot physically possess.

The destructive mindset of selfishness is associated with improper reactions, responses, and behaviors. The reactions might be uncalled for (as a result of misperceptions and/or misinterpretations); exaggerations that generate more mental chaos; or *"giving up"* unnecessarily.

Meanwhile, the afflicted individuals withdraw into themselves. Once in their self-centered world, the destructive thoughts and emotions associated with the trigger person or the trigger event start generating aspects located on the scale of hate — the shutting off of love, the attitude of indifference, the desire for revenge, and destructive conduct that ranges from ignoring, to neglect, to petty meanness, to attacks, and to death.

Mild Destructive Selfishness might be excessive self-indulgence in the pursuit of pleasures. Another is a non-productive "***WE**-ness*" — the hanging out with drifters as a lifestyle and thereby not developing one's gift to the world. By not doing all you can to get better and better every day, others lose and you lose by not reaching your potential.

Slight Destructive Selfishness is an entrance into a form of hatred, as in refusing to forgive and thereby freeing oneself to go to travel towards one's destination. A common form is envy — e.g. being unhappy about another's success. Still another form of Africans is that if one were to get rich by being stingy, he/she would be admired. But like other selfish people — no one would come to help out when the stingy was sick or come when his/her house was on fire, or come for his/her funeral. In short, all selfish people are avoided and excluded.

Moderate Destructive Selfishness displays, rather than doing personal physical harm, as acts of striving to thrive through dishonorable practices and thereby represents a further step into hatred. Typically, they do and say things to tear you down while they unfairly build themselves up. In doing so, they are bent on disrupting peace, harmony, unity, and disregarding what is best for the family and other loved ones. There is non-caring about others whether emotionally, socially, or materially; indifference to the suffering of others; not wanting to share time, money, or support; and having an "*all for me and me for me*" attitude. They deny divine supremacy and excuse their evilness and greed by such justifications as "the survival of the fittest" or "the struggle for existence."

Extreme Destructive Selfishness is usually thought of "hateful selfishness" by the public. Inside this mindset is an exaggerated regard for one's own advantages (entitled to the best of everything), accompanied by a sadistic disregard for the welfare or happiness of others. To this end, they have no moral conscious against stealing, cheating, or killing. They are the most obvious evidence of fallen human nature; are spiritually disconnecte from higher powers; and completely ignore the Bible's assertion (Eccles. 9:11) that the race is not necessarily given to the swift, nor the battle to the strong.

Managing Destructive Selfishness: Whereas constructive selfishness contributes to one's wholesome progress, destructive selfishness slows, stops, or reverses it. Constructive selfishness is a reality of birth but destructive selfishness is an individual's choice to exclude love. The absence of love leaves a void that is filled with spiritual pain, destructive thoughts, and Bad emotions (e.g. anger, fear). Because neither are ever satisfying, these unhappy individuals seek love substitutes (e.g. the greedy pursuit of money, possessions, and privileges) and/or a sadistic desire to hurt others.

At best, these approaches give only superficial pleasures and even those are temporary. As a result, there is not much left but to be envious. Perhaps the best stimulus to cause on to go into the win-win world is that the problems experienced in the destructively selfish world become too numerous, too great, and too overwhelming. Then if one reaches the point of knowing nothing better to do except to generate the courage to try something better, at that point one will start the process of evolving into higher planes of existence. One will learn to locate and appreciate ones Real Self and the spirit of other people and the beauties of life (Bailey, Selfhood Mastery). *Appreciation is the cornerstone for the re-prioritizing of one's destructive system of values.*

Constructive Selfishness

Selfishness is normal in children in that they seek their own good without regard to others. It this persists out of childhood, bad emotions result. By contrast, constructive selfishness generates good emotions.

Mild constructive selfishness is beneficial self-indulgence (e.g. vacations, frequent massages for purposes of getting refreshed. In short, some form of selfishness is beneficial—and this has nothing to do with other people.

Slight Constructive Selfishness—this is about doing WIN-WIN deeds — the deliberate planning and practice to make things better for oneself as well as for others—"I am lifting you as I climb." These adults are attentiveness to their own interest and well-being but without harm to others in the process. Sometimes it is best to make yourself a winner and then come back to help others. One reason is that people can take up much time and energy needed for life's preparation for material success.

Constructive Moderate Selfishness is about being a WINNER — one possessing healthy self-centered thoughts related to success within oneself, with people, with nature, and in possessing enough money and power to be comfortable. As long as one is not greedy and does not hurt others in the process, the right thing to do is to have ambition, get the proper education, and do whatever it takes to be successful. Of necessity in the USA, the pursuit involves leaving the crowd so as to discover and develop one's talents. Then one continues improving oneself educationally, mentally, physically, spiritually, financially, and cross-culturally so as to find the right place for sharing one's developed talent.

Extreme Constructive Selfishness is the ecstasy associated with engaging in SELFLESS SERVICE — doing things to benefit others at one's own expence. Yet, it is not wise for one to "over do it" to the point of personal hardship. A willingness to give all one has to save a life is what makes heroes and heroines out of ordinary people. Otherwise, if constructive selfishness can be defined as that which enables one to survive and thrive, then survival by any means necessary and thriving by honorable means is Extreme Constructive Selfishness.

Managing Constructive Selfishness: Focusing only on one's self-interest without regard for others is normal for children. If this continues on into adulthood, this "*normal childhood selfishness*" becomes "spoiled" and creates problems in increasing numbers and magnitude for others and for oneself. To avoid this, the maturing process out of childhood starts with CONSIDERING THE CONSEQUENCES OF ONE'S ACTIONS and that causes a gradual conversion toward a more balanced circle. Moderation is the key—not "too much" and not "too little."

THE BRAIN/MIND

Railroads and the brain have some things in common. Of course, in its simplest sense a railroad is a set of tracks over which cars can run. In a broader sense a railroad system includes the tracks, roadbed, freight and passenger cars, locomotives, bridges, tunnels, train yards and stations, repair shops and roundhouses, and signal systems. All of these things are necessary if trains are to work smoothly and safely.

By way of beginning stage comparisons, in its 17th century USA mechanical "babyhood" the railways consisted of horse drawn wagons so heavy that they broke down the dirt roads. Therefore, logs were placed at three foot intervals to which big planks were nailed — like railroad tracks. The wagon wheels ran over the planks and the horses walked between the rails.

Similar but more elaborated principles apply to the brains in humans. Like heavy wagons breaking down dirt roads, many human babies who start out life using emotions to solve their problems gradually discover emotions are not good enough. The weight of daily living problems placed in the "wagon" they increasingly face break down the helter skelter structure of emotions. Instead of relying only their emotions, they begin substituting "logs and planks" — better known as **"Thoughtful Impulsive" thinking** — in an attempt to get better results from decision-making.

This is somewhat like what railroad people had to do. Because even the wooden railways could not long hold up under the weight of heavy wagons, iron plates were placed upon the wood. This device proved satisfactory so long as horses were used to move the wagons. But, with the coming of the heavier and speedier locomotives, a new danger arose. Temperature caused the iron plates to expand and contract, which often caused these plates to break or loosen. As the train passed over these broken rails, the sharp ends frequently pierced the floor of the cars, endangering the lives of the passengers and even wrecking the train. The solution to this problem was the all-cast-iron rail.

In like fashion, *Impulsive Thinking* is not enough to stand up to the pressures of everyday life and, as a result, "brain wrecks" occur. Instead of the "brain train" getting to its goal or destinations, the weakness of Impulsive Thinking causes a splintering of the rails of emotions. Splintered bad emotions go out of control, add exaggeration and distortion, and thereby derail the "brain train."

We have seen railroad tracks coming in from all directions to enter big railroad stations. Perhaps the most well known is that of GRAND CENTRAL STATION in New York City — one of the busiest and most crowded railroad terminals in the world. A separate part of these stations is a circular garage for locomotives called the "*roundhouse*". Locomotives are driven onto a huge turntable — like the kitchen table's "lazy Susan" — where inspection, cleaning, and repairs are done. Then, as desired, the locomotive can be redirected North, East, South, or West. Meanwhile, railway cars, whether loaded or empty, can be attached.

Similar to the roundhouse where various railroad tracks come together, the "Grand Central Station" of the brain is the **Hypothalamus** where the psychological (mood/affect feeling tone) and physiological (autonomic nervous system) activities meet. What comes into the hypothalamus is information from the body and information from the brain (which in turn receives messages from the outside world).

We are aware that from brain cell activity a **Brain/Mind** interface is present — meaning that somehow *mental states are "cast" or "molded"* from the brain into the mind. If thoughts within the mind are harmonious and the feeling/emotional tone contained in the psychological brain component is pleasant, then the mind and body are peaceful. If thoughts are disharmonious and the feeling tone is unpleasant, then mind irritability (e.g. bad emotional states like anger) is present.

In other words, **the degree of ones mental peace or mental conflict depends upon the kind and intensity of thoughts and feeling tone one has**. This is a foundational concept for any selfhood mastery (Bailey, Selfhood Mastery).

Could it be that the same type of interface occurs with the Immaterial (or Sublime) Consciousness (where harmony, unity, and wholeness are present) with the "end of the mind"? If so, what enters the mind from the Sublime are messages based on love and truth. This would seem to be so if one were operating out of one's Real Self.

Experience tells us that just as the brain is linked to the mind, in turn the mind is linked to realms of higher power. The human capacity to imagine is an example of one's connection with remote fields of energy. If human consciousness is able to capture, and thereby understand these realities, then imagination and visionary consciousness are linking one to other types of realities, directly or indirectly (Some, Healing Wisdom p149). To these ends, Primitive Africans and Shamen and Ancient Africans used their emotions and *Sentiments* (emotions framed in intellect) to help them contact and then enter "other worlds" for religious purposes.

Emotional Thoughts (or thought/emotions or Sentiments) are an interweaving of thoughts with a primary, a secondary, or a tertiary emotion. Whereas thoughts are believed to arise from the forehead part of the brain — the cerebral cortex — at least Primary Emotions seem to arise from the lower positioned ancient parts of the brain.

Primary Emotions are the five basic emotions of Chapter IV.

Secondary Emotions are the acquired "normal" emotions of Chapter V.

Tertiary Emotions are *Complex Emotions* consisting of combinations of Primary Emotions among themselves or combinations of Primary and Secondary Emotions.

Brain Evolution: In briefly reviewing an over-simplified tiny bit of zoology, even the lowest form of animal life, the one cell creature MONERA, will *withdraw* from something irritating it. This suggests that its behavior is based on feeling with its senses. Apparently, as seen in the jelly fish, the feeling tissues give rise to nerves. *Nerves*, as first seen in the flatworm, have given rise to the BRAIN.

The formation of a brain allows behaviors to exist inside and outside the animal. "Inside" behaviors include impulses and urges that cause Instincts; "outside" behaviors allow for "fight, flight, or freeze" when one is put into a perceived danger.

Invertebrates (like flatworms) are below vertebrates (like reptiles of which snakes are an example) because invertebrates lack even an early cerebral cortex for generating thoughts. Perhaps emotions appeared somewhere between the first amphibians and reptiles. At least early mammals, like rats, possess a limbic system for emotions. Chances are that awareness inside consciousness arose when animals began to experience physical pleasure and displeasure.

Human Brain Anatomy: Current Western thought says that there are three brains-in-one, with each reflecting our ancestral relationships to reptiles, early mammals, and later mammals. The brain becomes increasingly specialized as we step up the evolutionary ladder. For example, there are two great nervous systems in the more highly evolved animals — the Central (CNS) and the Autonomic (ANS). The ANS controls things that are automatically done in our brains — like causing our heart to beat, our blood to circulate, and our lungs to breathe.

THE THREE BRAINS OF HUMANS

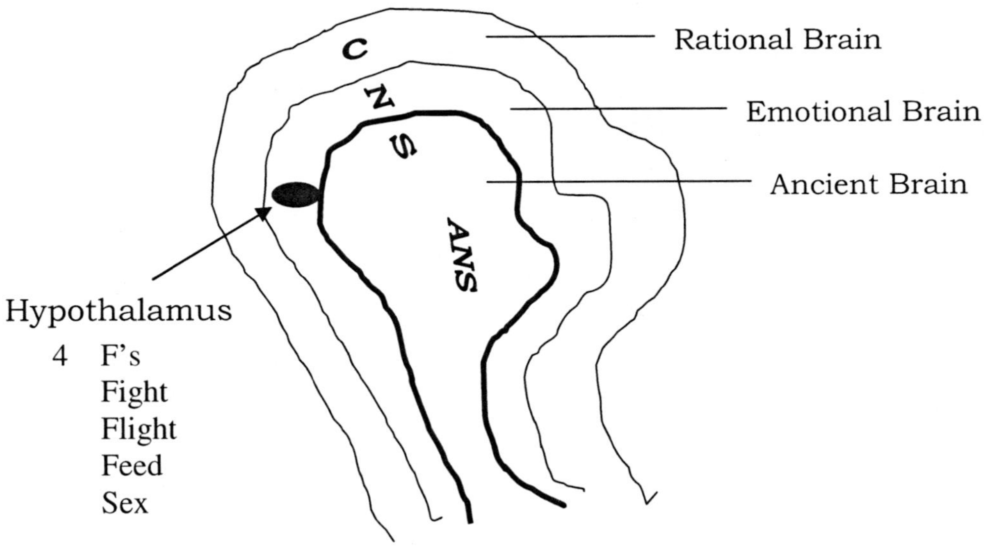

Figure 1
(Reprinted from Bailey, "*Creativity, Invention & Discovery*")

The CNS resembles a telephone system, with the brain as the central office, the spinal cord as the cable; the nerves as the wires; and our five senses (seeing, hearing, tasting, smelling, and physical feelings — as opposed to psychical feelings) being the "telephone receivers" for our brain. Our brains use the messages from our senses for feeling, thinking, and taking action. Looked at another way, our CNS can be compared with an ice cream cone — the cone, representing the spinal cord, and the brain, consisting of three scoops.

The first scoop of vanilla put on the cone is the ancient brain, the home of the ANS. The second scoop, strawberry, is called the limbic brain and sits on top of the vanilla scoop. The limbic brain is located behind our face and is the center of our emotions. Scoop three, chocolate, is the neo-cortex — also known as the rational brain (fig. 1). The word "cortex" means "bark" — the outer layer of any structure — the "bark" of the brain.

Brain One—the Ancient Brain—is the primitive reacting, basic reptilian brain located on the upper end of the brainstem where the head joins the neck. Within this ANS brain are the neural mechanisms responsible for behaviors involved in self-preservation and in preservation of the species. The first subdivision of the ANS is that of sympathetic nervous system (SNS). The SNS mediates physical reactions to stress in preparing the body for "Fight or Flight." Included in this reaction is the mobilization of the body's energy stores and in such a manner that a total body response occurs wherever there is an emergency.

By contrast, the other subdivision, the Parasympathetic system (PSNS)—the "Play and Stay" system—maintains homeostasis (a steady state of the body) by conserving body resources for rest and relaxation. Compared with the SNS, the PSNS is a more localized response and more designed for long-term use.

Brain Two—the Limbic System—the Emotional Brain—the Paleo-mammalian Brain is more highly developed than the Ancient Brain. Because it is the home of the hypothalamus and is concerned with regulation of the ANS, it is also called the Visceral Brain. Humans share this Emotional Brain, which give the packaged energy used for guiding our reactions and behaviors, with all other mammals. Whereas Pure Feelings (which connect the Real Self with the Sublime) are part of the Subjective Realm (see discussion elsewhere), emotions are part of the Objective Realm.

Brain Three—the Rational Brain—the Neomammalian Brain—is the cerebral cortex. It is the most recently evolved and the most highly develop, particularly the prefrontal cortex (frontal lobes). This is a principle of the human body as, for example, the vastus medialis of the thigh is the most recent in evolution and is the first to be lost when one stops using ones thigh muscles.

The prefrontal cortex is a special event in human existence and may well be the connecting link for those who believe in man's creation as opposed to man's evolution. For example, suppose that prehumans were created but became human with the development of the prefrontal cortex. We know that the prefrontal cortex is special because of the recent introduction of such brain test devices as MRI (magnetic resonance imaging; PET scans (positron emission tomography); and electrical sensing techniques to scour pockets of the brain where emotions dwell (and then develop detained schematics of the neural circuitry among them).

The palm-sized prefrontal cortex (gray matter), located just behind the forehead, determines both our general outlook on life and whether we respond positively or negatively to events and experiences. It problem solves and memorizes to aid the older feeling/emotional brain loops and still older reacting brain components in the overall struggle for survival. When properly developed, it is responsible for thriving. Because of the frontal lobes humans acquired the ability to have foresight and forethought ("I'll feel great when I achieve my goal"); to form beliefs; and to bring emotions into play that leads to judgments and guides behavior and other sophisticated aspects of the human mind.

In addition, the prefrontal cortex furnishes us with our most human qualities—our language; our ability to reason and deal with symbols; and our urge to develop a culture that is, at its best, about "win-win" and, if developed improperly, about "win-lose". If we did not have a sense of what would be wonderful or terrible in the future, our behavior would be very haphazard.

Similar to the links of a 3-piece chain, our three brains-in-one are so overlapped that one can predominate and control the other two. Yet, the central control for all three brains is the hypothalamus which, along with the brainstem, the PSNS, and the spinal SNS constitutes the ANS. Out of each of these three brains, similar to the off-ramps from a freeway, are nerves. Some nerves stay in the head to provide us with our five senses. Other nerves go into the body to allow a coordinated function of all the parts in our bodies as well as to give us the feelings we need to protect ourselves from injury.

Meanwhile, both the limbic and neocortex divided into specialized right and left parts. Our emotional responses are generated by the interplay of a number of brain structures, including the amygdala, the hippocampus, and especially the pre-frontal cortex. Brain imaging studies show that positive and negative emotions are polarized on opposite sides of the prefrontal cortex. Positive emotions outward-reaching emotions are governed by the pre-frontal cortex's left side; negative, inhibiting emotions by the right side.

One's natural temperament—optimistic, pessimistic, extroverted, or introverted—may depend on which side of the prefrontal cortex is more active. Babies who cry when separated from their mothers tend to have a dominant right prefrontal cortex; those who calmly explore the area where they had been abandoned tend to have a more active left cortex.

Brain Waves: States of awareness—whether ordinary or altered—occur inside four known levels of brain-wave activities— Beta, Alpha, Theta, and Delta.

Beta is the state of greatest and complete waking awareness and alertness. With brain waves ranging from 14 to 27 cycles per second, the lower end corresponds to linear thinking and problem solving; the high end, to anxiety and body tension which is difficult to control.

Alpha has 8 to 13 cycles per second—the state of brain "idling." At the low end one is daydreaming; at the high end, one is in a state of relaxed alertness and here material from the Subconscious is accessible. The brain is in alpha during light hypnosis, Meditation, biofeedback, day-dreaming, and the hypnagogic and hypnapompic states just prior to and after sleep. The optimum range for most awareness activity is between 8/9 Hz and 15/16 Hz. Alpha waves are inversely related to brain activity. Depressed patients have "high alpha" on the left side, indicating that this region of the brain is too inactive. Applying magnetic stimulation to the left side causes depressed patients to get better.

Theta, ranging from 4 to 8 cycles per second, one is in light sleep—a state of either semi-awareness (between sleeping and waking, as in dozing) or unconsciousness in which one is unaware of what is going on around one. Some can drop into theta in biofeedback and Mediation at a level just before sleep and without slipping into the brain-wave pattern of actual sleep. Athletes who do this have access to stored images of peak performance—like dunking over your top competitor.

The **Delta** level is deep sleep, unconsciousness, or coma with waves ranging from 0 to 4 cycles per second.

Brain Features: Sustained emotional stress damages the brain, and especially in children, by means of cortisol, the master stress harmone. In low doses it alerts us and organizes our behavior to ensure self-protection. But in high doses it disorganizes our thinking, prevents attention, and causes depression. Early sustained cortisol exposure also damages the hippocampus, a part of the brain that regulates mood and memory.

Our **Right brain** or hemisphere has characteristics which are artistic, intuitive, spontaneous, imaginative, emotional, and playful. It thinks in images, is involved in memory, and is sort of associated with "negative" emotions like sadness and anxiety. It has a greater ability to tolerated ambiquity and conflict (called liberals in politics) and are more open to new experiences. The part of the brain involved is the anterior cingulated cortex (the part of the brain that detects conflicts between a habitual tendency and a more appropriate response). It is more ready to accept new social, scientific, or religious ideas.

The Right brain is much better developed at birth—and is larger—than the Left brain. It is the vehicle for expansiveness into higher and multiple planes of existence regarding things like **Love, spiritually, compassion, peace, harmony, intuition, synthesis, nonaggression, and unity**.

By contrast, these are un-accessible to most White males in general because they have traditionally honored only their Left Brains and deliberately dishonored their Right Brains**.**

Our **Left brain** is not as well-developed at birth and it starts "catching" as ones rational functions are cultivated. It generates cheerfulness, verbalness, concreteness (e.g. mathematics), goal orientation, and a calculator type step-by-step (as opposed to right brain "flowing") preference. The left brain is the disciplinarian of the right brain. It has a tendency to block distracting information.

Every person has the ability to develop both sides of his/her brain and one side is not better than the other. Rather, they are complementary equals. This means that when the work together as a team the result is greater that the sum of its parts—i.e. 1 + 1 = 3; if both sides work in conflict or if one side is used without the other then the result will be a fraction of one. Individuals who have **the most powerful and creative minds use their right and left brains equally**.

Both sides are a "check and balance" on each other whereby one keeps the other in good balance while otherwise each side supports the other— similar to the way that one of our hands washes the other.

The most important site identified so far as an emotional (especially for fear) "center" (and there is no one center but rather a physiological loop) is the **AMYGDALA**. It is located behind the ear and acts like a video camera that scans for trouble every incoming signal from the outside world. It sends out warning of perceived danger and threat.

The amygdala, a word literally meaning "shaped like an almond," was formerly used anatomically to describe various almond-shaped structures within the body. The amygdala of emotions—the two almond-shaped structures in the brain sitting behind the eyes is located in the center of the brain and when a certain part of it is stimulated a state of intense *fear* results.

It is believed that the left cortex normally shuts down the amygdala's alarm signal by firing off a sort of "message received" signal to it. Without the left cortex, the amygdala runs wild, flooding a person with fear, helplessness, and despair. Failing to bring under control such negative emotions aggravates physical problems like high blood pressure and heart disease. If it is destroyed there is no longer a normal behavioral response to danger — like "freezing" or running as the need would arise for normal people. Nor are there the typical physiological changes associated with fear — like higher heart rate and blood pressure.

The amygdala is involved in other emotions as well. For example, Intense ANGER—an EMOTIONAL INFLAMMATION OF THE MIND—is an impulsive emotion that overrides reason.This happens because of the amygdala. In assessing an experience, it asks: **"IS THIS FOR ME OR AGAINST ME?"** If the signal is an anger producing "against me," then the amygdala sends out a crisis "may-day" alarm to all parts of the brain.

This emergency signal causes the brain to by-pass the thinking part of the brain and to react before the message even gets to the reasoning brain. As a result, there is failure to activate the thinking brain, especially its left pre-frontal lobe, in time for it to keep the emotional response in balance. Thus, emotionally oriented people react faster, not necessarily better, to emotional situations than do rationally oriented people.

The emotional system can work independently of the rational system whereas, except in logic, the rational system is always entangled with emotions. However, the emotional system reacts without being sure of what is going on. Its reaction is based on prior (as early as infancy) habits of reaction, even though the prior experience triggering the reaction is only vaguely similar to the present trigger situation.

Another thing the brain does is to produce biochemicals (e.g. hormones, enzymes). Too much or too little of a chemical can result in greatly disturbed thoughts, feelings, and behaviors. *Dopamine and opiates* are neurochemicals associated with pleasure and excitement.

Another chemical, the hormone *oxytocin*, is associated with friendship attachments, bonding, and sexual activity to the extent that it can cause the "chemistry" of "falling in love."

Serotonin is needed for communication between certain nerves. Low levels have been linked to depression. The gene, tryptophan hydroxylase-2 (TPH2) is a key to its production. Another gene, the serotonin transporter gene, is linked to developing depression in times of stress.

These and many other chemicals not only affect certain snapshots of our awareness but they are quite active in the movie we call "conscious" or "awareness."

In addition, there are environmental causes that have nothing to do with genetics and yet play a significant role in emotional health or destruction. The emotions you express on your face may affect how you feel. Perhaps those facial muscles feed information to the emotion loops of the brain which in turn responds with chemicals that produce happy or sad feelings.

III

THE DEVELOPMENT OF EMOTIONS

People are Bundles of Emotions

Bristling with

BIASES & PREJUDICES

and

Motivated by

PRIDE, VANITY, POWER

At the moment the sperm enters the egg the beginning baby is thereafter guided in its development by the mother's womb (i.e. the matrix) and mental and physical health of the mother. Eventually, while in the mother's womb, the fetus becomes affected by happenings apart from the mother — like the sound of soothing voices and music or reacting to loud sounds. What fetuses learn in the womb could possibly help develop their disposition and temperament.

The origin of these terms came from the Ancient Egyptian belief in the life and function of the universe being contributed to by four elements: fire, water, earth, and air (James, Stolen Legacy, p. 80, 142). The Greeks borrowed those ideas under the title of the Four Humors and proposed their vaporized state inside the body caused the following sequence:

(1) A Disposition (a way of thinking about things once aroused) triggers

(2) An Inclination ("to lean toward" what is preferred) which triggers

(3) A Temperament (an aroused person type of reaction) which triggers

(4) An Intention — the directing or "stretching" of one's thoughts toward a specific action.

Thus, in proceeding backward from an action to a thought—there is, similar to an emotion, a psychological component behind a Disposition that leads to a behavior; an Intention (deciding to take an action) affecting the psychological and the physical; and the physiological component (Temperament) (Bailey, Good Character, p. 33).

Furthermore, what first happens to babies immediately after birth is important — the types of shocks they experience, who holds them, and what those persons who handle the baby smell like.

Second, how growing babies are treated after birth continues to play an extremely dominating role. One of these areas is whether the child is given the necessary stimulations and opportunities to enable him/her to cultivate his/her curiosity and to develop those qualities which lead to maturity.

Third, is what they learn about emotions as they are developing. For example, American parents help fashion emotions by physically stimulating their babies until they reach peaks of delight. Thus, American babies learn that intense emotional expressions are all right as long as they are positive.

But a key feature about emotions is that they have a cycle range — going as low as they go high. Because Gussi mothers in Kenya hardly ever engage in face-to-face play of this sort, instead they seek to keep their infants as calm and content as possible. As a result, a low up-and-down cycle is shown in the Gussi babies by their learning to restrain both positive and negative emotions.

A fourth point is the types of answers children get for their questions. Clear, simple, and truthful answers are powerful building blocks for expanding knowledge. Any other type of answer leads to dead-ends of thoughts and often into bad realms of both thoughts and emotions. For example, if an adult tells a child that happiness is about money and power, that child is placed on a road doomed for unhappiness.

Fifth, babies learn from parents and other companions which emotions are appropriate and in which situations—especially those concerning conflict situations. This and imitating parents as to how to regulate their own feelings and behaviors is learned as early as 6 to 12 months old.

Six, **Love** is by far the supreme factor related to what the newborn, the infant, the child, the adolescent, and the adult require most of all for a healthy mind, body, and spirit. The child's *Love Platter* enlarges each of its own capacities for love, to be loving, and to be lovable by being loved. No matter how good every other aspect of a child's rearing, the child will not develop properly without the stimulus of love.

The child inadequately loved during the first six years of its life will be most seriously affected in his/her capacity to love and his/her ability to recognize love.

For example, infants raised in cold, impersonal institutions or in homes riddled with tension and anxiety tend to become withdrawn, lethargic, and actually waste away. This is called MARASMUS or MATERNAL DEPRIVATION. Despite adequate physical care, such children were deprived of "mothering" with its associated warm, personal attention, and similar "emotional supplies."

If this love deprivation does not begin until after the first year of life, the depression and arrested development of children may be reversed—provided mothering is resumed within three months. Otherwise, any one who is disconnected from Love will experience Spiritual Pain. Examples are sadists and masochist.

Flaws in **Self-love** are sure to fashion emotional problems (see later discussion). Lack of self-love causes defects in having an engaging manner toward others; lead children to become "cold people" or destructive people who lack tenderness and emotional bonding in relationships; and display as irritability and resultant periodic streams of bad emotions.

Whether highly intellectual or completely unintellectual, a common characteristic of "cold" people is the lack of an ability to love. For them, the need for love is so over-powering that they become totally focused Love seeking specialist. However, the best they can do short of reconnecting with love is to devote all their attention to gaining substitutes for love.

Specialization tends to shut off their wide-band tuning searches and thus prevents discovery of the all-powerful generalized principles of goodness and other aspects of life that are building blocks to maturity. Neither can they hear or accept pearls of wisdom concerning things of worth until they decide to definitely change and then muster the focused energy to do so.

Otherwise, they seek out or remain in areas that are familiar to them — even though those areas have not worked well for them. Since they have no idea what love is, the recommended first step toward change is to become familiar with love and with how love differs from emotions. This will be mentioned later.

GOOD EMOTIONS

Regardless of whether we started life on the right or the wrong foot, as we progressed through the maze of life we have sought out or have been drawn to things we like —whether good or bad. In contrast to the bad, it is proper to be drawn to what is good. But there is more to "good" than to that which we have been drawn. Besides, we are not sure of what all is embraced by the concept of "good."

Experience has taught us that some things we shun are good for us. We shun developing the ability to concentrate. The reason is that it is developed by prolonged focusing on what is boring rather than on what is interesting—and that is the opposite of what we like.

Some things we find pleasure in are bad for us—and we know what those things are. Maybe it is being with the wrong crowd or eating "junk" food.

Sometimes we choose things not bad per se but that are not in our best interest—as in spending time with superficial people who are going no where.

Sometimes we do nothing when we should do something—like not taking calculated risks so as to progress toward wholesome goals.

Sometimes we do something when we should do nothing—like not being quiet so as to listen to the "Voice of the Silence."

Sometimes we do not interpret things properly—especially when emotionally upset.

Sometimes we put the problem on the wrong person, as when we are part of the problem but blame others instead. To make matters worse, we do not always take advantage of learning situations. The point is that before blaming others we need to look at ourselves.

Sometimes we forget what we should not forget as, for instance, that our ability to improve comes from successfully managing the hard times of life; not the times when things are going well.

To answer the questions of: "What is Good?" and "What are good emotions?" requires starting at the top of the Cosmic Ladder. Things related to "Good" are lofty and lofty is about that which is in the Sublime. But what is the Sublime?

The SUBLIME of African Tradition: An Ancient African masterpiece for living inside life—and in preparation for reaching the heaven Afterlife—consisted of thinking, feeling, saying, and doing those things which would enable them to transcend into the Sublime. This involved a birth to death process of rising through the various planes of existence. Two requirements for entering this process included stepping into Reality and Truth in order to understand and operate out of one's Real Self. To know the contents of the Real Self— Reality, Truth, Beauty, Perfection, and Goodness—is to know the contents of the Sublime because each one is part of all the others.

Ancient African Sages said that the knowledge revealed to them from divine realms included the Sublime as constituting the connecting link between the heavens and the finite world. To be aware of the Sublime and its contents and to experience the wonderfulness of the Sublime is, they said, the ultimate "wonder of the world".

The word "Sublime" means "just under the lintel." When we walk from one room to another, we go under the cross-piece of a door. That cross-piece is called a lintel. Ancient Africans considered the sky to be the lintel which separated the Immaterial world (i.e. the Infinite world of "the heavens" above the sky) from the Sublime–the Intangible plane of existence in the Finite world.

Intangible implies the transition between energy and matter in the universe. This transitional shinny, pure, upper air "stuff" is called the "**ether**" and the space occupied by the ether is the "ethereal space." Other names for the "ether" are Universal Energy (Yogi), "Prana" (Buddhist), Chi (Chinese), and the "Lofty" (Europeans). The ether is presumed to be the ingredients of which the heavens, the lintel's stars/ planets, nature, and natural laws are made.

Whatever comes out of the heavens is in highest concentration in the Sublime. Those contents contain things of "**Supreme Worth"**—the **Reality** of **Truth, Beauty, Perfection, Goodness, Peace, and Love**.

Ancient Africans said the "ether" permeates and perfuses the entire universe. This means that a "piece of ether" on any plane of existence also contains a piece of the heavens and portions of its powers—similar to the way a drop of ocean water is made up of all that is within the ocean.

To be in contact with the source of the Sublime ether is to be energized; inspired; and aroused by sentiments of awe and reverence from its vastness and power. These beliefs spurred Ancient Africans to mathematically study the stars for purposes of learning God's (and nature's) laws.

Put another way, located at the place where the material cosmic mountaintop touches the sky, the Sublime embraces the core of the best of all there is in human awareness. The higher one ascends up the earthly cosmic mountain the more concentrated the "ether" power. The more concentrated the "ether" power, the more completely a human being can bathe in order to become thoroughly "Enlightened".

By stretching above cosmic space, above seemingly infinite distances, and above time, Sublime power outreaches human comprehension. It has no boundaries among any of its components (e.g. truth, beauty, goodness). Each component of the Sublime dynamically overlaps the others like the constantly changing color patterns one sees by rotating the tube portion of a kaleidoscope. In both situations the overall effect is a harmonious unification of the Sublime components.

While accessible to the human mind, the Sublime is above being understood, analyzed, or talked about with definiteness. Instead, it can only be experienced as a two-pronged happening—the happening of it being "out there and in here" at the same time. Consisting of magnitudes exceeding life, the entrance fee into the Sublime is that one's self-identity must dissolve into a Unity with everything real in the cosmos— while yet retaining individuality.

Good Emotion words used for Sublime experiences include "stupendous," "magnificent," "splendid," "wonderful," "elegant," and "exquisite."

People draw on lofty words in referring to the unspeakable beauties that emotionally bring tears to their eyes; that exhibit human perfection (e.g. a masterpiece painting of the rainbow); that are about "Perfect Moments" (like a flying flock of birds); that relates to the unity of soul mates; that are about people joined by a group spirit; that are acts of goodness and love done anonymously for people *"down on their luck"*; or that are ideal harmonious episodes—e.g. Truth, fun, play, humor, wit, and the highest types of pleasure.

Cultivating Good Emotions: The process starts, said Ancient African Sages, with self-knowledge because self-knowledge is the basis of true knowledge. As a result, they placed on their temples perhaps 7,500 years ago the admonition: "Man, Know Thyself." Part of the process used by Ancient Africans included Meditation (to rise above the physical world) and Martial Arts (to become peaceful enough and with sufficient inner strength to not be pushed around by the phenomenal world). The Buddhist speak of this as being in a state of "your face before you were born"—a state free of ripples which cause instability.

To "know" oneself is to connect with one's Real Self—that aspect which connects one's Soul with one's brain/mind interface (fig. 9). One's Soul is part of the Soul of Humanity. It is therefore in contact with the Sublime by way of one's "Pure" Feelings (i.e. Spiritual Feelings) and the Sublime is connected with the Amenta.One's Real Self contains personal powers, one of which is called Will-power and its subdivision called Urge.

By the use of Will-power, one directs one's constructive personal power to master one's passions and destructive emotions. This is done in order to make room for the occupation of unlimited powers coming in from the Sublime (James, Stolen Legacy p88).

One's passions and emotions follow Hermes' Principle V of Rhythm: "Everything flows, out and in; the pendulum-swing manifests in everything; the measure of the swing to right is the measure of the swing to the left; rhythm compensates" (The Kybalion, p35). Since this principle cannot be annulled or its operation caused to cease, by means of the Law of Neutralization one can escape its effects in certain realms by selfhood-mastery. What is neutralized is the destructive aspect present in passions and emotions so as to attain poise and mental firmness (The Kybalion, p37).

Yet, no restrictions are placed on the effects of good emotions or passions which lead to the application of Ma'at—whether for oneself, for fellow humans, or for nature. Thus, one uses one's personal powers to free oneself of bad influences; to control bad reactions to bad influences; and to fashion a force to rise above impulsiveness. Each of these is done so as to help correctly direct one's destiny in the direction of a masterpiece.

BAD EMOTIONS

The Story of Bad Emotions: From the dawn of man's existence there were all sorts of happenings that were good (e.g. food and water supplies), frightening (e.g. lightening, thunder), and bad (e.g. death, sickness, tornadoes). For things seeming to come from or were caused by the unseen spirit world, man used a vivid imagination and common sense to give explanations for the unexplainable in the form of stories — called Mythology. Whatever they could not understand was considered to be the work of a god.

Very Ancient Africans believed the source of all life was that of God— the One Universal Supreme Being. But between the creator and man lay many powers and principalities — good and bad, gods, spirits, magical forces, and witches — to account for the strange happenings in the world. In Africa where the days were always flooded with sunshine, it was natural that the sun—deemed the god Re (or Ra) — was generally adored as a good ruler and life-giver.

By contrast, the principle of evil and chaos was the Egyptian god Set (or Seth) — the god subsequently associated with foreign countries and with consorts coming from the Semitic pantheon. Because Set had a violent temper that caused upheavals and confusion, he was identified by the Greeks with their rebel-god Typhon. At times, his violent nature was put to good use, as in Egypt when he defended Ra from the coils of the serpent Apophis.

As Myths spread out of Africa, certain countries emphasized those that explained a time before man. Of particular importance in relation to the origin of bad emotions are myths of the Near East. Incidentally, the Near East was so named by Europeans in the 1800's in reference to the Turkish Empire that included Arabia, Egypt, and the Balkan Peninsula.

One of the best known Myths is the Arabian Nights—magical tales supposedly taken from the Persians by the Hindus and from India by the Arabs. The Jinn were magical spirits created out of fire, perhaps 2000 years before Adam and Eve. Living in the mountain of Kaf, which encompassed the earth, some Jinn were good and some were evil.

In the story of Aladdin and the Lamp, the good Jinn helped Aladdin build his palace. However, the evil Jinn hated mankind and could be controlled only by tricks. An example pertains to the story of a "bad" Jinn sealed up in a bottle for a long time. By promising riches, he persuaded a man to set him free. After the man released him, the bad Jinn grew very large and threatened to kill the man. This formed a concept of "Bad." Out of this world-wide mythological story arose "the bad" as being of the opposite of good.

The World of Bad Emotions: Bad emotions are those immature or hateful emotions which slow, stop, or reverse the wholesome progress of the individual and/or the people, animals, or nature under the influence of that individual. Bad is generally thought of as "*not good*"; *or* "*not as it should be, incorrect, immoral and not valid, and worthless.*"

If "*bad*" represented the hub of a wheel, its spokes radiate into all realms of life. For example, in Medieval European common forms were represented by deceit, fraud, and homosexuals. Obviously, there are degrees of bad along the course of each spoke—ranging from mild to slight to moderate, and to extreme. Whereas improper folkways would be mild or slight, improper conducts related to morals would be moderate or extreme. Floating in between mild and extreme forms of "*bad*" would be the illegal.

The same ideas apply to whatever "bad" emotions help cause those behaviors. Thus, examples of "*bad*" mild or slight emotions are shyness and timidity. Evil (extreme) emotions are rage components (e.g. intense anger, hostility, hate) which lead to deliberate destruction.

Causes of Bad Emotions: One of the first issues to address in selfhood-mastery is the ability to achieve stability of emotions and passions between the extremes. If your thinking is immature and you use emotions as your major thinking tool, then you are an untrained Right brain dominance person. As a group, these individuals I call Emotional Persons or **"EPs"**—and they share many features in common.

For example, "EPs" do not follow routine patterns in most aspects of their lives. Therefore, it is necessary to restrict selfhood-mastery practices in them to certain matters of serious business and otherwise go along with whatever route they take in applying their routine measures to every day life. EPs may cook the same ingredients different ways on different days and not be aware of the variations because to them variations are a normal way to do any one thing. What they do from day to day is not predictable (because it is a creative feature) and usually is not reproducible.

By contrast, Rational Persons or "**RPs**" generate a step-by-step process which is the same every time it is done and can be reproduced by most other people.

Whether an immature EP or an immature RP, the vast majority operate out of their Lower Self. The **Lower Self** is that portion of the Selfhood which has its Divine Spark lamp-shaded by the False Self. Inside the **False Self** are hate, envy, jealousy, revenge, lust, seeking hedonistic gratifications, and so forth. These animal and False Self forces constantly intrude upon ones attention until one puts in the self-discipline and work to master them.

Three general causes of negative, bad, and destructive emotions are losses, lacks, and blocks. But first understand that **"*Bad*" is not necessarily the same as "*negative.*"** For example, a fundamental property of Matter is its electrical charge.

Protons and the nuclei of atoms have a positive charge while Electrons have a negative charge. Charged substances have an imbalance of positive and negative charges—a net charge that exerts a force on other charged substances.

In the way that Yin and Yang are different but without one being better or worse, the same applies to the complementary equals of positive and negative. Emotions are usually thought of in relation to pleasure or pain. However, equally as important is to consider whether they are beneficial or not.

"NEGATIVE" EMOTIONS, like fear and anger, may be bad or good depending upon the circumstances; upon their degree; upon how they are used and when and where. Good "negative" emotions include: the fear that causes us to run from danger; the anger that causes us to attack in self-defense; the depression that helps us survive; the emotional pain in guilt or shame which makes us improve; and the crying that brings the much needed help. Children should fear running into the streets or fear jumping off high places. Anger is justified upon witnessing inhumanity or cruel actions towards people or animals. In other words, some negative emotions are reasonable but have to be guided into the right outlet.

DESTRUCTIVE EMOTIONS are present in people who care about nothing and who deliberately do harm. Destruction was born from some loss, lack, or block at a time when they were building their philosophy of life. Building a philosophy of life is a mental structure similar to the building of a house. A solid foundation of a house has a specific arrangement made of special of material. If that solid foundation rests on quicksand and/or if that foundation is weak, then the entire house will collapse.

When destructive emotions are part of the philosophy of life foundation, flaws in that foundation are difficult to get to because the house is already more or less built and because the foundation is buried underground. Nevertheless, it is from the mental material making up the foundation that generates mental activity like dispositions (mental leanings toward certain behaviors), thoughts, and feelings.

In contrast to the foundational materials in a house, the mental materials in a mental foundation grow and reproduce more of itself. Thus, if destructive materials are in the mental foundation, the destructive behaviors which spring from them will spread, as air diffuses into all parts of the earth world.

Furthermore, when neutral events or even good events happen to a "sick" mind, they are still carried into the channel of destructive mental activity— and on through its filter. The result is that the "sick" mind perspective transforms good into neutral; transforms neutral to bad; and transforms bad to something worse. In other words, the meaning of a situation is largely determined by being filtered through past traumatic experiences.

In summary, for Ancient Africans, **BAD** IS ANYTHING THAT IS ANTI-LOVE, ANTI-HARMONY, ANTI-FAMILY, or ANTI-PROGRESS. **Bad Emotions** are *the destructive forms of "Negative" Emotions (e.g. excessive acute anger) and the outright Destructive Emotions (e.g. Chronic Anger or Chronic Fear).*

THE BEGINNING OF BAD EMOTIONS: "*The projects*" is a colloquial term that originated in the inner city to represent too many apartment buildings in too small a space with too many people in a crowded condition. "*Putting up with*" all types of people around the clock causes "*project*" people to be socially shattered in certain respects.

Those same people are already feeling extremely stressed from situations outside of "*the projects*"—e.g. finding a job which pays a living wage. Furthermore, inside the "*walls*" of "*the projects*" are all sorts of destructive agendas going on as, for example, aggressive males defending their "territories." Other problematic agendas of "project" residents pertain to factors working against physical, mental, and spiritual health, safety, and philosophical values directed toward good character and a successful life.

Some "*project*" people display "*bad attitudes*" while others are passive and withdrawn. But the burning question is: "Why do certain youth want to and actually become 'somebody' — even though they live under these terrible circumstances which include abusive or unavailable parents?" Possible answers include:

(1) They have not developed the mind-set of hate or revenge;

(2) They see themselves as simply "*passing through*" their terrible circumstances;

(3) They have a strong desire to have a better life for themselves and for their loved ones;

(4) They have "*a cause*" — an intense determination to help their mother and other members of their family or the neighborhood be better off,

(5) They believe in their talents, skills, themselves (e.g. as having good character), and their capacity and ability to reach greatness;

(6) They view rising above poverty as a challenge;

(7) They appreciate things in life (e.g. nice things done for them) instead of cursing their losses, lacks, or obstructions — seeing the glass of life as half full instead of half empty; and

(8) Their minds are oriented toward a "win-win" way of living — a willingness to help others either while working toward their own success or after they have achieved success.

The extent to which a person may be judged mature is chiefly measured by the types of things which arouse his/her emotional reaction; by his/her behavior during such a reaction; and by maintaining integrity and excellent production during hard times.

Emotions are the automatic results of one's value judgments and value judgments are the automatic results of one's emotions. Both apply when used as an evaluator of events in the context of ones concerns and expectations.

A good or bad emotion **BEGINS** when the predisposing, precipitating, and immediate causes meet at one point and start the first part of a process. That point is inside the assessing of an event in the way that a video camera scans the people entering a store and what they do in that store. Part of the assessment is to send what was perceived through the filter of concerns and expectations so as to establish priorities.

Values of **high priority** are determined by: "*is it for me or against me?*" If "*against*" is the conclusion, then the emergency question is: "*What can be done about it*?" — not necessarily what is best in the long-run but rather: "*What will get me safely past this moment or experience*?" Meanwhile, the body is preparing for "*fight or flight*" and this physiological and psychological preparation is at the core of an emotion.

If you judge the bad trigger event as an accident, or if a little child was the cause, or if it is not in your best interest to do anything about it, then you are not likely to get real angry and hold on to a grudge. If you do, chronic anger—regardless of cause— eats your insides like strong acid will eat the insides of its container.

If your assessment leads to frustration as a result of an important goal being blocked or being caused by some type of loss — and if you believe that it was deliberately caused, you will feel angry and may seek revenge. Similar to children doing tit-for-tat on a small scale, seeking revenge at an adult level will set off a feud — and the stakes are big!—and revenge is a dumb thing to do. So how do you go about assessing what "*is it for me or against me*"?

SPOT-LIGHTING BAD EMOTIONS: "*Lay your cards on the table*" is an expression of the late 1800's which referred to showing one's hand of cards face up. Today, it means being open and honest through *Self-Introspection* (searching your own secret thoughts and feelings and then making known your position or intentions). Spot-lighting is about locating the "trigger emotion" as discussed previously.

The process requires writing out all of your good traits, limitations and weaknesses, and the "*dark*" secrets located in the dungeon of the castle in your mind. Look for those thoughts, impulses, and feelings which are in conflict with the values of your society and with the values and standard you have set up for yourself. Appreciating your good traits provides you with a stable mental base for making the good even better. It also lets you face your bad traits without feeling like a total failure.

After acknowledging your bad traits and freezing your opinions about them, explore your repressed thoughts and feelings. The reason is that repression is sometimes the key to understanding all other defense mechanisms. Denial can be equally as important as repression but it requires the help of others for you to bring them all to light.

Psychologists say that clues to your repressed memories (what you have been keeping from yourself) show as lapses of memory, curious dream symbols, slips of the tongue or pen (an inadvertent mistake in speaking or in writing), or strange blind spots (unable to see what is real out of ignorance or biases or denial) in your understanding of what is obvious to reasonable people. Here are some specific causes of Bad Emotions that may represent the "target emotion" you are seeking.

OUTSIDE CAUSES OF BAD EMOTIONS: Without question, the most powerful destructive materials in a "sick" mental foundation concern problems with Love. Very young infants build their philosophy of life with a great deal of speed and what is put into their minds can have a life-long effect related to thoughts, emotions, and behaviors. Regardless of cause, not receiving love or not being able to recognize love because of a destructive filter eats away at the foundation of ones philosophy of life. An analogy is the eating away by very hungry termites at the wooden foundation of a house.

There are innumerable other kinds of causes. Specific losses, lacks, or blocks may be in areas of abuse — neglect, rejection, ignored, or abandonment. Being harshly teased or humiliated or laughed at can cause wounds and scars in one's self-concept. For example, there may be a "bleeding wound" in one's mental foundation that gushes blood for a lifetime. Some ways of causing wound and scars from blocks that manufacture frustration and eventually destructive emotions include parental reactions of over-expectations, over-protection, or over-control of the child.

Or the parent, who tries to be a "buddy" or friend to the child, instead of a parent, will tell the child so much bad personal details of life's problems that the child is not able to handle it. I have seen cases where those children, as an adult, almost hated their parents for breaking the ideal image of a parent.

Improper teaching of children by parents may take the form of brain washing that concerns hate and evilness, as is done in racists socializing their children into "bully" tactics or destructive prejudices, or being greedy. By becoming part of the child's philosophy of life foundation, they are very difficult to slow, stop, or reverse.

It is difficult to determine which are the worse sources of what generates Bad Emotions within an individual—the family, the neighborhood, or a hostile society. But one thing I consider terrible is the tidal wave of violent and indecent content coming into the young person's mind from video games, movies, and especially television. As of this writing there is one instance of violence, profanity, or sexual content every 3.5 minutes of non-commercial airtime. Only one in ten television programs are free of objectionable content. There is even an increasing trend of having women bear guns. It is best either not to have television and video games in the home or watch only educational and clean comedy. Nevertheless, the following is a brief discussion of the more common types of causes of bad thoughts, emotions, and behaviors.

ABANDONMENT –there are many ways a person can feel a sense of abandonment. Examples include the divorce of ones parents; a father or mother simply disappearing; being removed from ones family and placed in a foster home; and being a latch-key kid—coming home every day to an empty house. Feeling insecure and unloved is a natural reaction to such circumstances— whether it happened in the past the present or the future.

Management: An approach for managing the sense of abandonment is to grab the trigger emotion; stay with it; and observe whatever pops up. There is truth that comes from the right and left brain about the same thing. Follow the right brain emotion to the path wherever it leads. At some point you will stumble upon the trigger event, the trigger person, or the trigger emotion as previously discussed.

Then determine what are your behaviors resulting from having a sense of abandonment. What is inside your target emotion that causes you to be fearful? For example, is your basic concern about the reality of what is going to happen to you now? Or, what will happen to you in the future?

Nevertheless, it is my job to be able to take care of myself when I feel abandoned. These are moments when my dog serves such an important role in my life. Because he comes through in being a good companion, I can better tolerate the things he does that irritate me. This sense of companionship enables me to realize that people do things for themselves and not necessarily against me. And they have the right to do that.

Attacks

Attacks may be verbal, physical, social, financial, emotional, or spiritual—and each of them cause a significant problem—and each must be handled in a different manner. Since this topic is too big to deal with completely, let us look at a tiny piece—i.e. how malicious attacks can help kill a youth's expectations for success.

Titan has discovered that Atlas has a weakness or limitation in a certain ability to do job. Titan attacks that weakness to the extent that Atlas feels even worse and becomes so insecure as to think he is a "*nobody.*" Then when a job comes up requiring Atlas to call on the thing he is weak in, Titan tells Atlas "*you're not good enough to that job.*"

Note how Titan has switched the focus from one weakness Atlas has to telling

Atlas that he, as a person, is weak. This causes Atlas to make the adjustments in how he thinks about himself. Atlas then believes he will fail in everything instead of working on his weakness in one thing to make it strong.

This belief of expecting to fail will cause Atlas to procrastinate in starting to do the job or will cause him not to try to do it. Or, if Atlas decides to try, his plans will create a bad outcome. He will be wishy-washy (or "*watery*") in his approach and make all types of excuses; will not rush to do it; and will blame others. Once Atlas starts the job, he will not give his best effort; will "*mess it up*," or will quit at the first signs of difficulty or setback.

Any or all of these delays in getting started or delays in finishing will cause Atlas to believe he is a failure as a person — as Titan said he was. Because Atlas did not do the job at all or did not do it "*right*," other people start believing Atlas is a failure and start treating him as such. Atlas then shapes his life around making his false belief about himself come true in other aspects of his life and therefore fails at whatever he attempts. This is called a SELF-FULFILLING PROPHECY.

In the meantime, Atlas reinforces his false belief several times a day by resorting to Self-Destructive SELF-TALK: "*I'm no good! I am a nobody!*" The combination of others expecting him to fail, of Atlas setting himself up to fail; and of his bad self-talk about being a failure — all meet at one point to form as "*attitude problem.*"

Inside that bad attitude is anger at oneself for failing; envy of others who succeed; and ongoing frustration over how to handle problems of a similar nature because of never having learned how to be successful.

Management: The correction is to return to the African system of everybody building up everybody else so that everybody benefits: "*I am because we are, and since we are, therefore I am*" (African philosophy). This implies that the more you understand about your spiritual connection with fellow human beings, the less angry you are likely to become. You also understand more about your self by knowing know what is and is not true. Correct the flaw and discard the rest.

What it took me until recently to learn is that people who attack me are merely using me as a shadow of something bad going on inside their selfhood. I can know this with certainty because I simply do not do or say things designed to hurt people in any way. Of course, as a physican I have an obligation to give them my best answer to their questions and that truth, as I know it to be, can sometimes hurt. Thus, if I am being attacked I will walk away but not get angry because my understanding of me being a shadow causes me to be more tolerant and more patient.

Child Abuse

In Medieval European society, both moderation and the proper use of the contents inside of moderation were parts of temperance. In other words, it was important, as determined by religious leaders, to use the correct "something" in a "*normal*" fashion. Otherwise, it would be abused—i.e. ill-used in the form of deceitfulness, a corrupt practice, a bad custom, rudeness, or engaging in mockery.

Two particularly enraging practices looked down upon with contempt were the selfish use of material resources (for to do so was an abuse of one's privilege) and homosexuality. Yet, the idea of abusing people in general and children in particular was not of concern to the vast majority of Europeans.

Over time, the word "*abuse*" was applied to sexual assault on a regular basis; then to physically "*interfere with*" (1948) and finally, to "*molest*" (1950). Meanwhile, when something was used for a purpose for which it was not intended, the term "***Misuse***" was applied. Whereas "*misuse*" may not lead to harm, in general, abuse carried with it some sense of harm. For example, "*abusive language frightened the young children*"; or "*child abuse leaves lifelong-lasting emotional scars.*"

Up to the mid-1980's the statement "*most parents abuse children at one time or another*" would have been accepted as an almost universal truth. After all, what parent has not spoken sharply to, smacked, or even shouted abuse at their children? Thereafter, "*abuse*" became a widely and inaccurately applied catch-all terms — usually with sensationalized connotations of shameful sex and sadism.

Today, child abuse applies when vengeance is part of the behavior. VENGEANCE is the combination of making severe demands or inflicting punishment in association with fury and maliciousness.

There is not much worse that can harm a child as being neglected, isolated, or ostracized by parents or peers. Deprivation—lack of love, comfort, safety, security—does the greatest damage. When parents feel vindictive and wish to seek revenge on things that have incited their rage, many use their children as **Scapegoats**. That is, they take their misplaced revenge out on their non-guilty children. Studies show that degrading treatment causes as much emotional suffering and long-term mental damage as physical torture. Effects are high rates of depression and post-traumatich stress disorder. The most important point is to what degree do victims feel a loss of control.

The fright and pain suffered by children when they are slapped, kicked, or beaten leaves permanent mental wounds. Furthermore, children over age 2 who lack secure attachments to their mothers have, during even mildly stressful events (e. g. receiving a vaccination shot), higher rushes of cortisol which bathe the brain and thereby *damage brain tissue.*

The abused child destined to follow the "Pain Approach" to life will, at some point, intertwine anger, anxiety, depression, and emotional and spiritual pain with any emotions present in the Compound Emotions. This has significance with respect to sadistic and masochistic behaviors—which are far, far more frequent than is indicated in the literature.

Hence, the memories children have about the cruelty they received are stored until the opportunity and their urge for reacting combine to allow a re-enactment on a "*symbolic*" substitute — i.e. a non-threatening person, animals, or thing. Then the abused, now teenagers or adults, can sadistically exert their power on a scapegoat and pay back on their symbolic weaker scapegoat victim the debt of days long ago when they were the weaker victims.

Then society takes over and gets criminal "*justice*" revenge—which is always worse when Black people are involved. The new abusers are thrown into prisons where they are further abused (sexually and otherwise) and learn the finer points of being criminals. Following release from jail, the embittered youth repays the punishing society with more sophisticated destructive acts. And the vicious circle continues.

With their defective will-power, lack of proper training, evil and sadistic nature, and basic wickedness pattern, these villains are in constant conflict with a cold, hostile, suspicious world which does not want them, which has few jobs ready for them, which expects them to find and keep low paying jobs incompatible with comfortable living, and which thinks they should restore themselves to sound mental and spiritual health when they have no tools to do so. These young criminals need properly guided restraints (e.g. on islands) until they have developed a loving philosophy of life and Ma'at behaviors.

Disrespect

There is nothing more upsetting to Black Americans as a whole—and from slavery to the present— than their ongoing experiences of disrespect received from Europeans. To help in understanding, let us review the subjects of respect and dignity.

The African Story of DIGNITY: Africa starts the earliest story behind the concepts present in dignity. At least a thousand years before the Jewish belief that humans are made in the image of God (Genesis 1, 27), African Sages said that the sanctity of life is the central pillar inside each human being; that God is Love; and that each human is made in the image of God. Thus, dignity—the spirit of God—is established in each person, including the ungodly.

Karenga (Ma'at, p. 318) says these concepts are introduced in the Sebait of Kheti for his son Meritkara on the First Intermediate Period, more specifically in the 19th Dynasty (c. 2140-2130 BCE). Kheti's comments not only provide the earliest known concept of humans as the images of God, but it also poses them as the children or offspring of God.

It was these concepts that evolved into concepts of human dignity and the sanctity of human life so that humans were seen as bearers of *Dignity and Divinity* — both characterizing what it means to be human.

In other words, dignity is the result of being a child of God and being the possessor of a divine presence within each human — both demanding a special status in the eyes of one's fellow man as well as a special moral consideration. Hence the respect shown to a fellow human being includes the determination to provide for the true well-being of the brother/sister, neighbor, and enemy (Harrison, p. 324). This is the core concept of the Offensive Non-Violence methods of Ghandi and Martin Luther King, Jr.

The African Tradition conviction that the dignity of the person is a natural endowment by God is summarize in the African maxim: "All persons are children of God; no one is a child of the earth." The possession of the divine spark disposes an individual to respect his/her own dignity by realizing his/her full potential as a person and functioning at his/her best in human society (Coetzee, p. 329).

In other words, in African Tradition, dignity is of a spiritual nature and this is as much a part of ones selfhood as is life itself. There is nothing degrees that any man can say because anything spiritual is above man's opinions or influence. Ancient Africans believed the moral relationship between one person and another ought to be that of the acknowledgement of the dignity bestowed on every person rather than on an appraised dignity. Dignity, they continued, is not achieved, as it is said to be in the Western world.

The Western Story of Dignity: Concepts of dignity were quite different outside of Africa. To the Ancient Greeks, dignity denoted an opinion, estimation, or repute (i.e. reputation and particularly a good one). Connotation terms for dignity at a Sublime level included magnificence, excellence, and a manifestation of glory — hence, being of angelic powers (2 Pet. 2:10; Jude 8). Still, these remained in an earth world—and not spiritual—realm.

In Latin, dignity (dignus) means worthy while in Greek (doxa) it means glory. Western dictionaries define "Worth" as the quality that renders something desirable, useful, or valuable in a material or market value sense; a quantity of something that may be purchased for a specified sum. By contrast, Ancient Africans considered worth as that which constitutes rays of love—peace, harmony, beauty, goodness, truth, and perfection.

Yet, even before the Greeks and Romans, one of the earliest ideas concerning dignity came out of ancient astrology. Here, dignity was considered a condition of placement wherein a planet's influence is strengthened— a condition considered "acceptable"; but if it was weakened the term "debilities" was used. In the New Testament, the astrological sense of "acceptable" and the sense of something fitting and respectable, dignified, dignify, dignity, and dignities were combined. The connotations springing out of this combination were always about good opinions, praise, honor, glory, and an appearance commanding respect.

For example, during these Biblical times, *Dignities* were considered persons holding a high position worthy of honor (see discussion on "Respect"), distinction, or merit. "Dignity" among Europeans was viewed as the quality of nobility, worthiness, honor, distinction, or excellence. Later, dignities declared to have dignity were called "the glorious ones," the "angelic majesties," the "celestial beings" — as in referring to "elders" and "princes." Part of this was about those deemed to possess *grandeur of mien* (a noble demeanor).

In the 13th century— out of the idea inside "esteem" and as a doublet of dignity —arose the word *Dainty* (that which is about delicate beauty—fresh and pretty). A *Doublet* is a pair of words from the same original root but which have evolved through different routes of transmission and thereby acquire significant differences in meaning. Nevertheless, dainty contributed its influence to ideas about Western dignity. Its miniature elegance implied that dignity is finely and skillfully made. The overlap of dignity and dainty became core concepts in *Etiquette* (i.e. the observance of the rules governing proper conduct within a given society).

Today, Western "dignity" refers to a state of being that arises from obedience to what one regards as elevated, noble, or in full accordance with one's rank, status, or position. In African Tradition, whereas how well you relate with real things is about **Respect**, *recognizing and appreciating the highest (i.e. the spiritual portion) that is inside a person is about dignity.*

The Story of Respect: When the word "respect" came into the English language (c 1380) it derived from Latin "specere" ("to look back at"; "to observe") with reference to an act of noticing with attention inside the context of "to honor." At that time, **Honor** signified an evaluation or estimation as the basis of recognition of the worth (pleasure or displeasure in a Western sense) or value (desirable materialism) of something.

As a result, honor was thought of as a fixed price for the purpose of ranking a given person or object on the proper rung of the Ladder of Importance (Bailey, Self-Esteem, p. 16).Whatever was on the highest rung was given the most deferential regard (16th century) because it was of the highest agreed upon quality by European experts and/or those in power.

This made "Respect" a somewhat "colder" term than either the Western terms "**Appreciate**" (the combined value and worth of something) or "**Esteem**" (the combination of regard, respect, and appreciation). The reason is that "Respect" embraced honor and confidence without particular feelings — whether referring to a person or thing. In other words, respect was based on the admiration of a person's desirable characteristics and competence— as determined by one or more observers who used their own man-made standards and criteria.

Among the Afrocentric the *theme of Respect* is to have good relations with and good behaviors toward other human beings. This implies that respect, as a form of Ma'at, is a symbol of harmony and unity pertaining to the human condition. Within this context, any application of the principles of Ma'at (i. e. love in action) is right as a form of Respect.

The World of Disrespect: In African Tradition, respect is a term referring to dignity—and this is fundamental to understanding Black people reaction to disrespect.

DIGNITY, according to Ancient Africans, is inherent in each human being; derives from being a child of God; implies the possession of a divine presence within each human; and demands both a special status in the eyes of one's fellow man and their special moral consideration.

RESPECT is a manner of spiritually relating to others based on principle of the Law of Sympathy (i.e. all God's creatures and creations are related and connected, no matter how remote in time or space). Thus, to have a respectful manner is to deal with God's creatures and creations as if one were to deal with God directly.

To repeat, of all the causes of anger related to Black Americans, none is greater than being disrespected. *What is being disrespected is a person's or a group's dignity.* In pre-colonial Africa, chances are that disrespect rarely occurred. By contrast, in the Americas, disrespect of Black people is a daily showering—either by Euro-American dominated institutions, by creative intentional design, or by good White people remaining silent. Disrespect also comes from within the Black community—particularly among subgroups (e.g. gang members) of the fragmented Black American "We" society. Such disrespect is a reflection of how slave owners socialized the slaves to be disrespectful to each other. This has been culturally transmitted.

Management of Disrespect: The place for Black people to start in the management of disrespect is with themselves as individuals and as a people. The principle is to stop all disrespect spewed out to anyone while cultivating personal and "We" Afrocentric respect. Once this is firmly established, then there is nothing anyone can do to take it away—and those who try are mentally, philosophically, and spiritually sick. Those sick individuals need to be pitied or ignored (because they are merely projecting how they feel about themselves).

African Tradition is the best model to study for gaining detailed ideas as to what to do (Donkor, p. 146). For example, the Akan (Ghana) protocol is based on three major interwoven elements: Spirituality, Humility, and Respect.

Akan spirituality is built into the "We" sense of community as a way of life. The key features are love, harmony, peace, interdependence, trust, honesty and other Ma'at traits which permeate the families, homes, and the environment. These values are reinforced through spiritual rituals, ceremonies, and festivals.

Humility, starting from the Afrocentric belief that no one is greater than God, means being "real" and with dignity and modesty. "Real" people acknowledge that: "All I have and all I am comes from God's grace" — and without implying a pious inferiority complex. That and the story of humility being associated with the good earth have been elaborated upon elsewhere. (Bailey, Good Character p101).

Respect for authority, position, the elderly, the spiritual, the mysterious, and the sacred— according to Opokuwaa (Akan, Protocol, p. 271; The Quest, p. 80)—is strict African Tradition which is taught from cradle to grave. Each person is respected for his/her uniqueness and importance to the well-being of the whole.

An obligation of each person is to *maintain a character deserving of respect.* Otherwise, in Akan Tradition, a loss of respect means the person, the person's family, and the village is viewed with pity and disgrace because the person was not taught the ways of the ancestors. The person must make the appropriate apologies and they must be accepted before atonement rituals are performed and things made right.

If Black Americans followed these principles, they would stop using offensive language (Table III) (Bailey, Self-Esteem); would stop degrading each other (e.g. male/females); would stop envying each other's success; and would band together so as to create, enhance, or maintain a sense of community possessed with "Black Power" strength.

ENVIRONMENTAL PROBLEMS: How would you feel if you were a "*human sardine*" packed into a human "*sardine can*" environment? Africans brought to the Americas as slaves and African American slaves living in ghettos on plantations knew what this was like. So as to carry the largest possible cargo to America, African slaves were packed on board ship during the "*Middle Passage*" so that they were wedged horizontally, spoon fashion, in the space the size of a too small coffin!

If bad weather or equatorial calms prolonged the normal one to three months journey, their twice daily ration of water and either rice, millet, cornmeal, or stewed yams was reduced to a starvation level. This plus no room to shift positions, sit up or turn over while in unbearable heat or cold, while lying in their own waste, and while breathing bad fumes in their unventilated crammed space, resulted in many slaves going "*crazy*" or dying from misery and suffocation. In their madness, some killed others in hopes of gaining more room to breathe.

These experiences, orally passed down to American born slaves "*from lip to ear*" along with the crowded conditions of large numbers of slaves living in a one room cabin, have created a special modern day setting that is not far removed from conditions on the Middle Passage. Thus, "*crammed living*" is valued differently by African Americans compared with Euro-Americans who do environmental research on the subject of "*crowding.*"

Although completely not applicable the struggling Black American Experience, Euro-American authorities define "*crowding*" as the psychological experience of distress that arises from the perception of restricted space. This perception affects the person's sense of privacy, personal space, and territory — the degree to which depending upon how each affected individual feels about it and then responds to it. How Blacks are affected by crowding is largely unknown.

When people are crowded in a ghetto there are associated mental and physical health risks factors that work against the person's ability to rise above poverty. Because politicians seemingly do not care about these neighborhoods, there is more noise, air and water pollution, lead poisoning from out of date buildings, poor enforcement of health safety standards, infections from disease carrying rodents and from sick people too poor to afford proper health care, and lack of open spaces (e.g. parks, lakes, forest) where revitalization can occur.

Threatening or potentially harmful conditions abound among the struggling poor. Many include interpersonal conflicts which generate varied coping behaviors (e.g. isolation, aggression), bad attitudes (e.g. anger, anxiety, frustration), and destructive physiological reactions (e.g. ulcers, irritability, fatigue-all due to over-stimulation of the automatic nervous system). Similarly, crowded prison inmates show higher blood pressure, more mental disorders, and an increased mortality rate than do uncrowded prisoners.

Even though the people are adjusted to it, loud noises and continuous distracting activities impair the ability to think and work. Children in noisy schools (as in being on the flight path of airplanes) have higher blood pressure, are more distractable, have more difficulty with puzzles and mathematics problems, and experience more hearing difficulties.

The survival stresses of daily life combined with living in an unhealthy environment may, in general, cause African Americans to be quite accepting of over-crowding if it helps them get through the day. On the other hand, overcrowding can make for poor social relations — more family fights, more husband/wife problems, and more "*turf*" wars. Overcrowding may tend to cause parents to find relief from having their youth out of the home, even if they do not know where the youth are or what they are doing.

Loneliness

Humans are social animals and this has its fullest expression in the "We" societies of African and Asian Tradition. But Europeans pride themselves in being an "I" (Individualist) society but they are going against what is natural. This unnaturalness drives many youthful Europeans "crazy" because they would rather belong than to spend all of their lives acquiring possession that they can not take with them when they die.

Otherwise, for many humans in the USA and elsewhere the nature of their lives, occupations, isolation circumstances, or being misfits and not liked necessitate spending time alone. Some are alone (a word meaning "all by oneself") while others are lonely (i.e. a desire for companionship).

Sort of a combination between the "We" and "I" groups is the **"Constructive I"** individuals—those who leave the crowd to cultivate their talents that will benefit the crowd. They need to be alone because they have so many things to do and have to travel unexpectedly and quickly. By being alone they get more work done and much faster and without interferences from the outside world — television, radio, talk shows, telephone ringing, people running in and out slamming doors or asking "just one more question." Yet, they spend time with people at every chance possible.

Everybody in the world is going to be alone for a small, medium, or large part of his/her life. The companion who spends the greatest amount of time with me is me. Whether we are alone or lonely depends upon <u>what we think about</u> when we feel isolated.

People who feel lonely are thinking about their feelings in a negative self-talk way. Usually, a common cause of LONELINESS is SELF-DISLIKE (see Chapter XI). People who do not like themselves do everything they can — playing music very loudly, watching television—to avoid being quiet and having to face themselves. Self-dislike can be so great as to cause people to withdraw from other people in order to prevent other people from seeing how unlikable they think they are. Or they fear not getting enough attention, looking foolish, or not liking what the crowd is doing. Any of these can cause them to feel "lonely in a crowd."

Then some youth are lonely merely because they imagine others do not like them, this answer is far too simple. More realistic options are:

(1) A tiny few may dislike you;

(2) You may not be correct in imagining others do not like you;

(3) You may not have made the effort to fit in;

(4) You and they may be okay and yet not be a "match" for each other.

MANAGING LONELINESS: Since you are going to have to spend the rest of your life with you, make the adjustments and do what it takes to like yourself. Start by thinking about a long-term goal, about creating ways to live well, and about how to help others. For example, "What skills do I need to help me and the people I love? This requires being alone and quiet in order to hear yourself think. Consider such life-shaping questions as a form of meditation as well as a form of philosophical thinking.

An equally enjoyable form of thinking while alone is CONTEMPLATION — mentally becoming one with something else and getting more and more out of it the longer you concentrate, like bird-watching or art.

Lonely people should force themselves to be good interviewers of others, to become good listeners, and figure out ways to make others happy. Learn to be eager to talk with others about topics of their interest. Discover how much fun it is to talk with children about true and real ideas. Engage in positive self-talk, like "how can I make today the best day possible?" Develop your wit by finding something amusing in looking at common things in an uncommon way and uncommon things in a common way.

Rejection

The Story of Rejection: Seagulls hovering over an incoming fishing trawler in order to feed on the tossed fish parts the crew has rejected ("*to throw back*") is perhaps the only useful illustration of the original meaning of "Rejection" back in olden times.

The Bible (Mark 8:31) says there were certain religious leaders who looked at Jesus, over-checked him out, and then deliberately rejected him. In other words, their rejection was about turning away from Jesus by not consenting to accept, receive, or consider him. This had nothing to do with who Jesus was as a person or his worth or his value. Instead, it was merely a non-acceptance.

In 1415 Europe, the word "reject" meant "to cast out" or "dismiss" and later "refuse to recognize." Other concepts arose during the Renaissance about "reject." One was a school of art, called "Rejective Art," that rejected non- essentials — those parts not allowed, gotten rid of, or refused to have anything to do with because it lacked essence and substance. **Essence** is what something is; **Substance** is the foundation making up the character of essence, which in African Tradition, represents the image of God.

Another meaning of “reject” was the sense of “throw back”— not because it is valueless but simply because one did not want it or had no use for it. An example is a manuscript that is declined or refused.

The ground-work was laid for a racial type of “rejection” prior to the 16th century, before Englishmen had had any significant contact with Black Africans. The Oxford English Dictionary definition of the color **“black”** was: “Deeply stained wtih dirt; soiled, dirty, foul — having dark or deadly purposes, malignant; pertaining to or involving death . . .” This set the stage for deep-seated hostility towards Black people.

Thus, when English voyagers to Africa first encountered dark-skinned people, they regarded them with distaste — as creatures less than human — the key point of racism. The Whites who showed *aversion* (“a turning away” from another's humanness) during slavery were the “Renaissance gentlemen” who financed the slave trade and then became USA “southern gentlemen”;

Adversion (a face-to-face opposition) was shown by the ex-convict slave overseers who had been released from European jails on the condition that they would leave Europe forever by going to America. These overseers became the “redneck racists”; the police of the slaves; and the Ku Klux Klan members. Meanwhile, the “southern gentlemen” spread their racist attitudes into the government and legal system and plantations and mainstream corporate America—each of which has maintained ever since the rejection of minorities.

The World of Rejection: From the story of the word “Rejection” we can see that there are several concepts contained inside it. Here are some types that are brought about by others and that are brought about by you.

I. REJECTION BY OTHERS:

A. YOU ARE NOT A MATCH for something you may desire. In other words, you or something may be all right or useful or valuable as is but it is not a “match” for the present situation. Two good people could marry each and yet get a divorce because they are not a match and could not figure how to make the marriage work.

B. YOU ARE REJECTED FOR REASONS UNRELATED TO YOU. Even though you may be a skilfull actor, the part of playing a Dwarf is not designed for you. I go to many book sales — books that sell for 25 or 50 cents — but I only buy those few which best “match” the subjects I am studying or am likely to study. The books I did not buy are quite important to other book buyers. Most of all of our choices in life are about selecting the one that best “matches” what we want and selecting that one means we are rejecting the others. This is extremely important in understanding that there is no attack on your self-esteem because you or your work product are not accepted.

C. REJECTION OF SELFHOOD—these are attacks by mean people that are directed trying to destroy who one is as a person, what one does, or how one appears. During slavery there was an intense programmed form of rejection set up by the captors to operate inside the slave community to destroy their entire selfhood.

D. INDIFFERENCE REJECTION—an example is when parents show no concern for their children's emotional and physical needs. It is believed that most antisocial, aggressive tendencies are the result of emotional insecurity incurred by rejection or loss of parental love.

E. AVERSION REJECTION. Understand that on a Hate Scale there are two main types of people—the Aversion and the Adversion sadist. To tolerate their own outrageously inhumane dealings with African American slaves, European "*gentlemen*" slaveowners "*turned away*" (Aversion) from considering the slaves as human beings. People who have an aversion to you are those who have been taught by racists not to consider you as human in order for them to be indifferent, with its lack of caring and affections.

F. ADVERSION REJECTION –an example of face-to-face oppositional hostility is evil people. They are so terribly disturbed in their minds with spiritual pain as to hate themselves (e.g. racist rednecks). Besides, they have overwhelming personal problems. In trying to get even a tiny bit of relief from their unbearable mental pain, they choose Black people to hate and to inflict sadistic acts and practices. Although they may say you are worthless or valueless, this does not make it true. They say this out of envy of you not experiencing their mental and spiritual pain.

Nevertheless, many people are almost destroyed by these sadists. It is typical for mentally weak people—those who are the "vicious cycle" poor—to believe that rejection is who they are as a person — worthless. They play the rejection scene over and over in their minds to keep fresh every detail that happened and even details that did not happen. They invite their friends to join them in a "poor me" party to wallow in how bad things are and "why bad stuff always happens to me?"

Being mentally weak does not have anything to do with intelligence or the ability to break the "vicious cycles." Breaking the cycle starts by locating the trigger person or the trigger event and the trigger emotion and then dismantling the happening for purposes of analysis and correction of the flaws. Since management is so involved, it is best to consult the section on "Tools" and tailor make an approach.

Keep in mind that views of outsiders — even authorities or experts—are wrong in their rejection judgment of you. After all, religious leaders looked Jesus over, checked him out, and then deliberately rejected Him. TO GET OFF THE FLOOR ONE MORE

TIME THAN YOU HAVE BEEN KNOCKED DOWN REQUIRES DISASSOCIATING (splitting off as independent units) what "they say" and then handling it so as to continue going where you need to go.

G. SLIDING SCALE REJECTION is commonly known as "*love/ hate*" relationships. These individuals will do nice things for you at the same time they are doing all they can to hurt you. A feature is them telling you how much you missed from not going with them—even though they did not invite you.

H. FAILED TEST REJECTIONS means that one does not win or qualify because of not meeting certain standards. When it comes to money, power, and education in the American marketplace, the standards are set up for Whites, by Whites, and based upon the system of values of Whites. Despite being unfair, "*that's the way it is.*" To successfully compete, Blacks must "*work twice as hard to get half as much.*" Most often, failing to pass the test is from lack of proper preparation. Or, what you have to offer may be good enough to win the city award but not the state award.

II REJECTIONS BROUGHT ON BY ONESELF:

A. SELF-DIRECTED REJECTION of this type began with your definition of rejection formed by the feelings you generated in your childhood magical mind. The seed for your self-definition was usually brought about by the opinion of others who gave you wrong information. Simply put, your definition was based on that whatever was not for you must be against you. Thereafter you engaged in "condemnation self-talk" which in turn resulted in an erosion (wear away) and corrosion (gnaw away) of your self-confidence, self-esteem, or self-motivation.

Perhaps your subsequent story went like this. There were two or more times in your early childhood that you perceived that you were rejected, neglected, or ignored. This has happened to each one of us and, at those times, we feel that every part of us and everything we do is judged as wrong or bad. Then we feel emotional pain down to the bone. It leaves us asking: "What did I do to deserve this?" Our resultant belief of worthlessness shouts in our inner ear that we could not pass the easiest of mental or physical inspection.

The more you and we wallow in this pain the worse our imagination makes it: "Nobody accepts me"; and worse of all, "God doesn't love me." These feelings are only the tip of the iceberg. We can go on to be destructive to ourselves (e.g. over-eating, lazy) or to others.

B. SELF-REJECTION FROM MISPERCEPTIONS results when you are irritable and filled with chronic frustration, helplessness, fear, anxiety, emotional pain, spiritual pain (an interference with the flow of love), and/or physical pain. These make it easy to take comments, situations, or actions out of context and misinterpret them as rejection when there was no rejection intended. A wife may do something for herself that is in no way directed against her husband. However, if he is hypersensitive he may feel rejected — and vice versa. When in a habit of thinking rejection, many go looking to be rejected just to prove their point.

C. REJECTION BY INVITATION. I am astonished by and appalled at the extremely common practice of people who receive gifts but fail to say "*thank you.*" Some even make the gift giver feel bad about having given the gift and by not having given more. The message of the ungrateful: "*I care nothing about you but just your money*" — a position that begs for the giver to "*reject me.*"

As a boy, I was taught nobody has to give you anything and, if they do, immediately respond with a letter, telephone call, or face to face expression of appreciation. I noticed that if I did things purely for people's benefit, they appreciate it. If one tried to control while benefitting from the gift, they reject it. If one tried to manipulate, one often got away with it because people are gullible.

D. REJECTION FROM IMMATURE THINKING—When the trauma of rejection and therefore insecurity happens to 3 year olds, their minds are forever attached to toxic "all-or-none" or "either/or" thinking. As a result of being correctly or incorrectly perceived as rejected, the 3 year old's way of thinking says: "I'll never take a risk again or even put myself in a position where I can be pushed away." They become very self-conscious and believe that if they make a mistake or if turned down by a potential dance or date partner, "everyone" will know they were rejected. Those painful feelings mushroom into: "everybody will be looking at me 'funny' and talking about me behind my back." They get stuck in "shyness cement" which prevents them from taking the risks that can give enjoyment to life.

One place to start shedding the "shyness cement" is to understand the word "rejection" (discussed above) and the word "problem." Originally, **"PROBLEM"** meant "something thrown in the way of the path" while REJECTION referred to "the path of something thrown across."

The World of Rejection: Feelings of rejection in inner city youth are a reflection of a sick society's problems. They are bombarded by a racist society that targets the poor by using the methods of rejecting, neglecting and ignoring. The effects are at a moderate or extreme level. Just as problems can range from mild to slight to moderate to extreme, so can rejections.

EXTREME (or severe) rejection is about brutal selfhood attacks. It implies that the attacker despises and loathes the attackee. The hateful power of the attackers causes little kids to believe and internalize self-destructive things. Such a scenario was quite common from the demeaning personal attacks on the slaves by the slave owners.

MODERATE rejection, rather than being a frontal personal attack, carries overtones of casting aside as useless or valueless behaviors or work products that is the victim of the attacker. It is the attitude that: "You are nothing because I say so." Then the attacker goes on to paint a picture of how great he/she is and how great is what he/she is doing.

SLIGHT rejection is the turning down of something and saying "no" to for reasons that may or may not have to do with the person making the offer. For example, scientists reject testing that is not scientifically done. Or, one may not be accepted because of not being qualified or of being over-qualified.

MILD rejection merely indicates that something does not fit. Rationally oriented people (who are very few in number) are generally not accepted into the in-group of emotionally oriented people because they are not a good match.

Managing Rejection In General: A giant step in handling your complex feelings of rejection is to realize that there are several shades of other meanings between someong being "for me" or "against me" and "either/or" and "all-or-none" thinking. What is in between may be the key to success.

Still, despite a lack of clarity, we can use any one of several well-known methods to break the habit of our own bad emotions. This frees us to work on achievements which establish self-worth and value to others (Bailey, Self-Esteem). Progress comes in little ways, step-by-step. It is best to start with the trigger emotion as, for example, insecurity.

INSECURITY, psychologists say, is THE SINGLE MOST IMPORTANT CAUSE OF SUBSEQUENT ADJUSTIVE DIFFICULTIES. Insecure kids feel they are getting much less than they need. From that point on, THEY STRUGGLE MORE WITH THE FEAR OF REJECTION THAN THE REALITY OF REJECTION.

Their defenses against rejection and insecurity wall off their inner self from the outside world. Anxiety (with hazy anger associated) from insecurity plays a large part in delinquent behavior (including cheating, stealing, and violence). It also accounts for many problems (e.g. promiscuity) in dating and marriage.

Thus, rejection can cause poverty as well as be the effect of poverty. The more passive kids develop an "I'm not good enough" (i.e. low self-esteem) depression; the more aggressive kids, greed (which is a kind of fear). *Both greed and depression might be narrowed by reducing the pain of insecurity*.

Otherwise, regardless of whether from society or parental causes, the rejected repress their feelings. Yet, those feelings continue to work in their unaware minds to create distortions of thought, hostile feelings, anxiety, bitter self-deprecation, low spirits, and insecurity. So, what can be done?

Step I— be clear about the term that applies to you. Whereas NEGLECT means to be disregarded with little or no attention or respect and IGNORED is to be left out or left unnoticed, REJECTION means "to throw away"—and this goes even deeper than these emotional pains — so deep as to affect our spirit.

Step II—Assess and examine the entire experience of rejection. Discover the trigger person and the trigger emotion. Often, our destroyed self-worth and self-value came from our parent's attitude denying our acceptance while treating us as an unwanted burden, a nuisance, and a source of trouble. Or, so we believed as little kids. But is this really true? Is there any way to ask the trigger person? If not, make up a story that explains away what you thought happened.

Step III— Youth or adults who resort to thinking as 3 year olds assume the extreme rejection category for themselves — even if the slight or mild or no rejection level was actually intended. A return to reality is about properly re-categorizing your prior rejections. Throw out the ones that were not real and deal only with the real rejections within their proper category.

Step IV— There is no better clue of future success in business, in social relationships, or in rising above poverty than the individuals who keep coming back after being rejected over and over. The guy who gets the best wife did not take her rejections personally but keep picking away at getting her approval. Causing them to get up each time they are knocked down is the "**NEVER GIVE UP**" philosophy.

Step V—The process of self-correction involves Self-Compassion — like putting aside the unwanted and unloved feelings with which we were viewed in childhood. Besides our not deserving those feelings, they really do not belong to us. Rather, they belong to our parents who were burdened with their own miserable problems.

Step VI—begin with **THANKFULNESS** for what we already have. Also, keeping a diary of the worthwhile things happening to us each day will teach us **GRATEFULNESS**. Our reward comes in taking a moment to enjoy particular satisfying achievements. For those who unfairly reject us, we might say "I've been rejected by better people than you" — smile — and walk away.

Step VII—forgive all who need to be forgiven

IV

THE FIVE BASIC NATURAL EMOTIONS

NATURAL EMOTIONS

Are the Naked Truth
about
the *Irrational*
and
the **IllogicaL**

Sometimes, not getting help is a blessing in disguise. In the 1980's there were various reasons I needed to know about emotions in general and the types of emotions in particular. The more I read in psychiatry and psychology books the more confusing the subject of Emotions became.

Some authorities said there are only two basic (elementary, primitive, primary) emotions — joy and suffering; others said there were three — pleasure, pain, and desire; still other said four — mad, sad, glad, or scared. From there, the numbers went into the hundreds and no authority seemed to completely agree with any other authority.

All of this chaos meant that I needed to find out as much as possible on my own and then reduce the information into an understandable and easily remembered classification. It took about a year to get comfortable in dealing with this impossible subject. The approach was to study the brain (to discover which emotions had "physiological loops"—that are incorrectly called "centers" for convenience) and to apply that information to Rational Thinking.

Second, knowing that many subhuman type animals (as evidenced by their expressions) simulate unconscious human reactions when faced with the same conditions suggested that such reactions were candidates for being selected as basic emotions. This became clear to me in observing my Pekinege dog—the most "emotional" dog I ever had (my other dogs were the somewhat rationally based German Sheperds).

Third, basic emotions seemed to be neutral in their orientation in that they arose from self-preservation instinct and without the input of thought. Thus, I eliminated Instinct Emotions as being of an abstract or of a Sublime nature, as conveyed in the term "wonderful."

Finally, it was apparent that different authorities were using different words for a given but fragmented emotion. Yet, certain synonym words belonged to the same emotion but applied to different levels of intensity. For example, "glad," "pleasure," and "joy" are words for pleasant emotions representing the same mindset. But since they imply different degrees of intensity, they belong on different planes of existence. Thus, they would not represent separate basic emotions. However, Critical Thinking causes us to look even more closely.

Some authorities use the same word for different emotions based upon the way they defined each emotion. For example, they might use the words "feeling good" to indicate "glad," "pleasure" and "joy." However, each of these words is on a different plane of existence compared with the others. Even though "good" is a common thread, the ideas inside each word has different features.

Still other words—like fear and anxiety—fail to be completely distinquished by most authorities because they may be triggered by the same mechanism. However, the "fear center" is inborn while "anxiety center" is acquired. Besides, some fears are natural and innate (e.g. self-preservation) while other fears are unnatural and acquired (e.g. feuds or greedy aggression). By contrast, anxiety is always acquired. Before proceeding let us look at Ancient Africans' Classification of the Universal Planes of Existence.

By using this type of reasoning and studying brain anatomy, I concluded, without being definite, that THERE ARE FIVE BASIC EMOTIONS: RAGE, FEAR, DEPRESSION, EMOTIONAL PAIN, and PLEASURE.

It is from combinations of these five primary emotions that all other emotions derive. Some of those emotions contain thoughts and some do not. Some of these combined emotions reflect simple feelings and experiences. Some of those combined emotions combine even more to produce more complex emotional states—like grief, disgust, or frustration.

When these emotions reach their limit inside the Tangible realm, the word "Feeling" better represents what is in Lofty realms. Emotions approaching the Lofty fade into "Feelings" simply because of their rapid vibrations that carry them beyond being stirred (recall that emotions are stirred up feelings).

If we assume that the instinctive requires no conscious thought, then basic emotions are instincts. Let us assume, therefore, that such a thing exists as the self-preservation instinct of "flight", as in running away from a bear, and that fleeing has some thing to do with being afraid.

In studying about fear I learned that it and other basic emotions are controlled by many different parts of the brain (a physiological loop) rather than by any single emotion center. To repeat, simply for convenience, I chose to refer to a fear "center" as that brain location which seems most commonly associated with the emotion of Fear. As a result of this approact, many stirred up feelings from other authority's categories of primary emotions were eliminated.

The Chinese speak of Instinct natural emotions as a release of Ch'I (Universal Energy). To me this implies that the **Instinct or Natural or Basic Emotions are of a finite Spiritual nature--with no degrees—and devoid of thoughts—and designed for self-protection**.

Some Instinct Emotions do not express themselves at birth—but rather some after birth (for which the term "Tarda" is used). For example, although fear is genetically based, it may not show for days or weeks or months after birth—which makes this post-birth display of fear a **"Tarda" Emotion.**

Some Basic or Natural Emotions are expressed in the womb (e.g. Rage) under special stimulation or expressed at birth (i.e. as pure expressions of human nature). Others await some trigger event that generates thoughts before they are expressed. Whenever that stimulus and its associated thoughts arise and then are expressed as one glob, they are called Sentiments or Thought/Emotions or Complex Emotions. Put another way, whereas Rage is an Instinct Emotion, Anger is Rage which has been diluted and polluted with acquired thoughts.

"So," you may ask, "since I feel all of these emotions at different times in my life, how do I know which emotional state I have?" Answer: first, the one that is of greatest frequency (Table II) with respect to the emotional state you deem of greatest significance. Second, the one that is present when you are in a "normal" functioning mindset.

Table II -- **Frequency Scale**

- Occasional (1 to 24% of the time)
- Intermittent (25-49% of the time)
- Prolonged (50-74% of the time)
- Constant (75 to 99% of the time)

Third, if you have a certain emotional state more often than intermittently, then it is dominant. INTERMITTENT means occurring at intervals that constitute about half of the total time—and presenting at more or less regular intervals (Bailey, Medical-

Legal Dictionary). If a certain emotion remains for a prolonged period of time (i.e. to the point that its duration concerns you) without letting up, it is "clinical" and chronic.

Whatever is spiritually based (i.e. instinctional as opposed to acquired) does not have degrees. By contrast, what is acquired has degrees of mild, slight, moderate, and extreme.

RAGE/ANGER

RAGE ("rabies" madness) is a reflection of our fighting instinct and its associated acqired emotion is anger. Though not nearly so common as fear, both rage and fear cause similar body "fight, freeze, or flight" reactions. In lower animals, the fighting instinct is particularly seen among mothers protecting their young, the future of the race depending on it. In such situations they are extremely powerful. They, like humans, show similar body expressive reactions — raising the upper lip and sneering and snarling to bare the teeth in preparation for biting.

Rage may have low and high forms, depending on the use or non-use of specialized cells of the temporal lobe — called the GOD MODULE – which concern spirituality, prayer, and religious experiences. In the mature who use these cells, courage, energy, and persistence spring out of anger and the fighting instinct for the purpose of noble deeds.

Being a normal instinct emotion present at birth (and even before), rage works through the sympathetic portion of the autonomic nervous system. Innately it is designed for self-protection anytime one has the perception of one's selfhood coming under threat, disturbance, or destruction. After birth it also develops an acquired humanitarian sensitivity to any acts of unfairness to oneself and/or to others (e.g. loved ones) but in a more tempered or masked or concealed way which therefore takes it into the anger realm. About 75% of anger-rousing events are interpersonal.

A STORY OF ANGER: In ancient Greek mythology the world of anger contained agony, anguish, despair, indignity, wrath, resentfulness, discomposure, hostility, brooding, irritation, annoyance, rage, and hate. Within this world the Greek god Zeus, for example, was said to breathe fire and sting others with his fiery tongue. Numerous other mythological figures, like the Furies and Gorgons, showed anger. The Bible has much to say about anger — that it stirs up strife (Pr. 30:33) and dissension (Pr. 29:22); that it is by nature cruel; and that it carries a person into the path of the dangerous. The hot-tempered say untrue or partially true insulting or ridiculous things about the opponent(s) or do something bad.

The reaction of the opponent is to assume the "inflamed mind" of anger which, in turn, produces intense passions for revenge for a perceived wrong or intentional injury. If an attack is actually made and the opponent returns the attack, there is raid after raid by both sides — a FEUD — for every real or fancied injury. Thus, the subdivisions in the world of anger are: (1) mild anger (e.g. annoyance, irritation); (2) slight anger, a short-lasting emotion readily experienced towards those we care about; (3) moderate anger with its thoughts of revenge; and (4) extreme anger, indistinquishable from HATE, is a lasting sentiment containing desires for deliberate destruction. EVIL is hate and cold rageful behaviors directed toward deliberate destructions.

AN ANGER SNAPSHOT

Definition: An inflamed mind causing physical agitation

Attitude: Unfairly treated; Denial of any contribution

Manifestation: A fighting spirit

Effect: Whatever angers you, wraps you in chains; also, anger eats away ones physical self, as acid erodes its container

Complications: addictions; unhappy; destruction to self and/or others

Cause: The bottom line is a disturbance in the flow of Love

Management: Cultivate the flow of love coming in and going out of oneself - - e.g. by appreciation, compassion, harmony, and unity orientations

The World of Anger: *Rage is to anger as fear is to anxiety.* Whereas rage and fear are instincts (that are closely associated), anger and anxiety are acquired states of excitement generated by the perception, memory, interpretation, and probably the addition of imagination related to some trigger person and/or trigger event (see later discussion). Rage and anger have been thoroughly dealt with in my book: Anger in Black Americans.

Mild and Slight anger (fig. 2) have the feature of clarity and certainty, whether right or wrong, and provides movement. If the intensity reaches Moderate or Extreme, that movement is in a vicious circle direction which, because of repetition, is a self-destructive habit. Anger is the one emotion that wants a fight. Through the ages it it is the only one that has given the nerve for one to take a stand against certain types of intruders.

Since anger is an emotion, it does not contain its own judgment or moral mechanism and is therefore dependent on a fellow constructive mind committee member to keep it under control. If the mind committee's commands are one of distortions and fantasy, then ones anger will react in the direction outlined by the committee's **Illusions** (mistaken or distorted perceptions or false impressions from faulty thinking); by the **Delusions** (false beliefs about something real but which remains resistant to contrary evidence or better reasoning); or by the **Hallucinations** (a lack of reality in the external world) (Bailey, Self-Esteem, p. 207).

THE STRESS CURVE

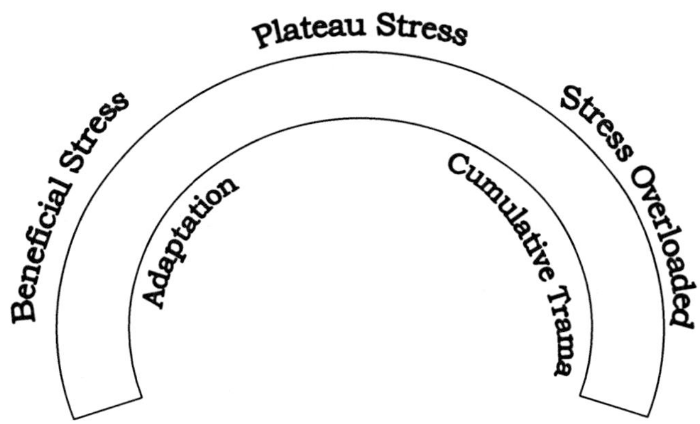

Figure 2
(Reprinted from Bailey – "*Anger In Black Americans*")

Mature Anger, under normal circumstances, lasts only as long as needed to provide self-protection. A crazy driver of a car comes at you and you jump out of the way. You become angry during the process but once the danger is over, your anger fades. When anger is a by-product of a duty generated by compassion for others, it becomes a motivating and driving fore for one to do whatever one can to help relieve the pain and suffering of others. Under these circumstances of compassion, anger is in the back of one's mind and is operating at a mild or a slight level—a level which sharpens the thinking processes.

But when your mind committee sends commands based on distortion or fantasy, the sympathetic nervous system and its associated anger go on an intense, steady, and ongoing alert. This is a tremendous waste of energy because the trigger person or the trigger situation is either exaggerated, hazy (distortion), or a fantasy. By staying on alert, the body remains at an increased protective mode of those spontaneous factors which are not under your control — more sugars pouring into the bloodstream (a fuel for energy); faster blood circulation (to remove waste products); increased force from a faster heart beat which increases blood pressure; more adrenaline outpouring from the adrenal glands to make your vision a bit sharper; and so forth.

Meanwhile, your anger remains at, say, a slight to moderate level which makes for “a short fuse” — a dynamite related expression indicating the chronically angry person stays ready to erupt “at the drop of a hat.” Incidentally, in the late 1800s, dropping a hat started immediate action related to a contest. When prolonged, this excessive production does damage to your body and causes you to get older faster. Furthermore, the combination of using up body reserves by the sympathetic nervous system staying on alert, and the muscle tension associated with chronic anger, causes physical ills — especially if the anger is unexpressed; if the body reserves are not replaced; and if the by-products of burned up body items are not flushed out rapidly enough.

Chronic fatigue is the flag bearer of chronic anger. Certain body language signs appear— perhaps clenching your teeth and grinding them down during sleep which, in turn, can cause pains in the jaws, neck, upper back, and/or headaches. There may even be ringing in the ears or biting of your lips or the inside of your cheeks. You may keep your hands in a clenched fist position; or change your stance into an “attack readiness” position; or lower your eyes, frown, or sulk. Some people get skin problems from chronic anger — hives, acne, itching, or premature wrinkling.

In my practice I was surprised to learn that people with **Psychosomatic** complaints — particularly resulting from unexpressed chronic anger — may have very real pain. My hypothesis is that muscles under chronic tension will leak out certain substances from the capillaries and those substances accumulate between muscle fibers, form scar-type matting, and thereby interfere with the smooth gliding action of the muscle fibers. In the process, tiny nerve fibers are entrapped in the “matted” tissue.

The *Outward Expressions* of Rage and Hate: ANGER IS EMOTIONAL INFLAMMATION OF THE MIND associated with a state of PHYSICAL AGITATION. If intense, anger is an impulsive emotion that overrides reason. Its outward expresions vary markedly according to one’s previous training, experience, and choice of power vehicle that makes up one’s philosophy of life. A common manifestation of anger is Offensive Language.

The Categories of Anger Manifestations are overt, tempered, masked, or concealed.

Overt Anger (“open”; uncovered; unfastened; evident) means those attitudes, feelings, and behaviors that are put into words (most commonly the use of offensive language (Table III) or acted upon rather than intimated or suppressed. In orthopaedic surgery, an example of overt is a fracture/dislocation of a joint compared with the tempered form as presented by a stress fracture. In law, overt means an open and outward act from which criminal intent is inferred. In behaviors, an example may be “flight” or “fight” or observable acts of violence or acts of abuse.

A most obvious form of overt aggression during slavery was the vast numbers of African American slaves who revolted. Some revolts were in the barracoons; some aboard slave trade ships; and some in the Americas. Other forms used by the slaves included physical violence, self-mutilation, suicide, and infanticide. These and others have been discussed in my book: "American Crime."

Table III — **A Classification of Offensive Language**

I	Blasphemy	Attempts to harm God's reputation
II	Profanity	Disrespect of what one holds sacred
III	Cursing	Calling on spirits to cast an *"evil spell"*
IV	Swearing	Calling on God to witness a non-truth
V	Obscenities	arousal of disgust
VI	Vulgarities	coarse and violent talk
VII	Malicious Name-Calling	attacking all dimensions of one's self-esteem
VIII	Maledictions	speaking evil of the victim

(Reprinted from Bailey – *Self-Esteem in Black Americans*)

Tempered Anger ("lessen"; soften) is from Latin "temperare". The *story of "Tempered"* was originally about mixing or blending in due proportions the elements of something. Then it came to mean controlled natural tendencies — as in toning down or reducing the intensity of something. For instance, when one's lower self (e.g. greed, passions, anger) was involved, to temper was to reduce the severity of their effects.

By 1828 tempered referred to an angry state of mind. Rather than manifest overt violence, people showed tempered anger through such measures as demonstrations, protest, or litigation. These are the measures Black people would greatly benefit from putting into action on a daily basis in order to move in the direction of obtaining their hard earned first class citizenship.

Masked Anger ("disguised") has many types of presentation. Some of these include that which gives a false impression (as in disguises at a Halloween party which cover the face); that which protects the face (as Egyptians placed on the deceased to divert bad spirits); that which camouflages (as when the chameleon blends into its surroundings); and that which shows as mimicry (as when the organism is not hidden but rather presents a false identity by its resemblance to another species).

An example of a "masked" concept in orthopaedic medicine is myofascial pain in the foot of a patient with rheumatoid arthritis. The tendency is to look at the most obvious (i.e. the rheumatoid arthritis as the source of the pain) and fail to continue to explore for other sources which are not obvious (e.g. myofacial trigger points).

During slavery, masked anger was extremely common in such caricatures (exaggerated peculiarities) as "Uncle Tom," "Sambo," and "Mammy." Other examples today are psychological abuse, insults, and ridicule (Bailey, Self-Esteem, p. 154). Since this is such a complex subject, let us step back to the first known use of the concept of masks and masquerades.

The **Power Approach vehicles** people choose are labeled passive, passive-aggressive, aggressive cowards (i.e. bullies), the arrogantly aggressive (*"little gods"*), and the non-aggressive. To better understand these five patterns, let us review a few basic aspects of power. **Power** is present inside and outside of us, either being used for good or bad purposes. Upon meeting threats, disruptions, or destructions to our power we can choose to get angry or not.

What anger does is to make one feel stronger—in the sense of a bully or of a victim (and deserving of sympathy and help). For the victim it is also an excuse for not getting back in the game; for the bully, it is to have the victim feel even worse pain than what the bully is experiencing. Self-anger is an excuse to not do what you could and ought to do.

PASSIVE PEOPLE are angry at others for blocking, neutralizing, or overwhelming their power. They have non-specific anger from their loss of power and are angry at themselves from their lack of power.

PASSIVE AGGRESSIVE PEOPLE who are arrogant become humiliated, enraged, and revengeful by those who take away even part of their power. Using the same anger pattern as seen in the Passives, they cultivate it into hate. The hallmark of their revenge is done in masked or concealed ways. This means that they do their *"dirty work"* either *"behind the scenes"* or as hypocrites — *"smiling in your face while stabbing you in the back."*

BULLIES (aggressive cowards) have lost power as a result of their mental conflicts and feelings of inferiority. Instead of turning their resultant self-hate upon themselves, they express their hate on scapegoats in order to justify their superiority complex.

"LITTLE GODS" (arrogant, aggressive people) see themselves as perfect; have a support system that enables them to make decisions affecting the lives of others, even against the will of their victims; and believe they are *entitled* to get the largest share of whatever is considered valuable in their society. Anything interfering with their power of having their way will cause fury (violent anger), which easily turns to hate and passionate revenge.

NON-AGGRESSIVE People are the mentally healthy who seek to replace anger with its opposite virtue, meekness. In the face of adversity, their *"manly resignation"* moderates anger by controlling its intensity. Neither do they allow their anger to be aroused over trivial things. Yet, they do take a stand when their moral values are threatened or disturbed.

THINKER'S SCALE

Figure 3

(Reprinted from Bailey, "*Creativity, Invention & Discovery*")

FORMS OF ANGER: Although there are as many forms of anger as there are people, certain patterns do emerge. These patterns (fig. 3) can be roughly grouped as mild, slight, moderate, and extreme — based upon the degree to which anger slows, stops, or reverses wholesome progress in one's life.

Mild forms have no effect on ones wholesome progress toward a given task

Slight forms are slowing to ones wholesome progress toward a given task

Moderate forms stop ones wholesome progress toward a given task

Extreme forms reverse ones wholesome progress toward a given task.

Of course, there is no definite line between these four. For example, a mate may tolerate mild forms of anger from but when you express those same "mild" forms to a boss, the effect of the boss's reaction against you may be moderate (e.g. you not receiving promotions), or extreme (e.g. you getting fired). Furthermore, the boss may display moderate or extreme forms of anger and you will not be affected. Besides, many features in one form may be seen in other forms.

It is important to keep in mind that the causes and expressions of anger in Europeans and Black people are quite different. Whereas fear is dominant emotion in Europeans, it is chronic anger (related to racism) that is the dominant emotion in

Black Americans. Hence to approaches to treatment are often quite different. What does not work well for either group is the Venting of Anger because whatever leads to talking fast and loud or punching a bag or pillow generates more anger.

Thus, there will be an attempt to fit the following into a classification. As a disclaimer, I have no expertise in dealing with angry people but have had best results from **letting them say what is on their minds without interrupting them**—however long that takes. Since that is too time consuming I simply try to avoid them.

TEMPER TANTRUM ANGER: Just as walking and talking around 12 months of age are normal developmental milestones for toddlers, so are temper tantrums. For some, it is an angry display of the child's sense of having realized the loss of his/her all-powerful status; for others, it is the result of frustration at not being able to get an adult to understand something; and for still others, it is from being denied something.

One management approach is to redirect the child's interest by offering an attractive distraction. A second is to ask direct questions as to what the child wants (e.g. hunger, exhaustion). If no response, do a quick physical check to troubleshoot for anything that is sore, or clothing too tight, or fever. If all is okay, put them in a bland place (where there are no things of interest) and leave them alone so as to get across the message that there are no benefits from being angry. When I was living in Wilson, North Carolina— with Mama Clara, Aunt Julia, and Aunt Cherry—when I got tonsillitis they were robot-like in taking care of me. They brought me food, said nothing, and left. From not being pampered, I decided to stop getting sick — and to this day I have not had anything more than a cold.

A third approach derives from the belief that the child is slowly realizing a loss of power related to controlling the world. A principle for dealing with children is to never give in, no matter what. To do so convey to the child that this is the way to manipulate you to gain what the child is after. Instead, do what is necessary for the child to develop a sense of power and importance. This can come from allowing the child to help do such chores as washing the car or helping to take care of the family pet.

But the bigger problems come when a child is putting on a public temper tantrum performance, say, at a grocery store. If distracting their attention, finding out what the child wants, and troubleshooting for physical problems do not work, then pick up the child and leave, even if the shopping cart is almost full. People will stare and form opinions. Avoid yelling or spanking and, instead, simply leave immediately. The key is consistently following the same routine and **not giving in**. To give in is to prove to the child and he/she has the power to get all desires met.

Adult temper tantrums have many patterns. In general they have strong opinions; get angry on impulse; hate incompetence; and may throw things.The "**Storm Out**" pattern consists of those who abruptly leave with hostility. Some lock themselves in a room (e.g. bathroom), move out, or go for a walk. The idea is to make their partners seek them out and try to woo them back. Or if the angry person returns without prompting, it is timed to ensure the mate is worried to the point of apologizing for causing the anger. A better approach is for the mate to defuse the situation by making light of it: "There he/she goes again!" It is not a good idea to tease. The angry mate needs to cool down and to examine "why" as part of troubleshooting every step of what happened and why the need to make the partner feel guilty.

Insults are a selfhood sting that manifests as surprise, wide eyes, blood warming behind ones temples, and perhaps a tight chest—together representing the emotion rather than responses to an emotion. Each dimension esculates the others as ones blood pressure and tone of voice go up, with each pushing the other to go higher.

"**Tearful Martyrs**" show a concealed pattern of anger. At the first hint that an argument is arising that they might lose, they hide their anger by turning on a faucet of tears. If that does not work, they "give in" with exaggeration: "Yes, you're right — you're always right and I'm always the one to blame." Thereafter, they mope around the house. A frequent pattern is that physical manifestations are used to mask their intense anger and thereby these people save themselves from being rejected due to their anger. Nevertheless, that anger causes immediate physical changes—e.g. blood rushing to the face (blushing); a quickened heart beat; a strong urge to yell and strike out at anything or any one; and active muscle changes.

Rather than give in simply to keep the peace, the partner should refuse to play the game by ignoring the tears and the silences. The "martyr" needs to discover that there are no benefits from this drama of histrionics. For example, people who hold in their anger are in a constant state of muscular tension as a means of trying to prevent their anger from showing through. This causes very real fatigue. Also, anger causes skin temperature to drop and this contributes to redness of the face, hives, acne, and even itching. Winning comes at a superficial level but real intimacy comes from being honest and open instead of "slipping and sliding, peeking and hiding."

Management starts with facing the source of their anger and handling that (as discussed in my book on Self-Esteem and in the chapter on "Tools").

SULKERS are the individuals who show obvious signs of being angry — a long face, sighing heavily, banging pots and pans — but when asked: "What's wrong?" they reply: "Nothing." The game is about: "*You should know what's on my mind and if you don't read my mind then you don't love me.*" The issue is almost always something the partner was perceived to have done "wrong" and there will be no inquiry to find out what happened because the sulker has already passed judgment.

These are immature individuals with an unnoble loyalty to stubbornness who fail to see the part they play. They believe they should be free to do whatever things they like but hold the partner to rigid standards. They have *no concept of fair play; are resistant to reasoning*; and remain at a childish level. They fail to ask if they are really getting what they want. The best the partner can do is to first ask what is the problem and if there is no answer then ignore the sulking episode. Being fussed over will only train the sulker to use sulking as a means of getting attention.

Management for some is coaxing so as to get the sulker to open up — particularly by starting with some unrelated "small talk." Otherwise, nothing else will work and thus let the anger fade away. For the chronic Sulker the problem is mainly about masking their real feelings and hence one might try appealing to their reason. The Sulker needs to know that constant, silent stewing (Passive Anger), even when not expressed, is self-destructive mentally, physically, and spiritually. It is also a major reason for alienating family, friends, and coworkers—and that is the opposite of what the Sulker is seeking because they want to love and be loved. They, like all people with problematic anger that is above self-help, need to have help from mental health specialist.

"LITTLE GODS" ANGER: A medical term for "little gods" is "*Oppositional Defiant Disorder.*" The public calls them "hotheads." Some children are socialized to be "little gods" (i.e. arrogant people with a sense of entitlement) and behind their anger is greed. Others become "little gods" from parents not imposing the guidance all children need. Still others are so scarred from psychological trauma that their inferiority complex is converted into a Bully type superiority complex. Anger for each type becomes an Addiction and serves as a means of sheer entertainment in the "power display" game. As is typical of addictions, there are combinations of bad emotions present (e.g. fear, hate, revenge); combinations of some type of abuse (e.g. drugs, alcohol, scapegoats); and perhaps some sort of organic (biochemical, anatomical) brain disorder — one or more of which can predispose to aggressive behavior.

Socialized "little gods" are greedy; lack discipline; are focused on a hedonistic lifestyle; believe they are too superior to show a good work ethic; deny their anger; and often engage in excessive drinking and physical fights. Otherwise, their hair-trigger tempers can erupt at any time for little or no reason and such outburst alienate family, friends, and coworkers. Although a few silently "stew," most scream and yell. Their "spoil-ness" causes them to be very hard on people who do not see things their way. Many know the proper solution but, when angry, they are unable to do it. They presume the world was constructed to specifically irritate them.

Little gods on the lower rungs of the social ladder are frequently introduced to "unnecessary acquaintances" — those who can put them in jail or "take them down." Otherwise, they are likely to wind up with apathy, hopelessness, promiscuity, and passive-aggressive behaviors.

Anger Manifestations of "little gods" include shouting insults and possibly throwing things. More often, they make biting comments by saying the worse possible things about the other's character — like sticking a knife in the heart. Shortly thereafter, they are likely to apologize and fail to understand why the other does not accept the apology and harbors resentment, if not fear. Perhaps it is best to treat "little gods" as if they are two years olds with temper tantrums. Simply leave them to have their tantrums until they calm down.

Management for these "little gods" has been devised by many experts but mental health specialists are not convinced any of these programs work. The general psychological principles include understanding; identifying and learning to control angry emotions; and employing relaxation techniques so as to minimize the physiological responses to anger.

A popular new arrival is called *Anger Management*, many forms of which generate confusing and even bizarre methods. It is unrealistic to think that a few dozen hours of anger management can somehow change a lifetime of destructive behaviors — behaviors that seem "normal" to those involved — behaviors that resist change under the best of circumstances — behaviors extremely likely to return when the "improved" persons return to the same environment that allowed it to fester in the first place. However, most little gods say: "I don't have a problem."

Nothing can be done to help these "little gods" unless they are absolutely determined to have a "character overhaul" and willingly go through the hard work required to switch habits. This is most likely to occur when their lives hit bottom and they know that they must change for the better.

For *socialized "little gods"* a change in their philosophy of life is needed — to make things of earth world value (e.g. power, money, possessions, abusing people) of much, much less importance than things of worth (e.g. love, peace, harmony).

For the *undisciplined "little gods,"* one approach is for them to learn self-control, self-discipline, and to step outside their own self-centeredness.

The *psychologically scarred "little gods"* need to become aware of the trigger person or trigger situation; gather more understanding about the truth of what happened; acknowledge their contribution to the problem; and forgive all who are involved.

The keystones for moving forward are to cultivate appreciation and compassion and shed unnoble loyalty to stubbornness and to immaturity.

Intermittent Explosive Disorder (IED) is a recent diagnosis that brings together those like-kind conditions which have been known under slighty different names because of slightly different criteria used for diagnosis. Both have contributed to misunderstanding and under-appreciation of IED. It is characterized by threats, temper outburst (e.g. as in Road Rage), aggressive actions throwing or breaking things, and even spousal abuse—although not everyone who does those things is afflicted. The average of onset is age 14 and it affects 5 to 7% of USA population, making it more common than schizophrenia and bipolar disorder.

Apart from those who have a biochemical disorder in their brains, anger is an addiction. This addiction accounts for many people's broken relationships, being overweight, substance (drug and alcohol) abuse, and clamoring to take antidepressants for feeling anxious, depressed, or controlled by mood disorders.

Management can work only for those who intensely desire to change. This will not happen for those who say: "I don't have a problem; it is people who are on my back that have a problem." The best attempt for possible improvement is to step behind their anger and explore the path that led up to their anger. At the core of the problem is that the chronically angry person is in spiritual pain—i.e. experiencing a lack of love. If these afflicted individuals can realize their lack of love—either coming in or flowing out of them—then they can be taught to give love to themselves and to other people. It helps to start by being in nature and learning to appreciate something—i.e. to see the dignity in it.

ACCIDENT PRONENESS: Originally, the undue susceptibility to accidental injury was attributed to the recklessness of some psychopaths. Today, "accident-Proneness" is thought of individuals, perhaps with psychogical problems, who demonstrate irresponsible behavior (Gregory p483, 133). The repetition of careless behavior comes out of a compulsion to re-enact certain life situations, regardless of unpleasant emotions or injuries and their consequences.

People who feel hostile or just mad at themselves and then engage in some aggressive action (e.g. sports or pertaining to their jobs) double their own risk of self-injury. The distressing emotions which range from irritability to hostility can give people tunnel vision. By not seeing the big picture makes them less aware of danger and less aware of the consequences of their actions.

Management is about prevention or "nipping the anger in the bud" (a metaphoric expression alluding to a spring frost that kills flower buds). Ways of doing this are discussed under the sections on Management. For example, those with accident proneness tendencies (a condition I learned about in my orthopaedic surgical practice), the idea is to avoid—or at least bring under control— being lonely, tired, hungry, or angry.

CHRONIC ANGER: When vicious cycle obsessions of thought and compulsive actions involve anger, the combination is called Intense CHRONIC ANGER. Short of obsessions, if you are unable to get anything out of your mind it becomes as unwholesome as any thought held continuously to the exclusion of goodness. This means the thought is ruling you instead of you ruling it. This is anger producing that has gone beyond prolonged (extended beyond a standard) anger.

The word "chronic" (Greek, time) implies anger that is deep seated and/or ingrained. It may be **Constant** (continually); **Almost Constant** (continually recurring); or **Recurring**. There are three commonly used words for recurring.

First is *Periodic*, or occurring at regular intervals—but those intervals are of varying lengths throughout the total time.

Second is *Intermittent*, or occurring at intervals that constitute about half of the total time but are more or less regular.

Third is *Occasional*, or occurring at infrequent and irregular intervals. Figures arbitrarily chosen to represent something that is chronic in medicine range from 3 to 6 months after an acute onset.

What chronic anger does is to elevate the heart on high idle which, over decades, contributes to premature death. Every anger outburst releases hormones that tighten arteries and hike blood pressure. Over time the artery walls wear out in the same way that squeezing and pumping will wear out the inside of a garden hose. Worn artery walls are prone to the scarring and fatty build-up that resage heart disease. Chronic anger wrinkles skin.

There are countless reasons for chronic anger and those who have it are mentally unhealthy. Causes include bad things that have happened in ones lifetime; or to ones family or friends; or to ones dead ancestors. Here are some examples.

Example I—The Emotional Scars of children's earliest years lay down a habit pattern. Because feelings from those scars are impulsive and chaotic, children have no words they can use for description. Hence, they cannot say what is bothering them. Instead, they make their anger known by "acting ugly."

Example II—An addiction to anger may be the result of apathy, helplessness, hopelessness, promiscuity, and/or passive-aggressive behavior.

Example III—When teaching "doctoring" to medical students I stress that patients "shut down" once they are told the bottom line of bad news — like "you have incurable cancer." **"**SHUTTING DOWN**"** means that they hear nothing else the physician tells them, no matter how encouraging, because of being filled with chronic anger.

Similarly, when inner city youth enter the first grade, many are already "shut down" to all attempts to educate them. Already they have chronic anger and/or hopelessness from believing that they do not belong in USA society. Already life seems unfair to them because of the various advantages of the rich, as seen on TV or in the movies—advantages that will never be available to them. Such attitudes are passed down from generation to generation as well as from neighborhood reinforcement.

Example IV— CHRONIC ANGER FROM A SHATTERED WORLDVIEW is a form of chronic anger seen most vividly in certain Black Americans, starting when the solid worldview of African Tradition was shattered when Africans were brought to the Americas as slaves.

A *Worldview* is like a blueprint (to serve as a standard) and like a map (to serve as a guide) regarding "how to live" in getting through the maze of life. A worldview is present when members of a "We" society or when members of an "I" (Individualism) society (who come together in an alliance) share: (1) a common body of meanings agreed to by practically all the members; (2) the same conclusions after reasoning from the same facts; and (3) the use of the same conclusions to handle any difficult problems, even if one of the group has not seen or heard of that problem before. For members of a "We" society, this is called a "*Group Mind*" or Intellectual Unity — as opposed to the Spiritual Unity which characterizes a peoples' ethics or *Ethos*.

The shattered worldview in each slave caused tremendous confusion, frustration, and an agreed upon way to figure out how to handle the evilness of the enslavers. Whereas bearing and caring for children allowed most slave females to retain many aspects of their worldview, the loss of manhood spirit, duties, obligations, and responsibilities — the loss of the African manhood tradition model — and the inability to have any manhood model except that of evil White male individualists has contributed to many Black males having an inability to re-establish a sound worldview in American society. It also contributes to chronic anger.

Management is about Black males becoming re-educated or educated about manhood in African Tradition; avoiding contact with the police and criminal system; figuring out ways to stay in school to obtain a sound education; using the education to become successful in the work marketplace; and the resumption of doing what it takes to have a comfortable home and family to return to at the end of the work day.

LOOSEN CHRONIC IMPULSIVE ANGER: In medical school, I urgently needed a car to get to and from the campus. The only car available for the $125.00 I could afford was a "hot rod." It was painted blue with big bright orange flames covering the hood. Since the car continually broke down I was constantly angry. One day, while waiting for a green light in downtown Nashville, Tennessee, the car backfired. Something in me "snapped." At that moment I got out of the car, walked home, and never saw the car again! That is a *moderate* degree of impulsive anger — the level of the mental state of many inner city youth.

Extreme anger is the "mad bull" level. In bullfights, when the matador shakes the red cape to attract the animal, the bull's impulsive anger causes him to attack the cloth. The attack is because of the shaking of the cape and, since bulls are color blind, not because it is red.

Humans easily stimulated to a "bull" state of "blind rage" have taken "leave of their senses." What happens is that a very strong or forceful thought of hatred arises within and totally overpowers the person's mind (see discussion of the Amygdala). Hence, in Extreme Anger THERE IS NO ABILITY TO JUDGE BETWEEN RIGHT AND WRONG. Nor is there the ability of the mind to think about the short-term or long-term consequences of the reactor's actions. When moderate and "blind rage" are chronic (i.e. a way of life), the power of constructive judgment can no longer function adequately; options are shutdown and situations are seen only from a selfish point of view. To say: "but I can't control myself!" is not true because "raging" reactions are a learned behavior.

The job of RATIONAL THINKING is TO HANDLE CHAOS INSIDE SERIOUS BUSINESS — like breaking up impulsive chronic anger. By using it to increase understanding of causes and effects, antidotes can be developed. Causes come from early childhood emotional scars, from the way we were trained to handle anger, and/or from the trigger event (i.e. "the shake of the cape"). For example, feeling rejected as a child may cause us today to be hypersensitive to rejection. However, to be distinguished are those easily correctable causes coming from following codes of one's gang or from a justifiable anger because a sense of fair play was violated. These causes can be differentiated by analysis.

For many, a common cause of becoming an addict to anger is as a source of entertainment. Reason can help these individuals understand that they are bored with life. Reason can then be used to lead them to discover their talents and discover their dream. Once one is known, the other is known and that will be the start of a life long and exciting journey to reach a satisfying destination.

Chronic impulsive anger experiences need to be changed by the *antidotes* (a state of mind that counteracts thoughts poisoned by chronic anger) of patience and tolerance. PATIENCE IS "BEARING SUFFERING" with calmness and self-control — whether enduring something unpleasant, or merely waiting, or doing something requiring steady effort. Without rejecting or accepting, TOLERANCE IS "PUTTING UP WITH" disappointments or violations of common sense and decency. A way to increase both is to rise above your opinions and beliefs and judgments to as to be free to interact with and live inside the selfhood of the troublesome person. Understand why that person chooses those particular think, feel, say, and do patterns.

A main thing to look for is: "**what benefit people get out of their actions** and reactions?" Such understanding helps shed anger and even hatred. The more we think about, learn about, and practice patience and tolerance the stronger becomes our desire to have both.

To begin substituting reasoning for reacting impulsively to anger, we can use the lever of taking deep breaths, counting backwards, leaving the room, or getting fresh air. After that, the loosening of chronic anger starts with self-discipline and self-control gained through improved patience and tolerance.

LOOSEN CHRONIC THOUGHTFUL ANGER: When I was 12 years old, a 16-year-old bully increasingly threatened to do me harm. On the day I predicted a physical attack, I flashed my Boy Scout hunting dagger as he came close. Surprisingly, he stopped and gave me a common sense lecture on how to handle my anger. He said that exposing a knife could easily have caused him to counter-attack with his own knife or use my knife on me. A better plan, he said, was either to avoid him, run away, or put up with his bullying. In short: "DISCRETION IS THE BETTER PART OF VALOR." This means that when we are in danger or trouble, using good sense helps more than taking foolish risks; it is better to be careful than foolishly brave.

To illustrate how potent our thoughts are, think of something that angers you (e.g. someone blaming you unfairly). After a few moments, notice that you actually are angry. Next, clench your fist, look angrily at your accuser, and "feel" the angry thoughts. Now, by smiling, observe the happiness coming in to surround you. Such positive and negative thought responses are the result of learning and can be dissolved by re-learning.

Re-learning starts with SELF-DISCOVERY — where did those feelings come from? Usually, anger sprouts from hurt feelings caused by FRUSTRATION or from some bad experience(s) in the distant past. Psychologists call feelings of irritation or hostility as ANGER-OUT; anger turned against oneself is ANGER-IN. Keeping these feelings inside us causes them to become dynamite ready to blow up at any time. Healing old festering emotional wounds can reduce any distress which generates a "short fuse."

The idea is to sift out the bad thoughts by the method of **THOUGHTFUL ANGER** — THE USING OF ANGER AS A STIMULUS TO THINK BEFORE ACTING. Whether from past or current distress, RATIONAL THINKING is a method useful for solving emotional problems. ANALYSIS breaks causes of anger into parts so that separate attention can be given to each part. We are looking to determine if the response to the cause was destructive or constructive and if our response was appropriate or not.

Assessing responses requires SELF-AWARENESS — the recognizing of all our bad thoughts without judgment. After acknowledging and accepting all of our thoughts, feelings, and responses, meaningful change can come from simply looking at the same situation from a different point of view. We can start practicing by seeing "the glass as half full instead of half empty." When a friend has made me really angry (actually, I make myself angry and not them), I struggle to shift my perspective. Instead of focusing on the bad things they did to me, my aim is to see the good things they have done and/or are doing. Yet this is very hard for me when they have shown themselves to be dishonorable (e.g. cheating and stealing).

Finally, the realization of pleasures from a disciplined and peaceful mind readily points out how dumb it is to mess this up by being chronically angry. Such anger damages me physically, keeps me from thinking clearly, and narrows my choices for making the best decisions. In addition to developing PATIENCE (bearing pain) and TOLERANCE (putting up with unpleasantness), the bottom line for loosening chronic thoughtful anger is to have COMPASSION in self-correction as well as being open to helping others with their fight.

MANAGING ACUTE ANGER: "When I get angry," Rambo says, "I seem to lose control and can't think of anything else but wanting to fight." Scientists have discovered that the way some circuits of nerves are set up in the brain give support to Rambo's statement. Sitting just behind the eyes is a "watchdog" that, like a video camera, scans for trouble each signal entering the brain from the outside world. For each signal the "watchdog" asks: "is it for me or against me?" If "against," the watchdog starts "barking" to alarm all parts of the brain to take emergency actions. The emotional part of the brain takes charge and reacts as if it is backed into a corner by an attacker and then has to fight its way out. Since it by-passes the thinking part of the brain, it has no plan for figuring the best way out of trouble. Therefore, it orders any "dirty" fighting that has a chance to win.

In the beginning, when the caveman was attacked by a wild animal he reacted like Rambo. Later, he found there was a better way to cause the least amount of harm to himself and his family. Thus, upon being attacked, he switched from his emotional to his reasoning system and followed a step-by-step plan—a plan which applies to this day. The following are suggestions for preparation and prevention; for managing anger as it begins to arise and for after it is present; and for replacing the addiction to anger.

Step III—stop making demands on reality. There is no reason why people should do things you want them done or to do things the way you do them. Shed delusions (believing in the unreal and not believing in the real) such as the world is designed to aggravate you. The truth is that people's focus is on themselves and the overwhelming majority of people care nothing about anybody else. Thus, the secret is to acquire inner strength and inner peace as you go about doing the right and decent things in life—and regardless of what others are doing to the contrary.

Step I— practice ways to escape without fighting when faced with any type of trouble. For most males, they need to defend their "manhood" when challenged. But, as stressed in my book on "Manhood," your manhood is not dependent on what anyone says about it. Rather, there are specific traits which characterize manhood.

Step II—take a deep breath so as to stop from immediately going into an emotional state and becoming panicky. Deep breathing can slow heart rate and lower blood pressure. When beginning to experience the impact that will lead to anger, count slowly to 10; when really angry, count to 100. Walk away from hot spots and, if not, thing of something you like—your pet, a flower garden, the big game.

Step III—assess the present situation based on prior research. For example, the caveman gathered details about the ways of all dangerous animals — their habits, strengths, and weaknesses. In non-threatening situations he devised plans for various situations about when and how an animal might attack — at home, in the open spaces, in the jungle. If the animal could not climb a tree then the plan would be for the family to climb a tree. Or they practiced standing perfectly still and staring the animal in the eyes if that was known to work.

Step IV—if there simply must be a showdown with another, first schedule it (to give each of you a time to cool down) and second, try to hold hands since that will keep both of you from playing "dirty." It also will keep each of you aware of each other's sensitivities. Never come from a position of "I know and you don't." It helps to have a common focus higher than either of you alone. For example, during a wedding ceremony the bride and the groom use their respective lit candles to light a third candle. That third candle represents the marriage structure which is more important that the individual personalities of the husband and wife.

The correct mindset is to be strong enough to admit you are wrong and the other is right when it is obvious and even hazy. This does not mean you are a jerk but simply that you made a mistake. Weak people can not do this because they must try to "save face." The idea is not to win but rather to come to some harmonious conclusion that is workable in order for both to win together as trust is re-established between all concerned.

Step V—For mean people who deliberately hurt us, our life improves immediately if we put in motion the mechanism to forgive them. In some instances it can also help to tell the trigger person quietly what made you upset—called "leveling." Then **Listen** with ears and heart to what they say without anticipating, interruptions, or judgment. Forgiveness is done for your benefit so that you can let go of your pain and move on with your life.

Step VI—Make a chart of your anger. This can start by writing out all of your bad emotions. Write what has hurt you and how you feel about it: "I feel angry when...." Write about the types of things that hurt your feeling. Make a list of the people against whom you hold a grudge and what each said and did. Try to recall if you were feeling particularly vulnerable so that you may have misinterpreted a "neutral" comment and made it personal.

Write down as many things you like about that person (if nothing else than that they are a human being to whom you are spiritually related) and see if what you like out-weighs what you dislike. Realize that there is something about everyone you dislike and therefore you can not let everyone go simply because we are social beings and need to relate to others. Also realize that you have your flaws that people do not like—flaws that may be identical to what you do not like in others (and that may be the reason you do not like them in others). Yet, some of those people you complain about show you patience and tolerance.

Write out where you draw the line on things that you absolutely can not tolerate. For me that line is anything evil done to any human being, to any animal, or to nature. Then write out what retribution they could engage in so as to get back into your good graces.

At some point in writing you will see that being angry has no benefit and that it does not make sense to continue being angry.

Step VII—avoid getting in threatening situations and avoid being around destructive and angry people or people who are going nowhere in life and are "about nothing."

Even when there is no "life-and-limb" type danger, hurting somebody because of anger will cause them to react with "tit-or-tat" — by "getting even" — by hurting back. To prevent this or to break it up, we must do the hard work to understand how it got started, as by asking the good person that you are: "what are the wisest approaches for handling this situation?" SEEING THE PART WE PLAYED IN CAUSING THE PROBLEM might indicate we need to stop blaming others as well as to apologize to them, especially to our parents who care about our feelings

In most situations related to anger, a reasoning mind will draw on creative ways to let tension out of the situation — maybe by agreeing that the opponent has a point worth considering; or maybe by coming up with a (practiced) humorous answer; or maybe by smiling and walking away. Any of these show everybody, including the opponent, that you are a person bigger than a foolish street fighter. When you are mad at the world that is the time to say: "I can't change the world but I can change me. So I'm going to a higher level and stay under control."

The ultimate cure for anger (or any bad emotion) is to adopt the Ancient African philosophy of shedding ones ego (e.g. selfishness) in favor of the concept of Wholism (the self is spirit and spirit is part of all of God's real creations and creatures).

MANAGING CHRONIC ANGER: If chronic anger is represented by the seed of an apple tree, then acute anger is like the leaves of that tree. When the need for handling chronic anger rises, it usually presents as a leaf situation that has little or nothing to do with the seed or the root of the anger. Very often that leaf of anger is a reflection of obsessional thoughts and compulsive deeds. *Obsessions* are urgently repeated thoughts and *Compulsions* are urgent impulses to action. Anger-related obsessive-compulsive defenses have to be repeated as overt or tempered outbursts of anger at a mild (e.g. raising one's voice) or slight (e.g. shouting, using offensive language) level in order to release the tension built up. Many of the reactions of angry people have no thoughts associated with their vicious cycle of responses.

Loudmouth jerks who spew out with violent outbursts from overflowing with anger have twice the risk of strokes than normal. It is not the emotion that is critical but rather it is what the emotion does — i.e. how it changes the chemistry of the body. Tavris (Anger, p. 158) says that the critical benefit of confessing lies is in reframing or reinterpreting the event; finding meaning in it; and putting it behind you. So what can be done?

<u>Step I</u> is SELF-DISCIPLINE AND SELF-CONTROL OF EMOTIONS.

<u>Step II</u> uses SELF-AWARENESS (looking at and accepting a feeling as it happens) and NAMING THE VARIOUS EMOTIONS. Typically, youth need help in saying what they feel.

<u>Step III</u> is BECOMING AWARE OF ONE'S THOUGHTS about the emotions being experienced but without passing judgment on either.

<u>Step IV</u> is SUBSTITUTING THE ANGRY THOUGHTS FOR GOOD THOUGHTS.

<u>Step V</u> is LETTING GO: "I can let go of my anger since it is not working well for me." Slowly, one can work up to the more intense destructive emotions. Hidden emotions can be grabbed hold of when they periodically peak into consciousness.

FEAR

In Western literature Fear is generally agreed to be a basic emotion which acts especially by *preventing actions* — the great controlling emotion that keeps people from doing things. It has always been used by masters and governors of all kinds as an instrument to prevent people from doing what they did not want them to do. Fear is essential to escape predators and other dangers by way of its flight, fight, or freeze response. We may fear for ourselves or others in this world or about something in the next world after death.

The Story of Fear: The caveman's main emotional problem, in contrast to people in today's world, was not anxiety. Instead, those emotional problems were about everyday fears—fears that were well defined dangers related to sudden and unexpected events of a life or death nature. Yet, instead of being calm, his reactions were probably one of terror by what might seem trivial to us. Perhaps, he was afraid of the dark — and various other-things — as we are. One group of fears related to threats, disruptions, or destructions concerning his immediate territory, as from enemy raids or animals on the attack.

Another group occurred on the periphery of his immediate territory — from things like forked lightning, thunder, earthquakes, and droughts. It was normal for him to believe that these were acts of angry gods and spirits. In light of today's knowledge, many of the caveman's normal and rational fears would be labeled abnormal and irrational anxieties. But keep in mind that the original fears were about the cause of a sudden and unexpected event. Gradually over the millennia, this idea of fear was transferred from realistic outside causes to the individual's inner world and manifested as anxiety more than true fear.

Originally, the word "Fear" was based upon the "Lucky Star" beliefs of ancient peoples. The belief was that discovery of one's "Lucky Star" provided safety in the form of loving guidance but failing to find it (a "disaster") would result in allowing evil stars to exert their influence and thereby create terrible events for the individual. The thoughts surviving out of this ancient belief concern the association of fear with either feeling unsafe (from lacking divine guidance) and/or from not feeling secure in having all of ones needs being cared for (as is implied in the word "Providence").

An early written form of how this transfer occurred can be found in the Old English epic poem *Beowuef* (700 A.D.). As a result of the hero killing a dragon and then being killed by a dragon, the emotion of fear shifted from the thing undergone to the dread of the event. For those who used their imaginations to fashion problems to worry about, the emotion of "Anxiety" was applied. The European Middle Ages were a time of all types of violence between neighbors capable of inflicting violence. This meant that anxiety and fear were associated with traveling or even stepping outside the home. Anxiety was shown as the dread of the event; fear from the likely chance of being robbed, eaten, or killed. These European ideas about anxiety and fear that centered on the anticipation of evil originated with the appearance of European 45,000 years ago persisted; became particularly noticeable starting in the 13th century; and is clearly evident to the present.

Meanwhile, modern authorities tried to distinguish anxiety from fear. They said that fear was bound to specific objects or situations whereas anxiety was a diffuse and undifferentiated apprehensive response to anticipated threats. In other words, when people are in a significantly fearful or anxious state, they see in themselves and in situations only what they want to see. However, this represented only the tip of the conceptual iceberg.

THE WORLD OF FEAR: You, like every individual everywhere, have a past, present, and future — each representing a world that was lived in, is being lived in, and will be lived in. Some people's worlds may be outside of their selfish minds (e.g. involved in charity); some, inside of their minds (e.g. living in the world of fear); and some straddling those two worlds. To illustrate, let us look at the world of fear. The setting of and framework for fear is that of danger, whether it is real or imagined. The psychological, physiological, and behavioral ways we have from simply looking at a possibly (e.g. mildly) dangerous setting is called Anxiety. The psychological, physiological, and behavioral ways we have from being inside the real or imagined danger framework is called FEAR.

To elaborate, the "*specific*" aspect of fear may be real, distorted, or fantasy, while the *"threat"* aspect of anxiety may have some basis in fact. Some distinguish fear from anxiety by saying that fear occurs in a limited situation, as being in the presence of a poisonous snake. One can escape the fear by escaping the situation. Anxiety, from possessing no obvious cause, is more hazy than fear; is longer lasting; and is not easy to escape from by a simple change of scenery. There is a connecting link, however, between fear and anxiety, as when a person has a good reason to believe something bad is going to happen unless that something is diverted. This form of anxiety is hidden justifiable fear.

There are *three main types of fear.* First is the fear present at birth. Second is the natural fear reaction acquired following birth. Third is Reactive Fear that results from doing something destructive to humans or animals or nature and, as a result, there is the threat of retialiation. The goal of the first two types fear is simple — it is to help us avoid or steer clear of danger.

Fear is one of the great emotions that decide the deeds of men and women and children in all places and ages. We may have fear for ourselves and/or for others; we may fear something in this world or something in the next. For good or bad, *fear sharpens the imagination.* Anxiety, when mild or slight, may focus and sharpen thinking and promote cautiousness. However, anything above slight tends to interfere with our normal effectiveness (fig. 2).

In putting all of this together, as reactions to danger, both anxiety and fear feel and act much the same — regardless of whether the danger in real or not. Any perceived danger affects a person's security. Anxiety comes from a threat to security;

fear, from being in a situation where there is a disruption or destruction of security. Thus fear and anxiety are emotions which also assess the nature of the danger situation and generate certain types of behaviors.

Broadly, **Behaviors** are self-protective actions and, as reactions, are detected via fight, flight, or freezing fright. Preparation physiological responses include: (1) increasing our heartbeat rapidly to pump more blood to our muscles; (2) releasing sugar by the liver to give more energy and to quicken our thinking processes; (3) enlarging the pupil size of our eyes; (4) breathing rapidly to bring in more oxygen; (5) putting out more platelets to aid blood clotting in case we are cut or bruised; and (6) many other bodily changes. The over-all effect is that our bodies are like a tightly stretched rubber band ready to be tripped into instance action.

PSYCHOLOGICALLY, PART OF FEAR DISRUPTS OR DESTROYS OUR SENSE OF SECURITY — either from a loss of power, a lack of power, or an obstruction to the use of one's power. SECURITY is the actuality of all one's needs being cared for—whether to get what one desires or to not get what one does not desire. Insecurity makes one susceptible to apprension and suspicion.

These draining effects on one's power cause frustration. Frustration gives rise to various degrees of reactions on the Rage scale (e.g. intense anger), and/or on the Emotional pain scale (e.g. feeling deeply hurt) and/or on the Depression scale (e.g. apathy—the cessation of responses that can show acutely as *"freezing fright"),* and/ or, for the mentally sick, pleasure from fear.

The attitude springing from a fear based sense of insecurity depends upon the magnitude of the perceived danger. If a person is *"backed into a corner"* and has no choice or if the person believes he/she can *"rise to the occasion"* (to get up off the floor and meet the challenge of the attack), that person will react by fighting.

By contrast, the fleeing (flight) attitude shows in the behaviors of avoiding, of retreating, of masking, of concealing deceptions, or of running away. Some people are able to neutralize these reactions by exerting extremely strong willpower. People with courage see pass their fears in order to get the job done. People who give in to their fears open the door to unhealthy psychological, physical, and behavioral states — mental illnesses, physically illnesses, and bad habits.

Mental illnesses can come from excessive focus on fear that is carried to completion (called *Phobias*); or excessive focus on one fear that branches into generalizations about similar situations or objects; or acquiring multiple fears at one time. For example, fear of a parent may generalize into a fear of all authority figures.

Physical illnesses resulting from fear overlap with those of extreme chronic anxiety and moderate degrees of chronic anger. There are numerous bad behaviors resulting from chronic fear — shyness, procrastination, refusing to leave the comfortable and the familiar out of fear of failure or fear of success. Victims of fear develop a way of living that is deceptive, safe, cautious, timid, dull, and unfulfilling. This pattern prevents spontaneity, learning, and growing. Many of these people are found in the groups that follow lifestyles of tradition.

MANAGING FEARFUL EVENTS: Contained in the psychological part of our emotional reaction to a fearful event is an immediate sense of insecurity and lack of safety. Both are based upon being in a disturbing or destructive situation and considering what could come next. At that point, if something suddenly and unexpectedly occurs, one may impulsively react by *"fight, flight, or freezing fright."* **Neurosis**—is the splitting off and temporarily suppressing a part of one's psyche. This implies that awareness is not unified.

If there is a time lapse between the sudden event and the need to respond — i.e. the *"fear gap"* — one could choose to do sound rational or immature rational or irrational thinking. Regardless of the type of thinking done in the *"fear grip,"* emotions are always present at some point within the "*gap.*" They may range in degree categories that are popularly called apprehensions, dread, or terror. Fantasy and distortion thinking done in the fear gap typically cause behaviors destructive to all persons involved.

<u>Each degree category may vary in intensity at a mild, slight, moderate, and extreme level</u>. For example, an extreme terror reaction may so frighten a person out of his/her senses as to cause any thinking to be irrational. Since there is a close relationship between fear, anger, and physical pain, the experiencing of a great fear may also cause physical as well as emotional or spiritual pain.

Some people deal with extreme feelings of terror and emotional/spiritual pain by becoming psychotic (fantasy—out of contact with reality); others by neurotic behaviors resulting from the excessive use of *"far out"* defense mechanism (distortions); and still others, in a self-controlled and rational way (realism).

By contrast, realistic and reasonable thinkers prepare to do constructive things. So how do you become a constructive thinker while being in the scenario of fear?

STEP I is to arrive at a courageous state of mind by means of the proper handling of fear in order to achieve what one wants and to avoid what one does not want. This is about change and change is about something new. The new is something unknown or unfamiliar and for most people (especially "We" and "Herd" thinking type people) the unfamiliar or unknown is scary anc causes the tendency to hang on to whatever one has, no matter how bad it is. This means being "stuck" in one place and in one mindset and the thought of letting go is a painful thought.

A first step out of being "stuck" is to **convert what you are scared about into**

Curiosity about the "why" of it. The more you explore that the more you are headed in the direction of cultivating courage. Part of that process is about shifting from trying to control things into trusting that you can handle satisfactorally unexpected and things you have never seen nor heard of before. Each time you achieve that little success you have created a prop or support for your self-confidence.

Table IV — <u>Self-Confidence Cultivation</u>

- Curiosity
- Multiple Small Successes
- Self-Trust (awareness of expanding capabilities)
- Self-Reliance (knowing and using what is available)
- Self-Appreciation (esteem of one's Substance)
- Self-Respect (honoring one's earned self-worth and self-value traits)
- Self-Confidence (sureness from empowerment)
- Self-Efficacy (believing one can get any unique job done)
- Empowered — a sense of control, a good direction, and inspiration

Since self-confidence is the keystone of Self-Esteem and therefore has been covered extensively in my book on Self-Esteem, only a few comments will be made here (Table IV). The process of building Self-Esteem begins with those forms of Curiosity—an essential for selfhood mastery— which lead to exploring the unknown. In such new frontiers one meets challenges and by means of trial and error starts accumulating <u>multiple small successes</u>. The stepping stones for building inner strength are like this (Bailey, Selfhood Mastery).

COURAGE is the action of going against your nature and rising above the belief that getting better is scary and then leaving the safe, the secure, the familiar, and the comfortable so as to put yourself in a position to win (or minimize losses) from a hard fought victory. It requires a solid mental, physical, and spiritual foundation. It is important not to confuse the idea of activity with progress and confuse the idea of change with that of growth. Being active and changing do not necessarily mean making progress or growing.

The resultant good character is used to establish capacity and ability competence in your education, training skills, desires, and willpower to get the job done right. "**Ability**" is having the physical or mental power of doing, without specifying the quality or degree. Health, strength, and fortune are abilities. "**Capacity**" is the state of being receptive — the power to acquire and hold.

All of these are used in the pattern established that makes up a generic approach to planning, preparation, practice and performance. Then, this generic pattern can be transferred to any fearful situation. The generic approach applies even if you have never seen or heard of this kind of problem before.

The process of becoming COMPETENT (i.e. *"good enough"*) includes knowing how to stay out of trouble or, if in trouble, knowing how to satisfactorily get out of it. Preparation for handling fearful situations is gathered from many sources — from interviewing people who have successfully and unsuccessfully gotten out of such problems; from reading stories about courage; from being in simulated situations with other people or in courageous virtual reality systems, like computer video games.

STEP II—SELF-EDUCATION is about all the components in the fear scenario. Within sensible limits the cliché: *"what is understood we no longer fear"* has significant beneficial effects.

STEP III— PRIORITIZE to determine which situations to stay in. You may stay because there is no viable escape or stay in order to learn from this experience.

STEP IV— PREVENTION concerns the foresight not to get into fearful situations in the first place. Foresight "sees" likely viable things in the future or "sees" into the Sublime, the Supernatural, and/or the Material realms. Forethought came to mean the ability to prepare for what is going to happen by doing the unpleasant things now for the sake of pleasant things in the future. Put another way, Forethought means thinking ahead to imagine events as they probably will occur and then planning accordingly to get what you want and not get what you do not want.

STEP V IS POST ACTION JUDGMENTS. Studying your prior reactions sharpens quick assessments about which situations you can do nothing about and which ones to run from.

PREPARATION FOR MINIMIZING FEAR: The boldly displayed sign on the freshly painted bench says with great authority: *"Do not touch"* but we touch it anyway. Our habit of rebellious curiosity is often carried over into situations that generate fear. Thus, the first pointer in preparation for minimizing fearful situations is to NOT MAKE IT WORSE. For example, do not give an angry person fuel to become even more angry.

Second is SELF-CONTROL — using whatever time is available to you within the fearful situation. If you were drowning, the best use of your time is to stop thrashing and screaming. Instead, figure out how to save yourself, as by "dog paddling" strokes.

Third is REALISM. What is the chance of something bad happening? Just like one can become "insurance poor" (i.e. buying insurance for everything), one can become "fearful poor"—i.e. being afraid of everything. After all, how often does lightning actually strike and kill some one in comparison to the number of people in the world?

Fourth, an UNDERSTANDING (being able to see things from all angles) of what is in the world of fear reduces the fearful reaction. This has been one of the most valuable contributions of science to human welfare. A child may be afraid of shadows on the wall until he/she understands their nature. A fear of thunder is not simply a fear of noise but rather the fear of a noise not understood. Part of understanding is having knowledge before the situation arises, of the dangers and limitations of the situations causing fear. This comes by learning from the experiences of others — by interviewing them, by reading about them, and by watching television programs about animals.

Fifth, MASTERY OF THE SITUATION reduces fear. In learning to ride a bicycle, children may experience fear until they have developed expert skills. So it is with all occupations or scenarios in which we see possible dangers.

The core of management for these five is to GAIN EMOTIONAL CONTROL:

<u>Step I</u> is learning as much as possible about emotions in general — about their causes, reactions involved, and consequences of emotional activity.

<u>Step II</u> is recognizing that fearful situations, being a natural part of life, are more easily prepared for by setting up pattern plans of actions. For example, fearful situations (1) and (3) and (7) may call to mind pattern (C) or (T) to see which one best fits. If pattern (T) works the best then it will probably need modification to be a good match with the situation (3)

<u>Step III</u> is to avoid getting into fearful situations if at all possible. This requires the COMMON SENSE that is interwoven with practical understanding (prudence) and good judgment that comes from good character. Such people show DISCRETION (caution, deliberation, self-control), FORESIGHT (seeing ahead), and FORETHOUGHT (thinking ahead).

<u>Step IV</u> is to use Rational Thinking (Table V) rather than emotions in fearful situations. People relying on emotions do not have an appropriate reasonable response ready to use in matters of serious business (see discussion of the Amygdala). Start by acquiring responses to apply when faced with relatively unimportant situations and learn lessons from your mistakes. For example, if someone gives a light insult—"you sure look awful today" respond with "thank you" for that takes the sting out of it

Table V — <u>**Rational Thinking Steps**</u>

I. Clearly define the problem
II. Gather pertinent information
III. Assess the gathered information

IV. Analyze the assessed information
V. Manipulate the analysis into cause and effect
VI. Maneuver creatively around obstacles
VII. Poetically synthesize options
VIII. Judgments into Plans A, B and C
IX. Troubleshoot the Plans A, B, and C
X. Post-action judgments

Step V is controlling outward expressions of emotions, as does the card player who keeps a *"poker face."* By so doing you lessen the chance of increasing the intensely of the fearful experience within yourself as well as lessen the chance of exciting other people and encouraging them to become (more) emotional. The vast majority of people — whether they are the prey or the preyor — are like sheep in that they are easily led by the *"shepherd."*

Step VI is the proper application of work and humor to reduce tension and help clear your mind for possible solutions.

MANAGING THE ADDICTION TO FEAR: Our reaction to fearful situations is a behavioral defense mechanism. Fear protects us by creating a leaning of the mind toward a withdrawal from dangerous situations. On the other hand, Anxiety, our most common and arguably most important emotion, is aroused by any threat to the private, public, ideal, or Real Self. Because emotions are about seeing things as *"all or none"* or either/or, the arousal of anxiety and fear results in fearing non-friends involved in the fearful event.

People in the ghetto often do not know much about the world outside of a few blocks from where they live and, through the media, conclude that "*outsiders*"—with much justification—are ultimately responsible for their struggling situation. Since their situation, is riddled with fearful things and people, the result is a *"We vs. Them"* attitude. No matter how legitimate this reasoning, the fact that a person has such hazy fears is an implied admission of self-distrust and self-incompetence. When situations like these become a habit pattern, an addiction to fear is present.

Originally, the term "ADDICT" ("to be bound over to") was a legal term meaning to *"deliver by sentence of the court."* Psychologists expanded this addict idea into one being literally sentenced or bound over to ones habit. The habit of fear is one of the most destructive influences and one of the most weakening mental states known**.** No matter how strong your otherwise positive mental outlook, fear can shatter it. Far more important than the thought about fear is the emotion that makes up fear. Thoughts are cold but emotions are warm, alive, full of energy, and act like a magnet. In other words, fear is an attractive force but in a negative or destructive way.

Just as strong desire creates the forces which attract the desired thing to you, having an addiction of fear creates the forces to attract more fear. The attraction occurs along the line of VISUALIZATION — the vivid mental pictures you are holding. Visualization always tends to make happen one's vivid mental picture. Uncle Cecil, by being addicted to cigarette smoking, was in a situation of fear. He knew it was worsening his emphysema (i.e. breathing problems) and thereby would greatly shorten his life span—and it actually did. Many women in physically abusive relationships are addicted to fear. Their needy desires to be with their man outweigh the fears of the consequences associated with the dangers they are in.

So how do you break up the addiction fear pattern? There is no easy answer. One approach from the science of Judo says *"to resist invader fears is a waste of precious energy while to examine them calmly and impersonally to the point of exhaustion as they pass through the mind is to get rid of them with the minimum waste of energy or time."*

The Chinese say: *"Let the thoughts arise within your mind without repressing them and without being carried away by them. Let not the passing thought be annihilated and let not a passing thought rise up again."* Refuse to let the mind become identified with these unwanted strangers, for they are but products of the mind and, as such, impermanent and fundamentally unreal.

If some particular problem persistently recurs at an inconvenient time, talk to it and say: *"do not interrupt me now. I will attend to you at 7:00 this evening."* Then keep the appointment and *"examine it, exhaust it, and let it go."* If it still persists, determine if it is within your power to handle it or not. If so, handle it; if not, give the problem to its owner or turn the problem over to a higher power and release it completely from your mind.

As discussed in the Anger section, a big part of this process may require writing out everything you can think of over a period of hours to weeks before you gain insights as to what to do.

LEARN FROM FEARS BEYOND YOUR CONTROL**:** After giving his daughter a talk on courage and bravery, the father answered her question with: *"No, I am not afraid of dogs and bees or thunder and lightening." "Gee, dad, I guess you're not afraid of nothing in the world but mamma."* There are many fearful things in life over which we have no control. Still, we can control ourselves. In other words, we can **separate the fearful happening from your reaction to it**. For the fearful situation beyond your control, a useless way of reacting is to yell and screams or beat on things or to give up and admit failure. Instead, extract lessons from the experience through the following steps.

Step I is defining why the situation is beyond your control. Did you underestimate the situation and become suddenly caught off guard and overwhelmed? Did you overestimate and fail to even try to look for a way to get around the problem?

In Step II, information is gathered about the strengths and weaknesses present in the enemy and yourself. Rational thinkers get rid of all distortions and see the problem for what it is.

Step III is assessing the information to see if you should have attacked or defended yourself, played dead, or run.

Step IV analyzes that information to decide what brought about your losses.

Step V is manipulation of the facts in order to determine what would have been the best next step — to BARGAIN (producing a series of offers in hopes of getting tolerable counteroffers); to COOPERATE (a combining for mutual benefit); to COMPROMISE (a mutual yielding of points); to ARBITRATE (submitting the dispute-to an impartial third party for a final decision); to CONCILIATE (appeal to the highest values within the enemy in hopes of establishing co-operation in reaching a settlement); or to ask for MERCY (the plea for compassion to relieve or prevent suffering).

Step VI is maneuvering information analyzed about the fearful situation so as to reduce the facts to a few basic patterns of what happened. Was there the pattern of INVASION; or EROSION (slowly eating away) of BOUNDARIES (as when supplies are-cut off); of DIVIDE AND CONQUER; of the BIG BANG DESTRUCTION; of INTIMIDATION; of SLAVERY; or of the ZOMBIE (as been pumped full of drugs or cult propaganda)?

Step VII is synthesizing harmonious packages from Step VI information to get Plans A, B, and C.

Step VIII makes troubleshooting judgments about what got you in trouble, what you can do to stay out of similar troubles in the future, and how to best prepare for trouble if you get in it again.

The purpose of troubleshooting your bad situations is to gain knowledge for changing how you think about fearful situations. It is human nature to fear the unknown and the unfamiliar. Such fear encourages ignorance and ignorance greatly increases your fears. Pertinent knowledge gives you the power to handle these fears. By believing you can win or minimize your losses enables you to at least win some of the battles, even if not the war.

Past experiences give transferable knowledge related to what to expect and the approaches to use. This is the purpose of preparation for the unexpected and then practicing all the possible problems that could be in Plans A, B, and C. Smoothness in practice is aided by keeping education and pertinent skills in good working order.

Preparation involves the best use of your energy so that it will not have to be drained in taking care of non-essential things. For example, avoid being in unnecessary debt because trying to buy your peace in a fearful situation may cost a great deal of money. Keep full the gas tank of your car so that in an emergency you do not waste time looking for a gas station.

TURNING BAD FEARS INTO GOOD**:** The mental state of Peace is one of happiness—a natural state of sound living. If we lack peace, there is no substitute. When love flows freely, peace is present—at least in the deeper realms of ones being. When fear is present, peace is absent. So what is Peace?

PEACE'S original Ancient African meaning was to fasten or fit things together into a Wholism, a unity, and a reality, so that the thing involved was complete and sound and harmonious. Wholism is the realization that all God's creatures and creations are related regardless of how remote in time or space. Peace conveys the idea of health, integrity, fulfillment, and prosperity. Biblically, righteous friendship with God and between companions was expressed by the concepts of peace.

So was the combination of contentment, happiness, well-being, safety, and security. Fear, resulting from some real or distorted or imagined danger, shatters the wholeness of peace. However, fear is beneficial when it sets in motion those mental activities designed to either return one to a peaceful state or to slow, stop, or reverse adverse progress (i.e. a downhill emotionally destructive course away from peace) which is preventing one from reaching a wholesome destination. Obviously, fear is bad when it is not beneficial.

The purpose of this discussion is to look at the ways bad fears can be changed to good fears and then to peace. The objective is to get to a healthy mental state whereby you deal with fears within a proper perspective and in a proper manner whenever they interfere with a lifestyle of peacefulness. The principle behind this desirable change is to TAKE ADVANTAGE OF THE CHAOS arising from the shattering.

The starting point is to know those components of bad fears which cause a mental state of chaos. The story behind this—called the Phoenix— began in Ancient Egypt where the people devoted their entire lives in preparing for the continuance of living in the Afterlife. The **Phoenix** was a symbol of hope—hope from the transformation of chaos into harmony based upon its pattern of dying, being purified, and rising anew. The Phoenix bird's regeneration and association with life was because the Sun flew on its wings through heavens while constantly being immolated and reborn from the fires of sunset and sunrise.

Since "Phoenix" symbolizes resurrection and immortality, in today's usage "phoenix" refers to a person, project, building, institution, or race of people who rise from the ashes of its own destruction—and then are vigorous enough to start anew as fresh, youthful, and strong. Rising phoenix-like into remarkable success with so little and so fast was what African Americans ex-slaves did in overcoming seemingly insurmountable obstacles. Otherwise, anything of excellence or beauty because of its harmony and unity might be called a "phoenix."

Whatever is CHAOTIC is so completely confused, disordered, and incoherent as to lose all relationships between its unified components. The shattering of peace creates chaos in the form of insecurity, either by designing a void or by removing all forms of harmony. If you can imagine the oxymoron (i.e. combining contradictory concepts) of formless pieces inside a void, then, by being a creative contractor, you can build what you want out of those formless pieces in the void.

The process starts by separating the good, the indifferent, and the bad pieces. Despite the number of bad pieces, there are always many more good pieces to use as building materials for your new structure of good character. Besides, <u>many of the bad pieces in and of themselves are "neutral"—neither inherently good or bad— are simply in the wrong form, wrong arrangement, or wrong combination</u>.

When Uncle Lloyd, a master brick mason, was ready to build a house, he inspected the materials used to make the bricks and then selected the best finished bricks. Next, on a solid base (the equivalent of love) he built the underground foundation (the equivalent of good character) before building the house brick by brick (the equivalent of a good personality). But he knew from past experiences and by gaining knowledge from other masons which bricks to avoid (the equivalent of irrational fears).

Thus, with respect to fears, there are two activities for converting the bad into the good. First is to know the best materials that go into the foundation built on love. These consist of all the traits of good character (fig. 4) — those traits which enhance one's sense of worth (i.e. those things which lead to peace) and one's sense of self-value (i.e. knowing that your works have marketplace value and that you are able to financially take care of yourself).

Second is the shedding of irrational fears — fears that make no sense and are not in your best interest. Such irrational fears concern things that interfere with your ability to make good decisions and fashion good solutions. In general, fears are irrational when things of value (e.g. money, possessions, fame, prestige, and *"looking good"*) outweigh things of worth or when they are self-created by starting a feud.

In short, bad fears are converted to something good through the process of good character and Rational Thinking. The cultivation of good character is the cultivation of wisdom. The display of wisdom is the display of good character. Thereafter, the cultivation of everything good and wise will restore peace.

GOOD CHARACTER WHEEL

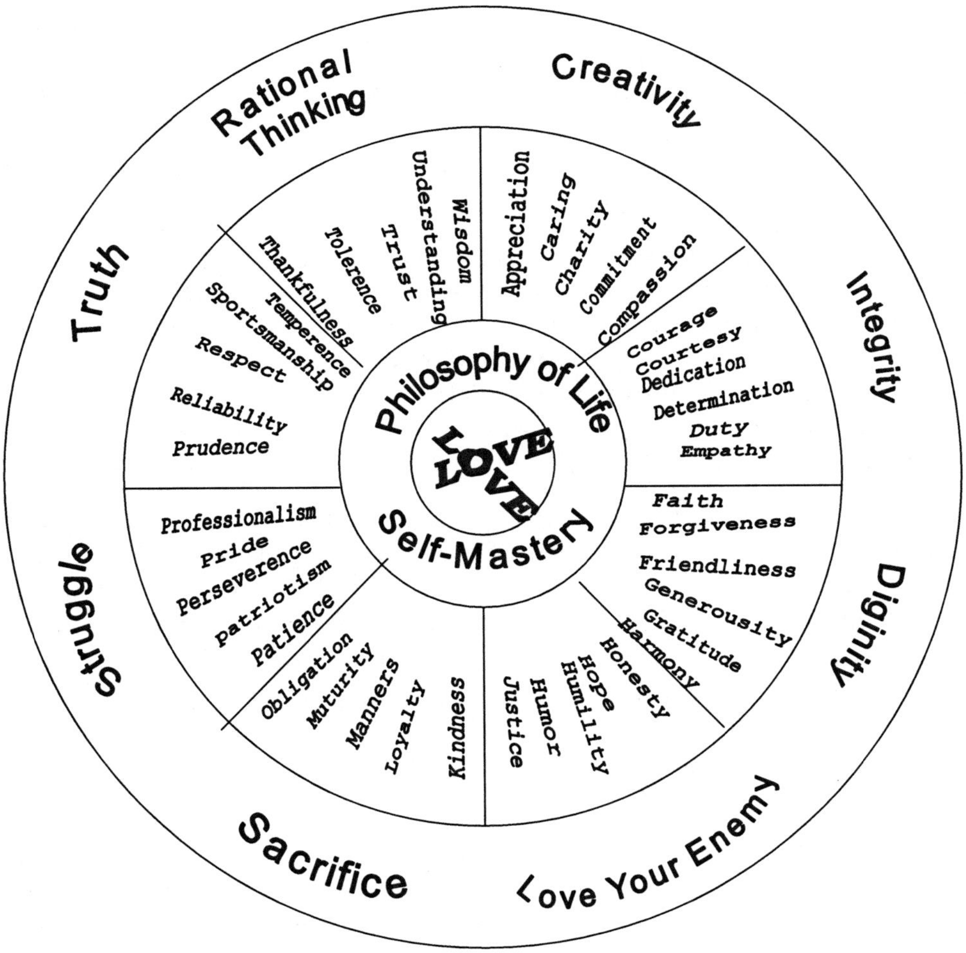

Figure 4
(Reprinted from Bailey – "*Good Character*")

DEPRESSION

DEPRESSION ("to press down" or "an area sunk below its surrounding" or "to exert a force, as in casting down") is the hardest of the five to label an emotion. Its word meaning pertains to a state of mind. Inside that depressed state are emotions which are capable of causing one to feel pressed down or casted down or sunk. In other words, the effect of an emotional state of depression is that one's spirit or thoughts or feelings are literally weighted to cause significant sadness, apathy, and a host of similar conditions. Each of these aspects is known by a variety of words.

In the animal kingdom, infant monkeys suddenly separated from their mothers will start with loud distress calls. Then from "*stirred down*" emotions of depression they withdraw, slouch, curl-up, and cease to play. This is a survival reaction designed to elude potential opportunist enemies. My toy dog Titan would hide behind the couch when I "disappeared." Of course this may be associated with fear. Humans use "instinct" depression as a cultivated extension for being in a state of meditation.

The Story of Depression: Saturn is the most beautiful and strangest of all planets of which we are aware. Its three broad, flat-looking rings are made up of millions of tiny bodies — like little moons — reflecting the light of the sun. Its eight fellow planets (a word meaning *"wandering"* heavenly bodies) comprise a planetary system called the solar system, so named because its star is our Sun (or sol). Whereas a **star** is a huge ball of fiery gases that gives off heat and light, a **planet** is a much smaller body that shines by reflected light. Planets travel around the sun in fixed paths called orbits. Our own earth is one of these planets.

Ancient Africans invented the science of astronomy to study the planets from a naturalistic and mathematical point of view so as to discover the laws of nature (Bailey, Common Sense). Foreigners who *"borrowed"* African knowledge accorded great significance to the planets. Most authorities associated those planets with divinities or gods. To Ancient Africans the major planets became symbols that represented the mixture and interaction of all the essential forces of the universe and nature. Thus, as supposed generators of life, each had a characteristic sphere of action, which they called its *"heaven."* Influences from each *"heaven"* could spread all over.

Furthermore, the orbits were conceived as so many envelopes around the earth through which a person's soul had descended when coming to be born. These and other concepts caused them to project a given mental order into the Celestial System (called *Catasterism*). From that order Ancient African Sages recognized and interpreted a moral planetary *"series"* capable of explaining things in the spiritual and psychological world.

For example, in the psychological world, Saturn was related to endurance and reserve; in the moral world, to subjective evil possessing a ravenous appetite. In order words, the bad aspect of Saturn was like an ancient "pac-man" (of the 1980's computer fame) devouring all its creations — whether they were beings, things, ideas, or sentiments.

Saturn's evil influence on a person, as it was in entering the underworld, was often experienced by the person as a *"sinking"* feeling, a *"letting go,"* a *"falling."*

This person's experience was accompanied by a lost vitality. The person also had a sense that everything of value to him/her in life had been seized and carried into the unknown.

The "sinking", the loss of vitality, and the disappearance of values were collectively called Terrible Depression *("to strike down").* At this underworld place, the ancients added, where the Soul's worth is lost, there is decomposing and death. Thus, the planet Saturn, representing the great bearer of misfortunes, was envisioned as the dark spirit lying captive and associated with dragons or vipers.

Subsequently, Hippocrates (460?-357) in Greece and later Medieval medical practitioners said that of man's four bodily fluids or "*humors,*" it was excessive BLACK BILE (consisting of dark blood plus other secretions) that released Saturn's dark spirit and created the melancholic or depressed person. By this time the word *"depression"* meant "to *press down,"* *"to lower down"* or *"to let down"* — as occurs to one's mind or spirit.

Otherwise, the *"sinking down"* or *"sunk down"* idea of *"depression"* was used up to the 17th century of material objects and as a lenient name for a human weakness. Meanwhile, the European ancients and authorities of the Middle Ages and Renaissance—under the belief of it being caused by evil spirits—were treated by whipping, bloodletting, and exorcism. They also started embracing methods used in Ancient Africa—things like the spirit soothing of baths, gentle words, and music. One of the African reasons for music was that the intricacy and the beauty associated with music led to insights into the mystery of music and that generated "aliveness."

Finally, depression— as a general word for "*dejection*"— was adopted in the 20th century as a clinical term — indicating by 1905 a melancholic state often accompanied by feelings of inadequacy, lack of energy, difficulty apprehending things, and making poor associations. In the 1950s psychotherapy and electroconvulsive therapy (ECT) were the major options for lifting people out of profoundly melancholic states. Then began the era of modern psychopharmacology and the development of drugs tha control the manifestations of depression—but not the underlying cause.

The World of Depression Types: In the broadest use of the word "depression," it is an umbrella word — a canopy word, under which is gathered a group of mood disorders — each with different causes, different symptoms, and different degrees of severity.

Depression is actually a group of mood disorders with different symptom patterns and different degrees of severity. This can be likened to a kaleidoscope of thoughts, feelings, and behaviors that are opposite to "Aliveness". Depression may *range* from mild (e.g. discouraged) to slight (e.g. the loss of an acquaintance), to moderate (e.g.

devastation from loss of a top value) to severe (e.g. feelings of utter hopelessness and despair, as from loss of a child).

Each mood can be expressed in concealed, masked, tempered, and overt forms and different features are present within each of those forms (Bailey, Anger). Furthermore, each mood disorder may have a preference for acute and/or chronic; for males and/or females; for the young and/or the old; or for a particular kind of frequency course (Table III) (Bailey, The Handbook, p. 72).

Obviously, it is essential to have the correct diagnosis—and this involves ruling in or out other conditions. For example, depression needs to be distinquish from people who are normal but seem sad and have an assortment of physical complaints. Patients with Alzheimer's disease may show depression type symptoms but which may not be true depression.

Depression may coexist with other diseases such as in patients who have had a stroke or diabetes. Knowing this is important because a lack of such information would probably interfere with management progress. Also, side effects used to treat chronic illnesses (e.g. high blood pressure) could itself cause depression.

So this brings up the challenging question of: "How do you discuss a problem with multiple variables?" What makes this an "impossible" subject to adequately discuss is that depression may be beneficial, neutral, or destructive at different times in a person's life and that no two people have an identical pattern. These variables make it easy to want to give up on discussing the subject but if that happened we could not make any progress in what is needed to help us understand what we have or what to do about each aspect. Thus, we must resort to an approach that works as opposed to what is "the truth" –an approach which obviously means there are exceptions that will not fit well into the following rough categories.

The "**What Works" Approach** sets as its standard how a person's life is affected by depression. It is against a standard of satisfaction (as determined by the individual involved) that what one thinks, feels, says, and does can be compared. The results of that comparison for each individual will allow for four categories — mild, slight, moderate, and extreme — with respect to what is not normal.

MILD DEPRESSION: Mild depression includes the realms of useful, of normal, and of abnormal which can be symbolized by the letter *"J."* The short stem represents useful; the curved portion, normal; and the long vertical line, abnormal; and the horizontal line at the top, destruction.

"Useful" Depression is most clearly seen among baby monkeys who have lost contact with their mothers and sense danger nearby. As a result, while hoping the mother will come back quickly, they will *"sink down"* so as to be hidden by

the high grass and then stay put. Another useful form is the human fear reaction involving fight, flight, or fright. Here, the *"freezing fright"* part, whereby one does *"nothing"* while conserving energy, is often useful. When I enter into a hostile group and have no idea what to do immediately, I will withdraw like a turtle retracting into its shell until I can figure out the next sequence of actions and reactions. At Duke University a study showed that mild depression could protect against death by slowing people down and thereby giving them more time to pay attention to their minds and bodies.

"Normal" Depression is a mental state characterized by feelings of sadness, hopelessness, and loss of interest. Often it *shows* as moodiness or brooding. The *cause* may be from inner factors, external factors, or one's natural temperament. For this reason, Depression may be part of the syndrome of other disorders (e.g. postpartum psychosis).

Management of Normal Mild depression: Some say an immediate relief can come from the mere act of **Smiling**. This is an age-old expression that has inspired countless wise song lyrics and sayings. Smiling works even if it is insincere — the "I don't want to pose for this photograph" smile. It is believed that the facial muscles feed information to the brain's emotional "center" which, in turn, responds with chemicals that produce happy (or if frowning, sad) feelings. It is known that facial expressions can alter heart rate, skin temperature, and blood volume. Similarly, the linking of facial expressions and mood is in the social feedback loop: "Laugh and the world laughs with you. Cry—and you cry alone."

The diagnosis between normal and pathological depression is made by comparing a person's behavior and talk versus what is the norm. *Depression becomes pathological* when any of the above mentioned manifestations are out of proportion to whatever caused it.

Abnormal (or "Normal Varient") Depression is unrelated to any loss, lack, or obstruction; or when its intensity and duration are grossly disproportionate relative to the cause.

An example of one of the numerous forms Normal Varient depression may take is what some call **"Mother's Baby Blues."** I have seen this in a number of my patients when I was a general practitioner. New mothers wonder if they are "good enough" to care for a baby and are concerned about a multitude of things — lack of help and support; what their new life will be like and will they miss their old life; do they really love this baby, etc. Much of this comes from the bleak picture other mothers shower them with. In "We" cultures (e.g. Africa, China), this is not a major problem. But those afflicted have trouble sleeping when there is an opportunity to sleep; worry excessively; and feel overwhelmed. It usually resolves spontaneously within a few weeks.

The "**Holiday Blues**" is another example of temporary Normal Varient depression. Contributory to its development include: conflicting family expectations and demands which create guilt and resentment; separation from loved ones because of distance, illness, or death; wishing in vain to recapture the "good times" of past holidays; unrealistic expectations of friends, family, job, or church; money problems; fatigue from addition stress; and so forth. Realize that "this too shall pass"; avoid isolating yourself; maintain moderation in socializing, eating, drinking, and shopping; weigh priorities to protect your health; continue participating in activities that bring pleasure—reading, sports, music; be a volunteer and do something to help others.

Seasonal Affective Disorder is a type of depression that appears associated with light deprivation. It can recur each fall and winter during the year's shortest and darkest days. Relief may come from frequent and regular exposure to lighting devices supplying full-spectrum fluorescent light.

Destructive mild depression is characterized by a sense of hopelessness, sadness, and problems concentrating or sleeping. However, a person may not appear sad but is usually quiet, unhappy, pessimistic, and inhibited — preoccupied with his/her own problems. Such states of depression result from some loss, lack, or obstruction in the course of our activities of daily living and cause us to feel sad for a period of time. Stressful events— such as failing to win, the death of a friend, being separated from a loved one— can lead to a loss of appetite, difficulty sleeping, fatigue, and irritability. But with the passage of time, that sadness fades.

Some physiological changes associated with abnormal mild depression are of an agitated or retarded type. The sources of agitated or retarded depression can be REACTIVE (a response to something bad) and ENDOGENOUS from inner problems.

With AGITIATED Depression there is increased muscle tension and heart and breathing rates, an imbalance in electrical changes in the nervous system arising from an increase in salt retention, and increases in cortisol.

In RETARDED Depression there is loss of appetite and weight, a coated tongue and foul breath, insomnia, fatigue, tightness in the head, and constipation.

SLIGHT DEPRESSION: There are numerous subcategories of Slight Depression and they over-lap. Some are the same condition with different names. Some are different conditions with the same name. There are no clear cut diagnostic criteria and no general agreement. This group is sometimes called "subclinical" or "subsyndromal" depression because the symptoms are not definite enough or significant enough to warrant a definite diagnosis of Major depression.

The causes may vary widely — from organic to philosophical to psychological.

Studies have recently identified a gene (tryptophan hyddroxylase-2, or TPH2) that is a key in making the brain chemical **serotonin** (needed for communication between certain nerves and related to moods). Low levels of serotonin have been linked to depression. So has the serotonin transporter gene which pours out in times of stress. These genes may or may not be related to environmental causes.

To be genetically susceptible means that certain brain circuits concerned with pleasure and rewarding experiences are chemically fragile and somewhat easily upset by whatever undermines confidence and erodes the props of self-esteem (e.g. a loss of or separation from a parent at a critical stage of development) in early life. Examples include the following:

The PASSIVELY DEPRESSED are totally overwhelmed and consumed by certain circumstances of daily living. They feel listless and inadequate, finding it hard to think, concentrate, and make decisions. They may become irritable and quarrelsome.

"DEPRESSION WITHOUT SADNESS" consists of depressed people who do not feel sad or simply can not put into words that they are feeling sad. Children and older men in this group who typically <u>lack the "feeling" or "emotion" vocabulary to describe their real mindset become quiet frustrated</u>. Children may simply be irritable and easily frustrated. Older men may say: "I feel lousy"; "I'm not sleeping well"; "food does not taste like it should"; "I'm having trouble concentrating." Younger men say "life sucks and that's that."

MALE DEPRESSION: In my practice I have found it extremely difficult to diagnosis depression in men because they generate around it a cloud of seemingly beside-the-point feelings like anger, apathy, and staying at a distance (i.e. hard to get to know because of the barriers they put around themselves). Or, they may present the false front of self-confidence, arrogance, and independence. Or, they may start losing interest in everything and have nothing to look forward to in their lives. They usually stop going out; perhaps stop shaving and washing; and have ongoing troubles with sleep.

Relying on male stoicism, workaholism, and social withdrawal instead, they do not seek treatment and even fail to acknowledge it out of a "manhood" thing. To bring some excitement into their lives, they may engage in the sexual pursuit of partners or compulsive gambling. For numbing the unpleasant state they may overindulge in alcohol or start taking drugs because they would rather not feel at all. Or, they may attempt suicide.

The causes are the same as for any depression. By viewing depression as a sign of weakness—i.e. "letting my emotions get the best of me"—men can get even more depressed from being depressed. In turn, that causes **Dysthymia**—chronic low mood.

Management is of course difficult because of the masks men place over their depression and are reluctant to seek help. Cognitive therapy (see later discussion) is a talking cure which enables men to reframe their bleak view of the world. For example, they need to see that if they killed themselves they might be ending their problems but starting a great deal of suffering for loved ones. *Interpersonal Therapy* (IPT) fosters better communication and conflict-resolution skills. Problem-Solving Therapy teaches ways of breaking down problems into units that can be handled one at a time.

Medical re-evaluations may be of benefit, as in changing medications. Increasing their intake of vitamin B12 could be tried as a "shot-gun" treatment. The entire family may need to be educated to what to do and not do as, for example, removing any guns from the home and focusing on the symptoms as opposed to the diagnostic label of "depression." Patients should be spared blame and accusations, if for no other reason than they feel bad enough without the added weight. When visiting the doctor, family members should remain to give the additional information that the patient avoids. However, it may help for the patient to know how his depression is affecting the family since depression can be an infectious disease.

Support groups can help, since men battle the world everyday and alone. Being in nature and exercising are particularly helpful. There is a stigma in the Black American community that psychotropic medications are being used as a social control mechanism.

Incomplete Mourning is complex subject that has roughly been subdivided as follows. Some say the five stages of mourning are alarm, numbness, pining (searching), depression, and recovery. Others say the stages are denial; sorrow; detaching from the loss; adjusting to life without it; and reattaching to a replacement. Still other recognize the types of Inhibited or Denied Losses; *Grief* (feeling terrible over the loss of something loved); *Mourning* (the 6 to 18 month process of resolving grief by relinquishing the loss); or *Bereavement* (the state accompanying the mourning process which may or may not be followed by attachments to or identification with a replacement).

Of course the causes are innumerable as, for example, over the loss of a loved one (e.g. one's mother). Some individuals may try to compensate (e.g. through laughter, being the office clown, or becoming a humorist). Some males tend to experience and express their depression differently — as in being more aggressive, irritable, and impulsive. Some girls show more helplessness, sadness, and leanings toward hopelessness.

Management is to, if possible and under the proper circumstance, get them to laugh. Laughter provides a sense of release of pent up emotions.

MODERATE DEPRESSION: Moderate depression is "clinical depression" – meaning that one's activities of daily living are affected; that there are diagnostic criteria in textbooks; and that treatment is required. However, any of them may step over into the Extreme Depression category. In Moderate depression people suffer from persistent feelings of unpleasant tension, anguish, and often both *"psychic* and Spiritual *pain."* Finding conversation difficult, they may simply complain that they are unwanted, unloved, and unappreciated. Examples of Moderate Depression are:

POST-PARTUM DEPRESSION which is in-between the "Baby Blues" and Post-Partum Psychosis. In this major depression, manifestations are more intense, are of longer duration, and cause more problems than the "baby blues." Symptoms include despair, hopelessness, failure to cope, withdrawal, and "too much" or "too little" concern for the baby's well-being.

Management starts with detecting pregnant women for unusual signs of stress or strain, and particularly if they are young and/or have had prior episodes of depression. Dads can become involved by attending prenatal classes to learn about the processes of birthing; what to look out for that might signal special problems; and the necessity for giving loving support in the event that the psychosis appears. As with all significant emotional problems, mental health specialists need to be consulted.

The AGGRESSIVELY DEPRESSED (called Masked Depression) grab for *"the tip of the sword"* in hopes of holding on to it for survival. Its opposite counterpart is PARALYZING DEPRESSION which can completely halt ones ability to function day to day and, at worse, can lead to suicide.

In both *pathological groups* there are a variety of causes, mechanisms of expression, and symptoms. The cause may be acquired poor thoughts, drugs, genetic (e.g. anatomical, biochemical), or from an interaction between biochemical sensitivity and life stresses (e.g. divorce, poor environments). Because of hereditary and cultural factors, different people respond to the same environment in different ways. Some of the neurotransmitters (chemicals between nerves) involved include serotonin, dopamine, and nor-epinephrine. If these three amines are too few they may cause depression; too much may produce a manic depression state.

EXTREME DEPRESSION: In Deep, Severe, or Extreme depression one gives up on life (e.g. apathy) or when one commits suicide because of being depressed. The facial expression is one of hopelessness and questions are answered in a halting, monosyllabic manner. They are preoccupied with thoughts of guilt, unworthiness, and self-accusation — often recounting their faults. All initiative is lost and suicidal thoughts are frequently entertained.

The weight or burden associated with extreme or severe depression becomes unbearable when there is *hopelessness*. Even more that emotional pain, it is hopelessness that crushes. This can come from overwhelming outside forces, from a misarranged worldview (which prevents figuring out answers), or from organic causes.

POST-PARTUM PSYCHOSIS is fairly common and has a wide range of manifestations. Several factors contribute but a chaotic state of maternal harmones following delivery—progesterone, estrogen, prolactin—is a significant factor. It can lead to such a sense of unreality, confusion, delusions and hallucinations as to cause a mother to put her child in an oven and cook the child. Hopelessness from other etiologies implies that one has lost the ability to look into the future and, in fact, can only see the present moment. In other words, there is a lack of foresight and forethought. The original concept forming the word "hope" came from the notion of "jumping to safety" or at least a "leaping into the expectation" of being safe from enemies. A positive attitude of expectation is a motivating force to push one in the direction of the expectations.

MATERNAL DEPRIVATION SYNDROME is about a loss or lack of mothering, even in 15 month old infants. This has deep and life-long consequences of depression and other forms of emotional disturbances.

Suicide is far more common in teenage boys than in girls but girls have more diagnosed depression and attempt suicide more often. Depressed boys show more aggression, anger, irritability, and impulsiveness but less overt hopelessness, helplessness, and sadness compared with suicidal females. Boys do not use girls' vocabulary or body language when they are significantly depressed.

Management includes psychotherapy, medications, electro-shock. Psychotherapy sorts out and changes destructive thoughts and provides beneficial structured life activities. Particularly with boys, there ought to be as much, if not more time spent in teaching them selfhood inner strength and inner peace and in their emotional, social, and spiritual wholeness and integrity as there is in academic and physical prowess. Parents must learn how to be sensitive to the depression and pains of their children—and each child shows pain and depression differently.

DEPRESSION IN NON-WHITES: Across racial and ethnic lines, the poor and the less educated suffer from higher rates of depression. Furthermore, they are largely undiagnosed and thereby carry the effects of slowing, stopping, or reversing their ability to adequately function in daily living. There are many predisposing, precipitating, and immediate causes for depression in minorities — and basically from the effects of racism coupled with other stressful life events and perhaps from genetic predispositions.

Successful minorities in middle and upper class marketplace occupations are constantly aware of being under a magnifying glass by a need to play a role for White co-workers and bosses. They hide their depression or pursuit of treatment for fear of damaging their status and job security. In the marketplace a rule is: "do not give anyone a competitive edge."

It is common for minorities to "work though" the depression — often to the point of exhaustion and to the beginning of substance abuse (Black Enterprise .com, August 2004, p. 103). Since diabetes and depression are common in most minorities — and both involve a common part of the brain — they can cause or enhance each other.

Because depression was essentially not present among Africans (before coming in contact with Europeans), to admit depression is to admit being weak –and that is a cultural taboo among Black Americans. They are also reluctant, because of the White medical profession's long history of experimenting on Black people (e.g. the Tuskegee Syphilis disaster) to go to the doctors' office and reluctant to take psychotropic medications.

There have been two times in my life whereby it is likely that I was depressed — once in 1969 from being overwhelmed with the racism forces being showered on me, and once during my divorce. The uncertainty about being depressed is that I lacked the classic features outlined in mental health textbooks.

As background, my boyhood dream was to be a physician. Following military service in the U.S. Air Force and working with the orthopaedic surgeons at Clark Field (Philippines) managing wounded soldiers flown in from Viet Nam, I decided to become an orthopaedic surgeon. However, orthopaedics had been essentially closed to minorities and despite my being accepted to a residency program, I was watched for even the tiniest of mistakes.

By entering this hostile "I" (Individualism) White profession, it was essential for me to do all the extra work it took not to make mistakes or to give the appearance of getting off track in any way. That, in addition to trying to learn all I could about the complicated aspects of orthopaedic surgery, were a great deal of continuous pressure.

Neither did the staff want to guide my training as they did for the White residents. Therefore, following the completion of my residency, I went to Johns Hopkins to take a fellowship in order to learn about genetics as applied to orthopaedics. By having known how to work hard at an early age, my hard work there put me out front of all the fellows and that was a threat to this racist bunch. They applied tremendous obstacles that brought me to a momentary halt.

At this point I think I was depressed but I could not afford to indulge myself because the necessity for achieving my goal. In order not to "go down the drain" it was essential to quickly regroup. But during that moment I was in a daze and was wandering around with no destination. I had absolutely no idea as to how to keep going or what to do. Although thinking I would have to give up, I did not voluntary think of quitting.

The second was during my divorce. This was my first experience being face to face with hatred from my ex-wife and her entourage and blatant greed from my and her attorneys, accountants, and all others involved. They kept me in court so often it was necessary to stop doing surgery. Everything was set up to put me in a deep hole that had no bottom and, at the top, all sorts of weapons were aimed at me. Without a doubt, the loss of my children was the worse. Nevertheless, I had to keep going and not make any mistakes in the process. Since everybody deserted me, I had to walk completely alone. The hostility directed toward me was shocking.

I think I became depressed because I had at least four of the signs and symptoms listed by the National Institute of Mental Health. One was difficulty sleeping past a half hour or so. Thus I would get up and work on researching some of the problems my patients had. Second was a change in appetite — mainly the eating of ice cream. Third I felt sad because of all the problems showered on me and because the hostility was so unnecessary. Fourth, there was not so much a loss of interest in daily activities — because I had no choice but to continue — but I was simply too tired to be an active dad whenever I had the kids for visitation. There was absolutely no time for any rest or recreation — and I was constantly in seep deprivation. On one occasion I did have a thought of suicide but that was when I hit bottom ad then the bottom fell out. It lasted a couple of seconds.

The way I handled this is what I now recognize as having risen above the mental plane housing my depression. The way this concept came about was on a particularly bad morning, I got up very early to drive up to the mountains. The higher the elevation the more I could look down on the smog. Then I got out of the car and related what I was viewing to the bad experiences I was having.

An insight came of simply rising above my problems into a higher plane of existence. This was readily understandable because during the night when I could not sleep, focusing on researching my patients' problems immediately took me into a higher world that was comfortable and exciting enough for me to completely leave behind my stress, distress, and worries.

Another effective approach was for me to work out all the bad emotions I was experiencing. This turned out to be seven notebooks consisting of about 700 typed pages. The first five were simply about complaining, blaming, feeling sorry for myself, and moaning and groaning. Then I got tired of doing that and said: "What are you going to do about it?" Thus book six went in the direction of self-help things. Meanwhile, because of my interest more in orthopaedic medicine than in orthopaedic surgery, I was investigating the psychosomatic complaints of my patients and realizing a connection to their orthopaedic complaints with the sort of bad emotions I was experiencing. As a result, book seven was entitled "Deceptive Orthopaedic Patients." Much information in that book is transferable to this book and its "bad behaviors" companion book.In putting this together, there seems to be several realms involving significant depression.

First is the **cause** with its predisposing, precipitating, and immediate subdivisions.

Second is the **happening** — that which has the potential to generate depression.

Third is your **interpretation of the happening**.

Fourth are the factors **contributing to the effect of the interpretation**.

Fifth is the **natural progression of the happening**.

Sixth is the **state of mind** of depression.

In applying these six realms to me, the fact that I chose to leave the crowd and pursue my own ambitions alone was predisposing. The precipitating causes were numerous and cumulative to the point of being overwhelming. The immediate cause is the **Proximate Cause** — the specific situation which unleashed a flood of thoughts and emotions that admixed. The result was to form that which "presses down" the plane of existence upon which the happening occurs.

Those situations were being overwhelmed by racism and by the hostility in my divorce with the specific immediate cause probably of a "straw" nature — the weight of which tipped the scale which opened the trap door so that a flood of bad memories were showered on me all at once. The mindset created by this flood was the happening.

The forms given to this happening was based upon my interpretation of the predisposing, precipitating, and immediate causes. However, there were several factors contributing to my interpretation — my pre-existing ambition; my presence in a hostile "I" society which left me isolated to the point of realizing I had to self-protect, self-produce, self-defend from outside hostility and "elbow" my way into a position where I could get what I was after; and the fact that I had a trained right brain and a trained left brain.

In the racism setting, my depression was from thoughtful causes ("what is going to happen with all my work products?") My environmental self was disconnected from my real self. In the divorce setting, my depression was from the emotional pain of my right brain (i.e. hostility) and from the spiritual pain (i.e. love flow interference deriving out of losing my children).

The natural progression of the happening would continue to generate those aspects designed to keep me depressed — and if I added distortions and fantasies the depression would have worsened. Fortunately, I took measures to release the tension present in the system generating the power to "pressure down" — keep working toward my destination; writing; and compensating by trying to help other people's children. To talk of the state of mind of depression brings up the issue of whether or not depression is an emotion (i.e. stirred up feelings) or a reverse emotion (i.e. the pressing down of emotions).

The stirring up of emotions and the pressing down of emotions (including suppression and repression) generates tension. Many thoughts and emotions combine to make up what is called depression sentiments (which are teeming with biological energy activity). This is what is considered as the "emotion" of depression while, following the weight of depression sentiments pushing down the plane of existence upon which it is operating, one is in a state of depression.

Yet, there are different levels of a state of depression. One is that state which involves only one plane of existence — equivalent to low self-esteem whereby one lacks confidence in one or two very significant aspects of life, as determined by the individual involved. By contrast, an inferiority complex is a generalized attack on confidence in more than one or two significant aspects.

If self-esteem problems can be thought of as occurring on compartments situated on the horizontal plane, depression states occur on the vertical planes. For example, a person may be depressed on the: (1) untrained right brain plane; (2) the trained right brain plane; and (3) the left brain plane (ranging between the immature and the mature). Thus, the combinations of state of mind depressions may be of seven types: 1; 1 + 2; 1 + 3; 2; 2 + 3; 3; and 1 + 2 + 3.

So what do these look like clinically? An **untrained right brain** receiver of depression sentiments shows as complaining; showing miserableness; having pain all over the body; resorting to drugs, alcohol, or food; unable to see what is available to work with; unable to produce useful or desirable work products; lacks the power to mobilize the forces to pull themselves out of their depression; has disconnected from one's real self; has an environmental self which requires outside support and/ or medications to function. They have self-esteem issues.

A **trained right brain** receiver of depressive sentiments are pressed down by their weight but have the power to mobilize their ability to step up from their depression to express at some socially acceptable form (e.g. art, music, or other forms of productive work) while keeping one's real self intact. These environmental self activities of daily living are "pressed down" to varying degrees — depending upon if the depression is mild, slight, moderate, or extensive. However, whether trained or untrained, the spiritual connection of the right brain means that spiritual pain will be present. This is especially true if part of the depression sentiments is somehow involved with a disturbance in the flow of love. Spiritual pain will cause a persistence of depression manifestations until love is re-established.

A **left brain receiver** of depression sentiments go into and clog the intellect "mechanism" by interfering with the progress toward one's work product distinction. To what degree and to what type is determined by one's societal common sense orientation, especially in relation to manhood/womanhood. Perhaps the reason pre-colonial Africans did not get depressed is because of the way the societal structure was set up whereby living up to principles of Ma'at were more important than any other type of work product. It was typical for people to have good relations with and good behaviors toward each other.

In considering that combinations may be present (e.g. 1 + 2, 1 + 3, 2 + 3, 1 + 2 + 3) there are different manifestations of depressive sentiments and if the untrained and trained parts of one's right and left brain are depressed, this is the most severe form of depression — one likely to end in suicide. If a person's mind's eye viewing stays on the same plan as the depression, one can not see what it is about and therefore cannot adequately handle it.

But, if one's depression is in the trained right brain or in the left brain, one has the ability to rise to a higher plane in order to get relief, to get a better view of the big picture, or to fashion a workable plan for handling it. If the left brain, the trained right brain, and the untrained right brain are involved, there is no place to rise above to and perhaps only the spiritual approaches one uses will help.

Managing Depression

The one thing all depressions have in common is the loss of "Aliveness." The one thing that will relieve depression is the acquiring of "Aliveness." So what is "**Aliveness**?" It is an experience better remembered, engaged in, or observed than defined or explained. Remember those times when, as a little child, you were totally absorbed in extremely busy play. Maybe you were playing *"hide-and-go-seek"* or *"hop-scotch,"* or *"catch- me -if-you-can."*

At any given time you can observe aliveness at its best by observing children at play. Following retirement, when I was a volunteer teacher's assistance at an elementary school, the 4th and 5th graders would engage me in their exciting play at recess. By participating, I instantly rose to a high level of aliveness. Being alive was not about how I felt because it had a greater scope and magnitude — like that of expanding loftiness. Loftiness is the expanding magnitude of the sweetness of an early morning sunrise or the beauty of a sunset, or the experience of a babbling brook transporting us into the flow of the best in nature.

The word *"aliveness"* comes into our language from its relationship to *"life,"* and *"love."* Originally, ***"LIFE"*** *("to stick to")* was considered to be the *"sticky"* glue that held love together and therefore would remain forever. Thus, aliveness was that which sticks to life and continues with it in a loving way. By allowing aliveness to fully express itself — as little children do — then the way you live your life is like the work the child puts in at play. For example, you are racing your motor to get started on today's work because there is so much to see and learn and do — and so little time. Time is precious and you do not wish to waste a moment of it.

Brimming with spiritual power, you creatively make fun out of hard work. But when you encage your free and creative mind by having and following a lot of rules and trying to make others follow your rules, you lose a substantial amount of aliveness. If carried too far, you become a slave to destructive thoughts and feelings — regardless of cause — and thereby enter the world of pathological depression.

Yet all is not lost because associated with the spiritual gifts of life and love is also the gift of guardian spirits to help each of us through life. My guardian spirit of named Jann — a buddy even more intimate than my dog (and my dog is my best friend). Jann will do whatever I ask and without passing judgment. As long as Jann is given a clear and precise command, he will go into any world to acquire the requested information. As a boy, I told Jann I did not want to be sick anymore and, up to this point, he did what was necessary to keep me well.

Depressed people ought to find their guardian spirit and call on him/her to pull them out of their depression, at least to some extent. Of course, they may need medical treatment. As a physician, I was certain that my post-surgical patients would get much, much better much, much faster if they worked with me to help themselves.

The same applies to the depressed. Similar to doing exercise, they must force themselves to do things that increase aliveness — like playing with children or otherwise being action-oriented. When alone, they should push themselves to do something creative — like drawing cartoons or making up funny stories. Such aliveness activities are to be done to immediately replace every destructive or negative thought.

It can not be too strongly emphasized that "depression" is a group of mood disorders with different causes, patterns, and severity. Failure to recognize that depression is a "glob" of different "strings" — with each string having different colors (e.g. from light blue "funks" to blackest despair) and each string has different shades of its color — means that every sort of treatment and management has been tried throughout history and none with any consistent results. There have been whippings, blood letting, exorcism, and methods of "spirit soothing" by music, prayer, baths, and gentle words. However, until the 1950s psychotherapy and electroconvulsive therapy (ECT) were the major options for lifting people out of profound melancholic states.

Next came the era of psychopharmacology, with its drugs that controlled the manifestations of depression, although not the underlying malady. Still, no expert knew which patient should get what, when, how much, and for how long. Today, we know that some causes of depression are cultural; some hormonal; some genetic; some are biochemical disturbances in the brain; and some are byproducts of organic, philosophical, and psychological factors.

Male stoicism acts as an important source of interfering with treatment because it considers depression a sign of weakness. After all, it says, emotions should not get the best of a real man. When some men realize they are depressed, they get depressed about being depressed.

Modern day **Psychotherapy** — the "talking cure" version — has three main forms — each designed to give patients tools to lift their moods. Cognitive-behavioral therapy (CBT) teaches how to recognize and successfully counter the depression sentiments that fuel depression. Interpersonal therapy (IPT) fosters better communication and conflict-resolution skills. Problem-solving therapy teaches ways of breaking down problems into units that can be more easily handled one at a time. Sessions vary from 10 to 16 weeks.

Antidepressants, rather than alter the mind, work to restore a normal chemical balance in the brain. Only one or none of several may work and it may take four to six weeks to know. Some have problematic side effects. Frontier approaches include deep brain stimulation (DBS) by placing a pacemaker in a key area of the brain. When effective, the patient experiences a "sudden calmness" and a "vanishing of the void."

Cognitive therapy teaches the depressed to reconfigure their view of the world and develop a more realistic perspective on the risks, losses, lacks, or obstacles they face (see later discussion).

MANAGING "NORMAL AND ABNORMAL DEPRESSION: Everybody has had "***Normal***" **depression** and they are something that one can do something about. Since it involves dejection, feelings of discouragement, a loss of enthusiasm, and a general slowing down of mental and physical activity, get interested in something that will generate aliveness—like playing with kids. Instead of carrying on a conversation that is in a monotone and instead of answering questions with a meager supply of words, vary the tone of your voice and increase the number of words, as in reading a story to a child. Rather than preferring to just sit alone and assuring yourself about the lack of hope for the future, go do something for the needy.

For me, during such "down times"—usually lasting from an hour to a few days—I push myself to keep doing some work — if nothing more than simply cleaning up my work station and putting things in order. Or, I will start reading some of the stack of newspapers accumulated, looking for information that might help me with an article or with a book. If I am tired, I go to sleep and will usually awaken before daybreak quite refreshed. Because of a great curiosity about life, my "down times" do not last very long.

Abnormal Depression is present when "*normal*" depression is lasting too long or the *"blue funk"* (the sunken ways of acting) is too deep or too widespread. It is serious when there is too great an interference with one's daily life progress; or there are delusions (e.g. *"I am rotting away");* or there is excessive guilt for imagined great wrongdoings; or there are hallucinations (e.g. strange body sensations). A major cause of depression is a family setting in which one or both parents treat the child as if he/she were unworthy of their love and affection. Here the methods used for handling spiritual pain apply. Any of these calls for the seeking of help from mental health specialists.

One of the major duties of mental health specialists is to distinguish between normal and abnormal depressions and between biological and purely psychological depression (e.g. by the dexamethasone suppression test — DST). Next is to decide which ones they *can do* something about and which of those *they need* to do something about. From a proper diagnosis it will be determined that formalized treatment (e.g. drugs, group or single therapy sessions) and/or self-help treatment are required.

EMOTIONAL PAIN

EMOTIONAL PAIN has a purely mental (psychical feeling) source and arises from some thought, feeling, or mental state that reflects a loss, a lack, or an obstruction. Both emotional (the Tangible type) and spiritual pain (the Intangible or Immaterial type) occurs when young children are deprived of "mother nurturing." Emotional pain is worldly suffering that can come, for example, from disturbances of basic natural feelings associated with a person's connection with people, things, or oneself.

Unlike spiritual pain, emotional pain can cause much of the same bodily functional changes as occur in fear, anger, hate, and rage. Painful emotions inhibit muscle activity which, in turn, cause changes in the exchange of nutrients and waste products. Both changes can manufacture organic problems, despite them being of a psychosomatic nature.

The Story of Emotional Pain: Whereas the one cell organism, Monera, experiences physical pain and whereas the higher animals also experience acute psychical pain, it is perhaps only in human beings where physical and acute (temporary) and chronic (enduring) psychical (emotional) pain are well developed. Egyptian dental specialist, at least by 3700 B.C., were treating patients with pain coming from their teeth.

Being a feature common to humankind, pain was referred to in the Bible by a number of Hebrew and Greek words. The setting for those words— and often those setting fashioned the primary meanings for pain—were in the realms of work, affliction, distress, tribulations, sadness, grief, and evil. Each of the words used in a given setting were considered to be caused by many things and therefore a category word itself had a variety of words to reflect the cause. For example, the pain subcategory of grief included sorrow and suffering.

The Bible speaks of suffering in both man and the whole physical creation because of man's original sin (Gen. 3:14-19). Thus, when man fell, the whole nature of humans became totally corrupt (Rom. 7:15). This led to suffering in the form of torment, anguish, pangs, troubles, agony, or an uneasiness of mind. Furthermore, there was a physical, mental, and spiritual price to pay — a penalty — for sinning.

For women, the throes of childbirth — *"her crying out in her pangs of birth, in anguish delivery"* — was an example of physical pain (Rev. 12.1-2). For men, the penalty was experiencing pain in their toil. In addition, individual sins were said to lead to personal guilt complexes (Ps. 32:51) and the excruciating pangs of *remorse* (deep painful regret for having done wrong), hopefully leading to acts of REPENTANCE (i.e. a *"change of heart,"* a turning to God — Is. 31-6). Those overcome with fear because of their unforgiven sins were experiencing SPIRITUAL PAIN — the penalty for violating morality and the divine purpose.

To gain a better understanding of the term EMOTIONAL PAIN, let us use as an analogy the story of Humpty Dumpty — the one sitting on a wall and who had a great fall and, as a result shattered into pieces. The "pain" part of Emotional Pain perhaps came from Hebrew "pena" (a root word for pain) referring to head, corner, and a parapet (a low wall at the edge of a balcony, roof, bridge, etc). Thus, Humpty Dumpty (the head or intact feelings) fell off a wall (the action of wounding feelings), and was broken into many pieces (the result of wounded feelings).

Nevertheless, the term EMOTIONAL PAIN was used for tragedies of the material world associated with causing wounded feelings in an individual. In elaborating on pain and pleasure being opposites, Aristotle (384-322 B.C.) said that pleasure is a perfection supervening (that which follows closely upon as an additional happening) on certain activities while pain was an imperfection. Spinoza (1632-1677) defined pleasure as the feeling with which one passes from a lesser state of perfection to a greater; pain as the feeling with which one makes the reverse transition.

The legal system, supposedly originating as an interweave with religious, has used pain in both a spiritual and a worldly way. In the spiritual sense the old legal expression "*on pain of death*" meant "*under penalty of death.*" This concept was influential in the rise of the Medieval European TRIALS BY ORDEAL. These were crude, unreliable, and extremely painful tests that accused persons were put through — tests believed to be controlled by God –in order to decide guilt or innocence of the accused. The belief was that if the person had sinned, God would not stop them from being killed by the ordeal.

A legal example of shattering people's emotions in a worldly sense is the SUBPOENA ("*under punishment*"). The fact that those subpoenaed are "*commanded*" to appear in court hurts their feelings. The reason is that people resist being "commanded" to do anything and to be forced against their will shatters the power part of their self-concept.

In putting all of this together, our feelings are like an eggshell surrounding our self-concept (who we think we are, what we think we do, and how we think we appear — all in the best sense). Emotional pain is the result of tightening, pressing inward, stretching, penetrating, or shattering the feelings contained around ones self-concept "*eggshell.*"

<u>EMOTIONAL PAIN</u>

Definition: Mind Suffering

Contents: Hurt Self-Esteem i.e. Hurt Feelings
Loss of Sense of Control
Guilt — Concealed Anger + Anxiety

Subtle Manifeststions: Picture Of Pain
Increased Activity — hard to sit still
Decreased Activity — listless blank stare, hands in lap

The World of Emotional Pain: Children have a staggering amount of learning to do before becoming full members of society. Much of this early learning occurs in the sometimes overly tolerant and sometimes unreasonably intolerant setting of the family. As children develop, their teaching becomes more direct and more varied — teachers, neighbors, television, videos, movies, books, and encounters from acquaintances and strangers. Some teachers are caring, some are indifferent, and some are mean in overt, tempered, masked, or concealed ways.

<u>Children have the best chance of developing a healthy emotional sensitivity when they feel cared for, accepted, respected and unconditionally loved no matter what</u>

they do. They are then better able, compared with the less fortunate, to accept being scolded or punished for specific bad actions and accept corrections for their errors. *"I love you but I do not like what you did,"* is a constructive discipline which helps build a strong and positive self-concept.

On the other hand, any rearing that significantly deviates from this ideal tends to create in children a weak and negative self-concept. It can start with conditional love — *"if you keep doing that, I won't love you anymore."* Bad name calling is worse — *"you're stupid," "you won't ever amount to much."* Here, the child as a person is being attacked rather than being made aware of what he/she did incorrectly. These are examples of wounding the feelings of children.

Some of those wounds heal over with "scar" tissue but when there are multiple slight or even minor wounds or when there are specific moderate or severe wounds, children's self-concepts and, therefore self-esteem, can be damaged for life. The *magical minds* of children ensure that they do not digest information exactly as it is given. Instead, they alter it to fit their state of sensitivity. For example, the *"scarred"* ones make worse whatever bad is said about them and the worse becomes real for them. Once they declare to themselves: "I am a stupid person" (or whatever else bad label was put on them), that emotionally painful label has a custom-made coloration, with a deeply social meaning. As with any internalized meaning, a child acts upon it—lives down to it— in such a way as to make it come true — a self-fulfilling prophecy (the *"aha, I told you so"* scenario).

Since little children lack adequate vocabularies to describe how they feel, their emotional pain, instead of being localized to one aspect, becomes part of all aspects of their lives. This is like causing the entire spider web to move by touching only one tiny part. Since there is nothing specific, trying to find out answers like: *"what's wrong with me?" "why are my feelings hurt so easily?"* are quite elusive. Rather, they experience hazy and non-specific anxiety. As a result of vulnerability, they put up *"a front"* — a facade — a *"mask"* to keep people from getting *"too close."* Thus, they are more likely to be lonely, preferring that circumstance to exposing themselves to others who put them down and are critical.

These children are deeply disturbed if they do poorly at some task or upon becoming aware of some personal fault or inadequacy. Thus, they stay with the status quo and fear leaving the familiar, because taking risks are too much of a threat for them. With respect to trying new things, the prevailing attitude is: *"I'm not going to go into water until I learn how to swim."* When encountering painful experiences (e.g. insults), they reject or forget trying anything of a self-improvement nature, even if it is relatively simple to achieve.

Such children remember the pain; keep it alive *"forever"*; and thereby wastefully burn up huge amounts of their daily supply of energy. The emotional pain in many people, like that just following a divorce, gives them such a sour disposition and narrows their enjoyment of life so much that they are often not a pleasure to be around.

Besides trying to rear children to avoid needless emotional pain, an objective of us as adults is to minimize as much pain as we can. Our first task in life is to live with a sense of well-being and the means for doing this is our ability to think. The basic guides we use to live are pleasure and pain. We use these guides to lead us into and away from certain situations. From these guides we learn to profit by the experiences they led us into and lessons learned largely determine our system of values. Both pleasure and pain are mental action words moreso than physiological descriptions.

Pleasure and pain—both being about emotions and both giving rise to individual and interwoven emotions—have defied universal understanding because they are on multiple planes of existence and their total involvement is so complex. This complexity persists even when we look at only two pieces of its whole—i.e. the pain and the emotional parts. The pain part of emotional pain imparts its features to the emotional part and the emotional parts impart its features to the pain part. In addition, the learned aspects of emotions and pain which result in habits combine with and often dominate the natural emotions and the natural physical pains.

The habit portions, typically filled with distortions and fantasy, can and do contribute, if not actually control, the interpreting of what comes into the mind. Those same habits frequently expand from imitating or copying the methods of others. How those habits are expressed may range widely within an individual as well as between different ethnic groups. An example of the latter is that given the same degree of physical pain, certain ethnic groups habitually show great expression while others show little or no outward expression.

The main point is that in each of us there are natural emotions and natural pains that are essential for self-protection and self-expression. Also in each of us there are acquired emotions stemming from real, distorted, and unreal (fantasy) interpretations.

Natural physical pain warns our bodies that something harmful is happening. When physical pain occurs, as in touching a hot stove, pain signals are carried through relay systems to the thalamus, cerebral cortex, and elsewhere. As a result, we have the experience of natural pain. Such pain we never get use to.

Meanwhile, during the same process of pain signals being carried through relay systems, specific pathways carry an emotional component of the physically painful stimulus to areas of the hind brain and reticular formation — thereby activating emotional responses. These emotional responses in the perception of pain suggest that neural mechanisms modify either the transmission of pain or the translation of central pain messages into negative affect (i.e. mood). Nevertheless, the emotional component retains many of the features of the physically caused pain.

Obviously, this is something humans and others of the animal kingdom desire to avoid. Thus, the drive to avoid pain and the drive to have pleasure is a most compelling drive to live and it is used by all animals. However, *humans have the capacity to merely avoid pain without seeking pleasure or to seek pain and avoid pleasure—and this is often seen in patients who exhibit abnormal emotional pain.*

On the other hand, as seen in Psychosomatic conditions, emotions can cause pain of a physical and of a psychic nature. Be it in nature or nurture, overly sensitive people seemingly ordinary stresses of school, or social life—academic disappointments, embarrassments, and romantic break-ups— trigger crushing emotional pain and even suicidal despondency.

The physical part of psychosomatic conditions coming through the autonomic nervous system, is stimulated at and, in turn, stimulates the hypothalamus and limbic portions of the brain. It then constricts blood vessels throughout the body. The resultant reduced blood flow to muscles causes a variety of changes (e.g. leakage of blood vessel contents capable of matting fibrils). These changes, when combined, generate muscle pain. In other words, emotional conflicts can cause organic problems.

To gain a glimpse of the purely emotional pain portion requires taking a step back in development to the time when the toddler's value system begins to form. They perceive experiences as "*likes*" or "*dislikes.*" As their experience accumulates, either the "*likes*" or the "*dislikes*" predominate. From these feelings (and here the word "feeling" includes emotions) they develop feeling oriented beliefs about what life is like (i.e. life-esteem), about what they are like (self-concept) and about how they like being the persons they believe themselves to be in physical, social, emotional, and intellectual realms (i.e. self-esteem). The feelings present in these perceptions gradually join with thoughts to form thought/feeling oriented beliefs. The presence of dominating thoughts compared with feelings is what forms "*values.*"

But when the feeling part of the belief is more prominent than the thought contribution, the result is a "*hypersensitivity*" to possible pleasures or pains impressed into the child's self-concept. This "*hypersensitivity*" –which is sometimes called the MEEE — is like the watchful eyes of the guards of a castle mentioned previously. The Meee makes immediate decisions of "*likes*" or "*dislikes*" about things and of whether someone is "*friend or foe*" — regarding whatever or whomever is approaching from the outside world.

The feelings in and around our self-concept are like the eggshell—like walls in and around a castle. Any violation of those "Feeling" walls cause emotional pain; any soothing reinforcement, pleasure. Some "*scratches*" on the walls are temporarily hurtful but are of no long term significance. "Holes" correspond to a person's moderately serious "*damaged feeling wounds.*" Although the wound(s) can be repaired with scar tissue, the wall is no longer as strong as it was. Extremely serious wounds, whether partially repaired or not, remain extremely sensitive because they have real, distorted, and fantasy "emotional nerves" trapped in the scar.

Some scars are like those on the elbow. This means that constant exposure to irritation—as occurs each time you bend your elbow and that bending keeps the wound open— prevents the wound from healing. Thus, an open sensitive wound persists—and this is what chronic emotional pain is like. Much psychic activity is used in guarding "wound damage" so as to prevent re-injury as well as to do whatever possible to bring relief.

Unfortunately, chronic emotional pain is very common. I have seen it most often with daughters keeping real, distorted, or fantasy psychic wounds open "forever"—even after their fathers are dead. Why this is so is unclear. Normal people do things repeatedly because they receive benefit. But what benefit is there to keeping chronic emotional pain? It seems to me that there should be a statute of limitations on how long you can be angry with someone so as to let it go and move on with your life.

Such chronic emotional pain is like a master/slave relationship. You as the enslaver are in control and the trigger person, the slave, is bound to you by your chain of emotional pain. By being bound to each other, neither of you are free. The master needs to watch and control the slave while the slave may not care or may enjoy the problems he has created for the master or may be totally unaware of the entire situation. The more the master feels that the slave is unaffected, the more angry the master becomes and therefore tries to perform more punishments. The more energy the master expends on the slave, the less energy there is to be about ones destination in life and/or to enjoy life.

This illogical and irrational reaction indicates that the master does not love him/herself because self-love does not allow one to hurt or limit oneself intentionally or needlessly. There is so much to gain by working together (1 +1= 3) or at least not working against each other (1 + 0= 1).

MANIFESTATIONS OF EMOTIONAL PAIN: As a means of display, many people choose **Histrionics**—which in females is somewhat like a "Drama Queen." Verbal Histrionics and "Drama" are vivid similies (e.g. "although he only touched me, it felt as if I was being jabbed by an ice pick"). Whereas the focus used by "Drama Queens" is more about exaggeration of expressions, the other type focuses on Behavioral Histrionics as, for example, deliberate and ceremonial type displays for expressions for their emotional trauma and emotional pain (Bailey, Medical-Legal Dictionary).

The documented story of Histrionics began with the ancient Greeks who believed that certain conditions in the female body were caused by a "wandering" womb (i.e. uterus) which could take different positions within the body. In the late 19th century European males believed mental instability among male artists was crucial to their capacity to create. However, unlike their male counterparts whose frenzied state could result in mystical insight, arrogant European men held that women could not channel their minds into creative activities.

The absurd reason is that the imaginative capacities of females were supposedly not harnessed and regulated by the intellect. Nor was mental transcendence of the material realm accessible to women. Instead, a woman's madness, as the absurdity continues, was evidence of the overpowering of her mind by the base instincts and drives of her sexuality — a mindset labeled **"Hysteria"** (Greek for womb) (Nelson, Critical Terms, p. 174).

Following this line of thinking, Sigmund Freud (1856-1939) who elaborated on the Ancient African use of psychotherapy, believed certain psychosomatic conditions were caused by psychological conflicts. Mental transformation of those conflicts showed as mental and physical symptoms which Western males characterized as a need for excessive attention and approval seeking; exaggerations of speech and expression; inappropriate and seductive styles of dress; and intellectual and emotional shallowness—all simply because this was not the way Western males would do it or the way would be in public. In short, the attitudes of "if you don't do it like me then you are wrong" and of "I know and you don't" are both signs of mental weakness and arrogance which characterize the judgmental.

Nevertheless, although the diagnosis of "hysteria" is no longer in vogue, the implication is carried in the revised diagnositic terms: **Histrionic Personality** style (for mild cases) or **Histrionic Personality Disorder** (for full blown cases). The term "histrionic" (Latin, "actor") emphasizes the often dramatic displays of word usage and body movements. I saw numerous examples in my orthopaedic practice and noticed their prominent in those cultures which are heavily Right brain oriented. Among the patients in my orthopaedic surgical practice I distinquished three major groups of patients.

First, the Honest and Straight Forward (honesty does not necessarily mean that one is right—afterall, "honest men differ"). These are the ones to which the medical text books apply. Histrionics is rare.

Second, the Self-Deceivers –those of the Somatoform Disorders who believe they have an organic problem but do not—or at least it is not as bad as they present. Verbal more than behavioral histronics is a feature. For them, a "hang-nail" problem is presented as a disaster; they talk a great deal in a rambling fashion about everything but the point. The idea is to impress rather than to connect.

There is much emotional pain and suffering being experienced by the Self-

Deceivers. They have a great sensitivity to being ignored (from lack of power) or rejected (not good enough) in all its real and imagined forms. Much of their attention seeking and perhaps sexual seductiveness is for the purpose of warding off their sense of inferiority and loneliness.

Third, the Conscious Deceivers are those who are lying for the purpose of secondary gain. They tend to be specialist in behavioral histrionics.

Freud said those with histrionic personalities are largely unaware of their own fearful thought and behavioral processes—employing instead certain characteristic mental defenses. Examples— as defined by psychologist A. J. Comeau (San Bernardino Sun newspaper 12/18/06), include *Repression* (unconsciously rejecting experiences); *Denial* (mental efforts to erase the factual and emotional realities of the past), and *Dissociation and Displacement* (efforts to replace painful memories, sometimes resulting in alternating expressions, such as painful physical symptoms or even alternate forms of identity and self-expression).

Note that these definitions have been created by Europeans, on Europeans, and for Europeans. These do not necessarily applied to people of other cultures. For instance, Dissociation in Black Americans is primarily a normal reaction to racism and pain and suffering.

Management of histronics requires a great deal of time, filled with compassion for the Self-Deceiver, but with a firm therapeutic confrontation. The idea is to get the histrionic prone person to develop awareness of and insight into his/her condition. As a physician, the starting point was to do a thorough medical evaluation to ensure the patient is healthy. Cognitive-behavioral interventions may help patients face and understand their fears and rejections and redirect them into a satisfying way of being and relating.

MANAGING EMOTIONAL PAIN: As is true of practically everybody I have experienced a wide variety of emotional pains of a mild, slight, moderate, and extreme nature. To be distinquished is Spiritual Pain—that which results from an interference with the perfusion of love into, inside, and out of an individual. Of course, I have had more than my share of the combination of emotional and Spiritual pains, as in losing my children in a divorce (Spiritual Pain) and for the wrong reasons (emotional pain). Nevertheless, the question addressed here is: "How do I handle emotional pains?"

The vast majority of mine were caused by racism and how these were handled has been addressed in some of my other books (e.g. Anger; Selfhood Mastery; Manhood). The extreme ones were most often caused by people close to me. The moderate ones were caused by the Black people I so intensely desired to help—and, in fact, I wanted more for them than they wanted for themselves. Most slight ones were caused by my omissions (things I should have done but did not do) and commissions (things I did but should not have done).

Evil people cause me the most trouble and I stay away from them. Their evilness implies they know well how to fight and therefore to fight them is foolish.

Dishonorable people—those who lie (of the type that causes great harm to people, animals, or nature), cheat, and steal—generate a dilemma. I simply do not want to be around them but I wonder, since one of my goals in life is to spread love, if I ought to be accepting of these individuals and yet keep them at a distance? Regardless of what they do, each has caused me emotional pain for about six weeks. In one instance I was stunned so deeply as to feel nothing for six weeks and then the emotional pain rose into prominence—for the damage done to our dreams for a pleasant future; for the damage (financially and psychologically) done to me; and for the fact that the person would remain "stuck" in a dishonorable mindset perhaps "forever."

Incompetent people who are resistant to self-improvement cause me emotional pain. Prominent examples are the tremendously bright and talented Black youth I have seen since high school who dropped out of school and proceeded down a "dead-end" road.

People whom I am close to but who demonstrate anti-harmony and an anti-cooperative spirit cause mild to slight degrees of emotional pain. For these and the other groups of people who really disturb me, the starting point for coming to a stable point for relating to them is that THE PERSON IS MORE IMPORTANT THAN WHAT BAD THINGS THE PERSON DOES.

Nevertheless, these four groups are only rough categories and there is much overlap. In every instance, I looked carefully at the part I played and, whenever possible, asked the people involved their opinion about my contribution to the problem. Nevertheless, simply thinking about putting this subject on paper has led me to consider the approaches, methods, techniques, and manners (the different ways a technique can be applied) I have used—and without self-judgment.

It is important to understand my setting—of being an independent thinker who was not defined by other people; of having a "live and let live" orientation; of possessing a strong desire to pursue goals, even if it meant leaving the crowd; and of striving daily to improve.

I left a very warm and pleasant "We" neighborhood in the all-Black community of Greensboro, North Carolina to enter a very hostile and racist and "I" (Individualist) society at the University of Michigan. Thereafter, I was forced to be an "I" *individualist* who was *isolated* as a result of gaining my education, training, and experience in an essentially all-White society.

It was essential to keep going straight ahead in the face of overwhelming obstacles and alligators in my path. Thus, the following comments may not apply to you. Yet, the point is that selfhood-mastery is required for whatever generates emotional pain in you.

Experience has taught me that failed expectations, disappointments, and wanting people to be the way you think they should be are among the most agonizing problems of the human experience. Each one causes frustration—a bitter frustration that "spits out" emotional pain with its associated bitterness.

From there it can mushroom in one direction or another — the drowning of the self in the deep waters of self-pity; or apathy with fatalistic beliefs that whatever happens must happen and all events are determined by necessity; or fighting the source; or through some scapegoat (taking out of ones hostility on an innocent and defenseless person). These reactions and actions poison the wounds and scar the personality even more — always harming the person to a much greater extent than the harm impart to anyone else. So what can be done? Here is my approach for managing emotional pain:

Step I is about being realistic. Look at the part you played, if any, in the attack, loss, lack, or obstruction which caused the emotional pain — an aspect of SELF-AWARENESS and SELF-RECOGNITION. It is a natural tendency to not digest information exactly as it is given but instead alter it to fit our self-concept. Then, with this altered information, we come up with SELF-JUSTIFICATION (excuses) to ensure that we continue to *"look good."*

We may overlook some of our bad points and not accept negative information. When something bad happens it is easy to blame someone else for our fault. Or, the problem may be that we are so opinionated that we are CLOSED MINDED (not open to different points of view or to new experiences that might have given pleasure instead of emotional pain). Or we may fail to remember that we are talented in some respects and either less talented or not at all in others. To not be accepting of this fact when others cross the finish line first causes much emotional pain. I felt this way when my poems and art works were not accepted by my fourth grade teacher. Now I realize that it was only her opinion which carried no more weight than my own.

Advertisements and the media bring us the mythical concept of a BODY IDEAL — the body type or appearance defined by a biased culture as "*attractive*" and sex-appropriate. They make money by telling you that you are not good enough and that you can be a winner by buying their product. JUST BECAUSE WHAT THEY SAY IS IDEAL DOES NOT MAKE IT SO. Make the most of what you have.

Step II—Shed distortions and fantasies that keep you trapped in ignorance. As mentioned above, in each of us there are natural emotions and natural pains that are essential for self-protection and self-expression. Also in each of us there are acquired emotions stemming from real, distorted, and unreal (fantasy) interpretations. *The distortions and the fantasies within our emotions and within our pains are what extend the boundaries of realistic emotional pain* and, in fact, may eliminate the boundaries so that there is no limit to the emotional pain experienced.

To believe in these distortions and fantasies is a *delusion* (believing what is not real and not believing what is real). Thus, the essential first aspect in handling emotional pain is to discover the truth.

Step III— INCOMPLETENESS means ones beliefs are not fully developed in relation to the big picture or that one is stuck in less than the best point of view. With respect to emotional pain one has the choices of doing nothing and just letting it hurt (passive); of going on the attack (aggression) directly or indirectly; of being "objective" and troubleshooting the experience (i.e. retracing the steps of what happened); or of learning lessons about what went wrong and what can be done to correct the problem the next time it is faced (non-aggression). Troubleshooting and learning lessons and information gathering help make for completeness.

Step IV—consider the possibility that you may not be right. Except when feeling guilty or showered with low self-esteem, it is normal for us to believe that who we are as a person is the right way to be; that what we do and say are right things to do and say; and what we think and feel is the right way to think and feel. On any one or more of these points, depending upon the situation, our beliefs are either correct or distorted or unreal or incomplete.

Step V is about intensely engaging in personally satisfying actions and accomplishments to the point that your mind is distracted. In the past, when my emotional pain was great, I rushed down to the bicycle path at the beach for an emergency bicycle ride. Or, I would get heavily involved in studying for a particularly difficult medical case. Sometimes I have resorted to certain "*compensation*" defense mechanisms of striving extra hard to become an *"overnight specialist"* in an area of my ignorance.

Step VI is philosophically handling the emotional pain. From my mother I learned and internalized the expression: "*everything happens for the best.*" If I failed at something important it was very useful for me to say: *"I did not prepare myself adequately"* or *"this was not the right time or the right person or the right place or the right situation."* It was absolutely essential that I not blame anyone and not look down on myself if I had done the best I could under the circumstances. A trait I have been most proud of is to not give up pursuing a worthwhile goal simply because it resulted in emotional pain. If nothing else, I tell myself, that if unsuccessful, I have still laid the ground work for someone who comes after me to pick up where I left off.

PLEASURE

Pleasure is Aliveness and Aliveness is High Positive Energy. It results from an agreeable activity stimulating the senses or the mind. One of life's greatest pleasures is being at play—and one of my greatest pleasures is being with children at play. Children at play are symbols of the free flowing enjoyment of life. Their abundant and overflowing cheerful energy, known as "Aliveness," shows in their jumping up and down—in their chasing each other—and in their giggles of delight. We adults know aliveness when we are happy.

At happy times we have a sensitivity to and appreciation for the overflowing of beauty and pleasures around us as well as for the experience of being loving and being loved. These energize our feelings for curiosity, creativity, responsibility and generating good works.

Whereas in its broadest sense Pleasure is a state of increased Aliveness, Primary Pleasure Emotions in the young are a purely normal selfish act — "I like to feel good!" Pleasant emotions are an individual's reaction to conditions and events which help him/her reach his/her goal. But with maturity they take on, like anger in reverse, higher forms. Those forms pertain to enjoying lofty things and/or to ensuring that all people concerned enjoy worthwhile things.

The Story of Pleasure: As discussed later (and also in my book Selfhood Mastery) in the Ancient Egyptian story of Creation the Ocean of Nun (i.e. Chaos) was the first of God's creations. It contained the Subjective Realm in which there are no things to be perceived (because nothing is formed in the Ocean of Nun). Yet, the Subjective Realm is the organizer of the Objective Realm, meaning the entire Subjective Realm remains in both aspects of the Objective Realm—i.e. in both the Noumenal (metaphysical) and the Phenomenal (object) planes. As a result, the core of the highest forms of Pleasure contains the Immaterial and the Intangible—both of which are imperceptible and concealed.

Different words are used to describe the Spiritual Pleasures as opposed to the Material world forms. In Ancient Africa and subsequently throughout the Eastern world there were words like bliss, ectasy, enjoyment, contentment, peace, harmony, and unity. In Ancient Egyptian teachings, the word-symbol denoting supreme and transcendental peace is Hetep. Ashby (Book of the Dead p362, 220) says it is much like the peace experienced in the dreamless sleep state in which there are no thoughts—just an awareness.

However, Hetep transcends the most pleasurable dreams and events of the waking state. When African Yogi were able to abide in this state of awareness perpetually and spontaneously (without any effort), they were considered to be fully **Enlightened**. This state of supreme peace and transcendence of body consciousness and desires is called **Bliss**. To summarize, we see that there is Spiritual Pleasure, with two types being birth gift bliss and bliss towards which one strives by means of meditation, contemplation, or yoga.

Western concepts of pleasure, pleasant, and please come from Greek "Flatness" and Latin "placer"—to be pleasing or pleasant like the flat, placid sea. The context was that Europeans attribute human-like characteristics to God. Hence, orginally these terms were used by God-fearing Europeans to appease God's presumed anger—as in "if it pleases you God"—or in doing certain things (e.g. sacrifices) for the prevention of God's wrath or to get to heaven. Later, in a worldly setting, pleasing methods were applied to enraged animals—smoothing ruffled plumage (feathers). In the Bible, "Please" has been often used to indicate "to give pleasure or to satisfy.

In Middle English period ((1066-1500) "please" referred to leisure—to be lawful. It was not until the 1620s that "please" (a shortened form of "if it pleases you") was first spoken of in request or as an indication of politeness—"pass the pie, please." The same sense was found in the legal system as Plead—"may it please the court." Otherwise, a high form of pleasure was that of "happy"— from "happ" (Old Norse) which meant "chance" or either good or bad luck. A person with good luck was declared to be happy — a sense surviving in today's idiom "happy-go-lucky."

In the late Middle Ages, a profound effect started throughout the Western world when the Catholic Church characterized pleasure (and even laughter) as a bad addiction. The teaching was that "Pleasure Addicts" had a duty "to work on and kick" this addiction if one desired to not have one's soul consigned to an eternity in hell.

The concept of a "Pleasure Approach" to life arose from a Western psychoanalytical doctrine that humans are governed by the search for pleasure and the avoidance of pain. They hypothesized the "*Pleasure Principle*" as being a regulatory mechanism of mental life whose function is to reduce psychic tension arising out of drives (e.g. libido) pressing for discharge. Further, the Pleasure/Pain Principle was about an individual trying to undo the effects of disturbing stimuli (pain) in a way that most easily provided satisfaction (pleasure).

The World of Pleasure: "Pleasure" is an umbrella term that has application on all planes of existence, from the earth world to the Sublime. Different terms have been fashioned for the higher forms of Pleasure as opposed to the material world (Tangible) forms. On each Pleasure plane of existence unique laws operate. Those on the higher (or Spiritual) planes are part of the natural laws of nature (which is in keeping with nature deriving out of the Nun).

So how can we determine which realm of the Pleasure planes of existence is natural in human beings? The answer was previously given. Recall in the discussion on the Brain that the Right brain is the vehicle for expansiveness into higher and multiple planes of existence regarding things like **Love, spiritually, compassion,**

peace, harmony, intuition, synthesis, nonaggression, and unity. Each of these is a natural feature of the mature. Some are naturally present in the baby's selfhood state at the time of birth, and even within the mother's womb.

Common sense suggests that the state of the child in the mother's womb is one of bliss and this state—a natural state— may be compared to the beatitude visualized for paradise. In the womb, the child is unaware of the alternation of night and day or of any of the images of temporality (Campbell, Prim Myth p65, 70). To indicate a post-birth moment of bliss, Ancient Egyptians depicted the original Madonna and child—Isis with the sun-child Horus at her breast.

From birth onwards, babies experience only pure and uncontrolled desire and they live for gratification of desire. Simultaneously, from the moment of birth onward *socialization* is imposing inhibitions and controls for the babies' expressions and actions. Thus, the babies' Pleasure Principle starts giving way to the Reality Principle. Slowly, the child comes to repress more and more of its desire for gratification in order to belong in society.

Despite some loss of power to socialization, children who realize that they still retain a great deal of inner power stop their downward slide, turn around, and start climbing up the power trail. These individuals will maintain a great deal of strength in their pleasure displays. An analogy is the way that a seed, when properly planted, begins to grow, bud, flower, and fruit. By contrast, children whose loss of power goes out of control in a downward spiral rarely have a life full of pleasure displays.

Nevertheless, Pleasure as a "Needy Want"—and which never diminishes— means that it is innate (and therefore containing a higher power spiritual component); and is about "Being" rather than doing; and is basic for ones mental health. It ranges from an awareness of contentment to the sense of happiness. Thus, it has spiritual (Intangible) and worldly (Tangible) components. It comes from simply indulging in pleasure, as done by children, and with no purpose in mind and from no attempt to achieve it. In other words, this is the pleasure one has because "it is there"—in the way mountain climbers decide to climb the mountain they stumble upon "because it is there."

Personal Pleasure: I will use myself as an example. As a boy, my thoughts consisted of a profound but simple answer to a profound but simple question. There were plenty of people around who did a lot of moaning and groaning about how mean people were, how unfair life was, and how they had aches and pains everywhere. By contrast, there were a very few people, like Aunt Cherry, who was full of fun and good humor, perhaps even when she felt otherwise.

From this and personal experience I concluded that it felt good to be around and a part of pleasure; and it felt bad to be around and a part of pain. From that point on, I started building a world around me that was peaceful and pleasurable. For example, I collected jokes and joke books and riddles as well as read pleasurable books, e.g. by Mark Twain and Will Rogers.

As a result of starting out life during the Great Depression and my parents being divorced before I started the first grade, I was forced into being alone for long hours at a time. Mother would lock me in the bedroom, keep the radio on the Italian opera station, and not allow me to have any toys anywhere but under the bed. While she was out working, I played all sorts of games with my toy soldiers; learned to sing Italian opera; and used my imagination to picture, in a funny way, what was said on the radio.

After we moved from Minnesota to Wilson, North Carolina, I learned the value of Wit and Humor. On the one hand, I had to be in a good mood, which I usually was, to see all the extra funniness in humor. On the other hand I could get pleasure out of Wit no matter if I was feeling down. Cherry, without trying, helped me develop Wit because, as she said, I played with her mind.

I focused on thinking up entertaining things that normally did not go together or that took an unexpected turn — similar to the answers associated with riddles. I never allowed myself to lose seeing ordinary things in a distorted or fantasy way and that would cause me to laugh. This carried over to my drawing of stick figures— which is actually the best art I can do.

Lofty Personal Pleasures: For me, lofty pleasures began when I was a boy working in flower and vegetable gardens (Bailey, Selfhood Mastery). For example, while delivering newspapers or working in the garden, I would watch what was going on in nature. A special interest occurred following a rain storm. It was always fascinating to see water coming out of a hole on the hill and observing its branching stream of water path and pattern. From seeing these and other patterns in nature I would look for interrelationships between me, people, or other things in the world.

From this I came up with the idea that **there are only a few principles in the world out of which all real things spin**. Since then I have always been eager to interrelate pieces of the puzzle. The bottom line is that I developed and maintained an *intense enjoyment for learning* and believed that anything I learned was important in helping me and others see life in a more simple and integrated way.

A major form of enjoyment comes from arriving at stepping stones related to my goal (pleasure + reason). This necessitates that the goal be clear and that it is constructive. The enjoyment is the greatest if the stepping stone achievement is in line with what I believe to be my purpose in life or if it brings the greatest good to the most people over the longest period of time. These forms of enjoyment take precedent over other forms of a more worldly or selfish nature.

As a boy I heard that if you truly love something you must be willing to let it go because to clutch it and squeeze it is to try to control it. Similarly, to try to grab pleasure and hold on will kill it—which is not necessarily true with enjoyment. Rather, it seems to me, pleasure and love must come freely and naturally—as when I am out in nature or when with my children. At no time have I pursued pleasure for its own sake and yet it comes several times a week. Enjoyment is the reaction to something beautiful or to some perfect moment.

Although Medicine taught me the value of maintaining an emotionally steady state in order to be able to make clear decisions, my pleasure has no bounds in studying to help my patients and seeing a good result from that information.

Of crucial importance in me liking myself was to use every opportunity to be creative and to remain mentally free. To do both required that I pay a high price to have my peace; that I rely on myself for doing what seems right and even if it goes against the way others do it; and that I keep away from people whose emotions are out of control.

Most of all, I like to explore any information just because it's there and follow the truth wherever it leads. All of these make my life predominately exciting but in a quiet way.

CLASSIFICATION OF PLEASURE (Table VI): Pleasure spans the entire range of Good Emotions and Spiritural (or Pure) Feelings. Pure Feelings connect ones Real Self with the Sublime by way of the "Silver Cord" (Bailey, Common Sense). Pleasure as a basic and natural Good Emotion is present at birth. One distinquishing feature is that Good Emotions have "loops" or "centers" scattered throughout the brain which can produce and reproduce them.

Table VI — **Classification of Pleasure**

A. Immaterial Pleasure
B. Sublime Pleasure
C. Tangible Pleasure
   1. Unbounded Tangible Pleasure
   2. Partially Bounded Tangible Pleasure
   3. Completely Bounded Tangible Pleasure
D. Pleasures of False Appearances
E. Pleasures in False Worlds
F. "Sick" Pleasures
G. Combinations

The major "loops" are located along the course of the medial forebrain bundle, particularly in the lateral and ventral medial nuclei of the hypothalamus. Specific aspects of the "Pleasure Loop" start with the potent "reward centers" in the septum, the amygdala, certain areas of the thalamus and basal ganglia and, from there, extend downward into the basal tegmentum of the mesencephalon (mid-brain). A significant part of this "Pleasure Loop" relates to the Right Brain.

As discussed under the three brains-in-one, the reward and punishment centers have "checks and balances on each other. For example, rage (a primitive negative attitude and reaction designed for survival) is predominantly held in check by impulses coming from the reward centers. This "check and balance" can get real close. Such an instance is seen in the lateral nuclei of the brain. Despite being one of the most potent of the reward centers, it will cause rage if stimulated strongly.

Pleasures of the Pure Feeling System—i.e. the Immaterial and the Sublime (Intangible)—are present in the baby before birth (Table I). Those of the Unbounded Tangible and the Partially Bounded Tangible planes can be considered "**Tarda Pleasures**" because they are natural but appear sometime after birth. The rest are acquired and therefore man-made. Anything man-made is not natural and is not about real harmony or unity.

It would not surprise me if the subject of Pleasure has never been classified because its family members, by being present on different planes of existence and being governed by different laws, are so very different. Perhaps the only thing they have in common is a Good Feeling (if of a spiritual nature) or a Good Emotion of "I like" (if of a worldly nature).

Certain family members have different names and other members are confused with each other by outsiders who talk and write about them. Some are ideal; some are good; some are neutral; some are bad (either immediately or in the long run); and some are evil. Different nations have different ideas what constitutes the features of those members on the higher rung of the Cosmic Ladder. In addition, there are complexities with respect to outside mental components and different combination of pleasures.

Outside Mental components contributing to Pleasure: Enjoyment, I believe, is a mixture of the highest degree pleasure with some other faculty (e.g. reason, spirituality). It results when one is released from the bonds of the body. Examples include being elevated by a painting or poetic work (pleasure + spirit); eating (pleasure + senses tied in with emotions); or the act of self-sacrifice (pleasure + belief). If it is present following a mystical experience, that enjoyment transcends into a blissful feeling as a continuation of the experience (Ashby, Yoga, p42).

Combinations of Pleasure on different Constructive rungs of the Cosmic Ladder: Emotional Pleasure is more associated with what is less enduring than enjoyment.

Of all the emotions in children, enjoyment and pleasure are prominent in their association with imagination—and they instinctively dwell imaginatively on whatever calls forth these emotions (Amen II:97).

I get pleasure from funny things kids do or something witty said or watching toddlers discover the world. I had, and continue to have, enjoyment from having written the classic book on Disproportionate Short Statute which changed the world literature on the subject and paved the way for Little People to obtain more beneficial surgery or the proper avoidance of surgery.

Within this context, to repeat, "Pleasure" is an umbrella term because it embraces all rungs of the Cosmic Ladder. "Happy" is also an umbrella concept but because it is not as inclusive as "Pleasure" regarding planes of existence, it is under the umbrella of "Pleasure" (see Amen I:96). Pleasure can be classified as follows.

I— **Immaterial Pleasure** is an unknowable Plane. Nevertheless, based upon the Ancient African belief that God is Love, I suspect that this realm is about what human beings intensely desire more than anything else in their lives. It is this realm that some refer to as Bliss. The more one cultivates whatever it takes to get to Bliss, the greater is one awareness of fulfillment, freedom, creativity, a sense of well-being, appreciation, and feeling special.

II—The **Sublime** Plane (**Intangible**) of **Pleasure** is like a kaleidoscope of Love, Goodness, Truth, and Beauty. It therefore has several terms. The story of the concepts contained in "Sublime Pleasure" starts much earlier than the word's appearance. It is associated with the Egyptians' Astroscopy (an observation of the visible appearance of the stars, planets, moon, and sun) done for the purpose of discovering the will of the gods. A "guesstimation" of its origin is 12,500 B.C. Astroscopy.

Eventually, by inventing mathematic from which laws of the universe were deduced, Egyptians concluded the whole universe, and particularly humans, were governed by the stars. Furthermore, each individual was believed to be influenced by a particular star (perhaps the one associated with ones dead ancestors). This was called ones "**Lucky Star**." To inform individuals of the course of their lives was Astrology's original purpose.

Lucky stars were considered holy. If one was fortunate enough to find one's "Lucky Star," it was said that the Divine Will would be manifest through it and thereby guide the individual through the maze of life. In the process one's life would be enriched as well as one being brought ever closer in relation with the Divine.

Locating and embracing beliefs about the lucky star (astro) was the background giving rise to the concepts found in the word **"Mystics."** When a person achieved unification with the divine, such mystics were "Illuminated," "Enlightened," "Happy," and therefore experiencing the ultimate in Pleasure. The effects of a mystical experience provided them with a sense of the **Fundamental "5Ss"** (Table X)—safety, security, sureness, stability, and strength. These five constitute the platform for evolving into a state of serenity or peace — a state known to Egyptians as Hetep.

When these African concepts were borrowed by foreign nations, the state of serenity or peace became known to the Hindu as **Nirvana**; and known to Zen Buddhism as **Satori**. To reach Hetep, the highest goal of meditation, and thereby acquire the root of all divine power, was believed by Egyptians to be the ultimate in Happiness or Pleasure (Amen, Metu Neter, Vol. I: 97, 162).

III—**Tangible Pleasure** (made of matter) is an innate/acquired Psychic Feeling/ Emotion reaction located somewhere on the positive/negative scale of the lower part of the Cosmic Ladder. It can occur with a good heart or short of a good heart. It can be real or faked. It can be healthy or sick. Things of lofty worth can be enjoyed as often and as much as one chooses but this does not apply to things of value. It has three subdivisions.

A. Unbounded Tangible Pleasure is reached through the practice of the Egyptian Ma'at values or the engagement of philosophical/rational thought. This almost lofty plane is known by such terms as Enjoyment, Contentment, Well-being, and Fulfillment. With respect to Ma'at values one fully experiences Spiritual Feelings and thereby one's capacity for pleasure has achieved a completely open condition (i.e. an "open heart"; an unselfish mindset). This can come about from giving pleasure to others or giving pleasure to one's own spirit.

Examples of giving pleasure to one's own spirit: "Aliveness" pleasure is being "full of life" and particularly if it is "just because...", as seen in children at play; as going on a nature field trip on a beautiful spring day; as enjoying poetry, art or music; or as contemplating in the context whereby only God is the proper object. Since this, too, has partial boundaries related to duration, the happiness produced is steady and ongoing as long as one is engaged in the appreciation of what is being done. Furthermore, like that of a tail on a kite, steady and ongoing happiness continues for as long as the temporary after-effects last (similar to the things you can still visualize for a moment immediately after turning off all the lights during the night).

Examples of giving humanitarian pleasure: This is the practice of making better the lives of others — perhaps creating an environment or atmosphere in which others can be productive; perhaps giving the hungry a fish; perhaps teaching the unemployed how to fish.

The engagement of philosophical/rational thought generates pleasure from speculative Intellect Creations. At a spiritual level such an experience occurs with an Epiphany (the radiance of splendor).

Otherwise, at a psychical feeling level, the emotional happiness from insights and intuitions is pleasantly felt but without displays others can observe. Another example is living the life proper to one's rational being. Even thinking of ideal possibilities without their realization carries the possibility of providing an intellectual freedom which translates into happiness.

Partially Bounded Tangible Pleasure is pleasure that is frequent but has a mid-range upper limit. An example comes from being a member of a "We" culture whereby fellowship and a sense of community are on display as an almost ongoing and steady experience. However, members of a "We" society are not completely free in spirit and in their true nature because of the necessity of substituting some of that freedom in order to gain the benefits of belonging to a group. But the price paid is a loss of a free mind and reaching ones potential, and especially among those with a strong urge to express individuality.

Another price is that those "We" societies who are obsessed with their children make this such a pleasurable state that many children remain fixed in this mindset as they leave childhood and enter adulthood. Thereafter, their interest and forms of pleasure are very child-like—to the point of them having a lack of interest in the more thoughtful subjects.

"We" members must abide by the customs, traditions, and expectations as well as play the social role expected of them. A bounded tangible realm is present when certain cliques in power positions have a greedy self-interest in taking unfair advantage of the unsuspecting and gulliable masses.To remove that restriction in order to gain full selfhood freedom would require one becoming a "Constructive I" (Individualist with a "We" society orientation). The "Constructive I" are not led by authority and will leave the crowd in order to follow their dreams or to do what they think is right.

Of course, "Constructive I" people are left on their own to find their way—sort of like an entrepreneau. This causes them to have to be extremely self-reliant and to work alone without support and often in spite of losses, lacks, and obstacles generated by envious people or people who do not like those who are "different." They find great depth in their successes.

Nevertheless, there are very pleasant times associated with being part of a "We" society. This involves little things like sharing a meal together, enjoying a family reunion, or playing with everyone's children. No one has to ask for trust or caring. No one needs to always be aware of what he/she wants because when another makes a suggestion, everyone tends to follow. For more information, Ani's Yurugu (p44, etc.) has a nice discussion on Humanness.

African Tradition has a "We/I" society. As close as can get to imagining such an atmosphere was in growing up in a wonderful all-Black "We" society. Nevertheless, conversations with native Africans confirm that much of their pleasure derives from being with each other, especially while sitting in the moon light, and telling stories.

C. **Concrete Tangible Pleasure** (completely bounded) is specifically defined by size, weight, number, mass, volume, height, extent, and/or capacity. People agree on definitions because the objects can be seen, touched, and measured. This shows in the Western world's obsession to have newer, better, bigger, faster, and a more powerful anything in the technology world.

A second form is pleasure from having reached a specific goal (e.g. receiving a scholarship) or having received some highly desired object (e.g. a priceless diamond). When this goal is obtained from good fortune, the term **Endaimonia** (Gr., "godly demon") is applied.

A third form is **Hedonism** (pleasure is the end of all strivings) — the esteeming of riches, fame, and pleasures of the senses (i.e. physical feelings) is the highest good (Runes, Spinoza Dictionary, p. 114). Hedonism is doing what feels good at the time. This, the lowest form of "normal" pleasure, is elaborated upon in an excerpt of "The Decline and Fall of the Roman Empire": "[European] history, which is, indeed, little more than the register of the crimes, follies, and misfortunes of mankind" (Brewer, p. 509) has been a driving force for the Western World to take on the sense of gratification of emotions and desires — both dependent on achieving or manipulating externals (e.g. riches, indulging the craving for food, sex, leisure) (Amen, Metu Neter, I:97).

Some Hedonists believe they should not work for what they get and enjoy. That attitude leads them to lie, cheat, and steal—even from close friends—because it is an addiction. This I would take very personally until it became clear that this was a problem with my ego: "How could they do this to me?" They do it because this is what they do and not because it is me.

Two common types are the "little gods" (who have riches and a sense of entitlement) and the Pseudo-Hedonist (who have champagne tastes but a beer budget). Ironically, the pursuit of pleasure by both groups is such an obsession that it becomes hard work. The "little gods" are never really happy because whatever they have is not enough and they strive to get more.

The Pseudo-Hedonist pursuit is about competing with those in the leisure class, with whom they show generousity. But with others they may act deprived. Such a pursuit means they slide into a dead-end where there is great unhappiness and desperation because of their lack of foresight and forethought.

IV— Pleasures of False Appearances are like an infectious disease which has spread and still is spreading all over the world. In essence, these are a form of ignorance more complex than simply not knowing because to overcome it requires shedding what is wrong and replacing it with reality. Three typical components of such ignorance (as discussed later) are *illusions* (wrong ideas about what is present); *delusions* (errors in judgment causing false beliefs); and *hallucinations* (seeing what is not there).

Ignorance is a clear destroyer of the truth — regardless of whether that truth pertains to things in the outside world or things already present inside one's mind. Such ignorance produces think, feel, say, and do activities that are headed in the wrong direction and that are self-defeating— the objective of advertizers.

Advertisers manipulate the "Pleasure Principle" to point out that *you are not satisfied with the way you are* but that you could find ever-lasting pleasure by buying their product. Advertisements entice the public in the form of what typically causes pleasure by tacking on what has nothing to do with pleasure per se as, for example, an attractive female in a male magazine related to any subject.

A destructive opinion pervading the Western world is that a thing is good for someone if it promotes one's pleasure; and bad if it causes one pain. Most people readily accept this at face value because it gives them permission to justify whatever they indulge in—whether good or bad. Eating too much candy, though it tastes good, is bad for you.

Another "down side" of advertizers advocating immediate gratification as the best thing is that they fail to carry it in directions of caution. For example, failing to engage in delayed gratification has been the source of untold failures and heart aches for countless numbers of people. If seeking revenge gives pleasure it is short-lived because one can expect the other to retaliate. A moment's thought can generate many, many other exceptions.

V—Pleasures in False Worlds are frequent in the ghettos. Here, individuals who have been shut out of the mainstream world of society at large (itself largely a false world) reconstruct their own standards and customs inside their new world. Pleasure comes through competition, based upon the Codes of the Streets (Anderson, 203; Bailey, Manhood).

A second example of a False World derived out of the ancient concept of **Lucky Pleasure**. Ancient Romans had great interest in the star's ability to convey ideas about the future as a prediction of good luck. To be lucky made for cheerfulness; imparted a contented mindset for what was gained; and led to an appreciation for bad things that did not occur. There is really nothing wrong with that as long as it does not adversely affect ones life. People who gamble and win have the experience of Lucky Pleasure.

VI—"**Sick Pleasures**" are associated with pain or harm or destruction. It stems from feeling good about another's pain; inflicting pain; or receiving pain. These three are philosophically and spiritually pathological. Since anti-social people lack guilt, they have no problem generating evil actions.

Those disconnected from love are attracted to "sick pleasures" as a hopeful means of trying to lessen somewhat the afflicted person's spiritual pain. Examples are seen in hate groups; Masochists (pleasure from feeling abused); in Sadist (those who inflict pain for pleasure); and Arsonist (who find pleasure in the power of destruction).

In the Western practice of associating pleasure with things of Value almost always leads to embracing an intense greed for money, possessions, and power—a greed which exceeds those virtuous qualities agreed to by Sages all over the world and throughout all ages.

In most cultures the vast majority of law abiding people engaged in the right and decent living will immediately convert when there is an opportunity to gain riches. They have no problem fashioning unfair advantages for themselves and putting victims at an unfair disadvantage—a scenario that repeats itself over and over every hour of every day in everyday life and on television.

VII—**Combinations**, of course, can include different planes of pleasure on the positive and on the "sick" and appearances scales. A reason combinations are infinite is that a laws of the earth world says degrees of things of matter can and do occur; and with variations within any degree; and with alterations within any variation. For example, each individual has a different concept of beauty and different people see different things as beautiful. What a person thinks was beautiful ten years ago may be quite different today. By contrast, the beautiful at a lofty plane is the same for everyone.

Managing Pleasure: If my assumption is true that Emotional Pleasure is a faculty, then it is part of our health maintenance system—for good or for bad. This determined by ones System of Values. If you are most attracted to material or tangible world things, then you are likely to choose forms of happiness related to things of value—and that leads to bad behaviors.

If you are attracted to the Immaterial and Sublime worlds, then you are likely to choose forms of happiness related to things of worth. Becoming a specialist of worth is the most difficult. However, it is far, far better than specializing in the world of value and appearances. A third option is to choose the best of "this and that" out of the immaterial, the intangible, and the tangible realms.

But what has a good chance of creating a balanced and mentally and physically healthy life is to realize the Yin/Yang factor with respect to Pleasure and Pain in its Polarity and Rhythmic aspects.

Ancient Africans believed that pleasure and pain are natural parts of life. By pleasure and pain being on opposite ends of the same pole, we are able to know one by being aware of the other—a Yin/Yang concept. Just as we know and read the words on this page, that reading is possible only because of the contrasting background of the white sheet of paper. If both contrasts were not present, then reading would not be possible.

In the Egyptian Tehuti's (? 5500 BC) **Principle IV of Polarity**, he states that "Everything is Dual; everything has poles; everything has its pair of opposites; like and unlike are the same; opposites are identical in nature by different in degree; extremes meet; all truths are by half truths; all paradoxes may be reconciled." (The Kybalion p32). In other words, there are some natural forms of pleasure where pain is associtated, as in painful operations to remove malignant cancer.

Another Yin/Yang aspect is that because of pleasure's background of pain and pain's background of pleasure, they are two sides of the same coin as they normally swing back and forth. This is based on Principle V—Tehuti's (the Egyptian Hermes) **Principle of Rhythm**: "Everything flows, out and in; everything has its tides; all things rise and fall; the pendulum-swing manifests in everything; the measure of the swing to right is the measure of the swing to the left; rhythm compensates" (The Kybalion, p35).

Balance in life, said Ancient Africans, is contributed to by not being overly concerned about pleasure or pain. When a person begins to hate discomfort and to seek pleasure, this leads the person to focus on pleasure and to try to wipe out pain—a pursuit that automatically agitates the mind—a pursuit that cause one to lose control of the real means of achieving abiding pleasure (or happiness), inner peace, and contentment.

But just as too much emphasize is not to be put on pleasure seeking, pain ought not to be allowed to dominate ones life. And this is easy to happen because a typical person has more negative centers of an inborn and of an acquired nature than there are pleasure centers. Therefore, it takes special attention to cultivate the pleasure centers or those aspects of the brain that lead to achievement and therefore to pleasure in order to maintain the appropriate balance in life.

Properly used, pleasure is a major contributor to success. But if used too much or too little, it does the opposite. TEMPERANCE is about "just right" pursuits—pursuits which start by realizing moderation in all things. It is an essential part of character building because it helps in the development of a sense of **Self-Restraint** — the idea of reasonableness needing to be in charge of moderating passions and limiting the pursuit of pleasures. Instead, there is much more to life than pursuing pleasure. According to Ancient Africans two are to *fulfill a personal purpose and to be of selfless service*. These pursuits ought to be checkered with pleasure because they certainly will be sprinkled with pain.

From reviewing the Classification of Pleasures it is evident that not all pleasures are desirable—the "sick" type in particular. Most people are addicted to the Appearance types and although they seem pleasurable in the beginning, they are not in ones best interest in the long run. Typically, they lead the individual away from the reality needed to live a balanced life that is about achieving a wholesome destination and instead put one on a road that is a dead-end.

For people who lose the experience of bliss, Ancient Africans believed that this could be regained by coming into harmony within themselves, the environment, and the Spirit. The means for doing this is meditation or contemplation (see Bailey, Selfhood Mastery for elaboration). This process leads to an ecstatic experience which not only transcends time and space but allows a human being to discover and experience the Divine. This experience, Ancient Africans believed, was to bathe in the Supreme Good, Beauty, Bliss, and Wisdom that is the essence of God.

When these concepts spread out of Africa, significant changes were made in different societies. In some, material world forms of Pleasure somewhat replaced the Spiritual forms. In some, the Spiritual forms have continued to dominate; in some, it is half and half; in some it is material world generated forms which took and continue to take priority; and in some, as in the Western world, it is all about material world forms of pleasure.

Constructive Pleasure is the result of either pursing a wholesome purpose and/or achieving it. In this context, a "**Purpose**" is, after going across the finish line, putting on a worthwhile performance that benefits oneself and/or others. Examples include productive works; maintainance of good health; good behaviors toward and good relationships with people; recreation; engaging in a hobby that takes ones mind to a higher level (e.g. art, music, poetry); and sexual expression.

Pleasurable experiences keep reflecting themselves in one's awareness, motivating one to renew whatever leads to the that experience. Amen (Vol. I:148) says this is the great secret for maintaining oneself motivated—which is a major factor to success in any undertaking.

To cultivate pleasure requires that you clearly understand what you really, really, desire. If it is *Things of worth*, the old song explains by saying "the best things in life that are free" — to love and be loved; to belong to a good group of people; and to have peace and harmony. The way to attract things of worth is to create, enhance, and maintain things of worth.

The approach to **Worth type Pleasure** is to have good character (always do the right and decent thing); to work hard at having the right relations with and behaviors toward other people; and to have a purpose in life. Happy people know they are free to go after as many things of worth—and as wide, as high, as deep, as long, and as often as they desire.

It is important to ensure that you get your fair share of pleasure—and this requires planning and work to make it happen. Since the other four basic emotions—fear, rage, depression, and emotional pain—have a large representation in the brain, they can easily crowd out the fifth—i.e. pleasure. Furthermore, the circuits of the brain particularly concerned with pleasure and rewarding experiences are chemically fragile and somewhat easily upset.

Fashioning a pleasurable childhood for children is a great gift to each child's life. Because of the magical minds of children, those on the road to the Pleasure Approach to life will distort and fantasize about what they like. This may extend to the point that it might help pave the way to a habit of pleasure, happiness, or escstasy.

The habit of displaying Pleasurable Emotions may or may not be beneficial in handling a tough problem but they are beneficial in the approach to such problems, if nothing more than in ones disposition. Associated with the best of pleasure is having a sense of complete trust in your ability—either to recover from losses and/or to provide to yourself the basic desires of living—safety, security, sureness, stability and strength. Even if you do not have most of whatever else you want, these five help fashion satisfaction with what you have. But having them does not interfere with you working hard to get more of what you want.

It is extremely important to pay close attention to these main forms of pleasure in order for you to select which one(s) best matches your selfhood and self-definition. Enjoyment can not occur for long if you are oriented to things of value and not at all if you are about "sick" pleasures. No matter what you choose, enjoy being who you are, where you are, what you are doing, what you have, and where you are going.

In summary, **Emotions of pleasure create, enhance, or maintain the "big picture" of pleasure; draw you to pleasure; draw people to the pleasurable you; and stimulate people to be pleasurable.** Satisfying pleasure as a way of life comes from perfecting Ma'at values, possessing moral integrity, belonging, making happy your own spirit, "aliveness," and feeling, emotional, and intellectual creations.

V

COMPLEX "NORMAL" EMOTIONS

COMPLEX EMOTIONS

are

Sentiments formed By

Crystallized Thoughts

and

Emotions

Springing from

the INTELLECT

Whereas basic or primary emotions are unlearned and universal in that they are found in all cultures throughout the ages, "Complex Emotions" is the name applied to all the rest. In animals and in children, emotions are not quite as hard to observe because they do not "filter" their feelings through mind committees the way adult humans do.

Whereas the five basic emotions pop up as automatic reactions, the Complex Emotions—the mixture of innate and acquired emotions in varied combinations and in varied states of development— entail mental processing to bring them into existence. This process is dependent upon the mental maturity in some things and the mental immaturity in others—the **Broken Tooth Comb Concept** (fig. 5). The degree of maturity relates to three groups of emotions.

Group I— are the **Primary or Innate Emotions** which are present at birth—Rage, Fear, Depression, Emotional Pain, and Pleasure. Technically, these are Tarda Innate

Emotions—meaning that the environment is a requirement for their expression and therefore they can not be separated from the environment. However, whenever they are expressed, that expression is complete because reason has not developed sufficiently for them to step down into a tempered, masked, or conceal state.

Group II — **Secondary Emotions** are Primary emotions to which reason has been added—reasoning from perceptions that may be real, distorted, or unreal. In other words, reason in the young child has developed sufficiently to not only initiate the production of protective emotions but, if necessary, to temper, mask, of conceal ones emotions. For example, innate Fear is tempered into Anxiety or Rage is tempered into Anger.

Group III — **Tertiary Emotions** — Compound Emotions — Acquired Emotions—are of two types—distortion and fantasy (as in presenting someone else's family album to represent ones own family).

COMB CONCEPT

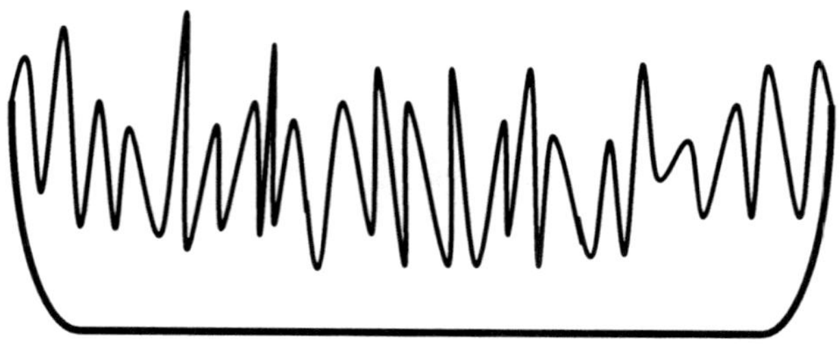

Figure 5
(Reprinted from Bailey - "*Selfhood Mastery inside African Tradition*")

Complex Emotions are innumerable (Table VII). Some have the same appearance but from many causes. Some have multiple appearances from the same cause. Some are mixtures of many emotions. Some of the same types are present in many emotions. Here are some of the Effects of combinations:

Type I—*Distortion* — the combination of real and distorted emotions. The word "distortion" is discussed under the Escape Emotions.

Type II—*Fantasy* (Greek "phantasia" — a making visible) is a complex word containing complex concepts and is tied in with a complex family group (see Bailey, Creativity for an extensive discussion). The word "Fantasy" is discussed under the Escape Emotions.

Type III—*Combinations of Secondary Emotions* which create a novel emotion. Examples: combining concealed anger with anxiety to create Guilt.

Type IV—*Combinations of Primary and/or Tertiary Emotions* added to reason to produce something normal or abnormal—a something that could be more fully expressed as an emotion—a something that could be tempered emotions. For example, Reason added to innate depression can either be a normal action leading to Grief or a psychopathological acquired depressive mood. Reason added to likes gives pleasure or enjoyment. Reason added to distorted or fantasy perception might cause paranoia.

Table VII — **Formation of Complex Emotions**

1) Primary emotions interweaving to give a secondary emotion;
2) A primary emotion with a secondary emotion or a secondary emotion with another secondary emotion to form tertiary emotions;
3) A primary, a secondary, and a tertiary emotion all combined;
4) A primary or secondary emotion with a tertiary emotion;
5) Any of the above four but with an added thought;
6) Emotions, thoughts, and spirituality;
7) Emotions, thoughts, spirituality, and things,
8) A primary, secondary, or tertiary emotion with spirituality concepts;
9) An emotion with a thing (e.g. ones hobbly);
10) A thought and/or spiritually with a thing.

The World of Complex Emotions: Common sense suggests that a baby in its mother's womb experiences a state of well-being. Yet, that en utero baby is sensitive to the outside world environment and to the affection shown by the mother. At some point before delivery, outside irritants, like a sudden loud noise, will anger and stir the baby to resist with a total body response directed by the autonomic nervous system (particularly the sympathetic division). But this *"war footing" anger* response quickly subsides.

Following delivery and during development babies are confronted by many situations they neither know how to respond to nor understand. These emotions of anger, sadness, and fear as well as the condition of surprise are *Tarda Instinctual* — an inborn response to act in ways essential to the babies' development or preservation but that are dependent upon the environment for expression.

Part of the on-going development of the baby is his/her mental, spiritual, social, and physical development. For example, the baby's muscles and nervous system, the anger response becomes more organized. Thus, by about five months of age, anger shows as thrashing, screaming, and stiffening of the body.

Meanwhile, psychologists say that surprise and sadness develop at 2 to 4 months of age; and fear at 5 to 7 months. SURPRISE is the momentary condition of the interruption of thought and emotions; SADNESS is the condition of emotional pain; and FEAR is the loss of a sense of security, safety, sureness (self confidence), stability, and strength.

Around 6 months of age they begin to learn to "*read*" other people's emotional reactions; start judging the possible consequences of events; imitate complex behaviors; and distinguish among and react to various emotional expressions. One of those reactions is to "*press down*" their stirred up emotions — called DEPRESSION. Also instinctual, depression is used when there is the experience of powerlessness, usually as a reflection of an impaired interaction, as when mother "*disappears*."

Gradually, getting into full swing after the toddler years and becoming well developed by *"the age of reason"* (5 to 7 years old), children's thoughts become increasingly more sophisticated. As the child begins to acquire rational thoughts there is an expansion of mental expressions. For example, an *advanced form of Surprise is that of Frustration*. Instead of there being merely a sudden momentary stoppage of thoughts and emotions, as occurs in surprise, frustration causes the organized thoughts resulting from reason to suddenly become chaotic. If temporary, the term acute frustration can be applied; if long lasting, chronic frustration.

Meanwhile, the addition of acquired thoughtful points of view, beliefs, and opinions superimposed on the youth's instinctual reactions expands the boundaries of and develops the contents within each emotion. As this is happening to each one, various emotions interlock and overlap as, for instance, in *Worry*. Those interlocked as well as individual emotions combine to form *Complex Emotions*. Here are three of the innumerable examples.

ANGST is a German meaning different things to different people (because of its varied content concepts). Yet, it generally denotes the deeper states of clinical anxiety, remorse, guilt, or irrational fear.

HATE is the result of the cultivation of Emotional Pain (from wounded feelings) with disharmonious thoughts. The threat, disturbance, or disruption of the well-being of one's self-perceived powerful state of being causes anger to develop into Rage and then into its complex partner, REVENGE, a form of hate. Evil is the behavioral deeds of Hate.

GUILT and SHAME—For either or both MORAL EMOTIONS to develop, an individual must have a belief in a higher power who represents goodness and love. Implied in a higher power belief is a self-promise to live up to its goodness standard. Then children must shift from obeying rules for external reasons (like fear of punishment) to obeying rules for internal reasons (because it is the right and decent thing to do). By failing to live up their highest awareness of goodness, they feel guilty or ashamed for behaving badly.

Of more importance than "acting ugly," as my Mother use to say, is the breakage of one's word to oneself and thereby breaking a bond of self-trust. If you cannot trust yourself then you have nothing to hold on to in troubled times. Therefore, you will start looking for some outsider to trust and guide you. Most often, that outsider is a controlling and manipulative person disguised as a "friend" but who will lead you astray.

ANXIETY

"There's danger in the air but what is it? And where is it?" If no one has an answer, then this raises the concern of Anxiety. Perhaps there were moments of such anxiety type thoughts in the minds of Primitive man—and before that, man-like species and animals. The repetitious question *of "will it happen?"* (with reference to the threat to security) is termed "Anxiety," while the *"the bad is actually happening!"* (the violation of security) is termed "fear." Everyone everywhere has had, has now, and will have experiences of anxiety.

The Story of Anxiety: The recognition of anxiety as a fundamental human emotion is recorded in the Ancient Egyptians hieroglyphics that related to religion, philosophy, literature, and art. In the Western world, like "anger" (acute and immediate choking sensation), the word "*anxiety*" came from a violent Old Germanic word which meant "*to strangle by choking.*" As a result, the person or animal who was choking became sick. When the choking occurred over a period of time, the resultant mindset was one of being worried sick, and sometimes worrying about choking until death.

In the 14th century, "*worried*" was applied to wolves who had the habit of seizing their prey by the throat in order to kill it. The setting up of sheep for the kill by a pack of wolves was called "*worrying the sheep.*" Sensing danger in the air caused those sheep to show signs of distress.

Eventually, it was necessary to make a distinction between "worry" and "anxiety." Hence, the milder distress of a prolonged choking type sensation was deemed to be "Worry" while the more serious type became "Anxiety. Subsequently, both worry and anxiety were expanded to include mental and physical sources of frustrations and insecurities. But a further distinction had to be made.

Whereas worry and anxiety were about the present or future "*something in the air*" (but lacking obvious cause), the word FEAR was distinquished by some"*right now*" threat, disturbance, or destruction danger quality about a specific thing. The implication was that *worry and anxiety had at least some magnification from imagination.*

By the 19th century, a main subject related to worry and anxiety concerned caring about the safety and security of a person, animal, plant, or place. SAFETY is a sense of being protected by something strong enough to survive any opposing forces. SECURITY is the actuality of all one's needs being cared for—whether to get what one desires or to not get what one does not desire. Soon it was realized that some anxiety was specific and some generalized. These, as with all other disturbing emotions of any type, are well covered in the Psychiatric, Psychological, and other mental health literature.

Then common examples of **Specific Anxiety** started being noticed in public performances as "Stage Fright" (which can hit people who otherwise have merely normal everyday anxiety) and "Test Anxiety" (as when a student takes an examination).

As a result, it became clear that the feature of **Generalized Anxiety** is a state of tension created by the possible happening of "what if" bad things. Because people with general anxiety seemed to be similar to worriers, they were so labled when they worried about many things at the same time and with a vague uneasiness about all significant present and future events.

Specific or Generalized Anxiety is ACUTE when it is temporary and troublesome; when prolonged to the point of causing continuing tension that constantly interferes with effective behavior, it is CHRONIC ANXIETY.

Chronic anxiety, whether specific or generalized, is like a low, smoldering fire. However, when that fire reaches a more active level, the state of NEUROSIS is reached. This means that at the level of neuroses there are more intensive *"premonitions," more "feelings of dread,"* and more of a sense of *"impending doom."* These insecurities call on more and more extreme defense mechanisms for the purpose of lessening the anxiety.

THE WORLD OF ANXIETY: A classification model is helpful for dealing, at one sitting, with all the countless concerns of your everyday life. Mine is the LIFE TRIANGLE CONCEPT (fig. 6). At the top of the triangle is Nature; at the left angle, People; at the right angle, Things (e.g. money possessions): and in the center the Self. The self consists of the body, feelings, reason, and spirit. To indicate that what affects one affects all the others, these seven categories are connected by a "*spider web.*"

LIFE TRIANGLE ARENAS

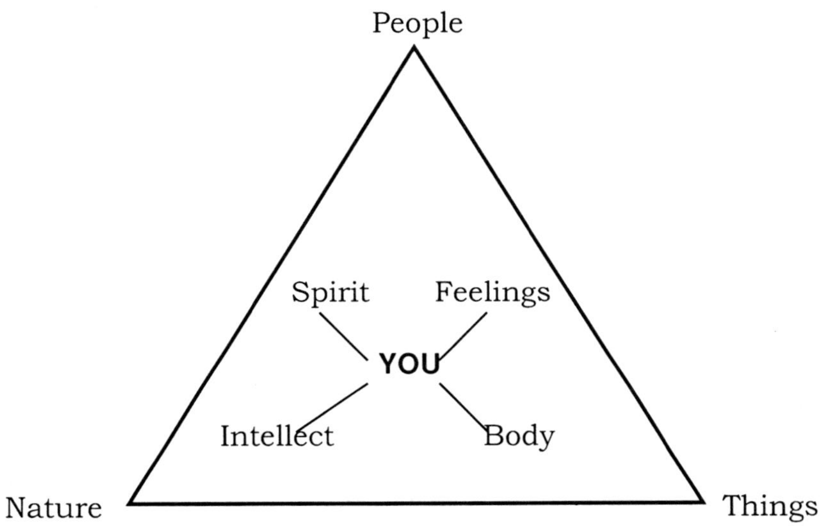

Figure 6
(Reprinted from Bailey –"Becoming a Champion somebody")

Anxiety, an emotion that vibrates the "*spider web*" connecting all the parts of ones selfhood, is a real or imagined threat to ones peaceful security. Anxiety-generated reactions are designed to help us escape from feeling overly insecure. In fact, much of all our behaviors — work, hobbies, social life, and relationships inside the family — are largely designed to prevent or relieve anxiety.

The contents of any anxiety mind channel is that of disharmonious thoughts and an unpleasant feeling tone. The thoughts are so hazy and full of disharmony that they bombard one's sense of peace, to whatever extent peace may be present within ones selfhood. The feeling tone is an emotion with such significant intensity that it shakes up our memory and our autonomic nervous system (which thereby affects all of the body).

The overall effect of anxiety, as with any emotional state, is to draw from our memory only that information which supports the anxiety we are experiencing. The linking of our mind's anxiety, our memory's anxiety, and our imagination join to create distorted thoughts and at least distorted, if not fantasy, emotions.

These combine to give a vivid anxiety force which varies in its power from person to person — depending upon age, gender, and the tendency to define problems in concrete or abstract terms. Concrete images produce the most vivid mental pictures. In general, the imagery of children, with their magical thinking, is more vivid than that of adults; women's more than men; and men's more than scientific and mathematical minds.

Nevertheless, when imagination becomes part of the anxiety force, it interferes with reasoning. Then, for the mentally immature, whatever it takes to keep from "*looking bad*," to reduce insecurity, and to prevent the increase in insecurity becomes more important than the calling on courage to seek the truth or to even face reality. Such self-defense involves coping through self-deception, avoidance, reducing undesirable information, and/or bias selections of only supportive information for decision-making.

Even if such defense mechanisms are successful in repressing the basic thought causing the anxiety, those repressed thoughts remain continually active — like the burning embers of a fire inside a balloon. This burns up so much energy that afflicted people almost always experience fatigue (from burning much of one's daily energy allotment) and unhealthy bodily tension, (as in muscle tightness). Furthermore, in most forms of abnormal behavior, anxiety is featured. The persistence of anxiety cuts a channel through one's mind. Then, into that channel drains almost all other non-anxiety thoughts.

For example, being the basis for all neuroses, anxiety causes people to feel both chronically threatened by life's hazards and to feel a sense of inadequacy in properly handling the tasks of coping. Despite being emotionally crippled by anxiety, neurotics continue to struggle through life in a "*so-so*" manner. What neurotics do is to imitate, degrade, or deform a reality that exists on another level (Choisy, p65).

Periodically, from the addition of added anxieties, the effects are like pouring gasoline on the burning embers so as to produce roaring and crackling flames. By already being angry and anxious, the extra burden causes them to commit some impulsive or foolish act which could have bad life-shaping effects.

Or, the extra burden may cause their life's focus to be shifted or diluted from outside goals to the pursuit of finding substitutes to lessen their neediness for love and affection. Experiencing such insecurity and having a driving pursuit for substitutes leads the person to experience an enhanced awareness of the need for love and affection.

Perhaps at anxiety's highest level are PSYCHOTICS (e.g. schizophrenia and affective reactions) whose distortions of perception and behavior reach such an irrational, fantastic, and out-of-contact-with-reality proportion that they withdraw completely from normal life. Some say neurotics dream in an unreal way about life but psychotics live life as in an unreal dream.

If anxious people's need for love and affection and a sense of belonging are not satisfied through their coping approaches, the result is a further increase in the sense of insecurity and anxiety. Thus, a VICIOUS CYCLE pattern results and it will persist until the spiritual need is satisfied. Mental health specialists who manage neurotics and psychotics are continuing to make refinements in diagnosis and treatment at various points on the complex scale of anxiety.

THE ANXIETY LIFESTYLE: Intense and prolonged insecurity can lead a person into to a lack of self-confidence, into low self-esteem, into depression, and into an increasingly higher susceptibility to anxiety and defensive behaviors. Causes of anxiety spring from a conflict between one's desires and values; from concerns about the future; from prolonged isolation, especially if prevented from being with others; from inadequate self-acceptance; from unresolved conflicts and frustrations; from failure to cope with overwhelming tasks in activities of daily living; from being overly pushed by parents to make great accomplishments; or from personal threats.

All of these concerns are met by youth as they go through their life passages, and particularly in teen age years. In the process, they experience some thrills of victory and some agonies of failure. Each passage—as they wade through the cross-currents of anticipation, expectations, and uncertainty— is filled with dreams, hopes and fears about possible successes and a dread of failures. This is a big deal because they do not have the experience to know that the good and the bad are normal. With each step, youth are hopefully searching, within the demands of society, for a solution to all aspects of their developing self. They try on many different hats but only one or two fit.

Their journey is made more challenging because, as adolescents, they are flooded with sex hormones. Sex hormones themselves cause think, feel, say, and actions and reactions of a particular kind. The undesirable patterns are about a mindset that generates bad emotions, frustrations, insecurities, and recurring dilemmas. For example, teenagers stand on the threshold of withdrawing from parents (in the interest of becoming independent individuals) while in an unstable emotional state. Yet, despite no longer being children but not quite adults, they must remain within the family to receive support. And secretly, they greatly desire the appropriate discipline from parents but only after they feel they have been heard with respect to what is on their minds.

Although there is no such thing, teens believe that their problems and struggles in every aspect of life are unique—"no body has ever had a problem like this but me." It is true that although the details of what, when, and where may be unique, the situation and the principle involved in the situation is the same as it was 5000 years ago. For example, in struggling with morality teens usually wind up feeling shame and indignation for any variety of reasons. Yet, how they come to feel about their actions and what they do as a reaction can be a critical factor in the development of a good or bad system of moral conduct.

Whereas the most common sources of anxiety during later childhood are family and school problems, and personal and social adjustments, teens develop increasing numbers of anxiety-producing experiences. BUT THE NUMBER ONE TEEN CONCERN IS TO BE ACCEPTED BY THEIR AGE MATES. Females tend to have anxieties about physical things (e.g. rape, fire), relationships, family, appearance, progress at school, and details of social life. For males, it is anxieties about their abilities in matters of sex and success. Anxieties resulting from a belief in being unable to make good in life and being unloved or misunderstood can lead to dishonorable (i.e. lie, cheat, steal) and generally ungovernable behavior — the "*I'll show them I don't care!*" attitude. Problems with these always cause bad emotions.

In the adult lifestyle, anxiety is experienced in areas of venturing into the unknown; by failing; by overwhelming and excessive problems occurring at one time; by problems in money, marriage, living arrangements, illness, old age, and death of loved ones.

DEEPER AND LONGER-LASTING ANXIETIES RESULT FROM ONE NOT DOING WHAT ONE STRONGLY WANTED TO DO IN LIFE—e.g. not having developed ones talent or not getting an education or not reaching ones destination. One have chronic low-grade anxiety regardless as whether these came from a lack of courage, out of laziness, or a "*shot-gun*" weddings secondary to unwanted pregnancies. People highly anxious about success and failure tend to adopt either a very conservative (i.e. settle for the "*sure thing*") or a very risky approach to life situations. Thus, success becomes such a remote possibility that failure can readily be justified to oneself — but never enough to fool oneself into being happy. Avoiding the "*too much*" or "*too little*" lifestyle is the way to avoid most "*ball and chain*" anxieties.

To understand the relationship of anxiety to fear, let us review my concept of the **Realms of any Emotion**.

First there is something that is *perceived* by the brain which is destined to begin an emotional process — a trigger, a stimulus, an activator.

Second, the trigger causes a certain emotional brain "center" to react. Actually, there is no "center" because multiple parts of the brain contribrute to the overall reaction in the form of a physiological loop.

Third is the reaction.

Fourth is what sustains the reaction.

Fifth is what determines the degree of the reaction.

Sixth is what determines the type and length of duration of the reaction.

Seventh is what shuts off the mechanism.

What anxiety and fear have in common is that of the same center (Realm two) and initially the same type of reaction (Realm three). Otherwise, anxiety is an environmental or an acquired offspring of the natural emotion of fear and may or may not show similarities in the other realms.

To repeat, the **Amygdala**, the emotional core of the brain, is located in the limbic system in association with the ancient brain. Information passing through the amygdala is tagged with emotional significance. This almond-shaped small brain structure situated roughly in the center of the brain forms a horizontal triangle with the two eyes. The amygdala receives the trigger — the inputs from sensory areas of the brain which in turn receive (1) raw sensory data from the outside world; (2) raw sensory data from the selfhood's inner world; (3) memory from the **Hippocampus** (named in the 16th century after the Greek word for seahorse); and (4) the prefrontal cortex (the rational thought "center").

Thus, the amygdala's primary role is instituting the fear response as a normal and immediate burst to physical danger — a reaction affecting both the brain and the body. Fear is a short-term physiological response which might be considered as a masculine principle. By contrast, anxiety is also instituted by the amygdala and thereby shares many of the same manifestations as fear. However, it builds more slowly and lingers longer — typical of the feminine principle. So what accounts for the slower build up and the longer lingering?

One theory for the slower build up is an amygdala which has been altered genetically (inheritance), congenitally (mutation, en utero disease or hormonal problems), or acquired (as by assuming a hyper-reactor role). Brain scans (e.g. CAT scan, MRIs) have shown some patients' amygdales to be of abnormal size or shape. One study related an enlarged amygdala with over-anxious young children — suggesting they have more fear circuits with which they must contend.

A theory on why anxiety lingers is that another mechanism — the bed nucleus of the stria terminalis, or BNST — takes over control of the fear reaction (Realm six). Another theory is that there is breakdown in the mechanism that signals the brain to stop responding (Realm seven). Normally, once the danger causing a fear reaction is over, the prefrontal cortex sends out an "all clear" and "as you were" message so that the amygdala can "rest and recuperate." But with anxiety, this process experiences interferences.

Anxiety Manifestations and Syndromes: Again, in returning to the stress curve (fig. 2), the "upside" is beneficial; the top is neutral; and the "downside" is destructive. WORRY of mild degree is perhaps the beginning anxiety syndrome on the "upside." It is an adaptation designed to allow for a greater sensitivity in anticipating danger for the purpose of taking preventative action (Bailey, I Am A SpecialSomebody, p. 116).

The umbrella term "Anxiety Disorders" is used when worry persists to the point of interfering with one's life. As a category, it is the most common mental illness in the USA. There are a host of subcategories but where each ranks on the "downside" of the stress curve depends upon which contributors to the emotional process are involved — and to what extent — and when — and how many.

There are many manifestations of destructive anxiety. For example, long-term, unrelenting stress on mothers — particularly those caring for a disabled child — can damage the DNA of their immune system cells in a way that may speed up the aging process. Studies of the blood's mononuclear cells, part of the body's immune system, showed shorter telomeres (bits of DNA that cap the ends of chromosomes).

Normally, telomeres get a bit smaller every time a cell divides. When they are worn out, cells can no longer divide and therefore will ultimately die prematurely. Most overly-stressed women also have lower levels of telomerase, an enzyme that repairs damanged telomeres. People with Progeria (Reichel, Bailey) — a rare genetic condition that reduces their telomerase production — tend to show outward signs of premature aging and often die young of heart disease and weakened infection resistance.

Generalized Anxiety Disorder is excessive worry about several things at the same time and occurring more days than not for six months. Yet it does not markedly diminish one's quality of life except for restlessness, difficulty concentrating or sleeping; fatigue, muscle tension and irritability. In my practice, unreleased excessive worry was likely to cause orthopaedic pain, particularly from "matting" of microscopic scar tissue between muscle fibers that interfere with the normal gliding mechanims.

Apart from muscles, most other parts of the body can represent target organ (e.g. gastrointestinal tract). Within that target organ the weakest link is attacked (e.g. causing a duodenal ulcer). If the afflicted persons stumble on a socially acceptable outlet (e.g. a work injury or some other sort), they may transfer the target organ from the unrelated target organ to the "supposed" or "claimed" musculoskeletal system and develop myofascial (or musculofascial) pain. For such a situation, rather than use a psychiatric or psychological term, I invented the term of a **"Tight Connective Tissue Syndrome."**

Frequently associated are biting of the nails; excessive smoking; and a history of tension headaches as a teenager. This is not common in "workaholic" Type A people because they release their excess anxiety into their work. When the anxiety burns out, the after effect may be depression. Significan depression associated with a "Tight Connective Tissue Syndrome" causes a Chronic Pain Syndrome.

Post-Traumatic Stress Disorder (PTSD) is a repeated, anxious reliving of a horrifying event over an extended period of time. It includes what happened to one in the process and perhaps what one did that should not have been done or what was not done that should have been done. Most feel emotionally and/or physically as if the past event is still occurring and is otherwise easily reminded of it. Studies show the afflicted have a smaller hippocampus (the memory "center") than normal.

Could it be that their stressful experience has somehow interfered with the hippocampus' ability to make new memories and/or to forget the old ones? Brain scans "light up" in areas where brain cells are using the most oxygen or the most nutrients. This suggests that the "lit up" area plays an important role in emotions. In PTSD the amygdala is more active (because of the trigger event?) than normal, while signals to the prefrontal cortex are weaker. Could this explain why patients still feel threatened even when they are perfectly safe?

Panic Disorder is recurrent, unexpected attacks of acute anxiety, peaking within ten minutes after onset – often appearing in a familiar situation (e.g. a crowded elevator). It is learned from repeated triggering of fear like reactions. The person feels a rush of fear or distress with no sense of cause. The first attack often makes people so afraid of another attack that they avoid anything associated with it. If it occurred in an elevator or on the freeway or in a supermarket, people thereafter avoid those places.

The cause may either be some deep psychological problem or some sudden alteration in ones body chemistry (a change in acid/base balance in the brain) or some disturbance in ones biological rhythms (since they can occur during sleep) or may reflect a family trait. Some people have an overly sensitive "suffocation alarm" system (the carotid bodies in the large arteries of the neck) that periodically cause the brain to perceive a shortage of oxygen when actually there is no shortage. Recent PET scan studies show that patients have one-third fewer serotonin receptors in their brains. Serotonin is a key regulator of mood.

Manifestations include palpitations; chest pain; sweating; chills or hot flashes; trembling; shortness of breath or choking; nausea; light-headedness or feeling of unreality; fear of losing control. Four or more of these in two discrete episodes could spell trouble. This "learned fear" triggers the amygdala's fear circuit to release warning messages to other brain areas to thereby cause "fight or flight" reactions. It is more common among women than men. Fortunately, the panic attacks themselves do not appear to be harmful and rarely last more than a few minutes. Yet they can lead to dysfunctional behavior such as substance abuse (e.g. alcohol, street drugs, prescriptive drugs); avoiding normal activities of daily living; and unnecessary visits to the emergency room.

Many patients respond to antidepressants which inhibit serotonin reuptake or drugs which boost the efficiency of serotonin. Some respond to cognitive behavioral therapy. All need to be made aware of how to deal with their anticipatory fear of panic attacks.

Social Anxiety Disorder relates to apprehensions of others and their judgments. Heisman Trophy winner and running back professional football player Ricky Williams was so badly affected he would not take off his helmet during post-game interviews. He would allow his mail to accumulate for days, afraid his neighbors were watching his every move and scrutinizing himi. He would hide from people in the store. As a child he was painfully shy, giving teammates the impression of being arrogant and not wanting to be a team player — but he desperately desired to be one. With therapy and medication, he has made dramatic steps toward a normal lifestyle.

Specific Phobia is an anxiety state with a consuming "fear" of a specific object or situation — often accompanied by extreme anxiety symptoms. People devise elaborate ways of avoidance and dread the next possible encounter. Even simply thinking about the thing generates anxiousness.

Obsessive-Compulsive Disorder is the exception to the fact that most anxiety disorders are more common in women. **Obsession** is the full and persistent concentration on an irresistible idea, urge, emotion, or thought which, in turn, directs its activities. The obsessive thought tends to fill up the "space" in the mind that could be better used for something else and the result is becoming a slave to that activity.

In ancient times this control of one's mind and the resultant bad actions was thought due to the presence of an evil spirit who took up residence in the afflicted individual. When bad actions are done irresistibly and contrary to the inclination or will of the performer and are associated with a sense of powerlessness and inevitability, they are called **Compulsions**.

Together, Obsessive-Compulsive Disorder is a preoccupation with specific thoughts, images, or impulses — accompanied by elaborate and sometimes bizarre rituals (e.g. excessive hand washing or praying). Much energy is spent, usually unsucessfully, suppressing the persistent, intrusive, and irrational thoughts. Obsessive-Compulsive Disorder, whether anxiety is the main feature or not, does respond to treatment.

MANAGEMENT OF ANXIETY: Anxiety is a normal part of life and much of it does not need management. A mild or slight amount of anxiety is beneficial (fig. 2). It sharpens our thinking, motivates us to be more careful with the feelings of others and to go to work on time everyday. These and thousands of similar instances of anxiety do not interfere with our lives.

However, moderate or extreme anxiety squeezes our minds and causes us to react with *"fight, flight, or freezing fright."* Anxious students often flunk examinations that they could pass with flying colors if their anxiety was under control. Promotions at work and family members at home can be lost because of anxiety reactions. So the question is: *"how do I gain control of my anxiety?"* Severe and chronic anxiety both require professional help while less than that may benefit from self-help measures.

Proper diagnosis requires realizing the different types and different causes of anxiety. Part of the work-up includes ruling out an underlying medical condition. Clinically manifest organic problems require specific treatment. Subtle underlying diseases must be kept in mind (e.g. subclinical hyperthyroidism) because they can use up reserves.

So, for purposes of management, here is a process to move the abstractness of anxiety into the somewhat concrete realm. ANYTHING THAT GIVES YOU SOME CONTROL OVER WHAT SEEMS UNCONTROLLABLE IS AN EFFECTIVE TOOL FOR MANAGING ANXIETY.

Step I—**Do the simplest things first.** See if the problem is from a poor diet and lack of physical activity. If so, correct either or both. It is worth trying to cut back or eliminate the use of sugar, caffeine, nicotine, alcohol, recreational drugs, junk food, or working at night.

Some people have a fear of looking foolish or going unrecognized in the presence of others and management for that is social skill improvement. For example, keep in mind the idea of doing what you can to make people feel good or that you are out to discover more about them or that your intention is to not show off your knowledge but rather to be of service or to benefit them.

An informal management of anxiety that can be administered without first going to a physician (if there are no health problems) is simple exercise — a brisk walk or a good workout for 30 minutes. *Yoga* is both a form of exercise and a way to quiet the mind (by focusing attention on breathing). *Breathing exercises* can slow a racing heart and lengthen the short, shallow breaths of a panic attack. So can Meditation. Benefit may come from massage, aroma therapy, guided imagery (a form of directed meditation), and acupuncture.

Maybe you need to make friends with or leave annoying people. You may need to find your talent and pursue the right job. Find a hobby that makes you want to get up and get to it.

Step II— RATIONAL THINKING starts with LAYING THE CAUSE(S) OF YOUR WORRIES OR ANXIETIES ON THE TABLE in front of you and really look at them closely. It is best to do this in writing. You may then see that going further is not worth it or is not in your best interest. Or you may choose to proceed but with less concern about winning. For the more serious anxiety producing causes, your efforts, with professional help, are to uncover repressed thoughts that now cause you to feel scared, insecure, and anxious. Discover also the defense mechanisms you are using. For example, your desire for approval may show as being the center of attention. List all of your bad behaviors and see, as you connect them with the causes of your anxiety, if they follow a pattern.

Next, look at the components of what happened. IT IS YOUR INTERPRETATION of a present experience or anticipated event that starts the anxiety process. If your interpretation is true then the problem needs to be handled by the rational thinking process; if less than true, analyze the misinterpretation.

Was the cause some physical (e.g. poor eyesight) or physiological (e.g. chemical or hormonal imbalance) disorder? Was the problem due to your overuse of *"what ifs"* — *"what if I don't get the opportunity for a promotion?"; "what if they don't like me?"* Was the problem due to looking to outside sources (e.g. friends, the coldness and indifference of authorities) rather than to the right and decent answers found within you? Was the problem from poor or inadequate information?

Step III—**GET TO THE TRUTH** and to what is real once the distortions and fantasies within your interpretation have been discovered. The reason thinking can be more clear now is that the unreal worries or anxieties are no longer taking up a great deal of space in the thinking and memory parts of your brain. After all, your mind can handle only so much activity and information at any one time. In other words, when anxiety almost fills the mind, there is not much mind available to handle the task at hand. A free mind allows you to not confuse imagined causes of anxiety with a reasonable concern about your obligations, duties, and responsibilities. Separate those aspects of what is really your involvement and, within your involvement, assess the portions needing attention. Let the rest go!

Step IV—PRIORITIZE THE PERTINENT INFORMATION known up to this point. What is the chance of something bad happening from each one? and what are the worse consequences if each one happened?. For example, the chance of getting in an accident while riding a motorcycle is quite low but the seriousness of injury (e.g. paraplegia) is of tremendous magnitude. If the chances of failure are low and the consequences are no greater than hurt feelings, then it is worth taking the risk.

Step V—Use Energy and Time wisely. Certain youth are so intent on being superspecialists in something or making top grades that they lose perspective concerning the number of different and difficult hats they must wear in life. This has been extensively discussed in my book: Becoming A Champion Somebody (p. 131). The key to being able to do a satisfactory job related to all the "hats" (e.g. a good mate, a good parent, having success in ones career, etc.) is the proper apportioning of your time and energy.

This demands effectiveness and efficiency in all you do. **Approtionment** is a proper balance in life which is designed by slicing the pie (which represents all your "hats") to fit the amount of time and energy that goes into each slice. Certainly, the two biggest slices are relating well and plentifully with family, and being competent in your career. Too much responsibility is a condition which burdened me most of my adult working life.

Step VI— SYSTEMATIC **DESENSITIZATION** is based on the principle that is impossible to be relaxed and anxious at the same time. Thus, stay calm and relaxed while being exposed to gradually more intense things of what makes you worry or anxious (see discussion under Tools). By so doing, you weaken your learned association between the hazy real or unreal cause and your anxiety.

The approach is to expose patients to a tiny bit of the very thing that causes them anxiety. Over a number of sessions, the dosage of the anxiety trigger is gradually increased. A patient suffering from a phobia to dogs might be shown a picture of a dog at the first session; a dog's collar at the next session; and so on until a dog can not only be brought into the same room but the patient gives him a back rub. Relief can come in as little as two or three sessions. Social anxiety takes somewhat longer and Obsessive-Compulsive Disorder may take a great deal longer.

Problems can arise if these procedures are tried by those who are not professionals. Or, they may occur if treatment is cut short—i.e. before the patient has become inured (i.e. habituated) to the anxiety triggers. Under either situation the anxiousness may be exacerbated (i.e. usually temporarily increased manifestations) (Bailey, Medical-Legal Dictionary, p. 172).

Step VII—consider specific types of management under the care of mental health specialist. Behavioral Therapy has Desensitization (Bailey, Special Somebody, p.18 and later discussion under "Tools") as its theme for dealing with such anxiety conditions as phobias, obsessive-compulsive disorder (OCD), and panic disorder.

Cognitive Therapy concerns the use of the power of the mind to reason through one's anxiety by reconfiguring one's view of the world and developing a more realistic perspective on the risks or obstacles they face. Patients with Social Anxiety Disorder, for example, may believe a group huddled in a corner is gossiping about them. The approach to this is to come up with other options (see later discussion under "Tools").

Antidepressants are usually resorted to when talk therapy does not work or needs support. The best known of the serotonin reuptake inhibitors is Prozac. It prevents the brain from reabsorbing too much of the neuro-transmitter serotonin, leaving more in nerve synapses and thus helping to boost mood. Another group of antidepressants — the serotonin-norepinephrine reuptake inhibitors — target the neuro-transmitter norepinephrine. Secreted by the adrenal gland, it triggers the "fight-fright-or flight" response which thereby increases anxiety symptoms. Yet norepinephrine helps control emotions and stabilize mood, especially when properly manipulated with serotonin. But the effect may take weeks.

Minor Tranquilizers work faster than antidepressants and thus both might be started together. However, drugs like Xanax, Valium, or Klonopin are highly addicting and may merely mask symptoms. As a rule of thumb, I believe far too many drugs are given and that those drugs have long term brain damaging side-effects. I recommend getting second and third opinions before accepting drug treatment. It may be that correcting emotional problems themselves is a better answer.

STEP VIII— TURN OVER THE PROBLEM TO A HIGHER POWER. Believers in the Bible, for example, find great relief from anxiety by reciting the 23rd Psalm (*"The Lord is my shepherd, I shall not want..."*). This was a frequent prayer of mine as a boy.

BELONGING

The word "Belong" means "having a rightful place" or "connected with." To belong is the feeling of being accepted by or a part of another person, by a group, or even of being identified with a group (see Hopelessness). It is the feeling of acceptance through friendly relationships with the community, social groups, friends, and one's heritage. In fact, the word "belonging" means "to go along with" in a way closely related to but must be distinquished from gregariousness.

Often called the HERD or FLOCK instinct, GREGARIOUS implies a desire which drives not only persons but animals to form groups with others of their kind. With gregariousness, although everybody tends to "stick together," seldom is there interest in others for such reasons as to enjoy a friendly exchange, a sense of being with one's fellows, or a belief in a win-win situation whereby everybody benefits as is typical of belonging to a constructive group.

A *Herd Mentality* in Western culture is about being polite and respectful but not considerate. People join their own kind because they prefer company to solitude — a point useful for separating members from the herd. In the ex-slave community, a Herd mentality was of a somewhat different nature compared with that of the West (Bailey, Rising Above Poverty).

When an entire community feels rejected and neglected, CHRONIC ANGER pervades the community. They as well as youth who join gangs tend to develop common desires, ways of behaving, and a pattern of absent or relative weakness in Rational Thinking. These human "herds" move around as a unit, respond in the same way to a particular stimulus, and blindly follow their leader — each member thinking and acting as one of their group.

The mindset of inner city youth's herd behavior, based on my observations, is the manifestation of mild or slight chronic HOPELESSNESS.

DISAPPOINTMENT

Disappointments have been present since the beginning of man. These feeling of earthly disappointments were the forerunners of emotional pain and they occurred in everyone in every age and in every culture. In 15th century Europe disappointment was attributed to many causes because not only had immoral and unethical behaviors become respectable in Europe, but deception, as in fraud, was rampant.

The deception leading to fraud (gaining an unfair advantage over bodies of people) involved those aspects of TRICKERY (deliberately giving the wrong impression) that included DECEIT (the pursuit of personal gain at the expense of victims) and MANIPULATION (hypocritical dishonorableness). When the victims' loss or failure was complete and final, the word "*frustrate*" was applied to the victims' reaction of being in a mental state of chaos.

One of the most agonizing problems of the human experience occurs in dealing with DISAPPOINTMENTS. The resultant frustration spits out emotional pain with its associated bitterness. From there it can mushroom in one direction or another — the drowning of the self in the deep waters of self-pity; or APATHY with fatalistic beliefs that whatever happens must happen and all events are determined by necessity; or fighting the source; or through some scapegoat. These reactions and actions poison the emotional wounds and scar the personality even more — always harming the person to a much greater extent than anyone else.

Management: What has helped me the most is certain of the sayings of my Mother: "Son, everything happens for the best"; "This too shall pass away"; and others discussed in my book "Anger In Black Americans", Chapter X, entitled Philosophical Management. Actually, that section applies to all the Bad Emotions.

EMBARRASSMENT

The Story of Embarrassment: When playing pieces for a board game were discovered in the tomb (1358 B.C.) of Tutankhamen in Egypt in 1922, it was supposed that the game was a form of chess. Although it is now assumed those pieces were of the Ancient Egyptian game now called *"Fox and Geese,"* it is still believed that chess originated in Africa. Yet, there is no specific evidence of chess before500 A.D. when a form of it was known in India as Chaturanga. The Persians adopted the game and much of its nomenclature. For example, "*checkmate*" derives from the Persian shah mat, *"the king is dead."* Thus, the chess game is over because the king has lost control. For whatever reason, to lose control by any king, the warriors of Arabia, the Vikings, and the "*polished*" knights of chivalry was considered embarrassing because the original meaning of embarrass was *"to put to shame."*

This meant that shame and embarrassment were associated, not with the wrong itself, but, specifically in the Greek culture, with the consequences as well as publicly being spot-lighted. Thus, the Greek (and subsequently European) individual's problem was not about having done wrong but in having been caught. The person who was embarrassed felt self-conscious. Such people's sense of being ill-at-ease ranged from *Flustered* (a condition of great confusion — as one might have from drinking too much alcohol) all the way over to *Mortified* (humiliated as a result of failure or inability to live up to what one feels he/she can do and ought to do).

The reaction from people observing the embarrassing event was to convey to the victim a loss of *esteem* (the enjoyment or appreciation of one who is honored). This combination of suffering from the dishonor of others and the process of self-reflection over one's failure or inability to succeed was like being put behind bars — whether in a mental and/or physical jail.

In this way both embarrass and shame were used in the sense of "*impede*," as in the way of an embargo. In fact, to this day the idea of impede or hamper remains in use, chiefly in the context *"financially embarrassed."* Possibly in the 17th century Europe, shame and embarrassed separated in the type of things they referred to. *Shame* went in the direction of having bad feelings about violating the rules of decency, at the core of which was whatever related to the genitals. Embarrassment started focusing on the doing of dishonorable acts (things not falling within the realm of virtues) and thereby the creation of moral repugnance.

Gradually, the setting of embarrass moved into the breakage of the rules or Manners. This trend had begun in the 12th century when the European idea of manners referred to the method of handling something. By contrast, in Ancient Africa, "Manners" were expressions of caring for the feelings of others. The reason this was so emphasized was that a fundamental of African Tradition is having the right relation with and behaviors toward members of one's society.

In the European Medieval period boundaries related to manners were placed on the knights. Their barbaric crudeness necessitated that the ladies of the court and the leaders of the Church fashion customary practices related to personal and social behaviors. These behaviors, in the form of assigned codes, came from members of the upper levels of the social European society who declared themselves "*gentlemen.*" Therefore, in keeping with African Tradition, any violation of the feelings of others was a cause of embarrassment.

Today, three major violations of rules involving things outside oneself are:

- Guilt from committing the wrong
- Shame from the consequences of the wrong
- Embarrassment from getting caught since it breaks a social custom related to civility.

The World of Embarrassment: The reaction — the mental state — occurring at an embarrassing moment is that *"flooding out"* of one's thoughts and feelings. In most social situations of the world, civility — including manners and etiquette (the social codes of good taste) — is the "*honey*" of friendly relationships and the oil of the wheel of civilization because they smooth over the rough spots and protect good feelings. People *"get along by going along"* — by avoiding *"rocking the boat"*; by avoiding appearing to doubt the experts; or by avoiding being rude.

The downside of *"getting along by going along"* is that the people involved become "*sheep*" by failing to stand up for what is right and by never developing their full potential. However, when "*normal*" people deliberately break the rules of civility, and without trying to be rebellious, they usually feel awkward and uneasy (i.e. embarrassed). In fact, many people will experience embarrassment when someone they care about is doing something foolish.

Black Americans feel this way about a fellow Black American's foolish acts that catch the public's attention. Acts of embarrassment — e.g. misnaming or forgetting someone's name, being "*sure*" that such and such happened only to be proven wrong — bring to the eye of the observer one's flaws in an almost naked state.

As mentioned, the mental state of embarrassment at the moment it occurs is a *"flooding out"* of all one's thoughts and feelings. Such a loss of control over mental processes can range from a fraction of a second to a *"long time."* What has happened at this moment of *"social frustration"* is that flaws in our **self-concept** (the set of characteristics which we associate with who we are as a person), our **persona** (that part of us we present to the public), and our **private self** (that part of who we think we are that we do not want anybody to know about) are spot-lighted for public inspection.

One's reaction to the mental state of embarrassment, so as to immediately reduce *"social anxiety,"* is some type of *"saving face."* Many show a lack of poise — spill a drink, stumble, drop a cigarette. Others, when facing lingering embarrassment, do foolish or irrational things to try to lessen their unfavorable image — e.g. perform immoral or illegal acts as a *"favor"* to the observer or take drugs or get drunk to distance themselves from a *"loss of face."* All of these *"face savers"* could become a habit.

Yet, because the underlying problem does not get better, this situation is usually handled by doing whatever it takes to avoid public exposure — like becoming **Shy** and not trying anything outside of your comfort zone. Commonly avoided situations include getting up to speak before a crowd; meeting new people of another class or race; going to formal events, like banquets, particularly if you are not familiar with proper etiquette; keeping quiet in class room discussions out of concern for the way you speak; standing alone for fear giving off a bad body odor from your social anxiety; or working on a creative project that will later be viewed by others.

To overcome shyness learn how to interview people and get them to talk about themselves. Then both restate what they said and ask them to elaborate on different points.

An approach to handling embarrassment and preventing the bad habits associated with it starts with thinking carefully about what you plan to say and do before presenting those words and behaviors the public. HAVE A WELL-THOUGHT OUT REASON FOR DOING AND SAYING EVERYTHING YOU SAY AND DO. Also plan, prepare, and practice before going public. However, some things are learned only with others — like dancing. Here, make a display of laughing out loud at yourself before anyone else does.

If caught at having a faulty opinion, say: *"well, you got me!"* If you made an error in judgment say: *"that sure was a dumb thing I did."* Or, if you have been put out of something, you might say: "I've been thrown out of better places than this. Or, "all great people have been laughed at." These and similar types of comments are effective. If you say it first, you immediately take away the agitator's upper hand of pointing out how dumb you were.

GRIEF

Grief (feeling terrible over the loss of something loved), Mourning, and Bereavement each overlap each other. They are most prominent, along with all sorts of negative or destructive emotions, when the trigger situation is one of death. The manifestations get increasingly worse with denial, embellishments, upon generalizing, and/or when enter-twined with delusions. Chronic Anger over what was done and who did what and Fear of facing the "cold cruel world" alone and Spiritual Pain (blocked love) are quite prominently associated with grief.

Grief can fall into more than one of the Formation of Complex Emotions categories, depending upon the person and the situation. When grief is related to the death of a child, parent, mate, or close fiend, the components of this type of grief are many. Typically, they embrace emotions (e.g. sadness), thoughts (e.g. of the loss), and spirituality (e.g. the passing into another world where bonds of affection and attachments are not readily available to human beings).

Animals' grief may not include the spirituality component but at least the emotion is present in those of the more highly evolved types. For instance, female sea lions witnessing their pups being eaten by killer whales are known to actually wail. When a goose, which mates for life, loses its partner, the bird's head and body droop dejectedly. There are countless anecdotal stories from some of the USA's 61 million pet lovers related to how their dogs became depressed or even died of grief after losing a beloved companion.

There is no time limit for deciding when grief is "normal" or abnormal. Some people grieve "forever" while others focus on the good memories. I have seen mothers die from grieving over a lost child.

HURT FEELINGS

Hurt feelings are the first stage of Emotional Pain and of Anger (consult both for the details related to hurt feelings). Everybody's feelings get hurt. This is particularly true of teenagers who nurse hurt feelings more than they let us know and more than adults can remember in their personal lives. They are desperate for relief and often are not able to reach out and connect—especially males. Boys do not use girls' vocabulary or body language when their feelings are hurt.

Thus, an easy next step is for them to turn to alcohol, drugs, sex, and dangerous activities (e.g. auto racing). Brain-imaging studies show that hurt feelings—the emotions that lead to anger or depression—stirs the brain at precisely the same sites as do physical pain. The more intense the hurt experienced by these individuals, the greater the presence of a spike in neuronal activity. In those with hurt feelins, the serotonin levels—the brain's mood harmone, are abnormally low.

Management is to know who you are. If what they say is not true, then what people say does not matter. If what they say is partially or completely true, then thank them for their assistance and correct what is necessary. However, when the vast majority of people say spiteful things to hurt your feelings it is an indication of their own mental conflicts and pain. Ignore what they said and have compassion for them by saying: "I'm sorry you are having a bad day."

MOURNING

Elephants may be nature's best known mourners, frequently trying to revive dead or dying family members or standing quietly beside an animal's remains for many days, periodically reaching out and touching the body with their trunks.

Mourning, **Bereavement** (the state accompanying the mourning process which may or may not be followed by attachments to or identification with a replacement), and Grief each overlap each other. Although 6 to 18 months is stated to be the "normal" process of resolving grief by relinquishing the loss, no one as a definite answer as to duration.

Some say the five stages of mourning are alarm, numbness, pining (searching), depression, and recovery. Others say the stages are denial; sorrow; detaching from the loss; adjusting to life without it; and reattaching to a replacement.

These are subjects people are familiar with—and usually from personal experience. It helps that instead of wallowing in the emotional or the spiritual pain that one celebrates the benefits of what was present before it was lost. With time, the emotional pain will disappear and the spiritual pain should lessen as you carry pleasant memories of them and how they influenced your life. Ancient Africans believed that cherished and honored ancestors remain available in the Supernatural world to be of assistance, if you but call on them.

NON-HATEFUL ENVY

Envy is at first a pained and concealed reaction to seeing others have something one wants for oneself. To not own what the other has is a reflection of a perceived loss of ones own omnipotence or a loss of some of whatever power one believes oneself to have. The companion of envy is jealousy and both are normal and are found in all humans as part of normal living. Whether envy and jealousy are "natural" or are learned is uncertain. Despite being two different arousals, both have in common varying degrees of the emotion of resentment.

The Story of Envy: *"Green with envy!"— "The Green-Eyed Monster!!"— "The Evil Eye!!!"* All three expressions imply a selfish desire, for one's own enjoyment, to possess something belonging to someone else. But why the color "*green*"? One reason is that people who are unwell are often said to look pale or green. The "*pale*" is plain enough to the observer, but the "*green*" takes a little imagination. The deeply envious feel unwell mentally and "*green*" has been historically associated with this mental state — perhaps because the Scottish verb for green means "*to yearn.*"

Certainly, yearning with an uncontrollable desire for what belongs to another — called COVETEOUSNESS — is at the core of envy. Another association was given in Shakespeare's (1601-1650) Othello. To make Othello mistrust his wife, Desdemona, the villainous Iago drops hints about her relations with Cassio by saying: *"O, beware, my lord, of jealousy. It is the green-eyed monster, which doth mock the meat it feeds on . ."* The allusion is to cats and tigers and other green-eyed animals which toy with their victims before eating them. In a similar fashion, a jealous (originally jealous, envy, and hate were synonyms) lover may both love and hate his beloved if he believes a rival is gaining her affections.

In the European late Middle Ages envy and jealousy somewhat separated from each other (and from hatred). Envy became more thoughtful than emotional and jealousy became more emotionally personal than thoughtful. In their full blown forms JEALOUSY WAS CONCERNED WITH "*LOOKING ON WITH SUSPICION*" in a relationship of two or more people while ENVY WAS MORE ABOUT THE EMOTION OF "*LOOKING ON WITH MALICE.*" Jealousy was about wanting to get or keep what one believed — true or not — belonged to him/her. Envy was about wanting to acquire what belonged to another.

In short, envy says *"I want what is yours"*; jealousy says *"Don't mess with what is mine."*

The World of Non-Hate Envy: During the normal socialization process, at some point children learn the envy concept of *"the grass is always greener on the other person's lot."* Today, this is greatly contributed to by the hundreds of advertisements (e.g. billboards, radio, television, movies) seen each heard day. Advertisers are quite successful at getting the public to feel dissatisfied with anything they have or in the way they appear or into believing that they simply are *"not good enough"* as they are. In turn, advertisers declare their product to be the answer. In other words, the whole idea is for you to become so dissatisfied as to want to be somebody else, be somewhere else, or so admire something else as to want to possess it or at least have one just like it.

Otherwise, it is well known that envy and jealousy can be taught when they normally would not exist. For example, during the times of American slavery, one of the brain-washing methods slave owners used to enslave the minds of African American consisted of creating fear, distrust, envy, jealousy, and hated among the slaves themselves.

The Manifestations of Envy can take odd twists. For example, if you help someone as a simple humanitarian gesture, the person helped may react by becoming envious that you have something he/she does not. Then he/she may hate you for needing your help. Enviers are usually people who play when they should be working and saving up for a rainy day. When that rainy day comes they believe that you, who worked while they played, should give much of what you have to them because you have it and they do not. They will start using ridiculous excuses like: *"You're my relative"* or *"I'm working to improve myself"* or *"remember when I called you on your birthday?"*

Dealing with enviors is a "no win" or a "losing" situation. If the rival attempts to help them, enviers interpret those attempts as trying to oppress them or to infiltrate their territory. But if the rival decides not to help them, they interpret that as a selfish act and that the rival is only seeking his/her own comfort.

If the rival presents both options, then enviors see this as playing games with them. No matter how much help you do, it is never enough. Furthemore, they will wind up hating the helper because the helper has enough to give of what they want—and they feel bad about wanting—and they hate that the owner is able to have it and they are not. All of this is a reflection of their inferiority. At best, the envious pay *"lip service"* (saying what they are expected to say but not meaning it) to being loving. One reason is that they wish they could be their ideal self. Another reason is their desire for you to believe that they actually are ideal. People in the system of hate — such as those with significant degrees of envy and jealousy — are not to be believed in what they say about who they are.

MANAGING Non-Hateful Envy: People are more ashamed of confessing to being envious than perhaps confessing to any other emotion. One reason is that envy is a definite sign of weakness. By contrast, a "*poor me*" person believes he/she is strong but has had a run of "*bad luck*." However, if forced into a confessional "*SHOW AND TELL*" (the displaying of their belittling emotions and talking about them from all angles), the envious presentation is veiled and incomplete. Management starts by "*getting real*" — by being true to oneself so as to discern the category of envy in which you operate. The categories of non-hateful envy include the mild, slight, and early stages of the moderate.

MILD ENVY is dominated by desire: *"how wonderful it would be if I could have or do what the other person has or does."* Such is a longing to have a thing, an advantage, a quality, or quantity belonging to someone else—but no action is taken. Throughout any of the "*normal*" day-dreaming of wanting of what someone else, there is no associated ill-will. In fact, the envior may desire to draw the rival into his/her territory so as to compete and prove to him/herself that he/she is equal to the other person.

Sometimes, envy may build up over a period of time. For example, if someone has perfected his efficiency (doing a job quickly and without wasted time or energy) and effectively (able to cause the desired results), then one may feel this is a good person to be around so as to learn some pointers. However, one gradually starts getting envious because one does not like another being more efficient and effective since it shows up ones own inadquacies.

SLIGHT ENVY is what might be suspected when some one does not like you "for no reason." A second common situation is present when someone tells another or even tells you that: "*You think you are better than me.*" Such envious reactions, present even in pre-school age children, are the feeling of displeasure produced by witnessing or hearing about the advantages or prosperity of others. One hopes and prays that some event will come along and cast down one's rival—perhaps by wiping out the rival's fortunes. But one would never take such a bold action oneself.

A third form of Slight Envy is one of: a "*keeping up with the Joneses*" type attitude — a sort of hunger for their appearance of having "*the good life*," as in the latest fashions. If you evaluate your value status in relation to the value status you assume others have, instead of competing with yourself to improve yourself, you confuse the value status of the Joneses with your basic worth — the misfit act of comparing apples to oranges.

If your self-esteem status is not strong, you will feel more "*worthless*" or "*no good*" if you do not have what the Joneses have. Such inferiority feelings are associated with insecurity, depression, emotional pain, anger, and sometimes will go on into self-hate. All of these increase the frequency, intensity, and duration of envy as part of a downward spiraling VICIOUS CYCLE — the making of problems worse and worse by creating a cycle of greater and greater problems in more and more aspects of your life.

The way out, Socrates counsels, is not to take delight in the envied persons' misfortune but to take pity instead. But if the pity is not sincere, this is where **Civility** shows—strongly disliking the rival while politely smiling in the rival's face. The Pretenders display a façade of "love" while trying to stab you in the back—e.g. making the rival the butt of jokes, the object of ridicule. Yet, the envior refuses to admit he/she harbors envy because it is such a belittling emotion. This makes these jerks and frauds difficult to spot.

On the other hand, it is far better in the long run to be glad for another's fortunes, even though it may be attained at your expense. Constantly practice this for the sake of climbing out of your self-centeredness. Meanwhile, gradually enlarge the scope of this practice to cover all who have had good fortune, for any reason — whether you view the cause for being glad as sufficient or not.

The summary point is to expect to encounter envy in various forms as you become more and more mentally healthy and financially better off. Possesing money or simply seeming to have the appearance of being "rich" cause even friends to do strange, and often, dishonorable things to "level the playing field" as they see it.

GREED

The Story of Greed: Comments made in Ancient Africans' "**Wisdom Literature**"—i.e. the Discourses and Instructions—clearly point out that Greed was an evil to be avoided. In Ancient African religion, including Kamit or Egypt, evil and suffering are ascribed to disruptive spirits and unrighteous living. For them, Evil is understood as the actions of people who are ignorant of the higher spiritual reality within themselves. Thus, afflicted people's actions are based upon egoism, anger, hatred, lust, jealousy, envy, and greed (Ashby, African Origins p197).

Discourses focused on the description of Order (Ma'at) and Disorder (Isfet). By contrast, **Instructions** were about making one wiser (e.g. a series of maxims on the "way of living truly"); about assisting ones breeding in polish and agreeableness;

and about causing one to draw out the good character one has inside. The most famous is the Instructions of Ptahotep (3000 BC).

But let us look at the words written during the 10th century BC of Amenemope, the African Scribe and son of Kanakht. In his Instructions—or Seboyet—what he says is the culmination of many ideas found in the the long traditions of Egypt. And this Seboyet served as a model for all ancient literatures of the proverbial type (e.g. the book of Proverbs in the Bible) (Asante, Egyptian Philosophers p107, 110). In Chapter Seven he dealt with the subject of Greed: "Do not strain to seek excessive riches when your needs are safe and satisfied. If riches are brought to you by robbery they will not spend the night with you."

In the book of Khunanpu, greed is condemned as "a severe and incurable sickness." It is the source of family disputes and division—"a collection of all kinds of evil and a bag of all kinds of hateful things...do not be greedy in the division (of wealth). Do not covet more than your share"—for sharing cultivates amity (peaceful relations; friendship), while greed undermines family and community (Karenga, Maat p333).

During Biblical times "Greed" was considered to be the desire to acquire and keep more than one needs—forms of *Avarice* (immoderate desire for riches) and Covetousness. As an unmixed evil (Lk. 12:15), it was on lists with murder, adultery, and malice (Mk. 7:22). Because desire for riches or possessions takes first place in the greedy person's heart, greed is equated with idolatry (Col. 3:5). The Tenth commandment forbids covetousness of all sorts when it speaks of a neighbor's house, wife, servant, cattle, or another's possessions.

During the European Middle Ages, Greed and its tentacles of Covetousness, Avarice, and Gluttony were deemed as vices and were included in the catalog of Deadly Sins (e.g. pride, covetousness (greed), lust, anger, gluttony, envy, and sloth) which Pope Gregory the Great compiled. Greed is evil, the Pope said, because it substitutes material things for the place of honor that the Creator ought to have in an individual's life. This was in keeping with the Biblical sense of greed being evil because it means worshipping an idol (Col. 3:5) instead of God.

During the European Renaissance greed was behind Materialism and Individualism rising into a place of high esteem. This process was about individuals being so motivated by destructive selfishness—by a fondness for dishonest gain—by an eager for base gain— as to sacrifice other people, places, and animals to possess things (e.g. money and property, power, extravagance, sex, and pleasure).

To achieve these ends Europeans used every method conceivable—methods done by any means necessary—methods which stirred up disputes, threats, disturbances, wars, robbery, or killing (including chopping up victims). In the 16th century, the word "Greed" came into English with the sense of "to be hungry"; "to be intensely desirous"; and "to step forward." The idea was about strong desires being more than is right or more than is reasonable.

Today, nothing has changed except that the means for pursuing greedy have become more "hi-tech", more sophisticated, and more subtle. Such afflicted spiritually disconnected people excuse their evilness and greed by such justifications as "the survival of the fittest" or "the struggle for existence." Yet, there is no valid reason to justify greed and greed invariably creates trouble and complicates ones life.

The World of Greed: "Greed" is a compulsive or insatiable desire to possess certain things that present an attractive appearance and that have an air of "scarcity." Its three components define a person's character.

Avarice is a greedy and desperate desire for money.

Gluttony is greed related to ones obsessive urge to consume food.

Covetousness is greed (Exod. 20:17) and an envious desire for the property or possessions of another person. It causes one to "keep up with the Joneses" despite knowing that by doing so extends one beyond ones means and causes one to purchase what one really does not need. Covetousness is also about idolatry and the worship of goods and possessions.

Afterall, "**The <u>love</u> of money is the root of all evil"** (I Tim 6:10). Note how this has been wrongly stated to say that "money is the root of all evil"—a misstatement that has had a profound bad effect on the lives of good poor people. By the misinterpretation that money is "the root" means that it can (and does) become the source of all kinds of evil.

The methods used today for pursuing greedy desires remain as those of the past. A typical USA pattern is to continually decrease quality as prices are continually increased. Poor service from the beginning gets worse. I have seen the switch over in my lifetime from "the customer is always right" to the present attitude of people in business: "to hell with the customer."

Let us suppose the situation of greed is that of one wanting more expensive items as a result of a mental obsession. Eventually one will reach a limit of what one can get—a fact of reality. When that limit is reached one loses all hope, sinks down into depression, and life becomes a drag. This is like a ballon filled with exaggerated desires and over-expectations and the wish for the ideal that lasts "forever and ever." Because that greed balloon will inevitably burst, one will automatically feel chronically unhappy, frustrated, and disappointed to an extreme degree.

Meanwhile, one will have a great deal of confusion as to what to do next and that shows as an attack against people who happen to be close by. The scapegoat victims will often be blamed as the cause of the balloon bursting. But before the balloon bursts, there is never any satisfaction with however much one obtains. Although the person's motive is to achieve "happiness," at no time is the greedy person happy, or even satisfied. The reason is that greed is about trying to fill a bottomless pit — meaning that there is never enough money, possessions, property, or fame.

Many believe that **Karma's justice** gives to each person just what is required to fill one's indwelling desires. For instance, if one is bound by a greedy desire for material riches, the Law of Karma will attract him to a rebirth in conditions in which he will be surrounded by riches and luxury until he becomes sickened with them. He will eventually find his heart filled with the desire to flee from them and toward higher and more satisfying things (Ramacharaka, Gnani Yoga p247).

The story of King Midus is an example. Midus desired gold so much that a genie granted him the wish that everything he touched would turn to gold. Because his "**Midus touch**" generated gold even when it was not desired (e.g. touching his daughter who instantly turned to gold), he lost everything important to him. Note that *desires related to Karma can burn out those bad desires holding one back while the same conditions and experiences can design the destruction of whatever will make for possible future advancement.*

Regardless of Karmic type, one has the free choice of continuing to follow one's Karma of past thoughts and actions or of resisting them. Only through a "*Purified Heart*"—i.e. ones conscious and unconscious mind—achieved by Karma reparations is it possible to go to a higher plane of existence in intuitive (above thought) understanding and Wisdom (discerning between the real and the unreal) about the nature of one's own existence Ashby, Yoga p90, 181). Doing loving things creates good karma and dissolves bad karma.

MANAGING GREED: According to Ancient Africans, as with all other sins, Greed is the result of separation between ones self and God—the state of ignorance about ones own spiritual essence (**Egoism**). Each person must take responsibility for his/her actions while striving to engender a sense of Divine Presence within him/herself. The approach is through that mentioned for "Man, Know Thyself" (Bailey, Selfhood Mastery). When this occurs, the very basis of sin and ignorance is dispelled from the mind. At this stage of spiritual development there is transcendence of the notion of good and evil.

Understanding all of God's creatures and creations to be part of oneself, there is no need to debate about ones treatment of others. Ones treatment of others becomes a spontaneous act based on love, compassion, forgiveness, and magnanimity—much like there is instant forgiveness of ones teeth when one bites ones own tongue. This is the true goal of religion—to rise above ignorance (evil, egoism) (Ashby, African Origins p197).

Most greedy people have no concept that there is any other way to be. Their idea of "changing" is trying other methods to "have it all"—and particularly methods featuring "short-cut" (because greedy people believe they are entitled to what they want, when they want it, and how they want it and without having to do much to get it).

"**And again I say unto you, it is easier for a camel to go through the eye of a needle than for a rich man to enter into the kingdom of God**" (Matthew 19:24). What does this mean? A rich man asked Jesus: "Good Master, what good thing shill I do that I may receive life in the other world?" Answer: "If you would be perfectly happy, go home and sell all that you have, and give your riches to the poor people. Then you will have riches in heaven. Afterwards, you may come back and be my disciple." But the rich man loved his riches more that he loved God and therefore could not be contented and happy without them.

Let us assume that Jesus was referring to those rich people filled with delusions about scarcity and thereby reacted from so much fear as to go about grabbing all they could—and by any immoral or illegal means necessary. Thus, for them to be happy it would also be necessary to shed these delusions; replace them with Ma'at (love in action) type values; and then modify, refine, or completely change their character to be in accordance with the ultimate of Ma'at principles. The objective is to become "no one" by being lost in the harmony and unity of all God's creations and creatures.

If you believe you are an incurable "Greed Addict" but are willing to keep trying to "shake the habit," then remember three things—reconnect with God; find and cultivate your goodness; and seek contentment by making easier the lives of the needy.

From an Ancient African perspective, the greedy voluntarily chose to separate themselves from God. However, by exerting free will, they can voluntarily choose to reconnect on their own or with the help of someone or some group.

Whenever one became greedy, one donned masks of arrogance, brutality, and individualism. Despite the reality of these masks, there is an unlying fragile goodness within them. By locating their goodness and focusing on it and enlarging upon it, one will gradually snuff out greed.

The **opposite of Greed is Contentment**. One way of achieving Contentment is to get everything you really, really want that is realistic. Once acquired, then contentment is a realist goal. However, to become content requires working smart, hard, efficiently, effectively, and with a sense of urgency.

A second way of achieving Contentment is to want whatever you already have. This is about Appreciation of your blessings.

A third way is to take advantage of what is available to you. This starts by learning to use both your Right brain and your Left brain. Your Right brain allows you to be motivated by love and love will cause you to sacrifice possessions to serve others. To make the lives of the needy either better or less difficult—"to bless others with the blessings you receive"— is a source of satisfaction. The gift was real and from the heart if you can have contentment, even if the people involved do not give thanks or ever realize how this happened for them.

GUILT

The Story of Guilt: Today, we think of guilt primarily as an inward feeling of remorse or a bad conscience—but in Biblical times it was a "*fact*," not a feeling. Many said (Rom. 5) that the sin of Adam, regarded as the human race representative, brought guilt not only upon Adam but upon all his posterity. This is known as *"ORIGINAL SIN"* or *"natural depravity."* From this there came to be an intimate association between guilt and sin.

The ancients believed that since all sin is an offense against God, guilt could only be understood by relating it to God. Therefore they emphasized that each human being is responsible; that responsibility requires sin or the fault to be voluntary; and that responsibility is necessary before proper punishment can be applied. Yet, the very imperfection of man's nature leads humans to deliberate wrongdoing and guilt necessarily goes with this.

The ancients believed in three distinct aspects to guilt: (1) there is an act of guilt; (2) there is the condition of guilt that results from the acts; and (3) there is the punishment that is appropriate to the act. The act was often called "*iniquity*" or "*wickedness*" — as determined by God, not man. The condition was the intention to sin or a disregard of what was moral. The appropriate punishment was determined by God. The fact that man has tried to influence the punishment is indicated by the long and widespread history of sacrifice and penance.

Ancient Africans, tens of thousands of years ago, originated the practice of blood **Sacrifice**. They agreed that since blood is essential for animal life, spilt blood must be the perfect symbol of sacrifice. The African purpose of sacrifice was not about guilt, as it was in other cultures, but about renewing and strengthening their relationships with the gods.

PENANCE ("*penalty*") was added to sacrifice as the European way of dealing with guilt. It originated in the post-apostolic period — that time after the lives of the 12 disciples chosen by Jesus to preach the gospel. Its purpose was to chastise church members guilty of grave moral offenses, such as apostasy (complete forsaking of one's religion) and sexual impurity. Offenders had to submit to a lengthy public regimen and could not be admitted to the church a second time.

Then, in the 5th century AD, penance became a private affair when confession to a priest was started. It was elevated to a sacramental level by Peter Lombard (1100-1160). The objectives were for the person to recognize the wrong itself and, in keeping with the meaning of the word "guilt" ("*paying*" for sin or offense), feel a sense of blame. Wanting to discharge self-blame by "*paying*" (so as to ease one's conscience) was accomplished by experiencing guilt and receiving grace simultaneously. GRACE removes condemnation but the mind continues to experience feelings of unworthiness and failure.

Because European religion and the legal system were somewhat closely related, the legal system stayed with the religious setting but with a shift of focus from the transgression of a moral failure over to breaking legal laws. While retaining the existential Biblical ideas that human beings are responsible and accountable for their actions, thoughts, and attitudes, they said, for example, that a state of guilt should occur when contract relationships are improperly broken between the parties involved. As a result, based on man-made rules, the accused could feel guilty but be blameless in the eyes of the state or, conversely, be guilty of a crime and yet be morally innocent.

The World of Guilt: Guilt is the emotion you experience when you have not lived up to your own internal standard. It is remorse for real or exaggerated or imagined wrong doings — a kind of self-inflicted punishment. STANDARDS are the ultimate rules that an individual sets up for his/her own behavior. They are the model against what we think, feel, say, and do is compared. Because children cannot have standards until they have acquired some fairly sophisticated concepts of what their society sees as the ultimate value and how it is used in various circumstances, standards are slow to be learned.

Until then, children start behaving in accordance with what they see their parents do and, to a lesser extent, what their parents expect of them. Eventually they internalize both and turn them into their own standards. Children most likely to have a well-developed sense of guilt acquire this from their religious training around age 4 to 6.

While cultivating moral standards, they are also developing the urge to live up to them. This process gives them their first ideas of guilt — representing that mysterious part of the self called CONSCIENCE. From people around them, children learn the good and bad of what to do and not do as well as that omissions (not doing what they should be doing) and commissions (doing what they should not be doing) result in punishment — all refinements of conscience.

Over time, children add their own concepts to both increased and decreased feelings of guilt. Standards too high or too numerous or too demanding mean that most or all cannot possibly be lived up to even some of the time, let alone most or all of the time. Some come into conflict with basic drives — like not stealing food when you are hungry or sharing when you really do not want to or being kind even to people to whom you feel hostile. As a result, shame and guilt develop not only regarding our conduct but also over our thoughts that go against our morals. Then too certain of our morals seem to have overly punishing consequences, as when a child feels he/she will go to hell for lying, cheating, or stealing. If this gets bad enough it can drift on over to DELUSIONS (firmly held beliefs that have no basis in reality), as in having committed *"the unpardonable sin."*

Nevertheless, people who cannot live up to their religious standards often feel the need to be forgiven — turning to prayer, to contemplation (becoming one with the truth in an attempt to obtain a mystical union with God), to the confessional, and the like. Not only can these methods reduce the guilt and anxiety brought about by violating religious or moral standards, but they can often reduce guilt originating in areas having little or nothing to do with religion or morals.

Guilt is positive when it guides us into self-correction. For example, guilt over being lazy, irresponsible, or engaging in avoidable misdeeds is healthy if it becomes a stimulus to improve and learn. Otherwise, it is necessary for our mental health to shed unnecessary guilt feelings which slow, stop, or reverse our wholesome work progress as well as to reduce or eliminate self-imposed misery, depression, and self-hate.

The aim is to have a sense of guilt that keeps us on the right track in the absence of authority figures who control the rewards and punishments in our lives. When shame and guilt become such guides, then we have established self-responsibility (shouldering the consequences for omissions and commissions) and self-controls for our own behaviors. Having such responsibility for yourself in past, present, and future behaviors implies that you see yourself as in charge of making good and bad choices.

GUILT BASED CULTURES: Throughout recorded history, shame and guilt have served as mechanisms of social control. Because both are painful emotions, true shame cultures (e.g. the Amish) rely on criticism to maintain good behaviors. A wayward member is shamed either by being openly ridiculed and rejected or through self-fantasizing about having been made to look ridiculous. Whereas *Shame is a punishment imposed from without and requiring an audience, Guilt is essentially punishment from within.* In cultures where honor means living up to one's own mental picture of oneself, a person may suffer from guilt although no one is around.

In the Judeo-Christian tradition the belief that God is all seeing and all knowing makes Western society a guilt culture. In fact, it was the development of the Catholic practice of confession, in which individuals of every social level examine their consciences and whisper their misdeeds to a priest, that was behind the rise of 14th century individualism in Europe. By becoming more aware of what was going on in one's conscious, meant that each person could get to know him/her selfhood better.

Confession and penitent behaviors were thereby added to all the other ways cultures had used to relieve their guilt — animal and human sacrifices, offerings of grain and money, as well as DEFENSE MECHANISMS — *denial* (often including actual loss of memory of the misdeed), *rationalizations* (justifying unjustifiable behavior), *Scapegoating* (displacing frustration from it true source), and *Projection* (blaming others for one's own real or fancied sins of omission or commission).

In England's 9th century high society, moral and ethical purity in matters of truth, honesty, and love were supposedly greatly valued. Women in particular were expected to have unassuming conduct (shy, bashful), modesty in covering their bodies, self-depreciation, inconspicuousness, and decency. Among those claiming high morals, to fall short of these attainments was to necessitate some sort of silent apology.

It was during the 12th century that disgrace, shame, and guilt were synonyms. By the end of the European Middle Ages, when **individualism and materialism were rising into prominence, the traditional vices became more desirable and respectable.** As a result, shame and guilt not only separated in meaning but were less of a problem, thanks to the flexibility had been put into European morals.

Meanwhile, historians generally agree that something like a "*mutation in human nature*" took place during the 16th and 17th centuries. People became more aware of their individuality, especially their inner psychological life. This new self-awareness, differing from the Christianity type, consisted of people emphasizing and valuing their unique individuality. Individuals became **preoccupied with pretense and false identity** — claiming to be someone other than who they really were. Naturally, the stimuli for inducing guilt became narrowed in scope and raised in degree of severity.

Today, it seems as if those who suffer the most from guilt have high ideals which conflict with their fundamental desires and/or have high morals based on their religious beliefs. For them, the emotion of guilt and the fears of sin are frequently the indications of a conflict between the desire to carry on the act and the standards preventing the act. The real fear in these cases is the fear of self (e.g. fear of violating of standards) on the one hand, and fear of not satisfying the desire on the other. The solution is to face the conflict and resolve it by deciding what will bring the greatest good to the most people over the longest period of time.

MANAGING GUILT FROM OMISSIONS: The framework within which guilt works is living up to and being responsible for the best of which one is aware (i.e. ones highest self). The "*big three*" of good care of anything, including your highest self, are obligation, duty, and responsibility. OBLIGATION is making a binding promise to take steps to get what you want and to not get what you do not want. The obligation involved in morals (i.e. right/wrong situations) is to live up to the rules of good character and to avoid dishonorable character. DUTY is the tasks that have to be done. Moral tasks ought to be discovered (e.g. compassion, kindness, patience, tolerance, meekness) and cultivated until they become habits. RESPONSIBILITY is shouldering the consequences for both successes and failures.

Moral failures are about omissions and commissions. OMISSIONS are a neglect of duty — wrongly leaving something undone or left out — the *"what I did not do that I should have done"* realm. COMMISSIONS are wrongly doing something that goes against good — the *"something bad I did that should not have done"* realm.

Startling findings in a recent study showed that 75% of USA college students believed it is all right to lie, cheat, and steal. This points out the scope of how people look at their *"highest self."* Those who believe in and use the divine power — God — as their ultimate standard have a high degree of morality and therefore experience guilt. Those with "flexible morals" or those who are immoral or amoral — like racists and the anti-social — use their "*lowest self*" (the destructive part of their selfhood) and are not likely to experience guilt.

For people capable of experiencing guilt, their process may go in opposing negative directions — omission and commissions. An example of the omission direction is that aspect of EXISTENTIALISM ("*to merge or stand out*") which says: *"I take responsibility for my choices in life, whether in spiritual or earthly matters."* The strongest and most chronic of any form of guilt occurs when you fail to make choices that take advantage of the opportunities to discover, develop, and find a niche (the right place) for your talent. That failure leads to a lack of self-fulfillment.

MANAGING GUILT FROM COMMISSIONS: The judge peered over his spectacles at the man accused of stealing a goat. "*Guilty or not guilty?*" he demanded. "*Well, judge, I think mebbe I'm guilty,*" said the accused, "*but I'd rather be tried an' make sure.*" This is an example of a COMMISSION GUILT — wrongly doing something that goes against the laws of right. Using *Incomplete Repression*, the guilty man pushed thoughts of his wrong deed out of his mind. Reasons for this repression included being embarrassed and angry, being caught and taken to court, and being fearful about the judge's verdict. At this point, dealing with the man's guilt is not complicated because the three bad emotions are from his wrongful act.

Properly dealing with the wrongful act as well as the cause of the wrongful act will soothe, if not eliminate, the guilt. The cause of the dishonorable act may have been that the man was going through hard times and needed the goat for food. But, creating a paying job for himself, would have been an alternative to stealing. However, if the cause was laziness or meanness, correcting those problems requires special work. Regardless of the cause, he deserves to be punished.

Throughout history, "*moral*" people have experience guilt from destroying holy things, cheating, robbing, failing to report lost property, swearing falsely in court, seducing slave females, and breaking trust (as in not keeping one's promise). Also throughout history, moderate or extreme dishonorable acts have called for death, Trial by Ordeals, or retributions.

At least up to the time of the 18th century European humanitarian movement, punishment for crimes involving morals was mainly vindictive. Thereafter, attempts have been made to match the gravity of the legal crime to the severity of the punishment. Such a matching is a useful guide for an individual dealing with his/her own ethical guilt when that individual freely chose to knowingly violate a moral law.

These kinds of legal, moral, and ethical guilt are to be distinguished from ENCAGED MIND GUILT — those alcoholics and drug addicts involved in the vicious cycle of poverty and crime. Their emotional and philosophical conflicts are so overwhelming as to cause them to act automatically from a position of self-defeating habits. Guilt comes from disappointing their family or from breaking up family relations. For example, a star college football player loses the opportunity to go into the National Football League because of positive marijuana testing. Therefore, he feels guilt for letting his family down.

The most important management step in moral and ethical guilt is to do what is necessary not to repeat the act. Guilt is good when your regret and sorrow serve as self-corrective measures to acquire and maintain good character. The act which winds up with a "*wrong*" or "*bad*" result does not make you an immoral or a "*bad*" person, even if you intentionally made the poor choice. The problem comes from letting that poor choice become a habit — the doing of more and more with greater and greater ease.

Desensitization to immoral and amoral acts gives you an unrealistic view as to how to solve your problems. It also causes you to stop thinking about how the consequences of your actions affect all people involved and therefore you become more and more self-centered. When disregard for the laws of right and guilt no longer inspires you to improve, evilness has set in. Otherwise, your job is to rebuild self-trust and re-establish the integrity of your "*self*" and "*self-concept*." All debts must be repaid.

HUMILIATION

MORES (moral common sense customs) and certain FOLKWAYS (non-moral rules for behaving) fashion humiliation, shame, and guilt. To feel humiliated means to feel as if one is reduced or lowered from a position of integrity type of pride, dignity, or self-respect to a state of being disgraced (a loss of honor). Humiliation is thought of as a form of Earth world shame. Whereas guilt focuses on the wrong itself, shame is more about the consequences of the wrong.

Although separated in the Middle Ages, shame and guilt retain many of the same features. Both relate to the involvement of the PRIVATE SELF — that part of each of us that we do not want to expose. Shame is hiding *"the skeletons in its closet."* Guilt is hiding its weaknesses in judgments or its wrongfulness. Spiritual shame, like spiritual guilt, is a violation of the total self as, for example, when someone says: "you are stupid" as opposed to *"what you just did was stupid."*

Althought today shame is defined as feelings of humiliation associated with exposure to one's faults and short-comings, humiliation may or may not result from a violation of one's moral self. Rather, it is much more frequent for humiliation to result from some flaw in the appearances one presents. This means it is like a bleeding wound to your self-concept from the belief that others will like you less for you having done something wrong or from not looking good.

Both shame and guilt have spiritual and earth world forces which knock one off ones self-created pedestal. Such can occur in one's own self-evaluation (and therefore a loss of self-esteem). Yet, it typically happens in a public setting and the result is as a BAD REPUTATION. Reputation is based on the public's judgment of ones *"persona"* (ones public presentation). Humiliation, Shame, and Guilt (see discussions on Shame and on Guilt) are essential to a socially moral (right/wrong) and ethical (proper/improper) life. The presence of one or more is a warning sign that all is not well within ones selfhood.

Management: For mild or slight shame—i.e. humiliation—an extremely effective and extremely commonly used method is to beat everybody to the punch at laughing at oneself for such a foolish thing one just did. If caught off guard, and immediate good comeback is to say to the person(s): *"well, you got me!"* (see Embarrassment). Most of the time you simply have to bear it.

Very often humiliation comes from you being overly sensitive and *"making a mountain out of a mole hill"* — discerning something big out of the insignificant. This requires discovering why you are hypersensitive — because you picture yourself as perfect; because you see yourself as *"not good enough?"*; because you focus too much on the negative parts of you while failing to appreciate your merits, worth, value, and good ways you relate to the world? Discover the cause and desensitize it.

JEALOUSY

The Story of Jealousy: Gods of Greek mythology were created in the image of those Greeks who showed total immorality and impulsive aggression–e.g. the conquering, mastering, smashing, and thrashing of others. Such is illustrated in the warrior frenzy of the god Ares (i.e. Mars); the poetic frenzy inspired by the Muses; the Bacchic frenzy of Dionysus; the ecstasies of the orgiastic rites of Pan; and, fiercest of all, the Cybele zealots' frenzy of lust (which to the ancient Greeks was called "*Love*").

Cybele, sometimes called the mother of the Greek and Roman mythological gods, was so superb at throwing wild parties in her temple of prostitution that everybody came. All the priests and goddesses, *"carried away"* with the mounting excitement of the party, engaged in such frenzied dancing and sexual activities that *"blazing jealousy"* occurred. Thus, each of the priests and goddesses could see the object of his/her love joining another with closer bonds of friendship than he/she had attained to. As a result, the jealousy expanded into hatred towards the loved object and envy towards the rival.

Thereafter, the link of hatred and envy formed the definition of jealousy. Associated with jealousy was great emotional pain from bonds being broken in the former love relationship. Subsequently, these emotions of hate, envy, and emotional pain have been said to dominate its victim's thoughts, often with varying degrees of fitfulness. The responses to this emotional state range from merely a tendency to grieve and to feel self-pity all the way over to vengefulness.

Understandably, these concepts of jealousy — also called "*zeal*" and "*ardor*" — spread into the Bible as a *"double-edged"* sword. People were supposed to have a zeal for God but, at times, even zeal of a sincere religious motive was deemed improper, as when self-mutilation was one of its expressions. The European anthropomorphic (human thoughts, feelings, and behaviors being attributed to God) practices spoke in terms of a *"jealous God"* for the protection and salvation of his followers (Deut. 4:24). Jealousy was feared in Old Testament times because of its destructive character, especially when present in the mentally deranged.

In the New Testament period it was the jealousy of the religious leaders in Jerusalem that caused Jesus to be arrested (Matt. 27:18). Therefore, jealousy referred to the relationship between one person and another or between a person and an object. For example, jealousy was negatively used to indicate a desire for something that properly belonged to another (Ge. 30:1); positively, as full commitment or intense love (Joel 2:18).

During the Middle Ages, jealousy was related to moral significance. Moralists of the 13th century considered good the inner feelings at the core of zeal (i.e. "*wholehearted devotion*" for a cause) but said that any self-destruction or trying to destroy another out of ill-will at another's good fortune were morally bad. As a result, jealousy, still interwoven with envy, was classed as one of the seven Deadly Sins.

Gradually, *envy* took the emotional aggressive route of ill-will directed toward a rival. By contrast, jealousy remained less aggressive and more personal —

concerning ugly attitudes of suspicion, fear, and uneasiness. Since then, jealousy has been thought of as setting up a tussle of rivalry with the person standing in the way of, or actually taking what the jealous person believes to be his/hers. The anger contained in the core of jealousy leads in the direction of revenge.

The World of Jealousy: In Central Europe, probably through association with "*yellow bile*," a symbol for jealousy is bright yellow — the counterpart of the English' "*green with envy.*" The idea of yellow dates to a belief of ancient philosophers that four liquids (blood, phlegm, black bile, and yellow bile) made up our **Temperament**. For example, too much yellow bile resulted in a short-temper characterized by excessive ferocity, enthusiasm, and zeal (wholehearted devotion). Thus, jealousy and zeal arose from the same source — "*to be aroused*" — and became like different surfaces of the same piece of glass. Subsequently, *zeal* went in the direction of the sentiment drive behind a persistent eager desire, effort, and devotion to a cause, institution, or person.

Such a zeal was shown in the European Dark Ages when wives suspected of unfaithfulness had to undergo a TRIAL BY ORDEAL — extremely crude and unfair ways of settling disputes. For example, in the presence of a priest, a couple was "*brought before the Lord*" and the wife took an oath calling for punishment if guilty (Num. 5:11-31). Dust from the temple floor and ashes from burnt barley were added to water from an earthen vessel. The combination was called the *"Water of Jealousy or bitterness."* The words of the curse were written down and washed off into the water. The wife then drank the water of bitterness and if no ill effect came upon her, she was judged to be guiltless. No penalty was prescribed for a man who falsely accused his wife.

If there was a continued *"spirit of jealousy,"* the husband used **Subrosa** (secrecy behind the scenes) techniques. For example, before the 12th century when glass came to be used in private English houses, windows in homes were simply narrow slits. Over these windows were slatted shutters — called strip, Louvered, or jealousie — which allowed in fresh air, filtered light, and yet kept out rain. The venetian blinds slats covering the windows also enabled a lover or jealous husband to look through them without being seen from inside. Eventually, these were known as *"jealousy windows"* because of their association with a painful emotion in the husband (the subject) about seeing the person he loved (the object) and a third party interacting.

Subsequently, jealousy has been said to involve three parties, compared with only two parties in envy. Jealousy is related to <u>possessiveness</u> of the other, envy to comparison of the self with the other. Envy has in it <u>coveteousness</u> (uncontrollable desire for what belongs to another) plus resentment; jealousy, suspicion plus resentment. We may be envious of those who excel us in fortune or quality or achievement and may even hate them just because of their superiority. We are jealous of those whom we suspect of taking from us something or someone that we regard as rightfully our own — whether that be our mate or our time. A free people must be jealous of their liberties if they would retain them. An almost sure form of jealousy is an older child's anger directed towards a new baby in the family. Such jealousy is linked with quarreling and stimulates hostile acts.

According to psychiatrist, inside the world of jealousy is:

(1) GRIEF — the pain caused by the thought of losing the loved object;

(2) NARCISSISTIC INJURY (i.e. a loss of self-esteem);

(3) ENMITY (hostility, ill-will, hatred) against the successful rival;

(4) SELF-CRITICISM in which one blames oneself for ones loss.

These reactions are distortions of what is true. Hence, jealousy concerns an emotional, passionate desire, whether positive or negative, to possess something. In jealousy, there is more selfishness than love for the other. The jealous mind is a poisoned mind and it always finds more than is real.

Manifestations of Jealousy: Jealousy ("*zeal*") in ancient Greece and Rome implied not only rivalry but emulation (striving to equal or excel), with a consuming earnest persistence in pursuit. This was best shown by ancient Roman priest who served the war goddess Bellona. Because of their fervent (strong feeling) affection for Bellona, their need to express aggression came from frustration generated by a sense of inadequacy in doing enough. To show *"whole hearted devotion"* as ardent fighters for Bellona, they did irrational (e.g. self-mutilation) and intemperate ("*crazy*" and extreme out of control) acts.

Nevertheless, both "jealousy" and "envy" probably come about from observing the liberties of older children, and especially adults, especially when those liberties involved what the child perceived as pleasure and excitement.Jealous children, the best examples of unmasked expressions, are clearly selfish and have feelings of fear, insecurities, powerless from believing they are *"not good enough."*

A second form of Jealousy concerns a fear of losing what one already has: "I want what is mine" and "looking on with suspicion" in a relationship of two or more people. "<u>Suspicion</u>" denotes an apprehension of injury and has more of distrust in it than envy. The suspicious person is altogether fearful of the intentions of another.

A third form is having fervent affections for some cause (e.g. the idea of romance rather than the practice of the romance); feeling inadequate to hold the affection of another; emotional pain from not feeling *"good enough,"* and subsequent irrational actions.

The degree of intensity of "jealousy," "envy," and "hatred" increases as distortions and fantasy start developing within *"the gaze"* of the envier. At that point, the envier starts thinking of the one being watched was *"agitating"* (a Southern term for purposely showing off just to be irritating). This interpretation leads the envier into an attitude of resentment. When it persists, it becomes chronic.

Chronic jealousy shows as a greater attachment for one parent compared with non jealous children as well as more irrational behaviors — like bullying, fighting over "*nothing*," destructiveness, nightmares, and attention-getting activities.

MANAGING JEALOUSY: Whereas ancient Greek type jealousy implied a friendly rivalry involving strong ambition and a zeal-like desire to achieve, its use in Christian circles related to *"Godly jealousy"* — *"Thou shall worship no other God."* Thus, we see the necessity for dealing with and managing jealousy at both spiritual and earthly levels.

The **spiritual correction**, in order to experience blessings, is clear and simple but the work involved is complex and hard. The Old Testament message for people uncommitted to God or who engage in idolatry is to be brought back to a right relationship with God. It adds that the positive side of spiritual jealousy is to be fully committed to and intensely love that which is right, beautiful, the truth, as well as do whatever it takes to maintain good family relations and good character.

In an **earthly correction** sense it is normal for jealousy patterns to occur in children at all levels of intelligence. General management includes measures to increase security, self-confidence, bonds of trust, and being shown socially acceptable alternatives to revenge. For example, their minds can be directed toward expressing whole-hearted pleasure at the news of a friend's success or happiness

For the more mature, jealousy problems in relationships are self-destructive and very personal. Most often, the personal aspect centers around sexual matters. Here, the third party seems to have more of an attraction to the loved one's sexual attention than the jealous person's "*right*" to it — that more is invested than the jealous person can afford to lose.

Look to see what it is costing you to be in the relationship. Have you communicated your needs and expectations and found them to go unheeded? Can you handle your perceived distrustfulness and suspiciousness of the faithfulness of the mate or will you come up with justifications for applying controlling and manipulative behaviors and the invasion of privacy? Is this relationship built on fantasy? If so, the place to start is to get real.

If the jealousy is at a moderate or extreme nature, professional help is needed. If the cause is unrealistic self-centeredness then start releasing this by having *"sympathetic joy pleasure"* at the other's good fortune, whether physical or mental. Then enlarge the scope of such thoughts to cover all of other successes, whether you feel it is justified or not.

PRIDE

The Story of Pride: Biblical thoughts about the Cosmos prior of the creation of man included the belief that pride motivated Satan, a powerful angel, to set his will against God's (Ezek.28:11-19) and thereby become a fallen angel of sin. The Old Testament words for the concept of pride includes swelling, "excellency," or "elevation" to emphasize arrogant behavior. Implied in these words was the idea of the sinful becoming "lifted up" in their balloon wrapping of smoke.

Back then, smoke was often associated with FOOLS. Hot air smoke produced from fireplaces was analogous to the "hot air" of the ranting and raving seen in the boastful and the conceited. So "puffed up" did these prideful people become that their delusions and thoughts of grandeur caused them to be considered as today's equivalent of mild paranoid psychotics. The religious dislike of such fools stemmed from them attributing their honors and glory to themselves and failing to recognize those accomplishments were grounded in God and his goodness. In other words, SINFUL PRIDE CAUSED FOOLS TO TURN AWAY FROM DEPENDENCE ON GOD IN FAVOR OF A SINFUL SELF-RELIANCE.

For this reason pride was assigned, in the 6th century, the first of the "Seven Deadly Sins." Under the canopy of pride there are several family members. For example, when pride becomes exaggerated or assertive or "high" the term applied to this is HAUGHTINESS (taking advantage of an established position while holding others in contempt).

When pride becomes overbearingly or insultingly superior, it is called SUPERCILIOUSNESS — the showing of a pompous superiority of disdain (rejection, as non-verbally conveyed in lifting one eyebrow).

VANITY (groundless self-admiration) is present when pride demands laudation (excessive praise) and admiration.

ARROGANCE, an aggressive form of vanity, consists of an offensive exhibition of assumed superiority because of riches, station, learning, achievements, or domination. Usually, these individual's superiority complex is a cover for an inferiority complex. However, some arrogant "little gods" have been socialized to believe they are superior—and because they did not earn it they must constantly try to reinforce their false belief. In order to get the kudos (glory) fools desire and think they deserve, their vanity deliberately claims it and THEY DECLARE THEMSELVES TO BE THE STANDARD AND THE JUDGE OF EVERYBODY ELSE. And they judge everyone but themselves.

Such arrogance is typically accompanied by INSOLENCE – a complex of ill-mannered rudeness (barbaric), impudence (without shame), contempt (despising and labeling their victims as worthless), and abusiveness (treating badly).

To repeat, because of individualism and materialism rising to prominence at the end of the European Middle Ages, pride and the other traditional vices started becoming desirable and respectable during the Renaissance. Pride, now based upon "price tag" value appearances, was seen as a favourable expression of individual power, money, and White racial assertion.

An off-spring of this "sinful pride" was that of the effort required for a tasteful appearance in clothing. THE APPEARANCE OF BEING WELL-DRESSED TENDED TO GIVE A PROPER ESTIMATE OF THE "PRICE TAG" IMPORTANCE OF THE WEARER. A different type of pride was also prominent during this period. It was associated with people paying attention to detail in order to give good and efficient workmanship as well as a delightful finished product were said to be deserving of "proper" pride.

Since then, at a deeper level, **"**PROPER PRIDE**"** has come to mean possessing those thoughts of rightness or wrongness that lead to good value judgments. As a result, without comparing ourselves with others, we can lovingly support others (Gal. 6:4) by taking pride in their accomplishments as well as our own.

When all of these aspects—those of a sinful prideful attitude, the focus on façade appearance, and the absence of a God notion— are placed into the historical setting of Europeans, the "**European Renaissance mind**" emerges. It was fashioned by the socialization practices of traditionally honoring only their Left Brains and deliberately dishonored their Right Brains. Because the Right brain is the vehicle for expansiveness into higher and multiple planes of existence regarding things like Love, spiritually, compassion, peace, harmony, intuition, synthesis, nonaggression, and unity, these aspects have been un-accessible to White males in general.

It is this "European Renaissance mind" that created and maintained African American slavery — that produced cruelties unparalled in history in its degree of horror, in its duration, in the number of dark-skinned victims involved, and in its lasting effects—-that has designed the subordination of women.

Management: Pride in a spiritual sense is something bad but in a worldly sense is something good. The favorable Pride is dignified sense of what is due to oneself or one's postion, self-respect, and self-esteem of a proper kind.

Its unfavorable connotation means a high and arrogant assumption of superiority in some respect. According to Ancient Africans "Sinful" Pride represents a disconnection from God—that one is responsible for ones benefits in life. Something significant will have to happen in ones life to change to the spirit of humility. Since greed is almost always associated with "Sinful" Pride, the management comments for Greed are applicable here.

SHAME

The Story of Shame: Starting in very ancient times one of the earliest of shameful acts was that of fraudulent tricks — those designed to gain an unfair advantage over a group of people while putting them at an unfair disadvantage. Perhaps around the same there arose the application of shame associated with defeat at the hands of foreign enemies (Ps. 31:15,17) because the defeated were humiliated and confused. This idea of disgrace (loss of honor) found in failure was extended into activities of daily living whenever something wrong (commission) was done or whenever someone failed to do something right (omission).

With public exposure of an omission or commission violation of one of its MORES (moral common sense considered vital to the well-being of the society) and, to a lesser extent, its FOLKWAYS (non-moral rules), the accused was subjected to ridicule and derision (jeering laughter). The fact of being spot-lighted caused the moral person to experience both emotional pain (from being belittled by others) and spiritual pain (from declaring his/her entire self a failure before God).

Biblically, although the Old Testament writers had no concept of "conscience, they did believe that there should be a natural sense of disgrace and unworthiness when one sinned against God or fellow human beings. The HONORABLE were those who worked for virtue and to be disgraced was to have violated their honor and therefore, through deception, God's spiritual rightness. Since the disgraced had not lived up to God's word, they were deemed UNWORTHY to receive God's blessings.

Worshipers of idols and willful sinners of the carnal variety were strongly stigmatized (Phil. 3:19; Jer 2:26). The worse of the carnal variety — that which relates to the physical `flesh" and especially sexual appetites — pertained to "heathen nakedness" or nudity (Rev. 3:18). Furthermore, it was considered appalling to lack shame for sins (Jer. 5). The reason, they said, was that shame is the appropriate evidence of conviction touching anything wrong in God's sight — a reaction against sin, which God himself gives (Rom. 6:21). But where sin is forgiven there need not be cause for shame (Isa. 54:4).

Christian Moralists of the 1st century A.D. declared women praying with uncovered heads or speaking in public worship as shameful (1 Cor. 11:15) conduct. During this time **CONDUCT** covered either the moral aspects of customs or any organized, formal, and public activity. The major reason for having such rules about conduct was to induce the shame aspect as something to be feared and thereby act as a powerful motivator for "*right*" conformity. Thus, shame in a good person would serve as a positive force — either by maintaining a right course of action or by leading to a change toward moral behavior. <u>The idea was to not only do right but also to take pride in the right action itself</u>, rather than to rely on the approval of others. For that to happen, a person had to feel shame at the wrong itself and not merely when the consequences of the wrong doing were experienced— or from "getting caught."

Regardless of whether shame resulted from the wrong itself (see discussion of Guilt), from the consequences of the wrong (shame), and/or from *"getting caught"* (embarrassment), it was a 16th century belief that shame was reflected in a person's face as a somewhat ruddy complexion. The terms *"shame fastness"* and *"shame facedness"* were used to refer to character and to appearance respectively. Meanwhile, the persistence of shameful acts by means of fraudulent tricks resulted in them being given the name SHAM (a mispronunciation of "shame") during the 17th century. Today, shame covers all of these concepts.

The World of Shame: Of the personal social emotions — social attitudes directed toward ourselves rather than others and existing only in a cultural context — it is said that shame, being more widespread, is more prominent than guilt and pride. Without culture, there is no occasion for such emotions — for they rest on thoughts, feelings, beliefs, and values used to interpret and judge behavior. Fear can be present when you are alone but only when other people are involved does shame, as from cowardice, occur. Of course, culture does not completely determine who we are but there is no escaping the dominance of social interaction in developing shame.

In the *Ancient African* shame-based society individuals were controlled by public threats to personal reputation and honor. Since they had no policemen and no jails, each Age-grade was responsible for the conduct of its members. *"Age-grades"* are organizations among certain African and American Indian groups representing a clear-cut division of society (Kenyatta).

From childhood on, each age-grade is allotted special privileges and responsibilities. Beginning at their adolescent initiation and continuing for life, members begin receiving a systematic education — duties of citizenship, tribal history and traditions of communal and individual life. An example is avoiding having babies outside of marriage.

Because all children are the entire tribe's responsibility (hence the African expression: "No child left behind"), sexual intercourse among the unmarried is very restricted. Any unmarried couple not conforming to tribal codes is dealt with by their entire age group. Penalties, lasting for varying periods of time, include not being called to eat with the others; not being allowed to attend dances; having to pay a fine; and enduring ostracism.

Cold-blooded murderers are treated with the greatest contempt because not only have they disgraced themselves but also their Age-mates. Since, public shame is reflected onto the violator's family and kin, they have a strong investment in controlling the behavior of all family members.

Similarly, the *Japanese* have a *"shame"* culture in the setting of harmony and hard work. Their concern for not acting in a dishonorable way partially explains why relatively little intra-group conflict exist in Japan. However, when shame is the major sanction, a person does not experience any relief when faults are confessed. The persistence of their emotional pain requires adjustment, time, and watchfulness. The reason for careful watchfulness is that shame, along with hopelessness, guilt, depression, and hostility, are important causes of suicide.

After following a winding history of *Western* concepts, today's thoughts about shame (and guilt) concern an unwanted exposure of one's private self— that part of each of us that we do not want to expose. Examples in USA society include disgusting exhibitionism, unwanted exposure of one's private body parts (e.g. genitals, even during coitus); and voyeurism (*"peeping Tom"*). Those <u>moderate</u> or <u>extreme</u> shameful acts which catch the attention of other people are likely to invite blame and ridicule. However, the societal consequences are no longer anywhere near as bad as they use to be. In fact, some people who do startling shameful things can become celebrities to the point of getting movie or book writing contracts.

People handle public disgrace in various ways — expressing deep sorrow from the humiliation (*"I did it and I shouldn't have done it and they let me know it and I feel terrible"*); making retributions to the victims or to the public at large through public service; buying off people, as the mafia does in supporting certain causes; staying put and enduring it; or moving away and starting a new life.

Managing Shame: As noted above, Shame-provoking situations vary widely among the different cultures. People are ashamed of things disapproved of by their particular culture. Since Babies show no evidence of shame, psychologists suggest that shame is learned as a fear reaction. The conflict is caused by either the fear of or the actual failing to meet expectations or ideals held by oneself or by others — and it is especially stressful when it is unexpected.

Hence, **training the child** includes those methods used for managing fear. Start by discussing what is expected and the "why" before the shame situation occurs. My mother would send me to my room with the promise to come up later to punish me. Besides *"dying a thousand deaths"* while waiting "forever," I had the time to think about what I did. Then she would recreate what the situation was, what I did wrong, and how I could have handled it differently.

Some Black caretakers I have seen, in dealing with impulsive children with a long history of getting into trouble, *simply hold them lovingly for an extended period while rocking back and forth.* Only when a **loving connection** has been established do they gently guide the child's behavior into a better way. Nothing works better than bonding through love!

Self-developed shame comes from over-sensitivities about the way you think and feel; what you say and how you say it; what you do and the way you do it; and how you appear because of your physical body (e.g. skin disorders) or what you are wearing. This is especially true of teenagers. Consider the possibility that there is nothing wrong with you but rather that you are so different that people do not know how to deal with you. If this is true, then maybe you need to seek out a different group of people with whom you are compatible. Otherwise, honor who you are as you are and make the most out of it. This adjustment is made easier by doing things to help other people.

Shame may be Created for You, as in making you the victim of rumors and gossip. Or, thoughtless parents may "show you up" by telling your secrets, and publicly blaming or criticizing you. Sometimes this problem can be handled by sincerely and calmly explaining the truth. Most often it is best to simply let it go. However, if enough is at stake, you can sue the false accuser—but this is inviting more trouble, time, and money than it is worth in the long run.

Very often the shameful feeling comes from you being overly sensitive and *"making a mountain out of a mole hill"* — discerning something big out of the insignificant. This requires discovering why you are hypersensitive — because you picture yourself as perfect; because you see yourself as *"not good enough?"*; because you focus too much on the negative parts of you while failing to appreciate your merits, worth, value, and good ways you relate to the world? To help institute the necessary corrections by bringing things back to realism and into a proper balance, write out all the good fortune you have and follow that with how to correct your limitations and weaknesses.

Maybe you need to start fitting your goals within the context of your abilities and determination to complete them. Maybe you need to do better planning, preparation, and practice for your performance. Maybe you need to get a cosmetic expert to show you how to take advantage of whatever there is about you that you are not proud of. Maybe you need to get a coach who can improve your education, training techniques, or competitive skills. Maybe you are in the wrong place to discover, develop, or apply your unique skills in a way that you are true to yourself and yet give people what they want.

Spiritual Shame results when you have not lived up to your highest self and have therefore interfered with your ethical (proper/improper) integrity or moral wholeness. The first thing to do is to stop making it worse. To say: *"since I have done wrong I might as well keep doing it"* will only multiply your trials and tribulations — your troubles and difficulties.

Eventually, the repetition of shameful acts—and especially your acceptance of doing shameful acts— will desensitize you to doing them. When you are no longer inspired to feel shame, you are well on the way to becoming an immoral or amoral person — like racists and the anti-social.

In summary, spiritual shame says: *"I have gone against my ethical codes of what is proper and I feel bad about the consequences and about getting caught."* Earthly shame says: *"I have wounded my self-concept of not doing the proper and decent thing. My feelings are so wounded that I do not want anybody to see me in my weakened state."*

Management includes correcting your tactlessness, your errors in taste, and your lack of skill in civility. Since you can do nothing about the spiritual pain that comes from spiritual shame and since you can not erase what caused the shame, the best thing is to learn the lessons it teaches; put those lessons into practice; and let of all else that was associated with the bad emotions inside shame.

VI

EMOTIONS INSIDE MINDSETS

Emotions are Heaven or Hell on Earth

EMOTIONS Gathered out of

Hate are HELL

Emotions Gathered out of

Tranquility are Heaven

A **Mindset** is that which produces a certain kind of reproducible thinking; is on a certain plane of existence; is either organized or disorganized; and is about the constructive, the destructive, or a combination of both. The main ones are largely influenced by ones philosophy of life and the type of desires springing out of that philosophy.

Some mindsets are about reality; some, about distortions of reality; some operate inside a fantasy or a delusional world; and some have combinations of the others. According to Ancient Africans, any mindsets that do not consistently deal with reality are in a condition of ignorance. There are instances, however, when one must develop coping and defense mechanism for purposes of self-protection—and either or both may not deal with reality.

Coping mechanisms are actions taken to make it easier to get along inside ones environment.There is a framework set up in most societies as to the nature and the degree of what coping mechanisms are acceptable. With respect to coping or defense mechanisms an individual in any culture or any subculture may follow one type, alternate, or compromise.

Defense mechanisms (Table VIII) are ways of handling philosophical and/or psychological concerns occurring within oneself. Those ways are either mature or immature escapes from reality. Their purposes are to preserve ones self-esteem—i.e. self-identity, self-meaning, self-image, and/or self-concept—in relation to worth (the best things in life that are free) and value (things money can buy or power can acquire) that make up ones system of values (Bailey, Self-Esteem; Bailey, Anger).

Some defense mechanisms are called forth "after the fact" — i.e. after we have accidentally exposed our private self (parts of us that we do not want others to see), or have created a flaw in our public self. Whereas your *Self-Concept* involves how you see yourself, your *Public Self* involves how you want others to see you. Your *Persona* is how they actually see you and that determines your *Reputation.*

Profound or deep Constructive Self-Esteem is the result of having earned multiple successes as a result of sound Common Sense and Rational Thinking skills. Profound or deep Low Self-Esteem comes from the child, before the age of reason, having such extensive damage to his/her self-worth and/or self-value system of values as to develop self-hatred and even hatred of his/her own social group.

Partial Constructive Self-Esteem comes from, after the age of reason, deciding that you are "almost Okay." This mindset is the result of believing that despite being really good in certain things related to worth and value, you feel bad about being "so-so" in others and not good in the rest of the things you do (i.e. partial poor self-esteem). But what you fail to realize is that this is the identical scenario present in those who *choose to believe* they have a complete and Constructive Self-Esteem. The distinquishing feature between these two mindsets is that the latter possess self-confidence and an intense desire to keep **getting "better and better everyday, and in every way"** (Couve).

Some self-esteem, whether constructive or not, can be boosted by certain successes or failures. But these— unless one continues to have multiple small successes and unless one benefits from ones failures—are only *Temporary Alterations in Self-Esteem.* Examples occur when one is shamed or when one has "talked oneself UP" through the power of positive thinking or with affirmations.

In fact, each of us has a number of edited and temporary public selves which we select from to present to different people in different circumstances. For example, you present one public self to your date, another to your friends, and still another at a job interview. Only to close buddies can you display your private self. Society seems to require that we tailor make our presentations to others — a means of "going along to get along." In reality, sophisticated people see through temporary alterations to who one really is.

Most people only see that part of us which is inbetween the public self and the persona, based on our calculated efforts to present a certain image. This is perfectly normal and all of us do it but yet it is still deceitful. That is the reason women use make up and do cosmetic things to their hair and fingernails; or why males do the "macho" things they do.

In other words, "Impression Management" is done as a self-defense mechanism to maintain self-respect and self-esteem as well as to make it easy for people to respect us, to like us (or at least not be against us), and to "buy" whatever we are "selling." Inside each "Impression Management" is some type of emotion.

DEFENSE MECHANISMS

In order to acquire or maintain our top values related to worth and value or to slow, stop, or reverse the adverse progress associated with losing things of worth and value, we resort to defense mechanisms — the doing of those things which *Save Face* (i.e. what ever we design to protect our self-esteem). The specific type of defense mechanism selected depends upon the type of situation a person is facing and the kind of self-esteem that person is trying to protect.

Defense mechanisms are used to prevent threats and the resultant anxiety to one's self-esteem; to assist in the rescue of a loss of self-esteem at the time disturbances are happening; to serve in a recovery capacity after self-esteem has been damaged to the point of death; and as emergency measures whereby one draws on a certain defense mechanisms as a coping techniques to get past the moment.

There are hundreds of defense mechanisms (Table VIII) and inside each there may be a large number of different emotions—any one of which may rise to a controlling power inside the mind. For example, *Deceptive Credit* — i.e. taking full credit for goodnesses or good works we did with others when others were significantly contributory may be about feeling the lack of a sense of power or having a poor self-esteem or as a form of revenge or an intense desire to be in the spotlight.

As a rule of thumb all defense mechanisms have in common the quality of: (1) self-deception (either as denial or disguise); (2) of being prophylactic (i.e. designed to prevent shame, embarrassment, guilt, or anxiety); (3) getting past the moment of shock or the lesser degree of shock called "frustration"; or (4) of allowing us to continue seeing ourselves as commendable, admirable, strong, and whatever else we see is needed to maintain self-respect as best we can. Here are some specific examples gathered from the literature and most have been discussed in my book on "Anger":

Table VIII -- **Defense Mechanisms**

I. Narcissistic Defenses
   A. Projection
   B. Denial
   C. Distortion

II. Immature Defenses
   A. Acting out
   B. Blocking
   C. Hypochondriasis
   D. Introjections
   E. Passive-Aggressive Behavior
   F. Regression
   G. Schizoid Fantasy
   H. Somatization

III. Neurotic defenses
   A. Controlling
   B. Displacement
   C. Dissociation
   D. Externalization
   E. Inhibition
   F. Intellectualization
   G. Isolation
   H. Rationalization
   I. Recreation formation
   J. Repression
   K. Sexualization

IV. Mature Defenses
   A. Altruism
   B. Anticipation
   C. Asceticism
   D. Humor
   E. Sublimation
   F. Suppression

EMOTIONS INSIDE ADDICTIONS

The Story of Addictions: Long, long ago when Religion and Superstition were beginning to untangle from each other, uncivilized religious brutes, in the name of some god, fanatically prosecuted anyone for not being a votary (one vowed to the service of a god) or for lacking religious fervor. Those showing fervor and displaying votary actions implied the *"giving over"* of themselves to a god — the early central idea contained in "*addict.*"

During the Roman Empire period (753 BC-476 AD), "addictus" referred to a debtor awarded as a slave to his creditor. The blending of the votary and slave aspects carried its meaning into Biblical times. The main idea was "to devote oneself" to any person or party as, for example, to the service of saints (1 Cor 16:15). The purpose of the devotion was for the arranging and ordering of a situation that expressed true love (I Cor 10:23-33).

Because some people expressed love in a good or a bad way, the sense of addict, as it left ancient times, pertained to a habit or practice of taste of expression. During the Middle Ages the Church's belief that an addict was one who had given oneself to something sinful was influential in having the habitual sinful being *"bound over to"* for sentencing by the legal court system.

The early 20th century saw the appearance of "addict" referring to alcohol and the various drug abuses (e.g. morphine, heroin) in those who had lost self-control. It became clear that the manifestations of **DRUG ADDICTION** (e.g. opiates, barbiturates) included: (1) a preoccupation with obtaining the drug; (2) a persistent use of the drug from an inner compulsion (or overpowering urge); (3) the use of the substance despite anticipation of probable adverse consequences; (4) repeated failed efforts to cut down on or control the substance usage; (5) a tendency to increase the dose due to increasing tolerance (i.e. it takes more and more to do less and less of the desired effect); and (6) both a physiological and psychological dependence on its effects.

The World of Addiction: Each of us is addicted to something. My addiction is to learning and writing and trying to help make the lives of others better. With other people, addiction occurs in those who are highly susceptible to something, most commonly to substance abuse (e.g. alcohol, drugs) or to those whose lives have gotten off track to the point of operating out of delusions.

Chances are that a host of bad emotions (e.g. chronic anger, helplessness, hopelessness, emotional and spiritual pain, apathy, etc.) led to an out of control Functional Philosophy. That Functional Philosophy then took on a life of its own and thereby detached or dissociated from one's Real Self. Meanwhile, all sorts of measures were tried to get relief from the glob of bad emotions and whatever gave even a bit of relief was repeated over and over with decreasing benefit as it was forming a bad addiction.

Still, those same bad emotions remain inside the delusional mindset that one has allowed to happen—and, in addition, new ones have appeared as a result of being a victim of the addiction. Usually, chronic anger significantly contributes to the addiction and then gets worse simply from becoming an addict.

Thus, chronic anger is directed at the abuser (i.e. the trigger person who is said to have caused the problem); at oneself for being a slave to the drug; at oneself for being too weak to let it go; at oneself for giving up one's destination in life; and at those who do not freely give money to enable the addiction to go on without a struggle to get money. Fear is an ever-present emotion. Self-hate causes one to willing accept self-destruction and destruction done to them by others. So does guilt.

There is also a tremendous amount of emotional pain and spiritual pain present inside the addiction. Both of those pains are so overwhelming in scope and magnitude as to cause the person to be willing to hurt others in hopes of either getting some temporary relief or because "misery loves company."

Managing Addictions: A turning point is for one to get honest with oneself by acknowledging the addiction and taking responsibility for persisting in an addicting state. These constitute a substitution of powerless to the stepping inside the power arena. Any addiction clouding the mind blocks one's awareness of what is meaningfully going on in one's mind. Hence, it takes help to gain mental insights.

What the addict then discovers is that he/she does not know who he/she is as a person because of being dissociated from his/her Real Self. Furthermore, it is typical for addicts to have told so many lies that they make those lies self-fulfilling prophesies by living the lie and then believing the lies they tell. As a result, they wear a thousand masks. Obviously, this makes correction very complicated. Substance abuse is an issue best handled by Alcoholics Anonymous and its drug equivalents.

This requires admitting one's suffering and then seeking a professional who can help—and without making things worse. The sooner treatment is started the better. The same applies to relapses.

Relapses come from all the things that caused the addictions in the first place and all the bad habits acquired while on the habit. Rehabilitation is merely a tool. It is important to find people around who show the addict how to use that tool and then help the addict continue to use it indefinitely.

For lesser forms of addiction, it is helpful to become an addict at writing in a journal everything that is on ones mind. The main point is to face reality and this requires courage and overcoming fear. Eventually one will stumble on the core thought or emotion related to the bad emotion causing the problem. When that occurs, one is likely to feel as if a "raw nerve" has been hit and this may bring one to tears. From this point on one can use any of the methods discussed under "Tools."

An essential tool for recovering from any addiction starts with Forgiveness. Both self-forgiveness and forgiveness of the trigger person are done so that the addict can move on with his/her life.

EMOTIONS INSIDE APATHY

The Story of Apathy: The word "Apathy" comes from the Greek apatheia, impassivity. Aristotle used the word as an antonym of pathos "arousing the feeling." To The Stoics — a school of Greek philosophers of 300 B.C. who believed that humans should be free of passion — apathy meant freedom from emotion. In his "Ladder of Divine Ascent", Saint John Climacus (A.D. 525-606) used apathy for the state of grace humans will reach if they make it to the top of the ladder.

In 16th century Europe, as the opposite of SYMPATHY ("feeling with someone else"), "Apathy" denoted an indifference to whatever appealed to sympathy or emotion or passion. Philosphers considered apathy necessary in order to make room for clear reasoning. By the 18th century, there were great efforts in increasing the number of words which attempted to portray feelings from within. Thus, the sense of apathy shifted to laziness of the mind; then to lack of concern, especially in matters of general importance;and then onto a heaviness and dullness that may at times amount to sluggishness and even stupidity. In psychiatry, the idea of a stuporous state (suspension of senses or feelings) characterized apathy as an absence of feeling from the psychical, not from the physical.

The World of Apathy: Today, one belief inside the word APATHY is fatalistic in that whatever happens must happen and all events are determined by necessity. An emotion characterizing Apathy is an indifference to or a LACK OF INTEREST IN or DESIRE FOR ACTIVITY, especially in matters of general importance or appeal.

To help illustrate what the emotion is like, recall that after getting in our car and starting the engine, we adjust the gear-shift to go forward, backwards, or into neutral. To go forward or backward means that two gears, which look like toothed wheels, engage each other so that one gear can push the other around. When the gear-shift is in neutral, the two gears are disengaged and are no longer interlocking.

In a way, our minds work like gears. When we are happy, our minds seem like they have been shifted to forward gear; when sad, into reverse gear; but when we have apathy we are in neutral gear. Apathy's features of indifference, withdrawal, inactivity, and inattentiveness are the opposite of Aggression and are not the same as passive. One can be passive and yet care about something but with apathy there is no caring. Apathy at least indicates that aggressive tendencies are being held in check or inhibited. The subject of Apathy is extensively discussed in my book on Self-Esteem and therefore only brief comments will be made here.

Much of my experience with Apathetic youth came when I did volunteer teaching bimonthly with the Los Angeles Conservation Corp—a program run by the city which hired youth from low-income families to help beautify the city. Some of these youth were soft and gentle while others were "tough guys." A burning question that arose from my association with the "tough guys" is "why do they not care what happens to them?" Surprisingly, many seemed to face with indifference their daily encounters with possible death.

Perhaps part of the answer relates to "burnout" and apathy. To survive in their environment meant they stopped being who they are in order to become tough, hard, and unfeeling. To repress emotions in one area means to repress them in other areas. Without realizing it, they probably came to act out that role all the time. In response to the daily "bad stuff" they have to deal with, while being someone they are not, it is conceivable that the accumulation of gradual mental stress **— BURNOUT** — overwhelms them.

If so, it then becomes an easy next step into the APATHY SYNDROME of being disengaged, indifferent, impulsive, irritable, suspicious, and unwilling to talk about stress or anything else — a defense mechanism of *emotional insulation* which helps youth maintain their stability in the face of stress.

The protective shell of indifference or cynicism is: "nothing really matters anyway." At first, retreating behind a curtain of indifference is beneficial for purposes of separating oneself from inhuman conditions. However, as it progresses into a way of life, it becomes more and more destructive towards the significance of others (e.g. "drive-by-shootings).

To be distinguished from Apathy are BOREDOM (which is due to blocking of expressive activity) and problems with hope and DESPAIR— the belief that one will not get what one desires based upon on a view of external circumstances — i.e. loss of hope. Whereas despair is associated with depression, DESPERATION embraces a HERD mentality — the tendency to think and act as one of a crowd (Bailey, Rising Above Poverty). Whereas extreme DEPRESSION may be combined with chronic HELPLESSNESS (a learned pattern of no longer trying to avoid negative events), a destructive Herd mentality concerns chronic rage, strong feelings of impotence, and reckless action or violence from frustration.

Nevertheless, the emotions inside Apathy include what is inside boredom, despair, desperation, depression, and helplessness. Whereas the apathetic mind is in neutral gear (having given up), the Herd mentality is in the process of shifting into reverse gear (in the process of giving up). Destructive feelings inside Apathy may be of several types as mentioned above. But those I have specifically noticed are those that involve different degrees of HOPELESSNESS (losing interest in living and giving up from a defeatist attitude toward life); DESPAIR ("they won't let me have it," as hope slips away); and DESPONDENCY (a deep dejection arising from a conviction of the uselessness of further effort to reach a secret dream). One belief that one will not live much longer and the threat of hopelessness causes DESPERATION (frustrations leading to rage with impatience, intolerance, and reckless or violent actions).

Management of Apathy: So how can these destructive mental states be slowed, stopped, or reversed? The fact that the youth have not given up hope completely is a place to explore. If their embers of hope glow to better the lives of loved ones, then fan those embers into a flame. However, because of their dimming ember of self-interest, inner city mentors are the best ones to fan the flame of hope. Any mentor willing to spend the time, give love, caring, patience, tolerance, and persistence to establish a mutual trust can be effective. Once bonding has been established, here are some additional suggestions.

Step I is helping the youth to feel SAFE.

Step II is applying the discipline needed to BECOME A REAL PERSON again to oneself (even though giving up the "tough guy" image to survive in the world of competition may not be practical). The process involves returning to ones Real Self—a subject extensively discussed in many of my books, such as Selfhood Mastery.

Step III is the establishment of a sense of BELONGING — the feeling of acceptance through friendly relationships with the community, social groups, friends, and one's heritage. Having pleasant experiences in nature helps one connect to the "soul" of the universe. Family and community need to do more things together — dance, art, sports, and fishing. It is particularly important to have a common purpose or goal whereby everyone contributes.

Step IV—To counteract apathy — the USA disease — is to shed unwanted isolation and excessive individualism.

Step V is to do what it takes to generate "Aliveness" and curiosity so as to overcome their difficult time finding energy for daily living.

In summary, apathetic inner city youth can automatically spin into despair, desperation, or depression—and vice versa, automatically spin out of despair, desperation, or depression into apathy. In anyone of those mental states a person's mind can go into any of the others, get worse (despondency, suicide), or get better. Thus, apathy is a sliding state of neutral, negative, and destructive thoughts and feelings that together cause people to have a lack of interest in what happens to them.

EMOTIONS INSIDE ARROGANCE

Arrogance ("to make great claims about oneself") is like the hub of a wheel that has many spokes, each of which has common features with the hub and its own unique features (see those discussed under "Pride"). One spoke is an aggressive form of *Vanity* (self-admiration and a desire to be admired by others that is groundless). A second spoke is *Dogmatic* in which one does not trouble oneself to give a reason—either because of the strength of ones convictions or because of ones contempt for those whom one addresses. A third spoke is a sense of *Entitlement* whereby one takes upon oneself more power or authority than is rightly justified.

The hub consists of destructive selfishness, Individualism, Greed, and Pride—all combining to fashion an exaggerated sense of self; fashions claims for the best; and consists of an offensive exhibition of real or assumed superiority, insolent pride, and domination.

The Story of Arrogance: The background to the ideas contained in arrogance came out of ancient times when the Egyptian king was the center — as a human representative of the power made celestially manifest either in the sun or in the moon and thereby making the king a man-god. By contrast, the much later appearing Mesopotamians (i.e. subsequently called Sumerian) kings were not deemed gods. Their critical dissociation between the spheres of God and man eventually decisively separated the religious systems of the Occident (only the "Vicar") from the Orient (god-king) (Campbell, An Introduction, p. 114; Campbell, Primitive Myth, p. 147).

Throughout history, people—mainly of the upper social class— who believe special privileges have been owed them reflect narcissistic entitlement. This means they expect to be treated as VIPs (an abbreviation for "Very Important Person"). In a Biblical sense, arrogance was "sinful Pride" and greed—and deemed evil because both were about worshipping an idol (Col. 3:5) instead of God. Obvious examples of arrogant little gods were those involved in the slave trade during African American slavery. Less obvious but equally evil are the vast majority of those who control the top power positions in the Americas.

As always, such individuals retain a sense of entitlement and are in a position to get and take more than they deserve. For example, top level Europeans have seen to it — by means of the gun — that they possess unfair advantages and immediately go on the offensive to attack anyone who threatens their greedy pursuits. In turn, they are characteristically quite fearful of their victims — the Amerindians (whose gold and silver they stole) and Black people (whose land, riches, and people they stole).

The World of Arrogance: Children who are pampered, catered to, and "spoiled" to the point of not only retaining their original self-centered mindset but also believing their omnipotence is real are beginning examples of "little gods." Thus, instead of the advancement toward maturity — from a childhood love of self to an expanding of this by embracing adult social concerns and love for others — from a hedonistic orientation to some degree of altruism— they remain immature with a "little god" mentality.

What was normal for these "little gods" as little children now becomes abnormal and disturbing when, as adults, they remain overly concerned with themselves. They escape responsibility and the risk of failure by being totally self-absorbed and self-involved while others take care of them and prevent them from knowing what it is to work. This keeps them with a very narrow focus and an absent of awareness of others.

At the same time, by not being liked by outsiders they compensate for those feelings of inadequacy by exaggerating their own personal qualities — and never admitting ever having been wrong or having made a mistake. Instead, they blame and project. They feel entitled to priviledges before others and take first whatever is the best.

The arrogant, by often being intelligent and in power positions, do a great deal of destruction to large numbers of people. Essentially, they have a philosophy of life (POL) based upon pursuing things of Value (e.g. money, possessions, power over people) in their self-declared capacity of "*little gods*." These are their only two friends.

By possessing a superiority complex, "*little gods*" have a sense of entitlement and a stubbornly childish mind set of "*I want what I what and I want it now*." They are a greedy bunch and will use any means nccessary — lie, cheat, steal, intimidate, kill — to try to satisfy their greed. But they never reach a state of satisfaction because greed is about trying to fill a bottomless pit — meaning that there is never enough money, possessions, property, or fame to bring them happiness.

Management: The arrogant and their practices need to be understood for self-defense purposes. Four major forms of selfishness are: (1) winner selfishness (self-improvement without hurting others); (2) win-win selfishness (self-improvement while helping others); (3) win-lose selfishness (greediness while hurting others); and (4) loser selfishness (the creation of self-suffering by a lack of caring for oneself). So why be aware of and understand the contents of these four forms? Answer: because the mind is often blind to the identification of the causes and effects to that for which it has no meaning or even no words.

For the arrogant who desire to change, Constructive Selfishness (i.e. the winner and win-win types) is to be cultivated as if they are flowers in a garden. Destructive selfishness (the win-lose and loser types) is to be weeded out of one's character. An approach is as follows.

Step I is to understand that "*little gods*" lack compassion for others. COMPASSION, the cornerstone of good character, is not based upon emotions but rather upon a very precise sense of belonging to the totality of the universe. This comes out of the Ancient African concept that all human beings are connected to each other and to God by the "*glue*" of love. Such a recognition of spiritual kinship of self and others is the beginning of EMPATHY. The "*Love*" connection part of compassion emits a sincere concern and heartfelt caring for the pain and suffering of others as well as inclines one take corrective actions.

Step II is to switch from hateful thoughts (anger at another's well-being) and evil deeds over to the cultivation of GENTLENESS — i.e. kindness, tenderness, quietness. Loving kindness, the opposite of hatred, is the desire for the happiness of another and being happy for the sources of happiness for another. Compassion, the opposite of cruelty (delight in another's suffering), is the desire that others be free from suffering and from the source of suffering. A Dali Lama method is to view an individual as you would your mother so as to bring forth the sense of gentleness; fondness, cherishing, affection, and gratitude. Do this until it becomes "*second nature.*"

Step III is locating all bad habits one has accumulated as result of evil practices as well as the associated bad attitudes. This requires keeping a diary in detail of all greed related activities and writing them out everyday. Even more helpful is to ask friends — and especially enemies — about what they observe about you and the bad experiences they have had in dealing with you.

Step IV is to consult the various books in libraries and bookstores on the mental health methods used by Tibetan Buddhists.

EMOTIONS INSIDE COMPLEXES

Two of the most complexes related to emotions are those of an Inferiority Complex and a Superiority Complex. Since both have been discussed in my book on Self-Esteem, only brief mention of them will be made here.

The Story of Complexes: The idea of the word *"complex"* arose from 13th century psychologist who used the *"four humours"* theory to explain human characteristics, traits, and features. They believed the mixing of certain humours in certain proportions caused certain definite body constitutions, complexions, dispositions, temperaments, and habits of the mind. Each constitution was called a *"complex"*. Thereafter, *"complex"* implied *"a whole comprising amounts of various parts."*

In the 18th century, psychologist defined *"complex"* as a group of related ideas, feelings, memories, and impulses which operate together and may be repressed or inhibited together. To be distinguished was a "**Syndrome**" — a group of related signs and symptoms in an unhealthy person. These syndrome groups of thoughts and feelings, consolidated into a complex unit mass, were not necessarily morbid or abnormal.

Meanwhile, arising from the same Indo-European root, *"inferior"* and *"infernal"* carried the idea of *"Hell"* in Western society and, when applied to humans, *"the Personality"* (or lower self) in Eastern society. Then *"inferior"* and *"complex"* were put together to designate the twine-like braiding of bad thoughts and bad feelings into a *"mental hell"* — *"bad"* being defined as that which slows, stops, or reverses one's wholesome progress. In 1907 this "braid" appeared in the English language as a psychoanalytic concept.

Alfred Adler (1870-1937), credited with coining *"inferiority complex,"* said it consists of strong feelings of inadequacy and insecurity stemming from real or fancied deficiencies of a physical, mental, or social nature. The overall result — when combined with anxiety, resentment, and over-compensatory drives — would be to adversely affect the individual's entire adjustment to life.

With respect to Europeans, Myers (Social Psych. P52) quoted John Powell as saying that *"all of us have inferiority complexes. Those who seem to not have such a complex are only pretending."* Humanistic psychologist Carl Rogers concluded, said Myers, that most people (again speaking of Europeans) he knew *"despise themselves, regard themselves as worthless and unlovable."* Myers added that many popularizers of humanistic psychology concur (those concerned with higher human motives, self-development, knowledge, understanding, and esthetics).

An Inferiority and a Superiority Complex both relate to **Self-esteem** (i.e. what you think of your worth and value). Worth is about spiritual things (peace, harmony, love) and Value is about worldly things (money, possessions, appearances, power over people, prestige). Self-esteem may be *Constructive* (i.e. living up to the traits of good character with a sense of self-confidence); *Arrogant* (being successful by means of bad character); or *Low* (placing a poor grade on one's self-worth and/or self-value so that one does not feel "good enough").

INFERIORITY COMPLEX: When Low Self-Esteem is present in multiple areas of ones life, it is an Inferiority Complex. There are three universal and consistent diagnostic criteria for an inferiority complex.

First is that a vulnerable patient declares some failure in some significant aspect of his/her life to be *"malignant."* Its malignant nature is easily detected during an open and honest discussion.

Second is the malignant force contained inside the declared failure.

Third is an attack of oneself as a person. This self-attack — whether detected at the beginning, middle, or end stage of an Inferiority Complex — is the most obvious diagnostic manifestation.

These three result in anger; fear (from a perceived inability to solve problems and thereby have ones since of safety and security threatened); depression; emotional pain; frustration; and helplessness.

An illustrative situation occurred during African American slavery. The methods used by the captors on the slaves were so devastating that varying degrees of psychic mutilation (among other terrible things) occurred to practically every slave. Following slavery, mental recovery began and progressed very slowly in Black Americans. Today, their recovery ranges from almost none to complete.

Many on the lower end of recovery have deflated self-esteem and (1) believe themselves to be a failure as a person; (2) engage in self-destructive personal attacks; and (3) malignantly tear down whatever self-esteem remains — the three fundamental features of an inferiority complex.

A step above an inferiority complex are people with a rather **Confined sense of an Inadequacy** type of low self-esteem. One of their features is a frustrated selfishness. Yet, they, like those with a full blown inferiority complex, fail to fully recognize their self-worth (e.g. peace, harmony, love, fellowship) or self-value (e.g. those talents and skills that can be sold in the marketplace).

As a result, they fail to honor or appreciate themselves. This leaves little or no room in their minds to do the necessary amount of self-love or to show compassion for others because of being overwhelmed with problems. Their focus is either on trying to recover from problems, on trying to escape from problems, or on feeling sorry for themselves. So how can these forms of self-esteem problems (e.g frustration selfishness) be corrected?

Step I is realizing that fundamental to human existence is the necessity of caring for oneself as well as caring for others. To leave out one or both automatically results in an unhappy life. Ancient Africans believed that love is everywhere and circulates between oneself and others. Thus, to help oneself in a loving way is to help others and to help others is to help oneself. Therefore, if one is blocking the flow of one's love, it also blocks love directed toward others. Similarly, if one allows love to be received from others, that love can help heal whatever is disrupting one's well-being.

Step II is the practice of aspiring to achieve happiness and to be free from suffering. Starting in slavery and continuing to the present, most Black Americans have made a habit of "*making do.*" This is essential for survival but is obstructive to thriving. During four centuries of the slave trade, Europeans taught Africans to be suspicious of, distrust, and fight each other. To slow, stop, and reverse the resultant social dissention, it takes the effort of all Black Americans.

Step III: Social studies have shown that demonstrating compassion to oneself and fellow suffers facilitates recovery from stress, trauma, and psychic mutilation. Inside the frustration selfishness of Black Americans are a host of bad thoughts and bad emotions. If one cannot afford to get professional help, then the hard work of discovering what these bad mental activities and eliminating them are will be well-worth the effort. In the process of discovery, this is done by getting the opinions of friends and enemies and writing out all bad thoughts and bad emotions.

Step IV is getting rid of bad habits by using the method of Step III. Hate, chronic anger, and a sense of powerlessness need to be replaced with their opposites.

Step V is to mature out of stubbornness through the process of developing Rational Thinking skills.

Step VI is working daily on a legacy purpose — the goal you want to leave to the world.

SUPERIORITY COMPLEX (also called Pseudo-Good Self-Esteem; the Aristocentric; and the "European Renaissance mindset") occurs when one disguises ones Inferiority Complex with an inordinate claim to superiority. They are of two types—the Façade and the Socialized.

The *Façade*—the false front—of arrogance shows as a reality of aggression. It occurs in those who have Low Self-Esteem and therefore these bullies select scapegoats to despise, beat up on, and look down upon. They feel "superior" when they can create misfortunes in their scapegoats.

The socialized "*little gods*" are at a development level as that of teenager "spoiled brats" which is characterized by an attitude of entitlement to the best or to whatever they want. Thus, through guns and a willingness to kill people, they take whatever they want and whenever they want it. They are full of fear, insecurity, envy, and hostility while lacking appreciation, compassion, love, and happiness. In addition, their greedy pursuits of money, possessions, power over people, status, prestige, fame, the most desirable sexual conquest, and other things of value related to the material world create for them many problems.

One of those problems is in causing resentment in victims and the worry of stirring victims to retaliate in overt, tempered, masked, or concealed ways. Thus, because of their evilness, Fear is their main emotional problem—and this has spread throughout the mindsets of Europeans.

Another is their unearned superiority places a constant burden on them to prove it with dangerous adventures (e.g. by auto racing). Even then, rarely, if ever being able to meet this burden of proof, they tend toward fantasy and secretiveness — fabricating stories to make them look good and/or to make others look bad. In addition, they fail to tell things that would cause them to look bad (e.g. their barbaric and savage history) or to cause their competitor to appear great. For this to happen requires lying, cheating, and stealing. When projected on to others, such dishonorableness takes the form of racial verbal attacks.

A third problem is the evil deeds they resort to in order to maintain their façade of superiority — stomping on, tearing down, grabbing from, and spreading vicious rumors or myths about those victims whom they consider their equals or superiors. They have left paths of destruction for tens of thousands of years. Envy drives the process of "I tear you down while I build myself up" and of to "win at any cost — and by any means necessary."

EMOTIONS INSIDE DELUSIONS

To watch a magician saw a woman in half is to observe an illusion. To believe the magician actually sawed the woman in half is a delusion. An **Illusion** is deception caused by something appearing to be other than it really is—so that what is seen does not exist the way it is seen. For example, the magician is performing an illusion because actually two women are involved — the one you see and the other one already hidden in the same box with the one you can see. Such appearances can seem very real to the naïve — so real as to require much proof to realize they are not real. Illusions are temporarily held mistaken or distorted perceptions of the five senses (sight, hearing, smell, taste, and touch) or false impressions of reality from faulty thinking. A mirage is an illusion.

Whereas the question of belief does not arise in illusions, *Delusions (believing what was not real and to stop believing what was real)* are false beliefs about something real and held on to in spite of no proof, evidence, or good reason. Delusions were a huge problem during Biblical times (see Greed, Matthew 19:24 regarding the eye of a needle). Furthermore, the vast majority of people have always believed in delusions, even in spite of seeing contrary evidence.

For example, for thousands of years, European experts and authorities believed the sun rotated around the earth — and hence the false terms "sunrise" and "sunset." Ancient Egyptian Science had shown just the opposite —that the earth rotates around the sun. Still, for a while many people continued to believe their senses — and the appearance of the sun going around the earth comes from our senses. To believe you can buy friendships or things of worth (e.g. happiness) is a delusion. To believe material things (e.g. money, possessions) are more important than good character is a delusion.

The 15th century word "delusion" (Latin "de", away; "ludo", to play or mock) meant "to play to one's detriment" or "the inability to distinquish between play and reality." Shortly thereafter, in 1433, European slavers started deceiving African entrepreneurs into believing they should help them enslave other Africans. Then the enslaved Africans were brainwashed with absurd delusions to some degree.

The slaves most affected—the "Ideal slaves"—adopted the slave master's teachings by coming to believe in slavery; taking pride in it; and assuming Blacks were born to be slaves. They surrendered to and used their whole mind to accept delusions. This acceptance —based on the necessity to adjust to the captors' dictates of the captors—led those slaves to be misguided into wrong and self-destructive think, feel, say, and do ways. As a result, they lost touch with the real world. The captors generated in the slaves **Delusions** of**:**

(1) **Persecution** whereby each slave was told fellow slaves were threatening him, discriminating against him, or conspiring to bring about his downfall—all for the purpose of creating social dissention, getting each slave to have inner resentments towards other slaves, and to fashion self-dissatisfaction;

(2) **Sin and Guilt** came from the White ministers telling the slaves they were extremely wicked and were committing unpardonable sins if they were not "Ideal slaves";

(3) **Impoverishment** trying to make the slaves believe they had no human or personal worth;

(4) **Jealousies** by forcing the wife or husband of one slave to breed with other slaves;

(5) **Reference** by Whites demeaning their beloved Africa;

(6) Influence to control slave thoughts and actions;

(7) **Superstitions**;

(8) **Controlled and Dependent on Whites**;

(9) **Systematization**— (e.g. Black is dooming)

(10) **Mental Poverty**—an inability to think, especially with foresight.

As a result, coming out of slavery and passing by way of the "ghetto tunnel" which connects the self-defeating customs of the slaves with today's struggling Black youth, a new world was created inside the unrealistic world of delusions. Because Black people are a tradition based people, there has been little change since slavery.

What this means is that of mental transformation in Africans brought to the Americas as slaves. Some of the mental transformations of believing to be right what they had always known to be wrong were seen in the following examples: those delusions in slave males which came from them losing or restraining their "manhood"; from being placed in an inferior position to Black female; and from not having what it took to fight the White man. Slave females had pains over being continually raped by White men, among others.

Following slavery, Europeans have done whatever it took for Black people to maintain these (among innumerable others). Even new ones were added—like them being "lazy" because of from an inability to obtain adequate or any employment. The overwhelming mental turmoil created inside these delusions fashioned a "**Special Mind**" in those Blacks who have continued to struggle from one generation to the next (Bailey, Freeing Enslaved Minds).

All Black people did (and do) have pain over being constantly insulted— e.g. Whites calling them by their first names, or gal/boy/uncle and insisting on Caste behaviors. A prominent Southern **Caste Sentiment** was the unpardonable offense in White people's estimation of a White and Black person sitting down to eat at the same table—or even sitting in the same dining room, though at separate tables. The Whites' believe was that they would sink to the level of colored people or without an attempt on the Whites' part, to bring the colored up to his level—a practice dating at least back to the way the scribes and Pharisees felt about Jesus eating with publicans and sinners (Woodson, 265). This and hundreds of other castes caused many Blacks to feel they were not respectable and not worthy of confidence of people in the community.

Inside the delusions of today's struggling Blacks are emotional and spiritual pains culturally transmitted and acquired. Together, they are denied, suppressed, repressed, ignored, compensated for, or dissociated. Ways they are dealt with are by denial, dissociation, suppression, repression or compensation (by "acting a fool" or fighting or "fleeing from" in by various defense mechanisms, including the engaging in superficial pleasures and "being about nothing").

Although these repressed emotions are beyond conscious awareness and hence out of control, they remain quite active in causing one to do weird and self-defeating things—things for which he/she can not account—things like getting in fights over "nothing".

Regardless of how many destructive emotions are present and in what combination in any given Black American, there is a lack of awareness about them. Yet, there is an accommodation to—and perhaps even the acceptance of— this "glob" of entangled terrible emotions and pains present inside delusions. Despite being considered "normal" for struggling Black Americans, the effects of this glob are overwhelming. It takes up so much mind space and energy as to leave little room for more constructive thoughts and actions. Hence, one is not in complete control of one's minds—a situation which can cause one to go "mad."

Besides, the glob may well explain many of the physical problems featured in Black Americans—strokes, high blood pressure, diabetes, and cancer. Many struggling Blacks are *mentally caged* by being unable to "escape" into a state of reality. Their only relief is to "escape" into more disturbing delusions or into superficial pleasures or activities that lead to "dead-ends." By contrast, when tired of all this mental conflict within themselves, "normal" people can "escape" into distorted or fantasy mindsets.

Pause for a moment to realize how completely caged you are by extreme anger. Suppose, as a way of life, you stayed in that mental state—conceivably as happens with many struggling Blacks. At some point you will decide to do something to get a little relief. If that something works even to some degree, it is repeated over and over until an addiction is set up. Under these circumstances it is remarkable that the afflicted get as much done as they do—and that they do not do things much worse than what they do. They need community help, if not professional mental help.

EMOTIONS INSIDE FRUSTRATIONS

The Story of Frustration: Since prehistoric times the snare trap has been a favorite of hunters. It consists of a noose of twine attached to the top of a bent sapling and held down by a notch in a nearby tree. When the animal reaches for the "bait," its movement springs the sapling free. Thus, the animal is snared by the noose and carried aloft to dangle helplessly. From the sense of victims being snared through deceit came the word "frustrate."

Naturally, the biblical experience of frustration was about spiritual pain resulting from being thwarted (defeated by a more powerful force) in attempts to interconnect with God. Its written concept can be traced to the Bible's statements in the New Testament (Mt. 15:9; Mk. 7:8) which repeated God's accusation that his people worship him "*in vain*" if they approach him according to made-up human rules. To believe "*in vain*" means to believe without the prospect of a reward. Therefore "*in vain*" beliefs are "*senseless*," "*worthless*," and "*ineffective*."

Examples include the worship of idols and doing things for mere glory instead of in humility — because both are devoid of substance or permanence. It is to be noted that biblical writings did not intend "*vanity*" to mean conceit or preoccupation with self. Rather, "*vanity*" referred to "*nothingness*," "*purposelessness*," "*emptiness*," and "*chaos*." These are the "*Big Four*" representing the experience of frustration at the time it occurs. Over time, the "*Big Four*" words were applied to matters of the material world.

In 15th century Europe, when immoral and unethical behaviors become respectable and rampant, the deception leading to *Fraud* (gaining an unfair advantage over bodies of people) involved those aspects of TRICKERY (deliberately giving the wrong impression) that included DECEIT (the pursuit of personal gain at the expense of victims) and MANIPULATION (hypocritical dishonorableness). When the victims' loss or failure was complete and final, the word "*frustrate*" was applied to the victims' reaction of being in a mental state of chaos.

If the victim was left with a loss but remained uncertain as to whether any possible new turn might be effectively met, the term BAFFLED was used. In other words, the situation which caused one to be baffled could, with the proper regrouping, still succeed. Whereas frustration would cause a person to "give up," baffled persons might simply work harder to achieve their goal.

Causes of Frustration: If all of our wants could be satisfied, then there would be no frustrations. Obviously, since we do not live in an ideal world, there are always obstacles to overcome — sometimes satisfactorily, sometimes not. Even when the sources of frustration are easily seen, it may not be in your best interest or worth your time, effort, and money to attack them. Not all sources of frustrations should be looked upon negatively. Some are normal, wholesome, and provide an opportunity for self-improvement. An example is the beneficial socialization practices instituted by parents for the purpose of building good character, good manners, and civility.

Some of the sources of frustrations are clear and definite while others are hazy. Example of the hazy, vague, and intangible sources include: "the economic system" or "the legal system" or "the political system" or "the prejudicial/discrimination system." Such sources are so unavailable, so powerful, and so nebulous that there is nothing definite to attack. Of course, "*bits and pieces*" of each can be attacked but this is like shooting an arrow into the darkness — chances are you will not hit the target and the constant failure attempts are frustrating.

Frustration, both a complex emotion and an obstacle, results from not being able to have something you really want. Psychologists define frustration as the blocking of efforts to attain some deserved goal and/or having the response feelings of aggression, depression, or withdrawal from obstacles placed in one's path. They categorize five sources of frustration:

(1) **DELAYS** — as in someone not arriving on time;

(2) **LACK OF RESOURCES** — as when individuals living in poverty cannot obtain proper food or medical care;

(3) **LOSSES** of people, places, or things — particularly from having no control over it (i.e. being helpless);

(4) **FAILURE** — whether from outside forces and/or self-induced ("if only I had done..."); and

(5) **MEANINGLESSNESS** — dead-end jobs, having no goals.

There, however, numerous others. One is the Realization of significant *Lacks* in ones own ability or resources or opportunity.

A second is having a sense of *Being Violated*—as will occur when one's home has been robbed, one's rights denied, or one's trust shattered.

Third, two people with *different value systems* and different ways of doing things can frustrate each other. One example is the couple in a relationship. Another is a teacher with middle-class values coming up against inner city youth with "street values." Both may feel inadequate. Both may not have the facilities or tools they need.

Fourth is *Not Enough Time, Money, or Energy.* As a result of needing to work, low-income parents may feel frustrated in trying of fulfill their idea of being good parents because they have to leave their children in the care of others.

Fifth is *Obstacles*, as when something or someone stands in the way and blocks the path to the goal. The same effect occurs when one experiences significant losses or lacks that interfere with attaining a goal. The intensity of the frustration depends upon how much one wanted or did not want something, the degree of interferences, and how often one has been frustrated in the past.

It is a *Self-Imposed obstacle* when a person develops a low frustration-tolerance and/or frustration-proneness. People with a LOW FRUSTRATION TOLERANCE (i.e. having a "*short fuse*"; a quick temper) easily build up a stock of aggressive type desires — meaning they are "*looking for a victim*" unless they otherwise properly release their pent-up tension (i.e. "*blow off steam*").

Sixth, *Self-Frustration* arises from conflicts in values within a person's mind. Conflicts from any cause push negative and destructive feelings to burst forth and then spread outward from one's mind. Frustrated people, especially if they are acting to their own disadvantage, get "fed up" with themselves and thereby develop a low frustration tolerance. They feel disappointed, harmed, and even injured from being rendered helpless or useless. Their frustrated ways of acting result in marked irritability, tension, anxiety, bad temper, rudeness, and often aggressive behavior.

Seventh are people with an *Overly Ambitious* type of low frustration tolerance. Just as certain people are ACCIDENT-PRONE (those with a variety of bad emotions which guide them towards the direction of some mishap), overly ambitious people are

FRUSTRATION-PRONE. They have set their ambitions so high above their abilities as to be perpetually "*refrustrated*" from "*biting off more than they can chew.*"

Thus, their frustration may occur in many different areas. For example, people with generally poor success related habits (e.g. laziness in living up to their potential) will create problems in all areas of their lives. Thus, their frustrations come from a source that is vague and intangible — like looking into fog and not knowing what to attack.

Eight, DELAYS typically have the same effect as obstructions.

Ninth, *Unfair Treatment* is present in normal people who deserve fair-play and in people with a superiority complex who feel they should get special—not just fair—treatment. Typically, frustration is present when one national or ethnic group feels hostility and practices discrimination towards other groups. This is particularly true when the outrageous rumors against a minority are scientifically proven to be untrue and yet the rumors are used to create a "revolving door" (like in a department store) with prejudice.

For example, European hostility toward African-Americans and indifference toward the poor have deprived both of educational advantages. Then it is claimed that both are "inferior"—a form of Projection. From the "inferior" belief, there is increased prejudice and indifference.

The World of Frustration: Ranging between mild and extreme frustration are all types of losses, lacks, obstructions, and delays — some concrete and some abstract. CHRONIC FRUSTRATION worsens the frequency and intensity of all these reactions and blocks the way to success.

The importance of frustration to bad emotions is the same as the relationship of the hub to a wheel. At the moment something prevents you from reaching your goal, there is shock, numbness, and perhaps the shattering of all your thoughts and feelings about whatever was related to your goal. Your mindset depends upon the significant of the goal to you and the degree of your frustration tolerance. The degree or intensity of your reaction to unsatisfactory circumstances depends on the value you put on those desires, needs, expectations, goals, and actions involved. The effect may be:

Mild — e.g. my teams fail to win often

Slight — many people will not help themselves

Moderate — e .g. interference with the top value just below the standard of love — be it money, possessions, or not living up to your potential

Extreme — e.g. being thwarted in the fulfillment of whatever pertains to love makes for extreme frustration.

Categories into which mild or slight frustrations fall into may be mental (e.g. failing a test), physical (e.g. obesity), social (e.g. insults), personal (e.g. limited capacities), or financial (e.g. limited resources).

It is the deep-seated desires and ambitions which cause moderate or extreme frustrations — those creating spiritual or emotional wounds — which need to be prevented or, if present, need to be handled. The "*Big Three*" painful sources are a loss (deprivation), a lack (privation), and an obstruction.

LOSSES are especially frustrating because we are deprived of something we have been accustomed to having — a loved one's death, a divorce resulting in the loss of one's children, a disability from injury or poor health.

LACKS can be devastating when they shatter hopes and expectations related to one of our values, as when we offer our life's work to the world and then experience its rejection or its lack of acceptance. Or, when poor people lack the necessities of life.

OBSTRUCTIONS that repeatedly stab one's spirits include racial or gender discriminations which prevent a person from developing his/her talent.

Regardless of the category of frustration, one or more **Emotional Reactions to Frustration** may spring from it –e.g. annoyance, anger, hate, a desire for revenge, fear, emotional pain, or depression.

MIND LEANINGS FROM FRUSTRATION: Babies are born with (and "little gods" acquire) the demanding attitude of: "*I want what I want when I want it and I want it right now!!*" But all sorts of blocks to this attitude pop up during socialization and thwart their imagined omnipotent (unlimited) power. Then they realize their **loss** of power as well as the **lack** of power to do anything about it. Part of socialization includes punishments and punishments and those can create fears about a loss or lack of love and caring.

Almost all of these frustrations produce a readiness to respond aggressively or passively. Such a predisposition to respond in a given pattern when faced with a frustrating situation is called "***SETS***" by psychologists. Each frustration is like a sharp jolt of electricity. The jolt causes children to take a step back to a fixed stage of personality development, a known stable platform at which time they once stood. This step back causes them to feel more powerful, somewhat safe, and less insecure.

Gradually, as the child's mind develops into a more thoughtful mode, they start developing patterns of reactions and of intensities. These developed and increasingly involved defense mechanisms are brought into a frustrating situation. Also, individuals carry over patterned arousals from one or more prior experiences into the new frustrating situation.

Typically, childhood frustrations have created such exaggerated emotional tensions, intense states of reaction to something or someone bad, and mental leanings (usually of a self-defeating nature) that, in later life, most people develop greater resentments and aggressions than warranted by their actual life situations. Thus, their reactions, when faced with a new frustrating situation, may go in two directions.

One is that their reactions become a super-imposed layer of frustration resulting from the new situation and thereby makes a bad situation even worse. Second, they may develop cyclic neurotic symptoms in situations which are not actually frustrating.

When they actually enter the realm of frustration, it is like what was mentioned as occurring at Grand Central station. Recall that in a separate part of this station is a circular garage for locomotives called the "*roundhouse*". Locomotives are driven onto a huge turntable — like the kitchen table's "lazy Susan" — where inspection, cleaning, and repairs are done. Then, as desired, the locomotive can be redirected North, East, South, or West.

Similarly, within the "station" of frustration there are so many North, East, South, and West type emotions. The emotions present in the situation of frustration come from the kinds of conflicts which the involved parties bring to the table— things like irritability, tension, anxiety, and angry surliness (bad temper). The more vivid the anticipation of reward prior to being frustrated, the greater the amounts of frustration and aggressive response generated by its delay, blockage, loss, or lack.

It is from this storehouse of emotions that the individual's mind committee selects one to direct the way the individual's mind should lean. For instance, one has the choice to go in the direction of the constructive approach, as a result of being challenged. This means a determination to work harder toward achieving their goal.

Or, one can choose to go in the direction of <u>aggression</u> (most commonly) or <u>withdrawal</u> or <u>regression</u> (going back to "*the good old days*" — to reaction patterns which were appropriate at an earlier level of development) or <u>depression</u>. The decision to go into the "*flight*" direction is the reverse of what leads to the "*fight*" response. Both mindsets then take on a lower level of aspirations.

Whereas some approach fear with a Selfhood Mastery Model (appearing the be completely without fear) and therefore deciding to fight, the "*flight*" group has a COPING MODEL for dealing with fearfulness (which worsens the farther they get into frustrating situations). Either approach closes down reason, opportunities for benefiting from the situation, and alternate peaceful ways for getting around the target of aggression.

To proceed in any direction other than the constructive direction, unless for survival purposes, is an act of mental immaturity. The decision to go down the destructive aggressive way, as opposed to the destructive passive way, is based on a variety of factors — the degree of arousal intensity, the tension in the desire for the goal, the situation, the cues in the situation, the prior events that went into fashioning their mind set, and the number of prior goal-response sequences interfered with.

Examples of CUES include the availability of guns or knives, or even the color of clothing present in the environment. The intensity of the negative emotions depends upon the number of punishments, insults, fears, and internalization of violence on television or participation in violence-oriented video games.

A common Effect of Frustration is LOW FRUSTRATION TOLERANCE. People with low frustration tolerance are mentally weak — which may or may not have anything to do with high or low intelligence. Their problems come from outside (external) and inside (internal) problems (or barriers). External causes of frustration derive from non-social (e.g. natural disasters, money problems) or social things.

Internal causes result from self-frustration — (self-generated problems pertaining to oneself) or from personal frustrations generated from encounters with the outside world. They are usually more lasting than the external types. In contrast to the internal, external barriers which the individual fails to recognize have no psychological significance. For those with low-frustration tolerance, internal barriers thwart their aspirations and prevent them from pursuing a fulfilling course of action.

So how does a low frustration tolerance arise? Before answering this, let us look at the subject of **FRUSTRATION TOLERANCE.**

The mid-1800's expression: "*the straw that broke the camel's back*" conveys a clear mental picture of an overloaded animal being given one slight additional weight. Similarly, in my medical practice I saw a number of patients called "*potato chips.*" The reason for this label is because the most minor of injuries would cause them to break into many pieces and affect every way they dealt with life. Tolerance is the bearing of those views or habits which differ from our own.

Since frustration tolerance is the amount of frustration that an individual is able to cope with, "*potato chip*" people have a low frustration tolerance — i.e. a "*short fuse*" at the slightest hint of stress. By contrast, those with high tolerance are able to function in reasonable ways under highly stressful situations. The probable reason for different degrees of tolerance pertains to ways — starting as early as infancy — that people learned to cope.

Frustration and its effects are a function of the differences between what one wants and what one can get. This means that the degree of frustration in a person depends upon what that person expects. People who take from life only what they need have reasonable expectations; those who are greedy have much higher expectations. Reasonable people who fail to get what they need, as with the poor, have frustrations of a different nature than the frustration that comes from an inability to satisfy greed.

The poor, for example, have specific reasons which set up tolerance as a goal. From a lack of frustration, tolerance in the rich may develop in many areas of their lives. Tolerances of differences in all people tend to be much greater among the poor compared with the rich or with racist.

Nevertheless, regardless of the nature of the people, the sources of frustrations can come from nature (e.g. natural disasters like earthquakes), social circumstances (e.g. racial behaviors), money and possessions, or from the self. Problems related to the self can be about the physical body (e.g. chronic illness); the reasoning faculty (e.g. unable to figure out a life-shaping problem); the emotional faculty (e.g. conflicts involving ethical values); and the spiritual force (e.g. the refusal of another to return our love and affection).

All of these LIFE TRIANGLE problems (fig. 6) occurs throughout the lives of each of us. When they cause you or me to react they are called SELF-FRUSTRATIONS. When you or I encounter Life Triangle problems as a result of our <u>actions</u> they are PERSONAL FRUSTRATIONS.

To return the question of: "how does a low frustration tolerance arise?" in most cases it is the failure of the baby's needs not being consistently met. This pattern of frustration results in the little child developing a sense of mistrust and both of these act to fashion FRUSTRATION PRONENESS (an easy susceptibility to chaotic upsetness).

Factors involved include the type of conflict or frustrating situation; how deeply seated the conflicts are in terms of one's desires and drives; and their frequency and intensity. If the nature of the conflict embraces the original trigger person or trigger event and particularly if the male's "*manhood*" is challenged, this is a situation of very great significance — his whole reputation being at stake. This mind set of early childhood creates such on-going emotional tensions that the person, in later life, shows greater resentments and aggressiveness than are warranted by their actual life situations.

A frequent result is PROJECTION of the hostile aggression upon others — saying that those others have the aggressive attitudes held by oneself. *"it's not that I hate her or want to attack her; rather she hates me and wants to attack me."* This projection leads to fear, mistrust of others, probably to hate, and the mixed-up justification of doing self-defensive aggressions. Lynching of innocent Negroes by White racists is an example.

Persons experiencing many frustrations accumulate a supply of latent (laying hidden) aggressions — like accumulating psychological "hand grenades." Causes for the accumulation include ongoing frustrations which constantly recur from being in the same situation (e.g. poor people's daily struggle for survival) and/or from problems in many different areas. Next comes the "*frustration straw that breaks the camel's back*" because it is associated with an opportunity for expressing one's pent-up feelings on a scapegoat. Such a meeting triggers all the "*hand grenades*" to explode at once.

Accumulating latent aggression is so common that probably everybody carries around some degree of GENERALIZED HOSTILITY. Although latent aggression expressions tend to be kept in check by the folkways of the group as well as by a direct fear of punishment, some "*hand grenades*" explode occasionally — as insults, cursing, and road rage.

Inner city and troubled youth, who have more than their share of frustration, do not handle disappointments and frustrations well. Apart from being poor and its associated social rejections, they have a host of frustrations— about how they look, insufficent skills and abilities, lack of social graces, awkwardness, shyness, fatigue, feelings of failure due to mistakes or inadequacies, deaths of their buddies, and feelings of isolation, loneliness, and alienation.

Since frustrations have shut down any desires they may have had to conform to society's values — including education — addressing their frustrations is a high priority. Although there are too many self-defeating emotions in each child to address, perhaps broad approaches exist for helping to establish sufficient mental discipline and mental toughness to allow self-growth or at least stopping adverse progression which lead to vicious cycles.

In other words, persons with low frustration tolerance generally have attitudes that are easily irritated. These attitudes sap pleasurable emotional energy. When upset, people burn much of their daily energy in the fire of hostility and that is very fatiguing. Furthermore, not having favorable attitudes toward others is picked up by others and, in turn, they often generate negative reactions — either with a return of unfavorable attitudes or deciding not to provide gifts or opportunities.

MANAGEMENT OF FRUSTRATION: We would never be frustrated if we got what we wanted and did not get what we did not want. But that never happens for anyone. Therefore, what one needs is to learn—as fully discussed under the Check Method—is how to minimize frustration on the one hand and how to achieve High Frustration Tolerance on the other. Both processes involve understanding of ones problems and having principles of management to use for customed designing to suit ones needs.

Let us start with **Understanding the Problem**. How do you know if a situation has frustrated you? Answer: pay close attention to your reaction and actions immediately after that situation. Frustration is present if you feel confused, then overwhelmed, and then have no idea what to do—an emotional state of chaos — i.e. utter confusion and disorder.

The DISORDER causing the frustration points to the lack of proper arrangement or combination of the parts making up the big picture of the frustrating situation — i.e. the parts are not in their normal places. The CONFUSION indicates that things are in such lack of order that it is difficult to identify the parts in the general clutter (i.e. the miscellaneous or various nature of the mess) and therefore has a strange form.

Thus, the first step in dealing with frustration is to identify the parts in the situations and put these parts into their proper order. Included in this process are three concepts:

(1) CLARITY — a "word picture" making each part definite and distinct enough for examples to be given or recognized;

(2) DISTINCT — explaining what distinguishes one part within the big picture from other parts; and

(3) PRECISION — using the words that say what you mean and mean what you say.

As mentioned, the sources of frustrations — temporary, semi-permanent, or permanent interferences between a person and that person's goal — may arise from one or more factors. Examples are inner factors (e.g. moral conflicts), physical-self factors (e.g. limited abilities for a given job) and/or outside factors of a social (e.g. a trigger person or group), government, legal, or physical nature.

Minimize Sensitivity to Frustration: ESCAPE ACTIVITIES, such as going to the movies, watching TV, or playing video, are not the best use of ones time. The main reason is that they do not promote a sense of self-worth or self-value. Both are so important in slowing, stopping, or reversing self-degrading beliefs.

Step I—The best way to discover the order of the parts present in the situation before the frustration occurred is to study all aspects of your prior experiences (Table XI). See the Check Method for details. Keep in mind that frustrated YOUTH HAVE LEARNED TO REDUCE THEIR EXPERIENCES OF PLEASURE. Perhaps the beginning reason is that, like in the stories of king Midas and Pandora's box, they were given a present of something special (e.g. life, curiosity, talents) that seemed valuable but which turned out, as they see it, to be a curse.

Step II— My approach for dealing with life-energy draining frustrations is to KEEP GOING TOWARD THE GOAL EVEN THOUGH IT IS A TINY BIT AT A TIME. If I just cannot bring myself to take positive steps forward, there are always files to put away, going through old newspapers to tear out helpful articles, throwing away junk, and doing whatever will help me move forward once my energy returns.

Step III—practice meeting actual stresses by allowing the child to face and manage frustrating situations on his/her own. The aim is for children to have independence, to take responsibility without blaming, and to continually improve problem-solving skills. For the best and quickest results, these approaches are started early in life.

To divert attacks or "acting ugly," teachers can help youth find different options for getting around frustrating obstacles. It is important for youth to know how valued they and their goals are, Shedding frustrations are of great practical importance for increasing intellectual and educational efficiency, improving the quality of work, and promoting pleasant and cooperative attitudes.

Step IV—establish a sense of security, self-esteem, and self-confidence through liberal expressions of approval, encouragement, and affection (Table IV). A place to start is with helping one's family and the needy. These are ways to generate love, if not from others, then from you providing you with what you need.

Step V—cultivate your abilities and skills through a graduated series of physical and social activities. Having a wider range of interest (e.g. music, drama, art, sports) partly pushes kids to improve. Networking helps children to better absorb the shock of frustrations, as does having a regular program for healthful living (e.g. good diet, physical activities, avoiding "poisons").

HIGH FRUSTRATION TOLERANCE DEVELOPMENT: When you can accept little frustrations with grace, you are ready to tackle bigger ones. This was a favorite principle of my mother: "*Son, if you handle small things well, you will be able to handle big things later.*"

To begin building frustration is to troubleshoot and correct the discovered flaws. THE RULES ARE TO BE EAGER TO TAKE ON DIFFICULT PROBLEMS AND TO NEVER TAKE SHORT CUTS. Blocks causing frustration usually develop from taking short-cuts or failing to pay attention to details.

Even the most mentally healthy people, upon encountering frustrations and failing to resolve all of them, create reactive emotions of anguish, guilt, emotional pain, envy, shame, aggression, anxiety, fear, and depression inside their frustration. However, by accepting frustration as a normal reality of life, they are able to develop a HIGH FRUSTRATION TOLERANCE.

This mark of a well-adjusted person occurs most easily from parents having given the young child constant, reliable care — the foundation for promoting the child's sense of trust. Part of that training includes the child learning that he/she cannot always have what he/she wants or at least not when he/she wants it — the *lesson of delaying immediate gratifications.* This is accepted because the child knows that the child-parent relationship is one of mutual caring. Being filled with this sense of caring is fortification for life. It enables the person to forever minimize fretting about what he/she cannot have. Thus, the child allows lesser essential desires go unsatisfied. Once accepted for what it is and from a "*cared for*" base, frustration is not nearly so frustrating.

Of tremendous help to me was that early in life I made a conscious decision that I would not allow material things to dominate my life. Instead, curiosity, learning, and enjoying things of worth (e.g. bathing in the beauty of nature) were far, far more important. Thus, when material things "disappeared"—and it is amazing how often this occurred in all sorts of ways—my frustration was not overly intense and not of an overly long duration.

If your original problem has come from poor choices when you were old enough to know better, take heart in knowing that high frustration tolerance, like any habit and attitude, can be acquired with practice. Start with little things. For example, the frustration of having to wait can be reduced by taking a book to read or using this as an opportunity to increase your conversation skills with any available stranger. Although there is the occasional failure in engaging strangers in conversation, most are eager to talk.

Despite the inevitable frustrations from the opposite sex refusing to date you, a principle of great salesmanship is that if only one in a hundred will be a sale then each rejection brings you closer to that sale. If you are having trouble finding a parking space, shift from being frustrated to viewing the situation as "*fascinating.*"

Unsolvable problems are best handled philosophically — "*I was either not ready to move to the next step or to continue going in this direction.*" Many times the cause of recurring frustration is from looking at the situation from a biased or narrow perspective. Since both are limiting, keep looking at the problem from many angles before taking action. Typically, more research is needed. Combining research with a different perspective allows you to draw on and organize information already in your mind. All of these work as a team to design a solution.

One of the things I really like about myself is how, ever since childhood, I accepted a frustrating situation as a challenge to get around what was blocking my path. Maybe for only a moment would I allow my thoughts and feelings to be chaotic (i.e. frustrated) before switching over to a problem-solving mode. If my goal had been worth pursuing in the first place, my job remains the finding of another way to get there.

If the frustration process originally started from a mistrust between you and your parents, look for the missing ingredients. Chances are that what you craved but did not get was an active affectionate relationship shared between you and your parents (especially a mother figure). Or, maybe you perceived that you had inadequate amounts of love with respect to quantity, quality (in the way you could appreciate), or duration.

When problems with love are the cause of your frustration-proneness, reconsider that your parents did show you love but in a way you did not recognize. Make a list of all the good things they did for you. Or, figure out ways to "create" an intimate but non-sexual relationship with another without it being a "*parent/child*" situation. The buddy chosen must be mentally mature, affectionate, attentive, and responsive. The amount of positive interaction between you two is the most important. A good model to study is the interaction between Black sports teammates who are great friends.

To understand the principles of life which fashion emotional maturity is also an exercise in developing frustration tolerance. The process includes self-evaluation to see the part you played in creating your problem. From further self-understanding make the necessary corrections. In short, the more you understand the more tolerant you become.

A major self-correction is to put meaning back into your life by becoming passionate about a worthwhile goal. Then develop a lifestyle to make it happen. You then become too busy to get frustrated over what others are doing to you. A wise move is to stop blaming anybody for anything and, instead, find ways to go straight ahead. This approach helps you to stop developing frustrating defense mechanisms to overcome frustrations. Perhaps all other approaches represent low frustration tolerance.

EMOTIONS INSIDE AN OVERWHELMED MINDSET

On the first day in class at the University of Michigan the history instructor told us students: "We will cover the time period from ancient civilizations to the Renaissance within the first two weeks"—and this was a very thick part of our textbook. The same day the French instructor said: "We will not speak another word of English from this point on"—and I certainly was not ready for that. At the next class, the English literature instructor said: "You will read 26 books and be tested on them at the end of the month." The same day the biochemistry instructor gave us a thick book of experiments we had to cover and said: "As background, I will assume you have had the following"—and she proceeded for the next half hour of the class to rattle off an infinite number of subjects. Everybody around me was nodding (indicating that they had had those subjects) but I have never even heard of them. I was so overwhelmed I went home and slept.

By the middle of the first semester at the University of Michigan, my stomach was really hurting from being overwhelmed by the difficulties related to all these courses and particularly in chemistry. I was anxious, scared, frustrated, disappointed in being so far behind, and embarrassed. Despite the university's assumption that what they were teaching me was the next step above high school chemistry, college chemistry was way too advanced for me. Instead of a "next step," it was a "Grand Canyon Leap."

Since this was a new experience of a school subject being above and beyond my understanding and level of competence, I went to the chemistry instructor for guidance—again my first experience of going to a teacher. Amazingly, she gave me one of the finest pieces of advice I have ever received. She said "**Start where you are**!"

As a result, I went home and started studying the assignment just handed out—paying no attention to yesterday's or last week's or last month's assignments. From that point on, I worked only on the assignment of that day but did so promptly and thoroughly. At final exam time, I made an "A."

But what is it to be overwhelmed? Although the emotions inside the word include being confused, frustrated, upset, and embarrassed, the meanings of these words in relation to each other have similarities and differences. In other words, several different ideas go into making up the concept of "overwhelmed."

The Story of Overwhelmed: An ancient concept was the energy contained in overwhelmed caused one's mind to swell up into the shape of a bowl and then that bowl would turn upside down. Thus, instead of one's mind looking toward the brightness of the sun, the mind's view from being turned upside down was to look over everything in a gloomy way. Of course, being overturned covered up any bright and clear thinking.

Another early idea of what happened to the mind from being overwhelmed was that of an overpowering mental force rolling into the thinking part of one's mind and burying everything in its path. This force was thought of as a mighty wave sending its power through, around, over, and under the mind so as to envelop all sides. Hence, the mind became suffocated and useless by three things — the over-spreading hurricane-like force; the crushing weight; and the cutting off the mind's thinking supply lines.

These three ideas were familiar to sailors in their navigations of ships, especially when they were unable to resist the combined forces of the weather conditions being faced. The effect was greatest when they were buried (i.e. covered and hidden) by an on-rushing and breaking sea, as in broaching (i.e. piercing a hole in the ship). The resultant violence and weight would capsize the ship.

In 1535, the Coverdale Bible defined "overwhelm" as "to be overcome completely in mind or feeling." Etymologically, the word root of "overwhelm" means "over," above in place; "whelm," to submerge, to engulf. One dictionary defines it as: "to defeat completely and decisively"; "to affect deeply in mind or emotion"; and "to present with an excessive amount."

From these stories about the word "overwhelm" we can see its operation at different levels. One level is merely to be turned upside down; another is to be "covered up"; still another is to be smothered by the sheer weight of numbers, amount, or forces. If you are "upside down" or "covered over" like I was in college chemistry, the approach to getting out of this mess is to "start where you are" and handle all problems as they come up. If you feel you are being overpowered by the sheer weight and forces of life so as to be crushed, then here are approaches that have worked well for me. Before discussing how to **Prevent Becoming Overwhelmed,** allow me to first give some background.

THE SIGNIFICANCE OF RESERVES: As a teen—working in downtown Greensboro, North Carolina, at Tuck's Photo Shop as a film stripper— my job was to take rolls of film out of their light-proof container while in the dark room. In hanging up each roll of film, like laundry on a clothes line held with clothes pins, a weighted clip with sharp teeth was fastened on one end of the roll and the upper end was connected inside a spring clip that was attached to a rack. There were six spring clips on one rack and each rack had to be placed on the corresponding right and left moving links of parallel chains of a film developing machine.

Every rack moved forward about every (?) 14 seconds so as to allow for a new rack to be filled with film and placed on the chains. Putting six rolls on a rack and placing that rack on a moving chain meant the film stripper had to be very fast, mainly to keep the sharp teeth on each spring-loaded clam from "eating up" his/her fingers (by clamping down on them and pinching off skin).

A point of interest is that my boss, who had been doing film stripping for decades, could not always keep up with the pace of the machine's progress. Thus, he and I had an unspoken competition to see who was the fastest by not allowing any gaps between the racks. Hence, I worked out a plan to get perfect results. On the machine there were three links on to which the racks could be placed before the hanging six rolls of film entered the developer. My boss always placed his first rack on the moving links that were about to enter the developer.

By contrast, I put my first rack on the link that was the third back— and that gave me a head start. They never could figure out how I was so fast as to never miss a space. Starting with some reserve has been a most valuable transferable principle for all large tasks which I undertake. This has been instrumental in my ability to keep going in the face of overwhelming odds. Starting with some reserve has been a most valuable transferable principle, as follows:

Example I—During medical school days we had 10 hours to complete 11 course examinations—and the time allotted was one hour for each course. The fact that I had made high grades on earlier exams in orthopaedics meant that I was exempted from taking the exam. Thus, I had a complete hour to take the remaining 10 exams.

Example II— As a boy, when traveling away from home, I always wore a money belt that contained money to be used only for the utmost emergencies. That same money belt was hidden and no one knew I had it. Experience taught me that if people think you have money they will come up with the saddest stories in the world. My emergency money was also used to prevent "late fees" and penalties but it was replaced as soon as I got any money later.

Example III—There was a long period (years) when I could only go grocery shopping four times a year. Thus, I would buy canned and non-perishable food and fashion this process like ants who store away food for the winter.

Example IV— In a few instances I wrote papers hoping they would be published (but most were rejected). Perhaps some were rejected because they were poorly written or did not have enough new information or there was not enough proof for the facts presented or the information was too advanced or the information did not suit that particular journal or because the reviewers were simply too lazy and never got around to reviewing or because the information was ahead of its time or at least not in keeping with its time. Nevertheless, these papers—complete with references—gave me a head start on that subject when I resumed working on it years later.

Of course, much information in those papers had to be updated and rewritten—work that was much easier than starting from "scratch." Incidentally, it really helps to write a paper and then put it aside because when I come back to it months later there is so much new information and so many new ways for saying what was said. Meanwhile, I would be jotting down notes pertaining to that subject.

Example V— For me to have been able to write 17 books in 36 months is a reflection of my having gotten a head start. Here's how! A quarter of a century earlier I had started researching Black history—with no particular order—and had written notes as to where certain information could be found. Meanwhile, it was my hobby to write the story of words—and I chose words I could not figure out what they meant (e.g. "appreciation").

Sometimes when writing on a very complex subject that was exhausting and overwhelming (e.g. Unity), I would remember having written on a small piece of that subject in other papers. Finding those former writings was like getting a "Helping Hand" from myself because it served as a stimulus to keep going straight ahead on my writing project.

Part of the process was to be so thorough in whatever I write—by researching everything available on the subject and by studying the story of the word—that years later I can pick up where I left off and build on the solid foundation I had laid prior. To be able to stumble on a pertinent paper provides a welcomed moment that often wipes out all feelings of being overwhelmed.

Of couse, there are some subjects (e.g. truth, Love) so difficult that I write about them every three or so years—and start from "scratch"—and usually not looking at what I had written before. The idea is to get a fresh start with a fresh point of view. This means I will look up the story of the word again in over 850 books. The reason is that from now knowing more about the "big picture" I see the same information differently now than I did in the past. Besides, some things that did not seem important then are very important now.

A giant step in acquiring information that reduced my being overwhelm by a subject came when I realized Western books were grossly inadequate for covering a subject. They fail to start at the source (usually Ancient Africa); fail to deal with the spiritual; fail to deal with the subjective; and approach a complex subject with a linear orientation (meaning dealing with only one spoke of a wheel and not showing how the other spokes are related).

To completely cover the subject it is essential for me to research out of African oriented material because that not only provides me with a higher quality of information that approaches the truth. Furthermore, it gives background to what Europeans were trying to say and then clearly explains it with a source, cause, beginning, middle, end, and result that was otherwise totally confusing in Western literature (e.g. "principle").

In other words, regardless of what I do I try to make it solid and the truth and keep it available so that it can be used to help me when I am particularly confused and overwhelmed. This is what I call, before starting a new project, HAVING A CHECKERED RESERVE—one that will give me periodic relief.

Managing Being Overwhelmed: The wise handling of the state of being overwhelmed involves both prevention and proper action to get out of it once it is present. For the latter, the basic idea is to do something every day designed to constantly give hope and direction and progress — even if it is in "bits and pieces" that help in "baby step" forward motion toward the goal.

Separate into pieces all the things you do in your life. Then take one tiny bit of one piece and, starting today, make it better. Tomorrow, take another tiny bit of another piece and make that better. And so on. To simply start this process is to take a step out of being overwhelmed. Gradually, as you proceed, you will become aware of being more and more "alive" and in control of your life. Such a sense of control helps build confidence, is satisfying, and makes for a happy life. Being "alive" stimulates curiousity and is a source of motivation.

In summary, my advice for dealing with being overwhelmed is "*to start where you are and move from there to your goal*" (see the Bridge Method). Keep in mind you cannot do everything or be all things to all people. Do the most important first but do something everyday.

EMOTIONS INSIDE SUFFERING

At certain times in my life I have asked: "Why do good things (like riches) happen to bad people and bad things (like poverty) happen to good people?" For most Westerners, answers start with the Bible. Since suffering (and pain) is an umbrella concept term that draws attention to how human beings are affected by the tragedies of life, we need to have some awareness of what suffering is all about in order to determine its relationship, if any, to poverty. Useful here is the "**OBMER**" method — an acronym for Origin, Beginning, Middle, End, and Result (See later discussion on SOBMER).

ORIGIN: The Old Testament (OT) portrays suffering as a human condition originating with the sin of Adam and Eve. Thereafter, as punishment, women experienced greater pain in childbirth and men greater difficulties in their work — both because of their own wrong choices and, as occurred with Jesus, because of the wrong choices and acts of others. Suffering was to be a reminder of man's shattered relationship with God. By contrast, Job, whom God himself called blameless and upright (Job 1:8), is the prime OT example of one who endured pain and suffering. His prosperity was suddenly transformed into tragedy. Wealth, family, the respect of his peers, and even physical health were torn away in a single day. We are left to our own reflection as to why and our answer can be applied to the cause of poverty today. For Job's temporary suffering, God may have had a purpose that is separate from punishment.

BEGINNING: One English meaning of "to suffer" is to experience something unpleasant. In cases of women struggling in labor or men struggling in a new job, distress pain causes their minds to pass further away from a state of well-being.

MIDDLE: Coming in from our memories to join physical pain are thoughts of sadness and sorrow. These apperceptions cause so much mental anguish that the volume of our physical pain is turned way down. Further deepening of emotional pain, called GRIEF, comes from the deliberate destructive acts of outsiders. It is our reaction to this combination of distress pain, apperceptions, and outside factors that determines how a suffering or poverty experience affects us within. It is our choice to allow in or keep out doubts, fears, trembling, and bad acts.

END: Suffering is temporary. The approaching increased pain, agony, and torment testifies to our need for deliverance. The essence of the ending is summed up in the writhing body and straining muscles of the woman in the pain of actual childbirth. Following delivery comes the pain of exhaustion. The "newborn" springing from the delivery suffering offers hope for the emergence of fresh life into the world.

RESULT: From the experience of suffering we ought to become better persons. But, we may blame others, consider the suffering beyond our control, and be bound by the experience of suffering, complete with emotional scars and hypersensitivity to the slightest hurt. Rightly approached, suffering produces perseverance; perseverance produces character; and character produces hope (Ro.5: 3-4). Perhaps, as sages have said through centuries, instead of answering the "whys" of suffering and poverty, God is to be trusted to make things right.

EMOTIONS INSIDE WORRY

The Story of Worry: Perhaps for millions of years, ferocious animals in the world would gang up on a larger animal. One would seize the larger animal by the throat and hang on with the intention of killing by choking, strangling, and mangling with the teeth. When humans came on the scene and then started domesticating animals, like sheep, a major problem was wolves or dogs "worrying" their sheep or similar animals, as in tearing out the throats of their prey.

As a result, the Old Germanic and related languages associated "worry" with "to strangle." However, a different sense was fashioned by the Ancient Greeks. To them, worry and anxiety were not distinquished in their definition of "to care" or "to be concerned about" — in the way shepherds cared about their sheep with an anxious expectation. The Hebrews' version was that worry contained a multitude of one's thoughts in a tumbling motion so as to cause a heaviness or vexation of the heart.

Biblically, worry was often deemed a legitimate mental activity because it indicated a concern for self and/or for others—and particularly concerning whatever is "about the Lord's affairs." However, the line was drawn on the legitimacy of the "worries of this life" if they dominated one's attention and thereby made God's word unfruitful (Mt 13:22; Mk 4:19). The idea was to link all legitimate concerns to God and thereby be free of anxiety and worry.

Meanwhile, the ancient physical sense of "to struggle" was continued in worry until the 8th century when it evolved into the concept of "to bind tight." This sense applied to a dog's tenacity as it harassed its victim by rough and severe treatment.

During the European Medieval period, one of the sports was hawking (hunting with trained hawks). Owners were always worried that the hawks would not return and for this reason they had to be "called back" by "crying out."

Because of the British prominence at sea and the development of the gun, continued trade and warfare resulted in thousands of foreign word infusions into English in the 15th and 16th centuries. The revival of classical African and, to a much less extent, classical Greek and Roman learning by Renaissance humanists introduced even more new words. These many many word tools opened up subtle distinctions.

For example, anxiety and worry began to separate somewhat. "Anxiety" was assigned to vague apprehensions — perhaps related to undue concern about past behavior or about anticipated dangers in future happenings. The apprehensions are hazily related to more than one thing but nothing really specific — and tend to be endured in silence.

By contrast, "worry" was assigned to mental turmoil over specific situations and conveying the idea of continuousness of sustaining bites or tears in a corrosive (i.e. gnawing) manner. The emotionally colored attitude of worry — whether depressing or exciting - was recognized as unpleasant. Typically, it was set up by some situation whose solution or outcome causes a baffled mindset containing indecision, conflict, uncertainty of one's ability to prevent some unwanted state of affairs, and a sense of trouble.

Another effect of new word infusions into English was that words started appearing that combined different ideas present in foreign words as well as different time periods in English—words which meant roughly the same thing (as opposed to synonyms). For example, one foreign word related to worry as a violent act ("to strangle" as if one's throat was grabbed or one's neck was twisted); a second foreign word was about "causing worry" (as in the sport of hawking); a third was being "inclined to worry" (as in showing concern for the welfare of oneself and/or others); and a fourth was that worry implied "to torment or fret someone by aggressive treatment.".

Besides words starting to appear which combined aspects of these three forms, there were different forms of worry by the time of the Renaissance—and some placed in synonyms. In other instances there was shading from one form into another.

For example, in the 1700s the adverb "worrisomely" pertained to harassing — in the manner of "to pester," "to plague," or "to annoy" by repeated demands. A "pestering" example occurs when the little boy says: "Mom, can I have that big elephant over there — huh? huh?" An example of "annoying" occurs when the thinker is around constant chatter.

The World of Worry: Even to this day there is no clear distinction between worry, fear, and anxiety. *Fear is about "Doing"* something (fight or flight or fright) as an action or reaction to a person, place, or thing. *Anxiety is more of a state of "Being"* resulting from a reaction to a person, place, or thing—and not something inherent in the thing itself. It starts when an idea of the trigger object enters ones awareness as a concept or as a memory of something bad having happened. The reaction to that idea is that there is "danger in the atmosphere" and that causes a mental reaction of a hazy, vague, or non-existent real threat. This can cause someone to take action (e.g. precaustions).

Worry, as distinquished in the 16th century, is now assigned to mental turmoil over specific situations and conveying the idea of continuousness of sustaining bites or tears in a corrosive (i.e. gnawing) manner.

An old Chinese expression is that anxiety thoughts are burnt. In comparing this expression with the "Stress Curve" (fig. 2) an analogy is to say that at the beginning of the Stress Curve is a raw piece of meat. The further up you go the more the raw meat becomes cooked. At the top of the curve the meat is well done and the more it proceeds down the opposite limb the more the meat become burnt and is therefore useless. In other words, burnt thoughts can not be used.

The emotionally colored attitude of worry— whether depressing or exciting – is more specifically unpleasant compared to anxiety. It is set up by some situation whose solution or outcome causes a baffled mindset containing indecision, conflict, uncertainty of one's ability to prevent some unwanted state of affairs, and a sense of trouble.

The experience of worry is uneasiness and restlessness and the mental activity of going round and round in circles. If excessive, one becomes maladjusted and disruptive. Plans are reformulated but no action is taken. Worriers tend to communicate what they are experiencing to everyone around, with emphasis on the suspense over the outcome of something. Worry can range from mild to extreme ("I'm worried sick").

Whenever the danger is imagined or has only a very small chance of happening the term "Anxiety" is used. As related to worry, "Anxiety is the use of the imagination to create problems to worry about." This is particularly likely in realms of safety and/or security.

People who believe they are "Nobody" have the sense of lacking safety, security, sureness, stability, and strength. As a result, they are actually aware of being unprepared to handle most of the more important activities of daily living and this causes anxiety and worry. This is greatly increased in those areas related to survival, if such a situation were to arise.

By being forced to compete for survival, the person defines it (e.g. as in mingling with strange people). The encaging feeling of being defined leads to an exaggerated worry that is about the emotion of Horror. The glare of a stare or a roaring tone of voice may evokd an emotion of Terror. Fright and a sense of Terribleness may result from situations perceived to be real but actually are not.

The major problem with worry is the tremendous burning of one's daily allotment of energy. Besides, there is the mental activity of helpless wasted motions of thought. One's mind is overwhelmed by obsessive concern over things one can not do anything about. The fretting about the future is without real or useful results. This energy would have been better used doing pertinent investigative hard work — if not to discover a solution, then to eliminate what is not the solution and thereby narrow the focus on where to investigate next.

Worry keeps people from doing whatever is beneficial that is part of the realm of fear and anxiety—even if success is almost guaranteed. When such a mindset is detected by unscrupulous people, this is an invitation for them to exert their skills of manipulating by charging a high price to prevent or reduce worry in their victims. Or, to escape from situations that could benefit the manipulators, being mentally paralyzed by worry may put the worriers on the run in order to avoid con-artist.

The objective of the con-artist is to get their victims so scrambled within their selfhood that they are unable to figure out what to do and thereby become so delusioned as to see the con-artist as a friend capable of leading them. Where those victims are led is into something harmful to them and rewarding to the con-artist.

MANAGING WORRY: To properly manage worry requires knowing what it is. So what can "worry warts" (one who worries excessively and unnecessarily) do? First, **face the problem** for what it is. If the problem can not be affected by anything you do, then accept it as something that will be resolved one way or another in time. If you can handle it then start planning immediately.

If you are overwhelmed with mental conflicts, this is a time to take advantage of meditation or martial arts in order to get centered and focused. Then start doing something designed to help the cause and/or effect of what you are worried about. Or, if that is not possible, work on something that benefits you and/or someone. Otherwise, rather than showing impatience, let time pass.

Summary Management of Emotions inside Mindsets: This discussion has focused on pointing out that labels like projection and rationalization only deal with a particular kind of behavior but such a description is not to be interpreted as an explanation. In other words, its relationship to behavior is "how it appears" rather than "why it is." The "why" understanding requires knowing what experience the person had that threatened or disturbed his/her self-esteem, how that experience affected him/her, and why did he/she rely on a given defense mechanism to get him/herself past the bad experience. Lines separating the various defense mechanisms are hazy and often a person's reaction will contain two or more different mechanisms.

Inside a given defense mechanism there may be a large number of different emotions. For example, Frustration is a mental state resulting from wanting something or wanting to get rid of something but being prevented from making these wants happen. All sorts of emotions, feelings, and thoughts are bubbling in the "soup" of chaotic thoughts and feelings that characterize the frustrated state of mind — anger, fear, emotional pain, spiritual pain, depression, apathy, fantasy, regression, restlessness, and varying degrees of destructiveness.

Any one of these mindsets may become dominant at any given time and proceed to generate a specific type of action or reaction. If anger rises into dominance, then the behavior it generates may be one of attack. To be able to recognize which mindset dominates inside frustration serves as something to hold on to while one is in the process of self-inventory and self-understanding for purposes of correction.

These reactions and general techniques are the first steps used to solve that person's problems and, if the same type of problem occurs, a given reaction and technique emerging out of the frustration may becom a habit. Thus, different people react differently to the same kind of problem. Nevertheless, a few modes of adjustment occur so frequently that they ahve been sorted out under the category of defense mechanisms and each one has been given names.

VII

ESCAPE EMOTIONS

To Simply

Flee From Bad Emotions

Is to

Miss the Point

Of **Being Human**

Originally, the 14th century English word "escape" meant literally to "take off one's cloak" to metaphorically signify "throw off restraint." Escape connotes danger and threat, especially in relation to personal freedom and the exercise of indedpendent movement. In other words, one escapes in order to avoid danger, pursuit, or observation; to get free from confinement; or to regain liberty.

The Escape Emotions are those vehicles one uses to gain relief from mental turmoil. But the question is: "What is one escaping into?" Is the escape into some constructive or into something as bad or into something even worse than from what one was fleeing?

Because emotions are not reasonable, the afflicted person perceives that the escape is into something better—and sometimes it is—either permanently or temporarily; sometimes it only seems so; and sometimes it is not. Within the escape into a fantasy, for example, any of these may pertain. Within the escape into distortion, one makes more room to maneuver and that brings some relief despite not being freeing.

Escape Emotions are forms of Defense Mechanisms. Because all defense mechanisms serve to disguise threatening impulses and thereby fool you, it is normal but not healthy to resort to them. In the process, you are unaware of your desire to want to forget the bad emotions. Furthermore, you want to do the unhealthy thing you are not aware that you are doing. As a result, you deny your bad actions. All of this requires mental energy and produces mental conflict. Both burn up a tremendous amount of your daily allotment of energy and that, of course, causes you to become fatigued more easily.

We better remember ideas and experiences which are colored with feelings — either pleasant or unpleasant — compared with those free of feelings. Furthermore, "*normal*" people remember pleasant experiences better than unpleasant ones — like *Shame* (a wound to the self-concept), or *Emotional Pain* (from a loss, lack, or goal obstruction), or *Guilt* (sorrow for improper actions). However, the defense mechanism most commonly used for attempting to forget the unpleasant is called *Repression.*

Features characterizing residents of the escape world start with wishes and progress to delusions and on to hallucinations. DELUSIONS (believing what is not real and not believing what is real) are imagined but fixed ideas of grandeur, jealousy, persecution, illness, or sin-based on simple coincidence or on a "*speck*" of the truth.

HALLUCINATIONS are even further away from reality — consisting of perceptions of sights, sounds, or odors which do not really exist, although they are very real to the fleer from reality. Usually, both delusions and hallucinations are merely extreme and lasting lacks, losses, or blocks to getting love or to the experiencing of overwhelming frustrations.

Of course, from time to time we all indulge in such flights from reality. Our reason is to weaken the effects of our emotional disturbances by recharging our energy and sanity batteries. After a temporary rest, we can come back with a mind clear enough to face the cause of the problem and handle it.

"*Regrouping*" is done in order to renew our vigor and strength as we return to reality to take on the problems we just ran from. But the problem with emotional escapes is that the cause of the disturbance does not go away and is not left behind.

There is always the danger of the escape being permanent. Permanent escapes cause one to spin off into another world away from reality and make a home there. The magic, fantasy, and distortions of reality are so attractive that one does not mind getting trapped and caged in this "far out" and unrealistic world. The fleer settles down as a more or less permanent resident in the escape world and sets up the rules and all else associated with creating a new world. An analogy is with run-away slaves (**Maroons**) who settle in remote areas where it is extremely difficult to make a living but where they are relatively safe.

Behaviors which come out of this escape world seems bizarre to reasonable people. Obviously there are all sorts of distorted and fantasy worlds people live in. Let us now look at some of these worlds of escape—those that are selective; those that are complete and temporary; and those that are complete and permanent worlds of escape.

DENIAL

The Story of Denial: The ostrich, the largest of modern birds, has a habit of poking its head in the sand. One explanatory theory is that the bird, since it can feed on almost anything, is probably eating gravel and stones so that these can help its gizzard to grind up tough food. An older theory in the early 1600's was based on the belief that ostriches burrow their heads in sand thinking they will not be seen simply because the sand obscured their vision and therefore they could not see!

Subsequently, when the idea of *"to bury (or hide) one's head in the sand"* was transferred to human behavior it implied refusing to face something by pretending not to see it. In other words, to ignore or hide from obvious signs of danger — to purposely ignore facts and sensations that one finds unpleasant so as to protect oneself from a great deal of stress.

The root definitions of the word DENIAL—each of which implies *burying one's head in the sand*"— embrace the concepts of:

To "*say no to*" negate (to make ineffective)

To"*refuse*" — "*there is none*" –i.e. not accepting something as real

To *"say something is not true*"—saying something never happened

The World of Denial: Denial ("no")— a word containing the meaning of "no" to reality and which declares reality as false and therefore is about a refusal to accept — without necessarily bringing reasons to bear. Based on the three root definitions it has three broad categories:

Category I— THE FAILING TO SEE: The trade-off for not seeing, knowing, or understanding something dangerous or unpleasant, is failing to do the essential foresight, forethought, adjusting, adapting, or accommodation for safety and security. Psychologists view the "*Denial of Reality*" as the denier simply failing to perceive that something exists. Such a person may be totally unaware that he/she has feelings of hostility or has actually committed a crime.Denial may be so complete that one may be in the process of stealing and shut out what one is doing so completely as to be unaware that he is a thief. He will then proceed as if nothing ever happened.

Amnesia (memory is temporarily lost) is the clearest evidence for denial of impulses, desires, memories, or behaviors that might threaten our self-esteem or cause us anxiety or might cause us shame, embarrassment, feelings of guilt, or belittle us. This means that if it is not organic then the offending thoughts and feelings are *Repressed* (i.e. conveniently forgetting what might otherwise be troublesome). In particular, some of the more personal memories are lost whereas impersonal memories are not.

Category II— THE FAILING TO ACCEPT WHAT IS SEEN: Or sometimes "deny" means to contradict or to declare the untruth of something—whether correct or not. An example is denying any memory, desire, or behavior that we or others might interpret as self-belittling or self-degrading or unethical (improper actions) or immoral or illegal.

One may fail to accept what one sees in oneself. It is human nature to maintain a self-concept that lives up to one's philosophy of life — and especially one's standard of goodness — even when it is not true. As a result, anything we think, feel, say, and do is justified in our minds so as to make us appear to our self as if we are "*right*" — despite being far from right. To JUSTIFY is to either present the truth or present something short of the truth(e.g. excuses, wishful thinking) to oneself and/or to others that what happened was a reasonable and decent thing to do.

Category III—THE SEEING BUT NOT BELIEVING: Delusions are examples. Failing to see, accept, or believe what exist also extends outside oneself. For example, though obvious to everyone else, parents may fail to see, accept, or believe physical or mental defects or the lack of superstar abilities in their children. Some senior citizens are prone to deny the evidence of their physical and mental decline. Having eyes that will not see or that change what they see are a great part of everybody's everyday activities.

People who experience "*seeing but not believing*" are not lying, or are not refusing to accept, or are not consciously dismissing it from their minds. Instead, they are saying: "*this really isn't happening to me*" or "*I did not believe what I just saw.*" In a severe crisis, such denial reactions may give the person time to face the grim facts at a more gradual pace.

This is certainly true for many Black Americans who leave the comfortable caring atmosphere of their home and neighborhood to enter the world where people not only do not care about them but find pleasure in inflicting pain and suffering on them. Even the reality of being around people who do not care is more easily dealt with by denial. Not until my senior years of life could I accept that there are people without compassion.

Management of Denial: Failure to see, accept, or believe becomes a problem when harm occurs. To deny is about fear and lack of courage. For management suggestions of both, see the indepth discussion of "Fear."

DISSOCIATIONS

Huggins (Black Odyssey, p. 49) mentions an impressive mechanism used by the slaves. After describing the African's capture from the motherland and the horrible ordeal of the Middle Passage, the slaves' sense of personal tragedy and private misfortune was diluted and washed away as one became mixed with and overwhelmed by the lesser and the prior ones. The slaves were kept exhausted and underfed in body and spirit — too benumbed to hope for more than the end of the ordeal and of the nightmare. *Besides the absence of hope which left a void in the slaves' minds, there was also the emptiness that came when their fear was gone as a result of having gone through the hour-glass stricture of apathy* (Bailey, Self-Esteem). Furthermore, since nothing of the worse of what had occurred seemed real, there was nothing more to fear.

They had already been transported beyond the bounds of known or imagined sensibility so that each new insult was like a load added to a camel's back on his way to giving up on life and becoming apathetic. Huggins continues: "the surrender of the spirit and the will to numbness was in its own way a choice of death, a retreat of the consciousness into a tomb of insensibility. Only the automatic, physiological reflexes acted on nervous response to keep the biological apparatus functioning." To me, this is the description of the mechanism leading to dissociation.

Dissociation is to many of today's struggling Black Americans as Repression is to Europeans. Although in Western culture Dissociation is considered a significant psychiatric problem, at least among many Black Americans it is a normal coping mechanism brought about by necessity. This is most prominently seen during slavery. Perhaps those slaves which did not internalize the Sambo role or its equivalent probably had varying degrees of dissociation. Those I have seen in my practice maintained close relation with their Real Selves.

Since dissociations are such an ever present state of being in Black people's lives, let us explore this subject in great detail. But first, what is dissociation? Suppose a "normal" person has some early traumatic experiences that undermine confidence and self-esteem (e.g. the loss or separation from a parent at a critical stage of development). Or, suppose at a later time in life an echo of the early loss occurs and places unusual demands on the already vulnerable reward system. That echo is particularly likely to affect people with few social supports—family, friends, or lovers. The brain's response to these psychological traumas is one of a diminished ability to experience emotion, including pleasure.

Paradoxically, this lack of emotion—this "**Numbness**"—this freeze—is deeply felt and is incredibly painful because it is a combination of Emotional and Spiritual pain. At the same time, ones activities, ones sociability, and therefore ones opportunity for pleasures and rewards decrease. One tries less; gets less; and feels increasingly worse. Eventually, one simply separates this painful part of oneself and retains the non-painful self—the process of dissociation.

As a freshman at the University of Michigan, a new experience—one of dissociation—occurred during my initiation into a fraternity. This was the experience of feeling no physical pain when it was being inflicted. In wondering how this could happen I thought about dissociations that many of us associate with sleep and what some people say about undergoing "out-of-body" experiences, particularly at the moment of being near death (Bynum, p. 81, 193).

Practically all Blacks are heavily into DISSOCIATION whereby the realities of life so painful that the individual *represses* entire episodes. In the Western world, the concept of **Isolation** (a variant of Dissociation where one keeps apart certain mental conflicts, desires, and attitudes because it would cause too much emotional stress to bring them together) is most prominently displayed in the story of "Dr. Jekyll and Mr. Hyde" by Robert Louis Stevenson. The entire topic of Dissociation has been fully discussed elsewhere (Bailey Freeing Enslaved Minds p307, 105).

Management of Dissociation: The type present in the Western world needs to be managed by mental health specialist. For those "normal" types in Black people, I suspect the problem would dissolve spontaneously once they are no longer affected by racism and the pain and distress emotions caused by racism. It is important to ensure that pleasure at least gets "equal time"—and that the pleasure extends over (unconscienously) into the dissocitated painful self once the source of the pain is gone. It may require a great deal of time and effort to make this happen.

DISTORTION

The Story of Distortion: No doubt, distortion (*"to twist different ways"*) began with the perceptions of the earliest ancestors of the human species—Homo Erectus. Chances are that perceived distortions were present wherever they migrated (in waves) out of Africa 1 million years ago. Colonizing Europe, the Middle East, and Asia, they lived mainly in caves and eventually learned to control fire. In the process, whenever dangerous animals appeared, they gathered a handful of long, dry grass stems out of the cave's store area; twisted them together; held one end to the fire; and then used this "torch" to scare away the animals.

This practice of twisting grass formed the idea that gave rise to a variety of words like distort, turtle and torture. The concept of the twist going away from the natural direction or posture of the thing involved meant that parts of the whole remained in order and the other parts were in disorder — that is, "twisted away" from its proper senses and direction.

During the period of the European Renaissance (16th and 17th centuries), there was great emphasis on etiquette and civil rules of conduct. Distortion was a word aimed—not so much at calling a lie a lie and telling speakers of falsehoods that they were liars— but rather at sparing the feelings of those prevaricators through hypocritical comments.

Since then, distortion in general has come to mean any twisting or contorting (bent, knotted, or warped) that alters the shape of something so that it no longer faithfully represents the object. For example, amusement parks have a hall of trick mirrors whereby full-length distortion mirrors make grotesque and ludicrous changes in the faces and figures of onlookers.

The World of Distortions: The thing distorted is like adding strangers to a family album and failing to distinquish the strangers as such from blood relatives. Distorted thinking may be a reflection of a deliberate purpose (e.g. for caricature, cartoons, and comic strips); of pathological thinking; of an intent to deceive; or of ignorance.

These are the measures which contribute to the creation of delusions. When children are given incomplete, dumb, stupid, or any other explanation that is not the truth, then the child uses magical or distorted thinking to taking what they were told and trying to make sense out of it. This can have lifetime adverse affects. For example, if a child is told that making money is the meaning of success, that child will go through life with this limited view and might spend all of his/her life making money.

A stimulus which creates real fear plus anxiety (e.g. excessive worry) typically leads to distortion, especially in the young child. Also, reinforcing the secondary emotion of moderate anger—like adding leaves to a head of lettuce—can result in hate, as occurs with feuds. Features of feuds are clannishness, problems causing scarcity and struggling (e.g. famine, poverty), and revenge.

Managing Distortions: To shatter distortions, the bottom line is to discover the truth. This requires not jumping to conclusions. Instead, I gather all available evidence before giving consideration to things on all of its planes of existence. In life-shaping and life-changing matters, I do not rely on anything even an authority or an expert says—and people's opinions have no meaning except to spur me to look at something from a different point of view or add something I forgot or make more clear some main point. Rather, an all-out effort is made to get back to the source of the information and evaluate that source for credibility.

Then the gathered information and the credibility of the source is examined by Rational Thinking. Pertinent information is **assessed on all sides—from the top down—the bottom up—each angle involving each side—and both sides of each side.** Next, a structure is built and tested. What is accepted is that the final product fits with your education, training, experience, intuition, common sense, and it "feels" right.

FANTASY

The Story of Fantasy: There are not many more complex words, containing more complex concepts, and tied in with a more complex family group than **Fantasy** (see Bailey, Creativity for an extensive discussion). Originally, the word "fantasy" (Greek "phantasia" — a making visible) was associated with a magic-lantern show. This came about because the fireplace in ancient times was the prominent method of heating rooms in homes of upper class people. As the physical center of home life, the floor of the fireplace was made of brick or stone and was "open." Therefore it was called a hearth.

Apart from the openness of the hearth causing a considerable waste of heat, water in a kettle was heated by the wood burning into a flame. Naturally, the heating of the water and the people in the room made the hearth the center of home life — meaning the common point where anything, like family discussions, occurred.

At night, it was the flame which gave the light that flickered with varying degrees of intensity. The flickers of fire coming out of the hearth produced dancing shadows and this appearance of an unusual or strange nature was apprehended by the mind as being a magic lantern show.

The result was that different family members in the room would sometimes see different things rather clearly. However, sometimes they saw something so hazily that they had to use their imagination to get an idea of what it was. The warmth and the dim light enticed family members to drift off into such deep thought that thoughts and things in the room seemed to blend together.

That point of blending between thoughts and things — between the subjective and objective — was called phantasia or fantasy or fancy. These words, synonyms at first, meant "*to make visible*" or "*to bring to light*" by means of imagining objects or events in terms of imagery.

In the 1st century A.D. the Greek word "*phantasia*" was predominantly used in cases where, carried away by enthusiasm and passion, you think you see what you describe, and you place it before the eyes of your hearers. The Greek word for "show or appear" is "phos"— indicating phantom, fantasy, and fancy.

Fantasia was used by the Greek philosophers when they referred to a power of the mind for putting things before its self. Our word PHANTOM (an image formed in the imagination and not from the senses) deriving from fantasia, illustrates this power.

Subsequently, "*Fantasy*" and "*imagination,*" both found in Chaucer's (1340?-1400) works, referred to "*a mental image or reflection*"— or more particularly "*an image of something which either has no real existence or does not exist.*" **IMAGINATION** was deemed to be a more seriously and deeply creative faculty which perceives the basic resemblances between things. This was because it can decompose its conceptions and recombine the resultant elements as well as with—or alternating with—combining previous experiences (i.e. the CREATIVE POWER) at its pleasure.

Meanwhile, although the sense of the unreal continued to survived in Fantastic, the showing of the face in an imaginative way or THE APPEARANCE OF SOMETHING THAT IS UNREAL, UNRESTRAINED, OR EXTRAVAGANT remained as the concept inside Fantansy. Whereas imagination was regarded as the superior faculty, Fancy (a contraction of Fantasy) and Fantasy (15th century) where considered as kinds of assistants to imagination. But Fantasy was more akin to Imagination than Fancy.

At this time (1490), "**Faculty"** meant the power or ability to do something; **Fancy**, an artistic ability to create whimsical and usually unreal ideas or decorations; and "*Whimsy,*" a fanciful idea that is quaint or odd or possibly amusing or playful in a child-like way. Of course, Fantasy was a foundational stone of Comedy. Fantasy has been in English for 600 years and for much of that time it has been merely a variant spelling for "Fancy." Fancy and fantasy then evolved as two separate words with separate pronunciations and with distinctive, although related meanings.

In John Milton's (1608-1674) Paradise Loss (V:100-106), Fantasy is the highest quality after reason itself. Charles Dickens (1812-1870), in "Hard Times," considered "Fancy" all the good and graceful impulses of warm human sensibility. Subsequently, Fantasy lost its equivalent to imagination and acquired a lesser, an even pejorative meaning of a ghostly figure.

The World of Fantasy: Today, Fantasy is thought of as the imagining of objects, symbols, or events not immediately present — a utopian or otherwise unreal play of the mind. Creative persons translate fancy and fantasy into and through their skill — painting, poetry, folk art, etc. Because throughout much of its history fantasy was the term for a mental image that takes the form of imagined events, daydreams, or night dreams based on wishes and unfulfilled impulses, it was embraced by psychoanalytical approaches.

Because fantasy's setting originated in an imaginary world and featured the magic of mythical beings, it was brought into literature as a general term for any kind of fictional work that was not primarily devoted to realistic representation of the known world. Its category has included several literary genres — fable, fancy tales, dream vision, romance, and science fiction — describing imagined worlds in which magical powers and other impossibilities are accepted.

Because fantasy artistically permitted seemingly unrelated objects to be brought together in a fine incongruity, as in Rousseau's famous "*Dream*" (1910) painting, modern painters welcomed it.

Nevertheless, *too little Fantasy stifles creativity while too much Fantasy is a psychological problem.* Mentally unhealthy people who engage in fantasy generate stories that are not in keeping with reality. If there is no realistic danger (and thus no grounds for real fear), then pure anxiety is a Fantasy Mental Image. When reason is added to a perception of pain that is a distortion or a fantasy, a psychopathological form of Emotional Pain is present.

Management of Fantasy: Something needs to be done about Fantasy it it interfers with in any way with ones life. Because it is an extremely common Escape Emotion, its management starts with facing reality and having a plan for handling any problem which comes up, even if one has never seen nor heard of before the problem being faced. This requires courage to face the fear (see discussion of Fear). In addition, the comments made for managing Distortions apply here.

"FRIGHT" EMOTIONS

"Numbness" and Anesthesia of Emotions are the intermediate—or "Fright"—part of the "Fight or Flight" reaction when one is backed into a corner. As discussed under Dissociation, this happened to me during the time of my initiation into a fraternity. It also occurred to a sublte degree throughout my orthopaedic surgical training when I was constantly in a hostile atmosphere. That subtle level was sufficient to keep me from feeling psychical pains to the point that I wanted to react with like kind hostility. In other words, it was like the reverse of stress but had the same effect of helping to increase my alertness and sense of control.

But psychologist and psychiatrist speak of the kind of selfhood "Anesthesia" associated with the degradation of love. Choisy (p62) states that prostitutes—and their partners, pimps, and customers— are afflicted with some lack of love. Examples include the father for his daughter or of the mother for her son. These frustrated children have recourse to a major defense mechanism—Security Distance—which they express as "Anesthesia."

Those who become prostitutes show a mock indifference to sexual activities as a result of their old grudges and pent-up aggressions. To gain revenge on her father, the girld seeks to debase his daughter—i.e. the girl herself as a prostitute. To soil the materal imago, the boy in his fantasies makes a harlot of his mother and debases her also. Hence, self-debased and debaser meet in sadomasochistic coitus. Two neurotics thereby unite for the sake of not creating but of destroying.

INSULATION OF EMOTIONS

The Story of Insulation: The shipwrecked sailor had been on the desert island for over five years when one morning he was excited to see a ship standing off shore. As a small boat rowed in and touched shore, an officer tossed the sailor a bundle of newspapers. "*The Captain's compliments*," the officer yelled, "*and he asks that you please read through these and then let him know if you still want to be rescued*."

Now the question: Will the sailor choose to stay and continue to reflect on his own thoughts, feelings, and experience (i.e. an INTROVERT) or will he board the boat to get back into the social world (i.e. an EXTROVERT)? The sailor made the compromise to re-enter the social world but to reduce his emotional involvement in the painful social situations he read about in the newspapers. Psychologists term such compromises as Emotional Insulation.

In 1538 the word "*insulation*"— as part of the process of isolating— meant to make into an island. By the 1700's its expanded meaning was "*to keep from losing electricity, sound, or heat*." When the mental health profession embraced the term, it became the quality or state of being narrowminded or circumscribed in outlook mentally and in character.

The lay public then got involved and applied the following names.

Ice Cubes are able to keep their "Cool"—their poise— all the time, even when someone is "in your face" and calling them bad names. Professional diplomats are in this category in order to conduct negotiations effectively.

The "*Blocks of Ice*" are those who stay insulated all the time so as to defend themselves against anxiety and frustrations

The World of Emotional Insulation: As a result of accumulating experiences of frustrations and disappointments, all of us learn to self-protect by lowering our expectations and by restricting emotional involvement in the attainment of our goals—maybe once or a few times.In an emotional sense, an insulated person shows a little bit of suppression, withdrawal, and a little of dissociation to the point of withdrawning into a sort of shell of passivity.

However, to remain stuck in that "*cool*" pose so as to avoid showing feelings of rejection, embarrassment or other bad emotions also shuts down ones feelings and expressions of affection and intimacy. For example, many inner city youth say: "*there is no point in even trying for that goal*" and then proceed not to care about any goal.

Many females (and males) who have been terribly disappointed in their first great love may be very careful not to allow themselves to become so emotionally involved on subsequent occasions. Gathering support from other wounded females, they may go on to hate men. Many children who have been badly bruised by sexual abuse or by other of life's blows become cold, detached, aloof. Thereafter, they are unable to either give or receive normal affection.

In more extreme conditions of long-continued frustration, as in chronic unemployment or prison confinement, many Black Americans lose hope, become resigned and apathetic, and adapt themselves to a restricted way of living — and with an extremely low level of aspiration.

Similar to the apathetic, these "*broken*" individuals self-protect from the bitter hurts of sustained frustration and disappointment by giving up and accepting whatever life brings them. Even worse is that they often cannot muster enough energy to help their own children. This lackluster way of living is then passed from one generation to the next as a way of life.

Another way that "*brokenness*" shows is by shallow living — the avoidance of healthy, vigorous participation in life's problems designed to lead to success. Self-protection is done by keeping their distance from all except close friends. They either will not try situations where they might fail or try something new for fear of being ridiculed. Either one prevents them from gaining the skills to overcome their fear of failure.

Management of Emotional Insulation: "If you can remain cool in all this confusion, you simply don't understand the situation." Many do not understand the situation with respect to the effects that their insulation will have on their lives. It might be helpful to have these youth take a tour of the homeless communities and talk to homeless people who insulated themselves.

Another problem is **Fear of Failure**. Again this has been discussed in the section on Fear and Courage. Briefly, failure is likely if one lacks the self-confidence and the planning and preparation to make success happen. Otherwise, if one has a track record of trying and failing, a starting point is a shift in thinking. For example, acknowledge that failure may need to occur if something is poorly prepared for or if the timing is not right or if one is in the wrong place. Or, perhaps failure results from "biting off more than I can chew." Or, maybe you "bit" into the "wrong" thing and now need to find something else.

Do what it takes to provide evidence that you have the ability to succeed. On the way to proper goals, failure never occurs unless one gives up. However, there will be frequent setbacks that are part of the climb to the goal.

As a result of low self-esteem they isolate themselves even more through having haughty and angry type behaviors. The secret here is to do things which build self-confidence (Table IV).

REPRESSION

The Story of Repression: In the 12th century, when medieval romance developed in Western Europe, the Old French word "*romanz*" meant "*the speech of the people.*" Thus, their early epics about romance simply told a story of what happened and had nothing to do with the inner workings of the mind, like motivation or justifying actions.

But gradually new techniques evolved that analyzed actions, motives, and states of mind — the beginnings of the modern novel. A leader of the analytical method was Chaucer's *Troilus* and *Criseyde* (before 1385). This love poem, within the setting of the legendary Trojan War, moves in leisurely fashion but is dominated by scattered introspection and psychological insight.

Parts dealing with *"restrain," "weaken," "check,"* and *"keep down"* were called *"repressions"* (*"to push back"* in the sense of exerting force). Thereafter, psychoanalysts embraced "*repress*" in reference to preventing the natural normal development of certain thoughts and to limit the spontaneous activity of those thoughts.

Today, "*repress*" means a form of inhibition by which a person denies or "negatives" a bad deep-seated impulse or emotion and treats it as if it never existed. London says that repression is the master defense mechanism [for Euro-Americans].

The World of Repression: Conveniently forgetting what might otherwise be troublesome is called Repression. Despite pushing this information out of awareness, the disharmonious thoughts continue to operate independently of any conscious control and can cause us to do things that seem weird even to us—"I have no idea why I did that!"

Repression is especially likely when a person feels guilty, shamed, or frustrated from some event. Such thoughts and memories cause emotional and/or spiritual pain. In turn, that pain causes anxiety and body tension. In the process, you are unaware of your desire to want to forget the bad emotions. Furthermore, you want to do the unhealthy thing you are not aware that you are doing. As a result, you deny your bad actions.

Nevertheless, what happens is that your bad emotions are "*pushed down*" into your sub-awareness but simultaneously it is always "*pushing back*" in order to return to your awareness level. This is like using your little finger to push a big cork underwater—a process involving a great deal of "*slipping and sliding.*" Suppose your little finger represents the mental force of repression.

Since the job of pushing down the cork (the bad emotion) is so great, it needs additional defense mechanisms for reinforcement. For example, if you are trying to repress the hate portion of a love/hate situation concerning your mother, that hate may be displaced to your female teachers. Then you design Rationalizations to make your otherwise irrational behaviors toward the teachers appear acceptable to you and to others.

Now your repressed hate for your mother (which periodically shows when your self-control is down) as well as your artificial hate for your female teachers create even more tension. That tension causes you to dislike your bad emotions and their expressions — both of which make your tensions and bad emotions even worse—the situation of a vicious cycle.

If your repressed hate for your mother is successfully kept out of your awareness, the activity of the repressed hate that you are not aware of causes a generalized and inaccessible tension that you are at a loss to explain. This tension remains as alive as it ever was and contributes to a lasting maladjustment.

Psychologists say that although repression is essential to normal functioning in activities of daily living, too much is harmful. When too much, repression calls in its buddy defense mechanisms whose job it is to distort, lie, and deceive the person. As a result, repression's purpose of protecting the individual against anxiety makes it the most basic and the most important of all the defense mechanisms. Complete repression is present when it has:

(1) Removed painful or threatening memories, thoughts, ideas, or perceptions from consciousness;

(2) Kept them in the unconscious; and/or

(3) Prevented unconscious but disturbing aggressive or sexual impulses from breaking into consciousness.

This means that the individual is unable to recall or recognize or believe what is recognized because of that person's need to "save face" — to preserve his/her self-concept.

An extreme example of repression is non-traumatic **AMNESIA** (a complete loss of memory) resulting from the forgetting attempt to escape from unbearable reality. *Partial amnesia*, instead of being selective forgetting, is more in the nature of selective remembering because the material denied admission to consciousness is never really forgotten. In fact, Freud said that repressed memories are "*virtually immortal; after the passing of decades, they behave as though they had just occurred.*"

That is why repressed traumatic events of childhood can and usually do cause psychological disorders (neuroses) in adults. Because the childhood trauma remains at such an intensive level, it keeps the person's psychological system under so much pressure that anxiety, felt but not understood, still persists. Besides being unable to remember the childhood trauma, he/she may not be able to see an object or person in plain sight that was associated with the trauma. Nor may he/she be aware of feelings that at one time he/she freely expressed. Some may experience frequent illnesses, sometimes to the point of physical disabilities without any organic reason (e.g. Conversion Hysteria).

Yet, repression is seldom complete. *Incomplete Repression* is like a damning up of a pool of mental energy. In this metaphor, just as water will leak through any crack in a dam, repressed thoughts, desires, and memories will leak through the walls of repression into conscious awareness wherever the barrier is not perfect. When such material leaks through, its ideas are distorted in ways that make them less threatening.

Since emotions are cyclic, by reducing the anxiety coming from psychic pain, one's pleasures are also reduced to the same degree. One reason is that the beneficial parts contained in the desire cannot be cultivated separately and failing to make that part flower reduces the person's opportunity to experience pleasure. A person has only a certain allotment of daily mental energy. Thus, if too much energy is bound up in the active process of repression there will be little left for other activities. People burdened with repression have so little energy left that they behave in a robot-like manner— and not spontaneously and not creatively.

Managing Repression: To paraphrase a passage in the Bible: Seek the truth and the truth shall set you free. Discovery what is causing you guilt, shame, or pain by any means possible. A place to start is with an in-depth analysis of the "weird" things you do but can not explain. Write out your thoughts, feelings, and emotions and follow them back wherever they lead (see the Check Method). This may require the assistance of a mental health specialist.

Once the discovery is made as to what is being repressed, healthy relief comes only by acknowledging the guilt, shame, or pain — whether brought on by anger, fear, or some other emotions. The problem can start to be dealt with by knowing what is feared or hated. Management starts with forgiveness of you and/or the trigger person. Next is to either to avoid it or learn a more constructive response.

WISHES

The concept giving rise to the word "wishes" evolved from the ancient practice of asking favors from the gods. Compared with reality, wishes range from distortions of reality to fantasy. Wishes are desires for distortions of reality or fantasies which are not possible to grasp. Wishing for realistic things may or may not be possible to grasp.

People operating in the world of wishes want things to happen that are either unattainable or probably not attainable. If they are attainable they want them to happen magically: "*it exists because I say so*" — the idea of thinking of something to be true simply because they want it to be. Evidence to the contrary is ignored, as with the statement: "*my mind is made up so don't confuse me with the facts.*" The arena of wishes causes people to believe that merely thinking about an act is the same as actually doing it. This is typical of young children who have not learned the distinction between thought and action.

As opposed to the magical direction that wishes can take, the world of wishes can be used as an escape from the frustrations of reality. Yet, wishing will never give them what they want because its colors do not match with what is reasonable.

Management is to learn to face reality and the truth. Then one must learn how to skillfully play the hand that one is given.

VIII

MASQUERADE EMOTIONS

Masquerades are performances while being masked

Physical Masquerades are **False Indentities**

Mental Masquerades are FALSE REALITIES

The Story of Masks and Masquerades: At least as far back as 30,000 years, African masks have been used for sacred purposes; as a conveyor of some deep symbolic meaning; or to teach certain life-shaping concepts to children of the village. Probably starting in Central West Africa, masks were originally markings applied to the face. Their colorful designs supposedly possessed magical powers to protect from evil spirits.

The combination of masks with performance in religious, healing, exorcism, and funerary rituals by these early Africans were the first "*masquerades.*" The masks and costumes of masquerade dancers conveyed the message that performers were assuming mystical roles and therefore were "*standing apart*" from the roles of their every day lives. In the early mysterious African initiation rituals, so awesome was the transformation occurring in each initiate that each reaction stage needed to be hidden by the appropriate mask.

As part of the practice of treating "psychological" problems, African "ritual specialists" wore masks to enabled African patients to **Personify** (to convert the invisible into being able to see something specific) that which they otherwise could not imagine. As a result, hidden fears located in the deep recesses of their psyche could be brought to light and handled — a practice picked up by innumerable Western psychiatrists (e.g. the Rorschach tests).

Situational Masqueraders (Bailey, Self-Esteem) have historically come into being when circumstances call for a form of self-protection having to do with disguising ones real emotional expressions (e.g. with flattery of someone disliked) or suppressing one true emotional expressions so as to have a "poker face". Humans and animals alike may resort to *"fight or flight"* self-protection; to **camouflage** (blending into the surroundings); to **mimicry** (presenting a false identity); and/or to **withdrawal** *"shell-protection"* (as turtles do because they are too slow moving to escape by running).

Since the beginning of African-American slavery, these forms of masquerades for the purpose of self-protection have been used by Black Americans. Because the typical situation of slaves was one of constantly being trapped while in the presence of a very evil enemy, the vast majority of slaves used the mental equivalent of the turtle's *"shell-protection"* method. When turtles sense danger their heads withdraw inside their shell and the upper and lower halves of the shell close tightly.

Let us suppose that one of the mental activities slaves perfected and culturally transmitted was a similar process any time they were around their captors. Yet, while in a *"mental retraction"* state, many slaves cleverly used deception. Such deception included various forms of personality and behavioral camouflage and/or mimicry to either enhance their chances of surviving or to lessen what they did not want. Perhaps the most common mimicry deceptions were the *"Uncle Tom"* and the *"Sambo"* caricatures (Bailey, Self-Esteem, p154-163).

Furthermore, masks and masquerades continued to be needed in the post-slavery setting because of the *"Negro Caste System,"* the Black Codes, the Jim Crow laws (pertaining to political, social, and legal systems), and terrorism. All of these systems, laws, and customs—representing extensions of the Slave Codes—reached a peak in the 1890's, lasted legally until the 1960's, and in a diluted form of custom, persist to this day.

Each system was designed to keep Blacks in a position of permanent subservience and to ensure Blacks would show no signs of intelligence, success, or anything above an inferiority complex level. Understandably, this generated every conceivable kind of self-destructive emotion in the Black people involved—emotions which were culturally transmitted into today's descendents.

Throughout its history, and until recently, this encaging context continued to be shaped and maintained by every form of intimidation, terrorism, and direct mob violence known to mankind. Examples have been lynchings of Black men and women at *"picnics"* (a word coined from *"pick a nigger"* to lynch). In an attempt at self-preservation from evil Europeans, it was typical for Black people to use every type of masquerade emotional expression.

Meanwhile, masquerade emotional expressions were extensively used in Europe and continue to be to this day. Some of the more prominent forms include courteous emotional expressions as acts of civility to hide how they really feel; disquise; and "deflection" emotional expressions designed hide how they really feel but projecting on to scapegoats their personal evils and then blaming the innocent.

BLAME

The Story of Blame: BLAME IS THE MOST COMMON, PERVASIVE, AND ENDURING CHILDISH TRAIT OF HUMAN BEINGS. In Greek mythology, Momus— the god of laughter, censure and rebuke— carried a club. The purpose of the club was to symbolize that when he hit the other gods with scornful, disrespectful, and slanderous words, that they would feel as if they had had a very painful clubbing. Because of the gods' outrage over this practice, he was banished from Olympus (the mountain where Greek gods lived).

Thereafter, any impious utterances or actions concerning gods or sacred things giving the appearance of blame were called PROFANITY OR BLASPHEMY – "speaking that hurts." As opposed to what the gods were about, "Blame" — as in "saying profane things about" — took a non-religious direction and emphasized humans. Whether by "mockery" or by "insulting," Blame's intent was to harm one's reputation.

Being a term of shifting denotations, it acquired many forms. Around 1200 A.D., blame referred to FINDING FAULT with someone; then (18th century) "to censure (expression of disapproval) or to CRITICIZE a person for something; then (19th century) holding a criticized or accused PERSON RESPONSIBLE for some wrong doing and, in legal courts, to the placing of guilt.

Since then, the concepts contained in these three have remained essentially unchanged:

The "Finding Fault" type of Blame is accusatory;

The "Criticizing" type is accusatory and judgmental;

The "Placing Responsibility upon" oneself or another type is judgmental. The responsible person's misdeed could be of an immediate ("you hit him") or ultimate ("you are responsible for what your kids did") nature — implying the meriting of an appropiate penalty. Sometimes we correctly or incorrectly place the responsibility on our selves.

The World of Blame: Blaming comes naturally. We do it several times a day and we have done it all our lives. Hence, there are innumerable categories in which Blame is featured. Here are some examples.

Today, an extremely common form is to accuse the poor of having faulty character and/or behavior as the cause of their problems. Called **BLAMING THE VICTIM** by psychologists, the poor are stomped on twice — first for being poor and then for being responsible for being poor by causing it or allowing it.

In Racism, blame is invariably applied to the victim—i.e. to the "scapegoats." Through the defense mechanism of the *projected type of Rationalization*, racists falsely accuse victims — "its their fault for not being any better off." To "prove" themselves right, many white racists have historically prejudicially defined non-whites as an inferior category of human beings — e.g. Chinese laborers brought in to build the Canadian Pacific Railroad.

This resulted in discrimination by which non-whites were denied equal access to jobs, income, education, and political rights. Such social inferiority confined many non-whites to poverty, low-prestige occupations, and poor housing. Then the victims were blamed for being poor although prejudice and discrimination formed a vicious circle — a situation that perpetuates itself overtime.

Brainwashing gullible Blacks into believing they are inferior causes those same Blacks to say: "I must have done something to deserve this bad thing." From there, they start degrading each other: "he is so stupid he deserves not to get a job." Meanwhile, victims are busy lowering their self-esteem and life-esteem to the point of hopelessness. Not now or for the future do they see themselves being part of mainstream America.

Thus, racist acts of oppression (e.g. deliberately paying victim workers less than a living wage) results in victim reactions (e.g. gambling to make ends meet) which, in effect, "prove" to racists that such oppressive acts were warranted — "pay 'em more and they'd waste it away" racists will say.

Why is it that victims allow themselves to be defined by victimizers and then adjust to the terrible world victimizers fashion for them and then start accusing themselves and each other for being victims? Psychologist propose as an explanation the so-called *"Just World" hypothesis*. It says that "**everybody" needs to believe that the world is fair** and that people get what they deserve. Both beliefs help people make sense out of senseless happenings and feel safe in the presence of threatening events.

But this is a very bad belief when dealing with people who have a non-worth type of system of values. Anyone whose system of values is based upon things of Value is to be watched like a hawk because they are prone to greed.

Eventually, after being beatened down for prolonged periods, history tells us that victims begin to start blaming the victimizers. This becomes a *double edge sword* — cutting in a good and in a bad way. The bad way is that to blame others gives others all the control and power and therefore one remains a helpless victim.

The good way is that correct finger-pointing indicates where the problem is coming from and helps clarify the problem. Things get better when the victims take charge and control of their lives by doing non-violent things that put the victimizers on notice that injustice will no longer be tolerated—things like picketing, boycotting, block voting, and stop spending so as to make the victimizers even richer.

Managing Blame: Bystanders verified that the tourist had the right of way and was driving slowly through the intersection when Titan deliberately ran into him. Yet, the police officer blamed and arrested the tourist. "Why?", asked the tourist. "Because," said the cop firmly, "Titan's father is the Mayor, his brother is the Chief of Police, and I'm going steady with his sister."

This scenario is actually the way it is in many situations involving blame. For the more fair-minded, as extremely important question is: "When things do not go right, where do you place the blame?" The Cause determines the approach to managing blame but sometimes that cause is not what it appears to be.

For example, the helpless have a tendency to blame themselves for their misfortunes but there are many factors which have led up to their state of helplessness. With struggling Black Americans, those causes can be traced back to slavery. To correct the struggling is about a planned approach to break up the vicious cycle; to discover all the problems; and to reverse whatever is causing each problem. If the issue is one of having trouble getting enough to eat, then focus on developing ways of making money and on developing forsight and forethought to as to handle the future essentials of living on a routine basis. For this to succeed requires breaking up many Enslaved Mind bad habits.

Nevertheless, the philosophy related to blame requires critical thought and flexibility. Whereas for healthy minds, blaming others is a block, for minds in poverty, blaming others may be what is needed to cope with bad life events. But once in the self-acceptance and receptive mood for self-growth, then taking responsibility, rather than blaming others, is likely to give the most progress.

For extremely troubled youth, blame must be looked at entirely differently — in the context of survival—as compared to those who are not struggling. Typically, many extremely troubled youth improperly self-blame for bad events beyond their control.

Habitual self-blame leads to depression and poor performance. Then they blame themselves as a person rather than blaming their bad behavior. This causes poor coping in later stressful situations. For instance, there have been times when I was so beaten down that for me to take responsibility for a problem I caused — which was actually the right thing to do — would have been "the straw that broke the camel's back" and greatly worsened my emotional state. Self-blame would have temporarily resulted in a serious loss of self-esteem and my fragile self-confidence would have been shattered.

For the poor, who are already over-burdened to the breaking point, it is sometimes better not to blame them, even though they are wrong. Furthermore, having them delay self-blame may be important for their survival. For similar reasons, even if not completely justified, by having the poor blame others—particularly if they are suicide prone— may be what is needed to get them through a crisis. Despite not protecting them from feelings of helplessness, this preserves whatever self-esteem is present. When they are emotionally stronger, they can face reality in order to see the part they played in the problem.

Otherwise, when deserved, it is best to self-blame *one's behaviors* as opposed to blaming *who one is as a person.* Yet, self-blame is only justified when one did something bad that one knew before-hand was bad. If one did the best one could under the circumstances, even if one now knows better, self-blame is not justified.

Success at doing something or multiple small successes help re-establish a sense of control, enable you to see things more realistically, and lift spirits when one is in tough times.

With extremely helpless people, even success may not give them faith in their ability. The challenge is to get their attention and to discover what will get them anchored into something. For some, being challenged to do better may work. For others it may be by learning about their rich heritage.

Something that can be tried with extremely helpless people is to put them on a winning team, perhaps as a rotating leader. The objective is to put them in the flow that may sweep them along into a success-oriented mentality. From there, they can be taught to assess their experiences more optimistically.

BLAME IS THE MOST COMMON THING WE DO TO OTHER PEOPLE. Except as mentioned above, it is of emince benefit to give up blaming anybody, including your self, for any thing. Two self-accessment questions leading to the start of self-growth are: "WHEN THINGS GO WRONG IN THE WORLD, WHO DO I BLAME?" and "WHEN I FAIL, WHERE DO I PLACE THE BLAME?"

As outrageous as it may seem to Black Americans, a giant step toward becoming free of an Enslaved Mind and to rise above racism is to STOP BLAMING THE RACIST! This does not mean accepting the evils they have done and "letting them off the hook." But realize that blaming them will do no good because they are too deeply evil to change—and they will never change!

Instead, to giving up blame is done so as to take control of our own destiny. I know that this is extremely hard to do — especially when we know we know we are justified. When I decided to break the cycle, it took me one year of conscious effort to overcome 85%; three years to overcome another 10%; and five years to overcome blame completely. My reward was the freeing of space in my mind for use in making my life better.

Remember: TO STOP BLAMING IS FOR YOUR BENEFIT, NOT THEIRS.

CIVILITY EMOTIONS

A Story of Civility Emotions: Civility is masked forms of behaviors that hide ones true thoughts and emotions. Whereas **Manners** reflect the feelings of one's good character and whereas **Etiquette** is personality conforming to established ethical behavior (proper/improper) related to appearances, Civility is a display of personality.

"**Personality**" is the part of ones character and self-esteem interacting with people in the outside world (as opposed to those within ones intimate circle). The emotions which come out of Civility are of a **Euphemistic** nature—i.e. the use of socially acceptable indirect expressions instead of displaying the harsh or unpleasantly thoughts from which the euphemistic emotions (of which there are many) derive. A broad ranging example of the euphemistic emotions is the word "Courteous."

Originally, the word "**Courteous**" meant displaying behaviors suitable to the social customs of a royal court. However, people in royal courts ranged from being shallow and concerned only about externals all the way over to those having firm convictions and principles associated with good character. Nevertheless, they all had the same approach — to please people of the court.

Yet, variations came in their *methods* (the choice of saying or doing something), *techniques* (what was actually said or done), and *manner* (the way it was said or done). Their success depended upon customs at a particular court during a specific time period. For example, Ancient Egyptians had a religious orientation whereby being **Cultured** (a real and high development of mind and soul) in technique was far more important than external and shallow appearances.

By contrast, for the barbaric Eurasians and Europeans, the highest level of interaction was on being **Civil** (i.e., simply avoiding being rude). Out of barbarism arose the **Feudal system** (900-1300 A.D.), which, in turn, gave rise to the **Age of Chivalry** — the codes of knights, which characterized "gentlemen." Chivalry's features were knights in the pursuit of courtly ladies, participation in the Crusade Wars (11th to 13th centuries) and engaging in warlike games of joust and tourney.

Up to the mid-1100 A.D., knights in armor were like modern tanks that walked. So, to let others know who was inside their encaging armor, they began wearing cloaks over their armor. These outer garments contained special patterns — called **Coats of Arms** — which were placed on the shields and banner flags of knights.

Probably the first families to use shield designs as Coats of Arms did so because they wanted everyone to know they were descended from those warriors who had declared themselves as noble knights. This was the beginning of **Heraldry** in Europe. Because of their association with the nobility, Coats of Arms eventually became a symbol of rank and evidence that the user and his descendants were gentleman. Thus, to bear arms became the mark of a gentleman, including those who owned castles.

Because it was routine in Europe for everyone to fight everyone –all the time—it was necessary for the castle owners to hire barbaric warriors. Then, as "barnyard courts" began to spring up out of the castles and evolve to serve as courtrooms, it was the king's council and attendants who decided what was "befitting a royal court." Since the barbaric warriors lived in and around the castle and intermingled with people of the court, the council, the Church and the ladies of the court did what they could to bring some civility to them. To this end they devised practices and codes (which had to be signed).

The *Knight's Code* — centering on honor, loyalty, religion, generosity, and courtesy — only applied to members of a knight's own class (i.e., other knights, lords, and their ladies). Otherwise, they disregarded the Code. Although they had no interest in religion, they remained civil to leaders of the Church by showing the approach emotions. Knights who disliked each still respected each other sufficiently to be civil. To everyone else, they were not even civil.

In legal situations, it was the king's council and attendants associated with the court whom criminal suspects **Flattered** in hopes those flattered would favorably influence the king.

Meanwhile, whatever behavior appeared in the king's residence was considered *Respectful* (appropriately measured honor given to others), *Polite* (following rules of conduct of high society as a habit of good manners), and *Courteous* (a positive show of consideration for others, especially on a specific occasion).

The World of Civil Emotions: Today, political candidates are experts at civility. They can publically attack each other, as in debating on stage. At the end of the debate or once a candidate has been chosen, some will say "nice" phrases, shake hands, smile, and greet each other's families.

Managing Civil Emotions: Obviously, in dealing with legal or political or high society, it is important to know how to play the game involving Civil Emotions.

Civility Emotions and behaviors are about acting, regardless of how you feel to the contrary, in a way that should please people as well as refraining from that which should displease them.

Personally, civil emotions are useful when there is no alternative but to be among unscrupulous people who are out to make life difficult for you. This is a time to "**Buy your peace**"—doing what it takes to minimize your losses by paying them off so that they will simply go away.

DISGUISE

"Disguise" is a 14th century European word that referred to someone wearing a masquerade as part of a performance. Later, psychologists adopted this concept in relation to people falsifying what they were after (e.g. Rationalization) or manipulating things they liked or disliked by assigning them to places where they did not belong (e.g. projection).

Rationalization consists of poor **excuses** (anything but what happened is presented as if it actually happened) and distorted "reasons" designed to soften the conflict and justify what was done.

Similarly, there are all sorts of words that serve as a disquise to ones emotions. In addition, the use of words can be used to divert one from realizing what ones emotions really are. These are so common as to not require elaboration.

HYPOCRISY

Hypocrisy is a form of dissociation, as when one asserts or believes in cooperation but behaves competitively; protects love but acts with hate; proclaims good-will but practices racism –all without being aware in part or in whole of one's inconsistency. Hypocrisy may range from it being done unconsciously all the way over to being deliberately designed to mislead.

Having a lack of awareness is the only way to satisfy two opposing urges and still maintain one's sense of fragile integrity and self-esteem. Even if we do not engage in such hypocrisy ourselves, we know many people who do. Examples: the bible carrying and church-going storeowner who gouges his ghetto customers with inflated prices and installment payments; or the lascivious judge who passes the harshest sentence on sex offenders; or the firm believer in democracy who practices racial discrimination.

These hypocrites maintain their equilibrium by compartmentalizing the contradictory aspects of their lives — isolating one from the other and any unacceptable contradiction from consciousness. Hypocrites are usually unaware of their inconsistencies. Even if the inconsistency is pointed out, one may still deny it by the defense mechanism of rationalization (using excuses for justification) to make such incompatible values seem more consistent. The subject of such dissociations has been discussed.

NAGGERS

Naggers are those whose emotional conflicts are so great as to cause them to find problems with others as a deflection from the problems they are experiencing. They go on and on about problematic "leaves" of a tree — a displacement for the real "trigger" which lies at the "root" of the nagger's anger.

Instead of talking about the "root," the nagger jumps from one leaf to another and then will step back six-twelve-twenty-four and/or forty-eight months to bring up every petty grievance they have been harboring. When a moment of calm pops up, the nagger takes a deep breath and starts again with: "And another thing . . ." Partners switch off listening to such negative talk.

This is tough for any partner — and the more the partner tries to explain or deny accusations, the more this invites nagging. There is nothing the partner can say that can make things better. However, to give in all the time to the nagger is to be considered "henpecked" for a male, or "roosterpecked" for a female.

Naggers can switch habits by realizing that they are just as annoying as the people they are nagging and by realizing that their nagging is an outward manifestation of inner conflicts. Naggers will be surprised by switching over to praising the partners for being what they would like them to become before they actually are. Elaborate praise is given for even little nice things that are done. Meanwhile, it pays to set the example of how you want the partner to be.

Such a retraining process for the nagger and the partner takes at least a year. This is about <u>giving up blame</u> — prioritizing what is most important (i.e. like the MVP or Most Valuable Player of the all-star game) and letting go of the rest.

PROJECTION

Projection putting one's bad mindset and bad behaviors on others— the act of assigning, in an exaggerated amount, ones dislikes or bad traits on to somebody else. All of us have things we dislike about ourselves which we will not admit even to ourselves. Instead, one may use projection and then start blaming and criticizing the scapegoat for having bad stuff that really belongs to the person doing the blaming and criticizing. In the same breath they make palatable their own failures by diluting them or by shifting from something significant to something minor.

A typical example is seen in a weak person's attempt to hide from one's own inferiority complex by such comments as: "You are bad [meaning I know I am bad] and therefore aggressing against you is not wicked or 'un-Christian' or unmanly". Or, by feeling extreme hostility and hate toward a Black people who did them no harm, Europeans began the pattern of stating that Black people hated them.

REACTION FORMATION

Closely related to **Projection** (attributing one's own shortcomings, problems, and faults to others) is Reaction Formation. This is a response that converts (at the psychological level) something desired and envied, but wholly unattainable, into something discredited and despised. For example, Whites, desiring to have skin color but unable to attain it, claim that dark skin is disgusting to them. Then they started attributing disgusting things to dark skin.

SUPPRESSION

The word "Suppress" ("*press under*") originally referred to the act of crushing, as when a military force would overpower and subdue the people they were fighting. From this idea of pressing others underfoot and keeping them down by sheer force, "*suppress*" quickly took on other applications. A beneficial suppression occurs in people who are **Meek** because they display the emotional discipline of restraint under provocation.

Socialization is a process of "*pressing under*" certain behavior patterns and promoting others—as when a parent suppresses a child when he/she attempt to do something that is definitely damaging or anti-social; or when sexual desires and physical aggression are brought under many social regulations and are generally inhibited.

If the child is relatively aware of what was being done—whether or not the punishment was fair, unjust, or brutal—the process of not reacting is termed "*INHIBITION*" by psychologists. Inhibition is the restraining of one's desires or impulses, as in keeping under control the urge to strike out at someone.

In contrast to inhibition, individuals engaging in suppression consciously "*put the idea out of mind*" — like putting it "*on hold*" in the way that "*call waiting*" on the telephone works. The person is not avoiding or denying the problem at hand but rather is waiting for a better time to deal with it. Friends use the same reasoning, at times, to keep some bad information from other friends.

Since practically everybody deliberately puts things "*out of mind,*" suppression, when used in moderation, is generally not seen as a defense mechanism but rather as a healthy and necessary form of self-protection. This is the reason our parents taught us that, when we are really upset, to count slowly up to 10 before having any reaction — a "*cooling-off*" period.

But sometimes suppression does not work. For example, society, in its efforts to suppress anger will actually punish the person, as when a bully is made to apologize. That punishment itself is anger-provoking as well as frustrating because it prevents achievement of the angry person's goal — namely to attack or destroy whatever or whoever is doing the frustrating.

Thus, punishment teaches not to express anger and so the anger merely smolders inside instead of being suppressed until it can be brought in the open in socially acceptable ways. Or, it may teach rebels to become extremely upset and lose their perspective by stubbornly allowing themselves to dwell too long or too intensely on their "*bad luck.*"

The "**POKER FACE**" is an extremely common example of suppression. The term "poker face" (1880) alludes to the facial expression of a poker player who is expert at concealing his feelings about the cards he is holding in his hand. In other words, it is a visage lacking any expression that can be interpreted.

Managing Suppression: In deciding which emotions to express or suppress, it is helpful to realize their degree of significance. When we were boys, my friend Kenneth Philips' philosophy was to handle everyday ordinary problems by "*shedding a tear and forgetting it.*" This works best for mild to slight problems –e.g. getting cheated or being snapped at.

Moderate emotional disturbances—those which slow you down and cause you to temporarily experience bad emotions — are handled philosophically (e.g. "*everything happens for the best*").

Extreme emotional disturbances are those which people push from their minds and in effect deny to themselves that they ever had such attitudes. Extreme use of suppression becomes repression.

In the mind's arena of repression there is also the whirling around of wishes, fantasy, distortions, and bits of reality. Whereas with repression, thoughts, feelings or memories are involuntarily kept out of mind, with suppression this is done from a voluntary choice.

Throughout the hostile environments I was in during my medical specialty training and medical practice (apart from my patients) it was essential that I keep a "Poker face." This means not letting my facial expressions of emotions convey to people what I was thinking. The situation was like sharks seeing blood and thereby being stirred to make a frenzied attack. If these hostile people saw any sign of weakness in me, as suggested by my emotions (e.g. getting angry or fighting back) they would have gone in for the kill.

WITHDRAWAL

The Story of Withdrawal: The European idea for the word "withdraw" (to go apart or away) was a military term associated with "*retreat*" ("*to draw back*"). However, the 16th century word "*withdraw*" referred to what we call now a living room. Back then it was known as the "*withdrawing room*" because of the now nearly forgotten custom of ladies withdrawing from the dining room at the close of dinner. The purpose was to allow the gentlemen to enjoy their cigars, brandy, and exchange of masculine banter — more like swapping lies — without offending the "*delicate sensibilities*" of any member of the "*fair sex.*"

Eventually, Psychologists took up the much earlier military idea of "*withdraw*" because of their awareness of the practicality of people withdrawing from a conflict in certain situations. Much too often they noticed that if certain people continued in stressful conditions and were not successful in coping with them, then withdrawal might deepen into apathy and then apathy would deepen into depression.

The World of Withdrawal: During a 40-year orthopaedic surgical practice, there were thousands of patients under my direct care who had had severe physical traumas. A feature common to the recovery of all was the withdrawing within themselves. Preferring not to communicate with others, they focused only on themselves and their problems. This form of selfishness is between constructive and destructive.

For centuries, the combination of depression, apathy, indifference, inactivity, inattentiveness, and withdrawal were grouped under the ancient title of "*Melancholy.*" Now we know that melancholy depression-like symptoms exist in apes and monkeys, the closest living models of our forebears. From this new information the question arises: "Do withdrawal and depression have survival value?"

What we know is that low "*energy*" reduces aggression, the risk of getting hurt or killed, and chronic stress from being in a bad situation. This is actually an evolutionarily sound strategy for simple survival. The important point is that if we retain genes for melancholia, repeated traumatic events could produce a more exaggerated response from them. This would trigger a deeper and longer withdrawal from life into the bottomless pit where there is a loss of "*aliveness*" called depression.

Such an explanation, if true, could shed light on some of the vicious cycles of bad behaviors seen in certain people. Most manifestations of constantly repeated traumatic events are most prominently seen in poor people and in minorities. Forced into having little or no control over their lives, these people are controlled by a complex set of rules within their political-economic-social-legal situations — rules they probably did not participate in making and, in fact, may not have even been aware of.

Besides, they have available many fewer options than others in their society as to where they will live, work, and play. Poverty makes education a luxury and being taught by teachers who have a different value system does not make education attractive to poor minorities. However, without education and the skills and "*certification*" it brings, poor minorities are "*the last hired and the first fired,*" even on menial jobs.

Withdrawal and apathy are often wrongly described by Europeans as "*lower-class people's lack of motivation to achieve.*" Instead, both are more realistically explained as a result of the disbelief that effort and education pays off. Their locus of control, they believe, is by Europeans who care nothing for them. Never committing themselves to difficult goals protects them from risk, frustration, and anxiety. Those who have withdrawn to protect themselves from assaults on their self-concept tend to expect further assaults in many life situations, including the school room.

By withdrawing, they seriously limit their possibilities for new learning, lower their level of aspiration, and give up even realistic dreams. Having loss a grip on reality, out of frustration emerges anger and fear — both increasing the further away they get from being in the outside world struggles.

Minority youth, although outgoing among their friends, retreat into a "*shell*" of psychological defenses and seek out those like them. Together they pursue their aggressive Lower-Self animal instincts rather than doing things of an intellectual or spiritual nature. It comes down to them drifting through life.

By contrast, temporary withdrawal can be healthful and productive when it gives us the opportunity to find more effective means of coping. The coping should include giving voice to pent-up emotions and having a socially acceptable outlet for draining off the energy associated with those bad emotions.

As a result of my experiences in a hostile Euro-American society, it became a habit for me to withdraw, as occurs when a turtle is hit at with a stick. The way this withdrawal reaction came about was from having been reared in and then leaving a warm "We" all-Black society in the South. Immediately upon entering the hostile "I" society of Euro-Americans, I had to become an individualist. To make matters worse, I was involuntarily isolated—i.e. having no contact with friendly people, and especially Black people.

The withdrawal was done in order for me to conserve and focus my energy. I needed to be alert so as to determine who was "for me or against me." This worked well until I retired and no longer had need for this withdrawal. However, by that time it was "second nature"—meaning it happens before a choice can be made, as when I am around unfamiliar people. As a result, it is customary for me to make the incorrect choice of waiting for people to show they are interested in me before relaxing from my tension of being their presence. Laughing and joking are indicators of my relaxation.

Managing Withdrawal: For most people, overcoming the Turtle-Withdrawal reflex is extremely difficult because part of all that is present in the mindset which causes it. Perhaps what is tied up in the withdrawal is a sense of a slight to moderate degree of abandonment in childhood and repeated experiences of being an "invisible man," as occurred throughout by stay in the hostile "I" society. Being an "**Invisible man**" means people acted as if I was not present—and this was aided by my placement of a veil around myself so that they would not know who I was—and thereby willingly contributing to being invisible. Nevertheless, I remain quite sensitive—in fact overly sensitive— to any one who might deal with me by way of abandonment or by the "invisible" route.

Still another approach learned from experience is to not expect anything from anybody and that may not always be in my best interest. Actually, it may even get to the point of having no expectation actually becoming an expectation.

A selfhood-mastery approach for overcoming my withdrawal reactions might start from doing what it takes to ensure my choice not to withdraw precedes my "second nature" to withdraw. A change of thought would include seeing the other side of self-protection by imagining that the people I am meeting may feel uncomfortable meeting me because of their shyness or from feeling intimidated for whatever reason. Thus, an immediate action of extending myself to them might reduce the tension present in those of us involved.

Another approach is for me to learn some fun thing that most people can relate to and that would give me "foot in the door" of an entrance into their lives and what they are about. It really helps to be able to speak the language of the people and about topics they relate to—and especially allowing them to dominate the conversation. Such has not been done up to this point because of my mission to put in book form my thoughts on what might help struggling youth. Although doing this is really fun for me, it is so different and detailed in its interest that it is not understandable to or cared about by most people.

IX

EVIL EMOTIONS

Love and Hate are not Opposites!

Love Is Spiritual

Hate is Man-Made

The Opposite of Love is the Absence of Love

The Beginning of Hate is Indifference

There are two systems in human beings which control all of human conduct — the system of love and the system of hate (with fear being at the core). The seed of Hate is ignorance.

Tremendous delusions have occurred throughout the ages and in all cultures by wrongly considering that Love and Evil are opposite. This a result of misunderstanding the laws governing **POLARITY** laid out by the Egyptian Hermes Trismegistus (? 5500 B.C.).

This law, elaborated on later by the Chinese under the title Yin-Yang, says that everything has its pair of opposites, that the opposites are identical in nature, but that the opposites are different in degree. However, in the process of being translated and being passed down throughout the ages some important pieces of information were apparently left out. What Hermes meant was that how humans use the systems of love and hate are opposite but they do not come from the same source.

The ancient Greeks, 65% of whom studied in Africa, got everything confused about what they learned in Africa. One was to consider love to be an emotion. This had to follow from their disregard of God and the subjective and the spiritual in favor of dealing with that which is objective (like emotions). This faulty thinking led them to believe that love (as an emotion) and hate/evil are opposites.

Ancient Africans strongly disagreed, saying that Love and God are the same and have no worldly features and therefore **LOVE IS DEFINITELY NOT AN EMOTION!!!** The key distinction is that loving spiritual forces do not have opposites. Ancient Africans said there are no degrees of God's love. Thus, at any given moment you either love someone completely or you do not.

In the way a light switch works by turning it on and off, love is either present or it is not present. Since conception that gives life is a spiritual event, a woman is either pregnant or she is not. Emotions have a beginning, middle, and end but Love has always been present, is present now, and always will be present. Emotions are man-made, Love is God made.

Ancient Africans said that although the human mind does not have access to the Heavens (i.e. the Immaterial World), Love in the finite world is most heavily concentrated in the Sublime just below. Being of an Intangible nature, anything in the Sublime has the same spiritual "all-or-none" features. To have it means you truly love unconditionally (meaning it is God-made. By contrast, things are relative if they are of a Tangible nature and/or man-made. In combining these features of the Sublime and the Tangible, we get Emotional Planes of Existence (Table IX).

Table IX — **Emotional Planes of Existence**

- The Intangible—the Lofty
- The Mature—the sound and solid types
- The Immature—those which slow ones wholesome progress
- The Bad—those which stop or reverse ones wholesome progress
- The Hate—thoughts and emotions of Evil
- The Evil—those that create disturbances or destruction

OVERVIEW OF HATE

Original synonyms for the word Hate included envy, sorrow, fear, abhor). Nevertheless, the System of Hate starts developing within a person when there is an absence of love. This system is kept alive either by living inside the world of Hate or periodically visiting the Hate world. Whereas the word "***System***" ("*a* *bringing together*") is individual things working together in a side-by-side position, a **Classification** is present when things are positioned top to bottom.

In a system, the "*troops*" communicate with each other and otherwise have ways of affecting each other. The system itself is always greater than the sum of its sub-systems. A living and active system like Hate is open to the environment because it takes in energy and information from the world and gives back energy and information to the environment. The system of the **Mind's Decision-Making Process**— whether dealing with hate or love— works through in the following way:

One's top values make up one's character;

One's character gives rise to mind leanings directed toward some type of conduct or goal;

One's mental committee determines how the mind's leanings will be expressed, if at all;

One's will power is the driving force to push what one's character and mind committee have decided to do; and

The resultant expression is one's Conduct.

If Love is orchestrating, the decision-making process designs actions to bring goodness, happiness, and well-being in the long run. There is an appreciation and enjoyment of home life; of trees, flowers, clouds, and winding rivers; of poetry, art, friendship, conversation, humor, reading, learning, and creating. Although the problems of everyday life are as difficult as when the system of Hate is orchestrating, the Love system handles them with non-aggression — compassion, kindness, patience, tolerance, and rational thinking.

If Love is not orchestrating the decision, then the system of Hate takes charge. In the hate system, all of this is reversed so as to cause, not preservation and unity, but separation and destruction; not happiness and well-being, but poor total health and misery; not the pursuit of helping others but self-centeredness by the greedy acquiring of money, power over people, fame, status, and special privileges.

The World of Hate: Hate is a very destructive negative energy that poisons, erodes, and corrodes the person who holds it. Such persons act in ways that cause harm to those towards whom hate is directed. The emotion of hate consists of ill-will (*"to loathe," "shrink from," "odious"*) — all that is the opposite of good.

Inside the emotion of hate is an intense desire to inflict injury upon any and every aspect that makes for the well-being of someone — the person's love, creativity, health (physical, mental, spiritual), manhood/ womanhood, energy, sustenance (whatever sustains life), faith, hope, profit, advantages, benefits, good luck, fortune, affluence, prosperity, ease, comfort, happiness, and everything the person cherishes or deems success.

One driving force of hate comes from desiring to belong by those who teach one to be hateful. More often, hate results from possessing so much unbearable spiritual pain and emotional pain that the afflicted person is driven to do anything that will provide some relief. One form of relieve is to impart at least that amount of pain onto others—evilness which flows out of ones rage.

This rage is a reflection of those mental conflicts which cause a desire to gain some relief from the expanding hate energy being built up. Wars, for example, have been the outcome of a desire to release hatred. Parents which give birth to that hatred include jealousy, envy, greed, and fear. Fear is the most inhibiting of all of these or any negative emotion.

SPIRITUAL PAIN is the Cause and the Manifestation of Hate: Whereas Emotional pain is worldly suffering from psychological factors, spiritual pain centers on a loss of love or to a lack of love fulfillment. Either of these may come from degradation within the *Love Platter*—i.e. an obstruction to give love, to being loving, to being lovable, or to being loved.

On the one hand, for some, there is nobody available to accept it. For others, the designated receiver fails to accept it. For still others, both emotional and spiritual pain occurs when young children are deprived of "mother nurturing." On the other hand, one may be the cause of a deqradation of the Love Platter. An example is the failure of an individual to do what it takes to achieve self-fulfillment.

A failure to become self-fulfilled results in both spiritual pain and emotional pain. On top of the pain is added SELF-DISGUST for missing out on the opportunity to be successful. Because your poor choices have stopped your emergence into your rightful place of prominence in the world, you experience a meaningless, empty, and lonely life.

Having a dismal life causes you to turn to others for answers. Others will have answers but putting their answers into practice will worsen your problems –either because the "others" are con-artist or mean or because of poor execution of the answers.

If the basic problem here is your laziness, procrastination, and scattered attentions on too many trivial things, all is not lost. Simply start where you are and go straight ahead in the right direction. That direction is to learn how to work and to do work right and with a sense of obligation, duty, and responsibility.

CAUSES OF HATE

Ignorance

Whatever man makes that is contrary to nature is a reflection of Ignorance and ignorance is a sure way to evil. Evil consists of such complex emotions as envy, jealousy, hatred, greed, lust, outrage (or chronic anger), shame, embarrassment, guilt, and arrogant pride. The reason ignorance leads to evil is that one lacks an awareness of the higher reality of one's own spiritual essence (which is the meaning of *Egoism*). Such ignorance is behind what generates a gap between oneself and God (Ashby, African Origins p 197).

Ultimately, **Ignorance is a lack of knowledge of the Self**. Ignorance causes the human mind to be fooled into believing that its thoughts are its own and that its memories and experiences constitute its unique existence. In short, this generates separateness from God.

Ignorance causes one to select a philosophy of life that is incomplete, weak, limited in scope, deformed, or destructive as a result of its distortion of reality or fantasy about what is important to have as a standard in and guide for life. Yet, some people do not recognize such features in what they believe.

The European Story of Ignorance: Upon entering the European Dark Ages, ignorance took the sense of "not to know." In the 14th century, the Latin "ignorance" (to not be acquainted with") was brought into English by Chaucer with the idea of ignorant meaning "to have little or no knowledge"; the idea of *Ignoramus* being "we do not know" (the first-person plural of ignorance). As the result of a popular play, it also took on the meaning of an ignorant person.

Ignoramus was adopted as a legal term in the 16th century, as when the grand jury refused to approve an indictment because of insufficient evidence ("we do not know"). A well-known expression in the legal arena is "ignorantia legis non excusat" ("*ignorance of the law is no excuse*" — i.e. the fact that the defendant did not think his/her act was against the law does not prevent the law from punishing the prohibited act).

The World of Ignorance: Similarly, ignorance powerful enough to become laws of our mind to shape our thoughts cause a reaction, whether we are aware of it or not. Hence, the very law which could produce freedom in one setting may produce bondage in another setting. An example occurs when wholesome "We" type non-spiritual faith is misapplied to members of a hostile "I" (individualism) society (Bailey, Freeing Enslaved Minds).

Inside the expression: "Where Ignorance is Bliss/Tis folly to be wise" is the implication that it is often easier to accomplish a difficult task if one starts off ignorant of the difficulties. By contrast, people extremely well informed and who anticipate every loss, lack, or obstacle, may end up hindered by expectations.

Thus, on the one hand, to follow this proverb may lead one to freedom. On the other hand, ignorance related to the education needed for a successful career causes unhappiness and suffering. This anti-education message was brainwashed into the minds of African American slaves and thereby represented a mind enslaving happening.

European men believe it is a sound practice to pursue things of Value (e.g. money and power) by any means necessary—even it means robbing or even killing others. For them, warring and destruction have always been a way of life, as seen in the Vikings and other barbarians—and it continues to be so to this day. Actually, money and power is all they have had.

What makes these destructive practices for the world a reality is the "manhood" refusal of Europeans to honor and use their right brains. Their definition of "**Manhood**" includes an orientation toward individualism, materialism, and separateness from other people and from nature. As a result of this orientation, European males view people not like them as threatening and the generators of constant fear (Sandra Harding in Eze p360).

The general belief of Westerners is that humans are born as "sinners" and that requires that differences be stressed. Another aspect is that by being born bad you can not trust yourself and therefore laws and rules and punishment is needed. By contrast, Ancient Africans and the Chinese believe man is born good and that philosophy generates an entirely different view of the world.

Human Love is expressed in the earth world as goodness and good works; hate, by evilness. In this way "*Good and Evil*" are on the same scale but at opposite ends of the same pole. This allows for a scale to be formed.

Therefore, **the OPPOSITE OF LOVE IS THE ABSENCE OF LOVE**. The absence of love cannot exist in the loving spiritual world. When the absence of love is present in the earth world, it starts as indifference and progresses from there to evil.

Revenge

Two Stories of Revenge: An **African** story is that Primitive (i.e. the first) Africans had beliefs in a world of spirits who appeared every moment of everyday to affect the earth world for good or evil. Thus, it was necessary to either pacify these superior spirits or to call upon their aid. For example, North Africans of the Sudan believed that evil spirits lived in the Paleolithic panther or bear. Since they needed these animals to live, they had a ritual of defense against the retaliation and revengeful magic of the spirits that included the thrusting of bones through the "*evil eye*" of the killed animals. Such a system of defenses to reduce the importance of "*spilling blood*" in order to live was a way of handling fear and anxiety.

Gradually, spreading out in circular fashion from these primitive Sudan methods, there developed new and varied depths of realizations against revenge. By the times of Moses, an expansion beyond evil retaliation and revenge there was in existence "fair-play" oriented good types termed vengeance and avenge. This was illustrated in Moses' early psalm which celebrated God's VENGEANCE — the appropiate handling of wrongs done to God (e.g. worshipping pagan gods). In this way, the word AVENGE (from the same etymological root as vengeance and vindicate) came to mean "*the righting of wrongs*"— the achieving of justice.

A **Western** story is that the Halloween customs that we observe on October 31 had their beginning from the beliefs of the **Druids** — priests of ancient Gaul (France) and Britain. The Druids said that witches, demons, goblins, ghosts, vampires, and other spirits of the dead — Revenants (literally, "*one who returns*") — would come back to earth on the eve of November 1. Their purpose was to engage in all sorts of mean tricks in order to have their wicked carnival of triumph.

The reason for their malicious mischief was to give TIT FOR TAT — an insult for an insult, a blow for a blow — in the spirit of "*to get at*" in order to hurt in return. Such a return of "like kind" — RETALIATION — was considered evil "*fair-play.*" Because the Revenants were evil, they retaliated against any who had not treated them well. However, when the Revenants were particularly angry with some living being, they built up an intense desire to inflict injury. As a result, their desire went beyond the bounds of "fair-play" and that was called REVENGE — a reaction to the "*environment*" instead of to a specific thing.

The World of Revenge: When applied in human-to-human interactions, vengeance implies the avenging of a wrong done to oneself or another by measures that punish the offender so that he/she suffers in the same degree as his/her victim. Whereas *Revenge* is an act of passion, *Vengeance*, its good counterpart, is an act of justice. Whereas to *Avenge* is to settle a score (get even) or redress an injustice as an act of deserved and adequate pay back for wrong done to others, *Retaliation* commonly, but not exclusively, refers to evil "tit for tat."

Because revengeful persons are resentful, spiteful, unforgiving, unreasonable, and lack a sense of fair-play, their behaviors to get back at someone call for revengeful behaviors from those attacked. Now a FEUD has started whereby there is raid after raid for every injury, whether real or fancied. A today's phrase for a feud is a "TURF WAR" and the bad emotions present in the participants are of a hateful nature. Besides, "Turf Wars" are present in both human and animal realms.

Examples: when two dogs reach a standoff over their territory, they face each other stiff-legged with muzzles pointed. Cats battling over turf present with their fur puffed to look twice as big. Birds engage in intimidating dive-bombing for the purpose of trying to force "the enemy" from their perches.

TERRITORIALITY is the tendency to occupy, mark, and defend a particular space. Thus, a bird may, by its singing, indicate to his rival: "*this is my territory, stay away from it*" and to a female: "*please come and look at what I have.*" In my youth, boys who defended their "*turf*" would threaten, "*posture*" and occasionally fist-fight. Defense became more violent around the 1970s.

Today, individual rage has expanded into gang rage. Gang rage, as a result of one side presumably violating the other's space, shows as "*turf war*" revenge. Gangs choose turf because that is all they believe they have. So how do turf wars start?

Since WE ARE INCLINED TO EMOTIONALLY EXAGGERATE THE WRONGS DONE TO US and to feel that no punishment is too severe for those who have offended us, Revenge has connotations of hateful cruelty. This ranges from VIOLENCE (e.g. the cowardly "*drive-by*" shootings) to PETTINESS ("tit for tat"). The great amount of CONTEMPT (meanness) behind pettiness generates conflicts with others.

When engaged in "*turf wars,*" gangs are in a peculiar master/slave relationship. Opposing sides, considering themselves masters, are actually slaves. Not being free from raging and hateful thoughts and feelings makes people powerless to control their emotions. This keeps them slaves to those they are trying to harm. Furthermore, having a dependency upon "*the enemy*" for their purpose in life means both opponents are tied to each other. Neither side can walk away from the other; and neither side can ever win—"Lose-Lose."

The mind-set of hateful revenge is that of MALICE — a deep seated and often unjustified desire to kill, wound, or hurt other's feelings and reputation (e.g. by gossip). Malicious acts done with delight and for no good reason are the purest form of hate. These people have spiritual pain and activating love is curative.

HATE robs one of compassion and showers minds with a bitter VINDICTIVENESS (Latin, "to speak with power"). Vindictiveness implies not only being enraged about some real or imagined actions "the enemy" did but being even more enraged with "*the enemy*" him/herself. Prolonged dwelling upon what one regards as a personal injury is called RESENTMENT.

After the "*attitude problem*" of vindictiveness, resentfulness, and malice — which together deliberately shape an opportunity for exercising revenge — comes REVENGEFUL actions designed to cause actual harm. This mind-set of hate is what many youth of the "*pavement jungle*" bring to the table of school and of society. Expressing Revenge is the display of Evil deeds.

MANAGING THE REVENGEFUL: Revenge is a bad habit! It results from socialization or a choice. Such a mind-set of hate must be understood for self-defense preparation; to foster compassion; to help generate insight into how and where to try to help them; and to serve as motivation for increasing ones patience and tolerance.

Thorough investigation determines how hatefulness shows itself (in mild/slight/moderate/extreme forms); in what manner (overt/tempered/masked/concealed behaviors); and to whom it is directed (to oneself and/or toward others). Then the thoughts behind Vindictiveness (being enraged at the enemy), Malice (desiring to hurt the enemy), and Revenge (taking action to hurt the enemy) must be replaced with thoughts of peace.

The bottom line for why disturbed youth have hateful revenge is <u>THE ABSENCE OF LOVE IN THEIR LIVES</u>. As a result, they feel their dignity is not respected and that makes them hypersensitive to any type of situation they consider disrespectful (Anderson, p203) as, for example:

(1) Competition perceived as unfair;

(2) Being exploited or deprived;

(3) People who have not proven themselves to be trustworthy;

(4) Faulty communications of the superficial or deep variety.

SUPERFICIAL FAULTY COMMUNICATIONS include misinterpretations — an intended compliment or joke is heard as a snide remark; constructive criticism, as a personal attack.

DEEP FAULTY COMMUNICATIONS relate to the words used (as rational people do) and the feelings behind those words (as emotional people do). Emotional People (EP), through stirred feelings, share a common communication; Rational People (RP) have little awareness of such non-verbal communication. EP do not have a developed rational Left brain and that means their Right brains are "wild" in that there is no check and balance on what is thought and felt as emotions.

Inner city or struggling youth, lacking a faculty for words, are basically EP. RP do not always connect with what EP say (and vice-versa). Since inner city or struggling youth believe no one listens to them, they see no point in keeping their word when they make a promise. Instead, they choose bad behaviors as a more practical and effective tool to get attention. If their attention can be gained and if the situation is a "*stand off*" with another youth, then try **BARGAINING**.

Step I—It is essential that the opponents be heard—allowing them to say what they have to say. If what they say is either unclear or very important, then the arbitrators should repeat it in more simple language.

Step II—each side produces a series of offers and counter-offers until a solution emerges acceptable to both. The idea is for EACH SIDE TO RECEIVE WHAT IS MOST IMPORTANT AND GIVE UP WHAT IS OF LESSER VALUE OR WORTH. Even though both sides remain a little dissatisfied with the solution, they will better understand their opponent's position.

Step III—if bargaining fails, an outside source is needed to help focus on important issues, defuse emotions, clarify positions and proposals, and make suggestions that allow each side to compromise and yet "*save face*."

For Deeper Communications a useful place to start is with the Check Method (see "Tools").

Step I—troubleshoot the vicious cycle of hateful revenge by discovering the thoughts that are generating resentment.

Step II—a clue that one has touched on the core thought is that one responds with a great deal of energy at its mere mention. Then discussing it may cause one to cry. After the cry, one feels a sense of relief, unlike one has had in a long time.

Step III—a simple approach to management is to start by substituting the hateful thought with its opposite and constructive one. To find the "*right*" thought, a process of hard work, requires many "trial-and-error" combinations.

Step IV—since good feelings follow good thoughts, the presence of a good feeling indicates that a plan can be worked out for a goal.

Step V—to make the constructive thoughts a habit requires at least 30 days of staying with it. An indicator that one is continuing to be motivated requires at least a year of daily progress or until the goal is achieved. Once one has a success rate of 75% good results, the chances are good that one will complete the journey to the goal.

In constructively dealing with the "Enemy" what works for me is to THINK OF "THE ENEMY" AS A TEACHER. From a teacher I can learn more about self-discipline, self-control, compassion, patience, and tolerance. The process includes focusing, not on "*the enemy*" as a person, but on that person's behaviors. I can totally dislike those behaviors but not the person because the "enemy" and I are related at a spiritual level.

Forgiveness: It takes a strong person to admit the part he/she played in causing the problem and to look at the enemy from the opposite point of view what has been customary. The key is to develop compassion. As ones compassion grows in strength and as ones inner strength becomes stronger and as ones love for oneself increases, one can both forgive "*the enemy*" and forgive oneself for hating. Sincerity for my wrong doings is shown by making restititution.

CATEGORIES OF HATE

Indifference starts the system of hate at one end of the scale of Hate and evilness is on the other end. In between indifference and evilness are located the various destructive emotions — each with their degrees and shades of intensities. Indifference implies a lack of feeling, interest, attention, caring and discrimination. It is a neutrality that keeps one detached from the spirit of people and aloof from compassion, harmony, or unity.

Since fear rushes in to fill the void vacated by love, fear is the predominate emotion which seeds in Indifference. Fear brings with it a self-centered and destructively selfish focus as well as all types of self-defense mechanisms. Both pave the way for all bad emotions (e.g. rage).

Aversion, say Europeans, is at the core of hate but this is not exactly correct. The aversion ("*a turning away*") of Whites seeking to enslave Africans, for example, consisted in Whites shutting down all beliefs of their own actual shared African ancestry (all humans derived from Africa) and culture as well as of the fact that Africans were (and are) "fellow human creatures." This means that aversion is a more thought out action of not caring about who another is, what another does and/or how another appears.

Adversion is the deepest form of hateful opposition. The mind set of adversion is ill-will from correctly or incorrectly perceived omissions and commissions — the realm of injustice as determined by engaging in injustice. The mind set for aversion and adversion is usually for the purpose of gaining an unfair advantage and/or putting the victim at an unfair disadvantage. Both aversion and adversion consist of hateful thought and both can and often do lead to indistinguishable evil actions.

Racist "*red necks*," like the KKK, showed adversion in their face-to-face encounters with ex-slaves. The difference today is that the hated is less overt. A practical example relates to the Michael Vick dog-fighting tragedy which has struck a nerve and generated unprecedented emotions. Based upon television and newspaper comments, the overwhelming majority of Whites are appalled with "righteous indignation" while many Black people are nonplussed.

In a Western sense "**Righteous indignation**" is anger felt by Whites which makes them eager to punish because, rather than the act itself, *the Black offender has done something which Whites have forbidden Blacks (but not themselves) to do.* In America, everybody loves competition—and Euro-Americans crave brutality.

In analyzing the tragedy there are "four courts"—the Federal legal system, the Virginia legal system, the NFL system, and the system of public opinion—in which the football quarterback Vick has been tried for one crime.

The NFL (needing to protect its reputation) and the animal rights groups had just cause for their reactions. Regardless of race or status, I am totally against evilness done to humans, animals, or nature and thus agree with those who recommend reasonable and proper ending punishment for Vick.

But what Black Americans know for sure is that the legal system dispenses unequal justice—and with Blacks typically being treated unfairly. History documents that Whites stirred into raging emotions by the actions of a Black person are out for total destruction (e.g. a lynching) of that person. If the courts do not "make an Example" of him, then public opinion certainly will.

In other words, accused Blacks, simply by being non-White, are too often deemed "overly guilty"—guilty beyond the crime— and in need of punishment beyond the boundaries of their crime. The reason is that the irrational and illogical racism "baggage" Europeans attach to Black people is full of hate and destruction—and who knows for what?

This "baggage" and its fantasy European causes put many Black Americans at a loss as to what to think, feel, say, and do about a fellow Black person accused of a crime. Yet, most Black Americans carry the African Retention that all God's creatures and creations are related in spirit and because of that dignity are therefore deserving of respect.

But in addition to this "baggage" I am particularly concerned with the associated "Deflection" and "Projection" tactics Europeans use to perpetuate racial delusions and unrest. An example of "**Deflection**"—a throwback trick to the ancient Greek Sophist—is seen by the media steering a specific crime topic to appear as if it is "normal in Black culture."

To the end of magnifying the actions of one wayward Black man as representing all Black Americans, talk show hosts interview many Black Americans to get their conflicting comments on dog-fighting. They ask "no win" questions like: "are you people still engaging in dog fighting?" No matter what the answer, Whites gain their objective of implying that this is part of the Black Experience (as if it is not present in the White and Brown and Yellow communities). Comments selected to support their position are broadcast over and over again on different television and radio stations throughout the world and throughout the day.

It serves to "deflect" public attention away from the evils of White culture—things like wars (over 37 in the last 50 years); crimes around the world that bring misery to millions of people; animal hunting for "sport"; bull fighting; or the daily killing dogs in dog pounds? Over three million pit bulls a year are euthanized because they will not be adopted. (Bailey, American Crime). Dogfighting—a cruel, menacing, and illegal activity—takes place in basements, barnyards, clearing in the woods, and abandoned warehouses all across America. Dogs are ripped apart, in the way "Negro dogs" of slave owners' used them to rip apart runaway slaves.

At least what Black athletes can learn is to be more responsible; make better decisions o what they do and how the conduct their life; and the need to make better choices on who their friends are.

HATEFUL ENVY

The Story of Hateful Envy: The significance of Envy dates back to Ancient Africans. They believed that the great disease of the soul is denial of God; next is belief in appearances; and accompanying these are all evils and nothing good.

Ancient Africans said: "The heart of the envious is gall and bitterness; his tongue spits venom; the success of his neighbor breaks his rest. He sits in his cell repining; and the good that happens to another is to him an evil. Hatred and malice feed upon his heart, and there is no rest in him.... Envy is the daughter of pride, the author of murder, the beginner of secret sedition and the perpetual tormentor of virtue. Envy is the filthy slime of the soul; a venom, a poison, or quicksilver which consumes the flesh, and dries up the marrow of the bones" (Ashby, Egyptian Yoga p 150).

The Egyptian Hermes (? 5500 BC) told his son Tat that all humans have twelve tormentors. The first torment is IGNORANCE; the second is GRIEF; the third is INTEMPERANCE (excessive indulgence of a natural appetite or passion); the fourth is INCONTINENCE (lacking a restraint, especially over the sexual appetite); the fifth, INJUSTICE; the sixth, AVARICE (greed); the seventh, FALSEHOOD; the eighth, ENVY; the ninth, GUILE (cunning, deceit); the tenth, ANGER; the eleventh, RASHNESS (impulsive, acting without due consideration); the twelfth, MALICE (desire to inflict harm). Under these twelve are many others but all begin to depart — although not immediately — from him who has obtained the mercy (or Grace) of God. The twelve tormentors, Hermes said, prevent us from conceiving anything beautiful or good. Yet, the greatest evil is to ignore what belongs to God.

The ancient Greeks thought envy (phthonos) weighs down the soul like lead and causes a wicked mental pain. An example of extreme envy was mentioned in the Bible (Genesis 37-39) where the story of Jacob and his envious sons ended with the supposed sale of Joseph to the Ishmaelites and Midianites. Joseph ended up in slavery in Ancient Egypt. The Gospel records indicate Christ was arrested because of bitter envy and hostility on the part of the religious authorities (Matt, 27:18).

In the 6th century, because of the evilness connected with envy, Pope Gregory declared envy to be one of the seven "*Deadly Sins*." The reasons for this were several. One is that the twelve tormentors of the Egyptian Hermes (?5500 BC) provided the model for the SEVEN DEADLY SINS — pride, covetousness (greed), lust, anger, gluttony, envy, and sloth. A second is that envy is not only a serious offense morally but also because they gave rise to others sins. A third is that envy generates domination based on its moral significance and destructive results.

Like Ancient Africans thousands of years earlier, Christian moralist recognized a distinction in bad emotions that were and were not associated with hate. Yet, Christian moralist struggled with exactly what constituted envy. By being unclear in definitions, European etymology originally linked envy and jealousy. They were aware that what envy does is to select and react to a target person, place, or thing and then that process carries the envier into the system of hate.

The downside of envy was repeatedly pointed out in religious preachings as eating away at the spiritual center of medieval life because its motivational aspects invariably led to destructive actions. Since then, envy has been defined as wishing for or desiring something possessed by (or presumed to be possessed by another). Whereas jealousy refers to relationships, envy is more about malice in the emotional aspect of *"I want what you have!"*

Meanwhile, other forms of Envy of a lesser nature were recognized and they too needed to be distinquished from jealousy. When these envious well-known concepts of ancient time continued into the European Dark Ages, even further distinctions were made.

"**MALICE**" in the 13th century continued to carry the ancient meaning of "*looking at someone with resentment or even malice*" — the selfish and unfriendly grudging in view of what another enjoys. It was applied as an epithet to particular parts of a person's character or conduct and often associated with a "sick" pleasure in seeing the distresses of another.

COVETEOUSNESS also continued with the Biblical concept represented in the Tenth Commandment: "Thou *shalt not covet thy neighbor's wife"* (Exod.20:17, Deut. 5:21). This was expanded to include the combination of a greedy desire to possess some animate or inanimate thing belonging to another, followed by attempts to take possession of it.

In the visual arts, envy and the other deadly sins were personified by ugly persons, often doing battle with the pleasant looking virtues. Envy was often displayed as a woman riding a dog with a bone in its mouth. As the European Middle Ages became less agricultural and more mercantile (industrial), envy rose to commercial importance.

Since market economics was based on the ASSUMPTION OF SCARCITY (i.e. human wants will always exceed the resources available to fulfill those wants), the envious, driven by greed, created immoral business and social relationships.

Members of high society were forever scrambling to keep up with "*The Joneses*" — i.e. trying to match the lifestyle of one's more affluent acquaintances.

The World of Hateful Envy: Of the complex emotions (Bailey, Self-Esteem p 61), envy— when fully expressed—is the most bitter; is the orchestrator of the associated complex destructive emotions; and is a reflecition of one's inferiority complex. Ones attitude is: *"I want what is yours" (with malice).* This is to be distinquished from jealousy ("Don't mess with what is mine"). At its worse, based on one's own judgment of what is good, envy is hatred of the good for being the good, as when one hates another for possessing a value or virtue one regards as most desirable.

In general, mentally healthy people are not familiar with moderate or extreme envy and many are not aware it even exists. Therefore, they have no idea how to ideal with it. Thus, they are quite gullible and can become easy victims.

Previously, mention was made that Envy has four major categories—mild, slight, moderate, and extreme. The Non-Hateful forms are Mild, Slight, and the beginning of Moderate. The Hateful forms pick up from there, with no clear line of distinction between non-hate and hate.

MODERATE ENVY is characterized by progressive steps that border on hate and then progress into full blown hate. It seems that each step reflects that individual's perception of an increasing loss of power—and this perception of loss may vary from one situation to another.

Every individual is born believing the world centers around him/her and therefore anything desired, despite belonging to others, is viewed as "already mine." Besides, they continue, anybody available has a "duty to supply me with whatever I want and whenever I want it."

This is a "little god" mindset of being omnipotent (unlimited power). It is human nature—part of self-preservation— to resist any loss of power. Fortunately, the majority of people evolve out of this to an acceptable degree.

But those who are highly vulnerable to envy are inclined— upon perceiving a threat to their power—assume a fighting mode and as if their "life or limb" or self-esteem is in jeopardy. The nature of that fight can be:

O<u>vert</u> —as in total all-out war where "anything goes"

T<u>empered</u> —as in striking back only when struck

M<u>asked</u> —as engaging in behind the scenes passive-aggressive attacks

C<u>oncealed</u>—as in designing destructive plans and then enlisting the help of evil spirits

People with any of these *"twisted"* extreme manifestations of envy can be extremely dangerous and may appear in any person who possesses Moderate or Extreme Envy.

Those approaching the Hateful level starts out with desiring something corresponding to what another has without implying the other should no longer have it. It progresses to being about the selfish and unfriendly grudging in view of what another enjoys. There is the hoping and praying for their rival's good fortune to be wiped out. However, they would not help in making this happen.

Another problem is that their emotional range is limited and they tend to remain somewhere in the range between indifference to almost Hate. This range is in keeping with the concept that the opposite of love is the absence of love (i.e. indifference) and that the opposite of indifference is hate.

Those who have stepped into the Hate arena consider ways of making life more difficult for the person envied and this is the beginning of hate. From there it progresses into carring the emotion of malice, as mentioned above.

Passive-aggressively they politely "*smile in your face while stabbing you in the back.*" This means one has reached the level of a typical self-centered thought process like: "*I begrudge you what I see you have, for you possess it merely to torment me*".

Their features are the total reliance on their left brain (analytical of everything and everybody); having no God or higher power connection; and the absence of compassion or caring. In fact, the afflicted may find pleasure in your pain and suffering. They are about the triad of *"me, mine, more."*

Management follows the same pattern as for slight envy or handling jealousy. For defensive and offensive purposes regarding you and/or others, it is essential to learn to understand both mindsets and then learn how to properly handle both.

Start by never wishing bad luck on anyone because this will boomerang and return to harm you. Socrates counseled that the only way out is to not take delight in misfortune. Take pity instead. The management comments for Extreme Envy apply here. For those desiring to change, any of the methods mentioned under "Tools" may be of benefit.

EXTREME ENVY is hatred at the sight of whatever is good and with an intense desire to destroy it. This includes one hating good people for being good and for doing good things. In fact, one's mind becomes twisted enough to feel emotional pain at one's own few virtues.

The extreme envy mindset derives from feelings of inferiority; from self-hate so severe as to cause the afflicted to want to inflict injury and misfortune on one's victims; and from being overwhelmed with *spiritual pain.* These three are so terrible as to keep one on the *"self-escape run." Yet,* ones weakness as a person leads one to strongly *deny* that the object of one's hatred is oneself.

Such people have passed the point of wanting to survive and thrive or just wanting your values because they are an enemy of life itself — wanting to destroy all values related to surviving and thriving. This attack on the successes and achievements of others is generated by their lack of not having their own successes and achievements (the envy portion). Therefore, they do not want others to have what they cannot have (jealousy).

"*Sick pleasures*" are gained from their rivals' misfortunes — the fact that rivals have lost their fortune; the fact that they do not want rivals to succeed. They, the essence of evil, keep running so as to avoid facing the realization that the object of their hatred is themselves.

Management is of no benefit to attempt unless the individual decides to change. Those whose evilness is caused by organic problems (e.g. biochemical imbalances or structural brain defects) are not likely to change. It is best to stay out of their way. Those who made a voluntary choice to separate themselves from God have a chance. Such does happen with a few who have been imprisoned for prolonged periods. This is usually helped along by a religious teacher who helps the afflicted come to the point of starting to see life differently. The Muslims in particular have had success by challenging the afflicted to be better than they are and by using the approach of "*only love conquers hate.*"

The only cure for Moderate or Extreme Envy is to overcome spiritual pain. This is done by re-establishing one's flow of love in, around, and out of oneself.

MASOCHISM (Self-Defeating Personality Disorder)

The Story of Masochism: It just could be that in the very early history of human beings on earth there was a woman who provoked her mate into abusing her so that he would show her how much he cared about her. No doubt, masochism has subsequently been present in all cultures and in all ages.

The early Christianity characterized *Sadism as aggression turned outward and Masochism as aggression turned inwards.* Homosexually oriented masochistic practices were widespread in monasteries, convents, and boarding schools. Then too the religious atmosphere was one of imparting guilt in people so as to keep them under control.

In the 17th and 18th centuries a number of English women became addicted to flagellation or whipping and even formed clubs to indulge their "sick" pleasures. Such clubs were instrumental in ushering in the Victorian Period—the entire second half of the 19th century which featured stern morality. Nevertheless, Pornography of the English Victorians was shot through and through with sado-masochism. Some reasons derived from "treatments" they had previously received at the hands of their parents and teachers.

Perhaps the uninhibited sexual acts occurring during the Victorian era designed the background for the term "Masochism." It was coined from the name of the Austrian novelist Leopold von Sacher-Masoch (1835-1895) because of his preoccupation with sexual pleasures of pain mirrored by his characters. Starting in early childhood he was weaned on tales of violence and cruelty told to him by his wet nurse and his father, a chief of police. The tales of cruel, dominating females inspired him to fantasize. As he grew up he began to act out his fantasies — entering into slave/master relationships with a number of women. He sought out beatings with studded whips and other instruments of sexual cruelty.

The World of Masochism: Like Sadism, in recent years the meaning of masochism has been broadened beyond sexual connotations. Today, Masochism refers to pleasure from one's own pain or humiliation; from self-denial; from expiatory (atoneing) physical suffering (e.g. religious flagellants); and from hardship and suffering in general. By permitting oneself to suffer is a way to convince oneself of being strong and the ability to take punishment.

One set of theories on causation include: Conditioned Learning; an expression of a more generalized masochistic attitude toward life; and by the individual having serious questions about his/her worth and value.

Another set consists of a deep sense of guilt, shame, and self-disgust—each of which calls for paying a penalty of suffering to make things right. To this end it is a mechanism of self-punishment designed to reduce feelings of guilt. Certain of these individuals believe they can build up a reserve of retributions which can be drawn upon when one yields to temptation in the present or future

A third set is about the pain from being abandoned, neglected, or rejected and having the experience of getting some attention from being spanked or punished. Here, punishment is looked upon as evidence of love and affection.

Otherwise, Masochism is said to come from childhood experiences that associate pain with pleasures (e.g. the combination of pain and sexual arousal). Although (sexual) masochism fantasies may begin in childhood, activities with partners usually begin in early adulthood. Adult male masochists—as a reflection of varying degrees of psychosis— indulged their perversions in brothels equipped with a variety of ingenious machines on which they could be flagellated or tortured.

Forms of Masochism are wide ranging. *Mild* forms are seen in those who desire to be bitten lightly in order to increase sexual pleasure. *Slight* forms include physical pain (by being beatened, pinched, and/or pricked to the point of bleeding) or desiring psychological distress by disparagement, condemnation, or humiliation. The Mild and the Slight forms are so common as to be "normal."

Thereafter, the boundaries between "normal" masochism and the pathologically abnormal are even more vague. *Moderate* forms perhaps begin with the invitation of pain and degradation by such measures as humiliation; beatings especially while bound; trampling; semi-strangulation; spankings, switchings, or sticking with pins; and verbal abuse. Usually these occur in an obedient slave/superior "disciplinarian" relationship. Such behavior is repetitive and intentional.

Extreme, chronic, and addicting forms are seen in those who attempt to inflict pain on themselves to such a degree as to occasionally cause genital mutilation or castration. Others ingest excreta and engage in certain aspects of necrophilia (Gregory, 512). They have a need for increasing the potential for self-harm and to increase the severity of the acts, even to the point of death.

Non-sexual forms of sadomasochism are spoken of by psychologist and psychiatrist as a kind of selfhood "Anesthesia" associated with the degradation of love (Choisy p62). Examples of such situations can be seen following some new achievement by certain people (e.g. winning the lottery). Then those people engage in self-defeating behaviors that not only produce personal problems (e.g. pain, guilt, or depression) but that incites anger or rejection from others. As a result, the afflicted people feel hurt, defeated, or humiliated by people's responses and wind up worse off than they were.

In my observations and from trying to help some of the struggling poor (e.g. the "Make Do" members) it seems that they are drawn to situations or relationships in which they will suffer. Then they will put up all kinds of resistance to anything designed make their lives better.

Or, they may reject opportunities for wholesome pleasure or advancement and, instead, engage in excessive and needless self- sacrifice (Bailey, Rising Above Poverty). It is my impression that simply giving these individuals money for self-help purposes is doomed to failure because some type of masochism is involved.

Is this the result of socialization or, in the case of struggling Black Americans, a reflection of the traumatic events that occurred during slavery and the subsequent cultural transmission of "zombie" customs (i.e. the custom continues but the reason for the custom has long since faded away)?

At a carnival event, I once saw a motorcyclist drive through a burning tunnel of straw; stop and turn around; and then drive back in, never to come out again. This has forever bothered me—first from the suicide and second as to what could be going in his life to cause it.

Nevertheless, Masochism is more common among women. Earlier psychoanalytic literature attributed it to "feminine nature," perhaps because suffering is associated with submissiveness (Thorpe p368). To minimize the association with a trait more characteristic of females, the psychiatric literature now designates it as a **Self-Defeating Personality Disorder**.

However, many women have protested this term because it leads to "blaming the victim." They agree that some women do act foolish in self-destructive ways; that some stay in bad relationships; that some do not take advantage of opportunities; and that some tolerate heaps of verbal, emotional, and physical abuse. Yet, there is no proof that these are necessarily masochistic people. Many women remain in bad relationships for situational and economic reasons. The point is to beware of being gullible to science (Wade, p573).

Managing Masochism: Without their desire to change, management attempts are almost doomed to failure. One reason is that, as a feature of experiencing emotional or spiritual pain, the afflicted expect failure from every effort intented for improvent. Stubbornly, they often act in a fashion that will increase the likelihood of failure. Though similar to Passive-Aggressive people in being pessimistic and undercutting, their defeatist style is more of a reflection of a gloomy sense of hopelessness and helplessness than a vindictive attitude. They often feel guilty and undeserving of any better life.

Some ray of hope for helping comes from getting them to recognize the part they play; taking responsibility for their misery; and help lead them out of stubbornness. Sadomasochists need professional help.

SADISM

The Story of Sadism: Originating in antiquity among people in all cultures, Sadism tended to be preserved mosts strongly in totalitarian, militaristic, and patriarchal cultures. Floggings or torture were frequently the lot of animals, captives, slaves, servants, children, and wives or concubines. Such treatment has been a male prerogative. However, in the beginning of the 18th century, extreme Sadism became recognized as evidence of insanity.

The word "Sadism" derives from the name of the French man of letters (literature), and libertine (without moral restraint), Count D.P.F. de Sade (1740-1814) who described a variety of sexual perversions in his novel "*The Curse of Virtue and the Blessing of Vice.*" Most of his adult life was spent either in prison or in asylums for the insane. Shortly after his marriage into a wealthy family, de Sade began a series of liaisons with prostitutes, luring them to one of his residences for sessions of sexual abuse. He advocated sexual violence as a way of life.

Thereafter, a Sadist, by the infliction of pain and suffering, was known as one who received pleasure through the practice of cruelty— either mentally or physically. Some societies continue to tolerate or even institutionalize the sadistic treatment of minority groups up to the present (Gregory, p510) and thereby geneate the state of masochism in some of their victims.

The World of Sadism: It is common to find both sadistic and masochistic behavior in the same person. Whereas experiencing pleasure from receiving cruelty is called PASSIVE ALGOLAGNIA in medicine and Masochism by the lay public, the experience of pleasure from inflicting cruelty is known as Sadism in medicine, and BULLYING among the lay public.

Both sadism and bullying may be an expression of a more generalized hostility and hatred experienced by individuals who have been neglected, rejected, or frustrated. In some instances, when these are caused by their wives, men have displaced their anger against their wives by attacking other women.

Or, some women displace their hostility for their husband's lack of consideration by verbally attacking other men — perhaps in telling them how bad they are in what important things they left undone) or what bad things they did but should not have done.

These "**Bulling Sadist**" have more than the ordinary Sadistic Personality Disorders. On the one hand, they are aggressive or violent in the pursuit of money, power, and possessions (the Bully) while on the other hand they are cruel for its own sake (the Sadist). Typically, these "little gods" are domineering, controlling, and judgmental. They surround themselves with symbols of aggression—such as weapons, violent movies and television programs, and military paraphernalia.

Fascinated by violence, injury, or torture, they are amused by or take pleasure in the psychological or physical suffering of others (including animals). Lying for the purpose of harming or inflicting pain on others (not merely to achieve some other goal) and resorting to intimidation or terror to get people to do what they want are routine. Mental pain is usually inflicted by humiliating, derogatory remarks made in the presence of others. Physical pain may be inflicted in a great variety of ways: whippings, biting, pinching, sticking with needles, choking, and branding.

Causes of Sadism are many—with most yet unknown or denied (because they would be incriminating). The form known as *Selfhood "Anesthesia"* Sadomasochism is thought to be caused by the degradation of love (Choisy p62).Sadism is sometimes interpreted as a *Reaction-Formation* against Masochism (deriving pleasure from one's own pain or humiliation).

Reaction-Formation is a psychological response that converts something desired and envied but remains wholly unattainable, into something discredited and despised. As a defense mechanism it is used for self-protection from dangerous desires. Then it develops opposite conscious attitudes and behavior patterns. Usually they can be easily recognized by their extreme and intolerant characteristics—both of which are out of all proportion to the importance of what happened.

Thus, in a sadomasochism situation the masochist attempts to deny the desire to be injured and by reaction-formation the person goes to the opposite sadistic extreme of inflicting injury on others. Or, as a result of guilt and an unconscious need for punishment, there may be a turning of those sadistic impulses against the self. Or, that same attitude may be turned outward on whoever is close by.

Cruel behaviors that characterize sadism and bullying are obviously fashioners of severe emotional disturbances. Such behaviors come from uncontrolled and distorted thought processes stemming from philosophical and emotional disorganization, unrestrained impulses, and absent or "*flexible*" morals. Being in the category of violent, these individuals have no honor. They need professional work-up to rule in or out some organic (e.g. biochemical, tumor) cause. Therefore, avoid them if at all possible.

Managing Sadism: Professional treatment is indicated—either for medical or psychiatric (to focus on the unconscious awareness and motivation for being abusive and to explore their vindictive envy arising from repressed self-contempt). Behavior techniques that develop alternative, socially acceptable outlets for aggression as well as nonaggressive ways of being assertive, may help.

Since most causes come from socialization (and therefore having quiet acceptance in European society), an approach is for the afflicted to change their system of values. A place to start is from exclusive pursuits of things of value (the Materialism Elites) all the way over to the embracing things of worth (love, peace, harmony) and their internalization. A giant step occurs when things of worth orchestrate and restrain things of value.

GENERAL MANAGMENT of HATE

Arising directly out of Ancient Africa or indirectly from seeds of thought borrowed out of Africa were the ideas that one could wipe out all hatred and evil by the one virtue of Love. This message of Hermes Trismegistus was spread forcefully throughout Asia when, in the 6th century B.C., the king of Persia (529-522 B.C.) drove out the Black Egyptian priests.

One of those priest started Zoroaster in Iran, Buddhism in India, and taught Confucius in China (which Confucius readily admitted). According to Buddhist scripture, the sources of evil are desire, delusion (or illusion), fear, and hatred. To remove evil, it is necessary to remove all the vicious qualities by dissociating oneself from the undesirable quality — i.e. "*objectivise*" it, as if one is an observer reporting what is happening — and then eliminate it.

The sages have said that all we regard as independent of ourselves we can master, but over that which we believe to be ourselves we have no power. For example, if Titan says that he cannot understand mathematics and calls himself "*stupid*," then he has made his lack of understanding mathematics a part of him –the part whom he believes to be stupid. But if he keeps his problems with mathematics separate while recognizing that his mind is not blind to everything, then with the right books and/or the right tutor he can eventually master mathematics.

Meanwhile, and throughout the ancient world, Hate has been so universal since so early in the history of mankind as to be part of all the mythological stories of all cultures. For example, the Homeric poem about the Greek god Thanatos — the hard-hearted one who is hated by the immoral gods — center around a perceived sense of injustice.

Justifiable hate, according to Christianity (Exod. 18:21), applies to hating covetousness (jealousy leading to a greedy desire to possess what belongs to another); hating all the bonds of ignorance which cause one to do evil for want of appreciating what is good; and hating evil itself (Ps. 45:7). Christ taught his disciples to meet unjustifiable hatred from others with goodness (Matt. 5:44), and especially from one's enemies.

Unjustifiable hatred comes from those sadists who have set themselves up as the judge and jury of what is just and unjust, based upon their own non-loving standards. To victims they declare to be guilty, they dish out hateful punishment. According to Christianity, this is tantamount to murder (1 John 3:15) — one of the moral evils (Gal. 5:20). The correction of unjustified hatred, Christian moralist continued, is to simply follow the revealed nature and purpose of God — i.e. having love at the core of all decisions and all problem-solving.

The ones engaging in unjustifiable hatred and who over perceive injustices are either imitators of what they have been taught or full of emotional turmoil. For these individilals, Medieval Christian moralists (Europeans who declared themselves qualified to fashion concepts of right conduct) outlined for the understanding of the masses of people the "*seven moral virtues*" and the "*seven Deadly sins.*" They said <u>those fourteen factors cover the whole range of human conduct</u>.

The **SEVEN MORAL VIRTUES**, causing humans to live well with God and with other people, are (1) Faith; (2) Hope; (3) Charity; (4) Prudence; (5) Justice; (6) Fortitude (endurance in facing serious and difficult problems); and (7) Temperance.

Anything opposed to these, the moralist said, could be grouped into the **SEVEN DEADLY SINS**: (1) Vainglory or Pride; (2) Wrath (anger); (3) Envy; (4) Lust (understood as excessive or illicit sexual desire); (5) Gluttony (including drunkenness); (6) Avarice (covetousness); and (7) Sloth (lazyness, especially in pursuing the virtues). These vices are the producers of evil and some form of hatred is present in any form of evil. Evil (or sin) is said to be a violation of divine law in such a way that it causes a disordered relationship with God.

Similarly, before we can begin to remove an unwanted quality, like the desire to inflict harm, we must become an observer of it — i.e. stand back and look at it. However, if we identify ourselves with hatred we cannot manage our hate. Instead, lay the fear, the insecurities, the emotional pain, the depression, and the anger on the laboratory table. Then examine each one from all angles — analyzing its cause, its nature, its effects. Face the fact that you are allowing it to dominate your mind and that you have become what you have been constantly thinking about up to this point.

Understand that the management of hate depends upon its presenting cause — from a perceived earlier childhood sense of injustice, from being taught to hate, from feelings of inferiority producing mental conflicts, or from developing a superiority complex.

This brings us to the way to **CHANGE A HABIT**. The principle for any type of cause stems from the truism that THOUGHT IS POWER. To continually think of a quality tends to strengthen it. Do what it takes to constantly think hard about the best destination you want to arrive at in life.

Meanwhile, let the old bad thoughts die by simply leaving them behind. Even to occasionally revisit those bad thoughts keeps them alive. From that point on, the general principles of switching from bad to good emotions apply — by avoidance, by replacement, and by sublimation.

X

SELFHOOD TOOLS FOR HANDLING EMOTIONS

***Be Drawn** to Lofty Pleasures*

***Be a Center** for Lofty Pleasures*

***Contribute** to Lofty Pleasures*

***Attract Others** to Lofty Pleasures*

The setting out of which the words "*handle*," "*manage*," and "*tools*" arose was that of a farm, with its horses. Obviously, farms require a great deal of "*hands on*" work and, dating back to antiquity, working with the hands included the use of tools. TOOLS consisted of anything used to make, prepare, or do something. A HANDLE was nothing more or less than "*something of a tool to be held in the hand*" but then the sense of "handle" was extended into different realms. One of those embraced the idea of handling a horse.

Such hand activities involved in handling a horse were, in the 16th century, grouped under the term "MANAGE." The horse trainer would use a rein (a long narrow leather strap attached to each end of the bit of a bridle) to control the horse. Thereafter, the words "*handling*" and "*managing*" referred to devising and contriving ways and means by which one gets another to comply. An example of this was applied in medicine in order to distinguish managing from "*treatment*." Yet, both "*managing*" and "*handling*" meant "*dealing with*" by exercising control ("*to have power over*").

The original idea behind "*treatment*" was to restore health — i.e. "to cure." But the nature and complexity of certain types of medical conditions — such as Self-

Deceivers (e.g. the Somatoform Disorders) and people with bad emotions — often showed that the ideal of "*cure*" was not a viable option. Thus, it was necessary to figure out ways to keep their problems under control through "*management*" –e.g. the "*handling*" of all pertinent problems of their home and family situations, money and relationship problems, etc., by dealing with the entire individual.

A parallel situation is seen in the legal definitions of "Impairment" and "Disability." Whereas "*Impairment*" in an injured worker is that which causes a loss of function of the body in whole or in part, "*Disability*" is defined in terms of that same patient's relationship of "Impairment" to the patient's environment. Those varied medical effects that significantly disturb this relationship are called a patient's overall "Disability" (Bailey, Medical-Legal Dictionary, p37, 63). Hence, treatment would be like "Impairment" and management (or handling) would be like "Disability."

In medicine, there are some patients who need to be cared for by non-surgical as well as non-medical means. These patients require management, not treatment.

MANAGEMENT is the on-going handling of the patient as an entire individual. After a thorough evaluation ensures that the patient is not in trouble as a result of some disease, the additional performing of diagnostic tests, giving prescription medication, or doing invasive therapeutic procedures are avoided unless obviously indicated. Management is done to keep patients from going elsewhere for medicines or surgeries that are not needed and/or that are likely to do them harm.

Similarly, managing "difficult" students has as its first aim, not the teaching of school subjects, but keeping students from doing harm to themselves and others. After slowing, stopping, or reversing bad down-hill progress, students are helped to maintain a steady state in hopes that they will eventually "see the light" that gives them a passion for getting an education.

Managing the "Big Picture" of Emotions: Although there are good and bad emotions needing to be managed, the process starts by taking charge and taking control. A teacher may be in charge of unruly students but is not in control. Taking charge and taking control of emotions means to discover what they are and to acknowledge their good and bad aspects. This opens the door for them to be managed.

Some forms of management require a generalized change in ones system of values and in ones character and self-esteem. Other forms of management require a specific change in some flaw, as with chronic anger. For both groups, certain Selfhood Tools are needed.

Handling bad emotions is deemed successful when individuals, without necessarily being cured, no longer allow their emotional reactions to slow, stop, or reverse their "*good works*" progress. Of course, this includes the stoppage of doing harm to themselves and to others. The objective is to establish a habit of success along stepping stones present on the right path and make it so attractive as to kill one's bad emotions from a lack of desire to use them.

In managing a generalized change for those who have Bad Emotions, there are certain mental orientations and certain methods applicable to practically all people. By contrast, in managing flaws that generate Good (those of an intemperant nature) or Bad Emotions custom tailoring is required.

GENERAL ORIENTATION FOR MANAGING EMOTIONS

As is true with anyone desiring to live a Masterpiece Life whereby constructive things are done for ones selfhood, for other people, and for nature, it is essential to start with a solid philosophy of life. To do this and to do whatever it takes to keep going straight ahead requires Courage. Hence, these two topics will be covered before discussing General Methods for Managing Emotions. The General Methods are of two types: one is a complete overhaul of ones System of Values and the other is a partial overhaul. They are presented in this order.

Philosophy of Life (POL)

At age 6 the core of my POL was formed in Sunday school at AME Zion church in Wilson, North Carolina. Our teacher, Mrs. Dobbs told us little kids that "God is Love and God is within you and you and you" as she pointed to each of us individually. This was so awe-inspiring and fulfilling that I used it to formulate the three parts of my POL—which is likened to a sky-scraper building (fig. 7).

On top of the concept of **Love** (the base of my POL structure), I built all the **Cherished Values** (the underground foundation that constitutes my character) and, on top of that, my **Power Approach to Life** (the above ground structure that interacts with people). From then onward, my primary pursuit in life has been to get to know what Love is and how it can be correctly spread. But I have learned that to do it right, spreading Love is very, very difficult.

Your POL is formed either by you accepting what you learn from people in the outside world; from what you decide is the best standards and guides to get through the maze of life; or from a combination of both. **If your POL is sound and solid, all other aspects of one's life will fall into place.**

SKYSCRAPER BUILDING CONCEPT

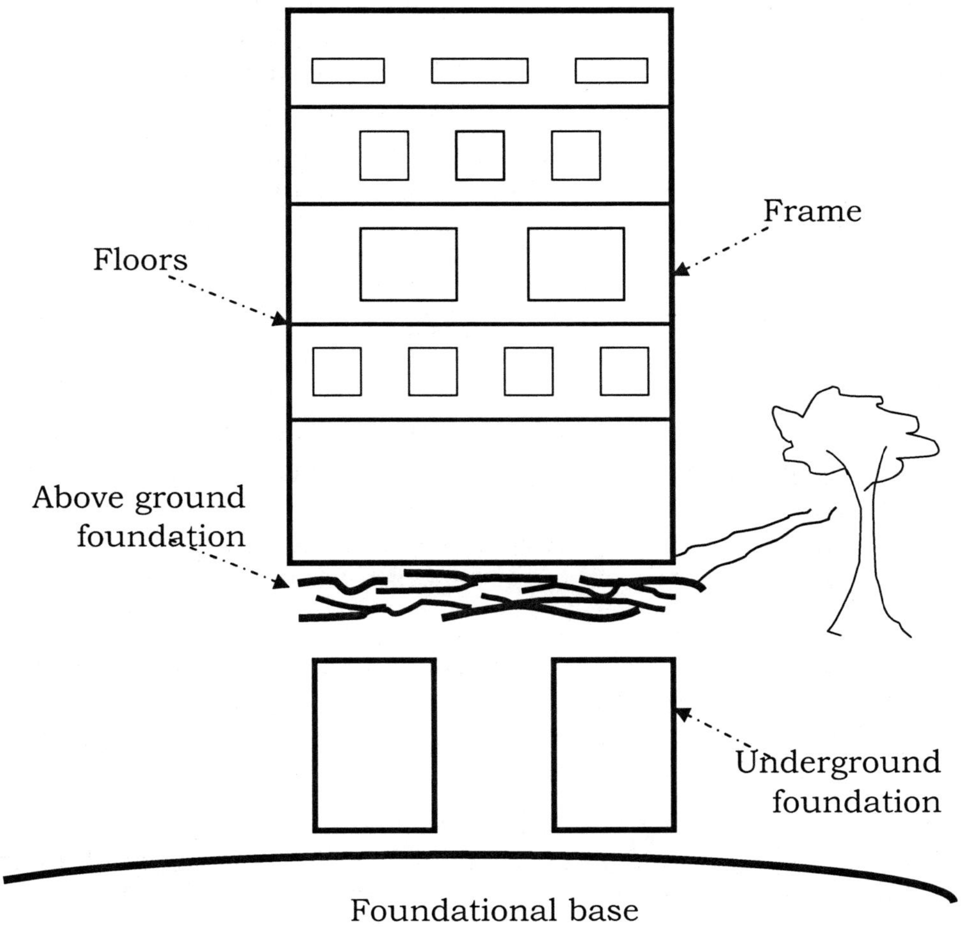

Figure 7
(Reprinted from Bailey, "*Afrocentric English and Critical Thinking*")

So how is a philosophy of life put together? Our mother's womb— the "home" where each of us as fetuses were protected and nourished— was also the beginning school "classroom" of socialization instructions. What mother thought, felt, reacted to, ate, drank, listened to (e.g. type, tone, and volume of conversation or music), got angry about, was stressed out about, or was happy about generated harmones that were all internalized by us. All of these things molded some of what we liked and disliked before our birth.

After birth, we "learned what we lived and lived by" as a result of conforming to socialization. In other words, we also internalized much of what our loved one's liked and disliked. Meanwhile, our genes contained things directing what we liked and disliked — some of which were made known at birth while others did not present until some time after birth (called "tarda" manifestations).

These same genes also contained things directing self-protective and self-exposure mechanisms. Whether expressed at birth (called congenital) or later (i.e. tarda), they fell into the categories of **"is it for me or against me?".**

In early childhood, we expanded our selfhood by selecting our top likes and "things that are for me" as well as our top dislikes and "things that are against me." These were based upon our prediction of what might be useful in getting through life.

Aside from likes and dislikes, we considered items for selection into our system of values from the perspective of "worth" (things money can not buy, like love, belongingness) and/or "value" (things that can be bought or sold as, for example, the products resulting from our genius, skills, talents, or appearance). Once we decided which things of worth or things of value would dominate our lives, our basic system of values was formed.

Perhaps around age eight, I made the decision to not let money be a dominating factor in my life. This decision was made despite having special needs for money at that time to help the family and to get a college education. Thus, my decision was to have a system of values dominated by worth.

Our System of Values, as mentioned, are our life-shaping guides that influence or affect all of our significant choices, decisions, and solutions. Each of these we choose or allow others to choose for us. When these values are prioritized, based upon what we consider to be solid principles, they constitute our Philosophy of Life (Figure 8).

In my opinion, the absolute best POL that ever existed was that of Ancient Africans. They had God/Love as their standard; Ma'at (love in action) as their Cherished Values; and Nonaggression as their Power Approach to Life.

ONE'S ACQUIRED NATURE

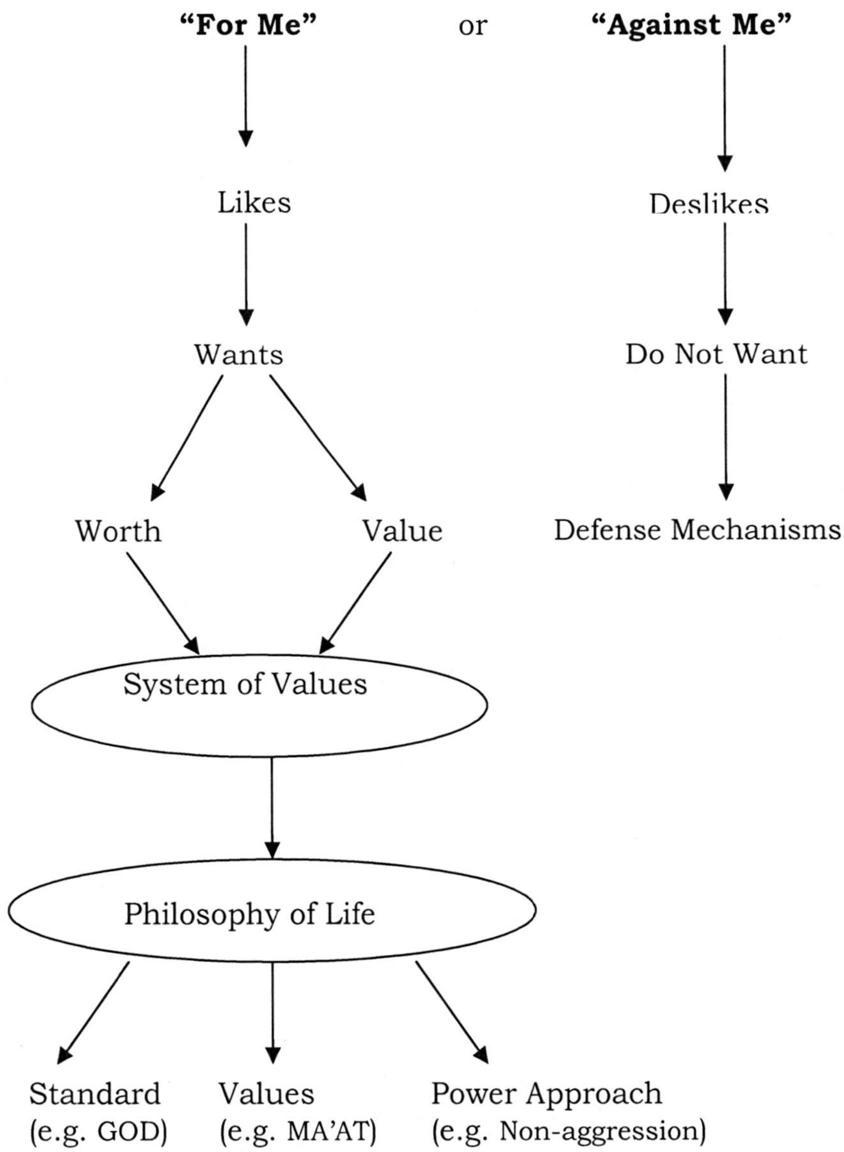

Figure 8

(Reprinted from Bailey, "Self Esteem in Black Americans")

God/Love as the Standard of African Tradition requires elaboration. It is in marked contrast to the Ancient Greek's belief that love is an emotion. The Greeks also said that love exists in degrees— Agape, Philia, and Eros. In Latin, the words are Caritas, Amacitia, and Amor.

Erotic or Amorous love are of the "need" type in that they relate to sexual desire and activity. Philia refers to personal friendship with "Storge", a subdivision, pertaining to loving persons and things close to us. Agapa, originally an orphan word regarding natural affection, rose to royality status by New Testament writers to convey to future generations the unique magnitude of God's love for mankind.

By contrast, African Tradition says that **Ultimate Love** flows out of the mind or nature of God and that this is above the capability of man's mind to grasp. Nevertheless, it seems to be the "glue" of Wholism and, says, Amen (Maat p77), an executive force of our oneness with all. In the discourse on the Law of Sekher it was explained that the Love force can act directly to affect physical objects and events and, in addition, is the dominant force amongst all others. To love your enemy, therefore, is an act of conquest—not submissive resignation.

As understood by Ancient Africans, the spiritual goal of Ma'at is to perfect the *Love Platter*—enlarge ones own capacities for love, to be loving, and to be lovable by being loved. It is to develop a "heart" that is filled with Love for all. It is the inner peace and inner strength resulting from a "heart" filled with Love that generates the Love to be summoned in adversity—a love that manifests the ability to act as an independent force in the Cosmos. This Love that flows out of the divine aspect of ones selfhood is a power that subdues the unrighteous (see Amen, Maat, for elaboration).

<u>The Ancient African view of Love as the perfect and all powerful force springing from God's mind, as opposed to the European view of love is the most fundamental difference between African and Western World philosophy</u>.

Cherished Values are those which flow out of one's Standard. Ancient Africans termed them the "Love circle of values" because they consist of those values which make up African Ma'at (i.e. love in action). Examples of Ma'at are truth, justice, righteousness, fellowship, harmony, unity, peace.

Nonaggressive Approaches were chosen by Ancient Africans Power Approach because it was "natural" and automatically flowed out of Ma'at Principles with ease. The Nonaggressive are gentle, kind, compassionate, affectionate, helpful, sociable, and empathetic. The emphasis is more on "Being with" than "Doing with" each other—in the sense of having good relationships with and good behaviors toward fellow human beings.

The values we choose to form our philosophy of life and how we prioritize those values are what give rise to our character (who one is); to our world view derived from paradigms (our life-esteem); and to our self-esteem (who you judge yourself to be). Our character, world view, and self-esteem determine what we do (work products) and how we present ourselves — the result of which gives rise to our Reputation.

SPIRITUAL FEELINGS CONNECTIONS

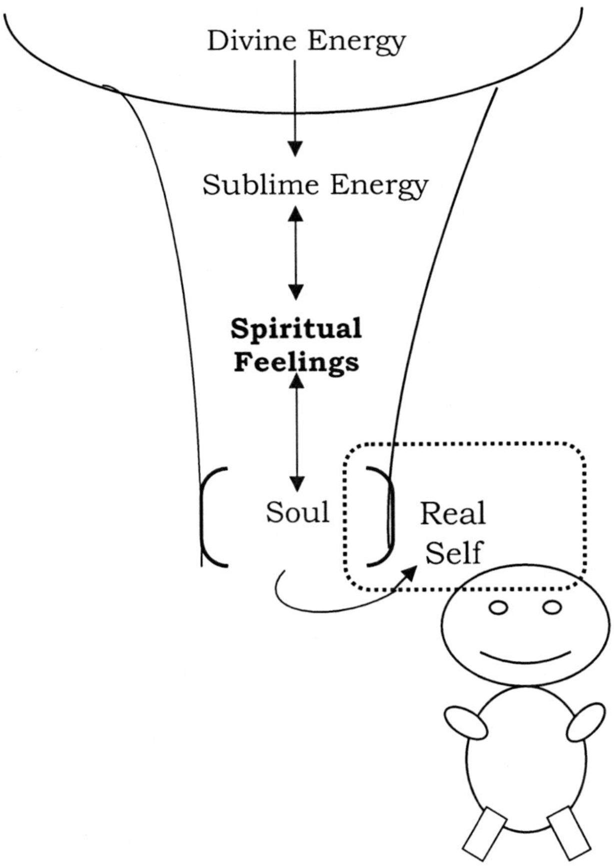

Figure 9
(Reprinted from Bailey, "Creativity, Invention & Discovery")

RECLAIM YOUR REAL SELF: This is a partial overhaul of ones orientation to life in that one has a sound POL but has put barriers around it. As a result, ones False Self has become dominant over one's Real Self. But what are these selves about?

The Real Self is that part of Selfhood which remains above the everyday concerns of the Lower Self (also called the "Personality"). Ancient Africans said the Real Self is the Divine Spark sent forth from the Sacred Flame as the Child of the Divine Parent. It is Immortal—Eternal—Indestructible—and Invincible.

Like interlocking rings, the Real Self (the Intangible part of one's Selfhood) links the Immaterial heaven or the Intangible (or Sublime) with the Tangible (material) part of one's Selfhood (e.g. thoughts, feelings). In other words, it is the transitional part of one's selfhood—that portion between one's Soul (i.e. spiritual self) and one's brain/mind (i.e. physical self). This means that whatever flows out of one's Soul then flows into the Real Self (fig. 9). The **Naturalness** in one's Real Self stems from a direct connection with the ultimate Creator source and therefore is bursting with a "bucket full" of the power obtained out of God's ocean source.

Besides its residents of Reality, Wisdom, and Power, the Real Self contains one's Life and Aliveness; one's consciousness and unconsciousness; one's Will-power and its Urges; one's human nature (e.g. self-preservation and instincts); one's loving character; one's purpose or mission in life; one's creativity; and one's natural rhythms. Each of these natural properties of the Real Self has Feminine and Masculine principles at its core.

To a partial or complete extent, the individual is typically unaware of the latent and potential qualities of the Real Self—and also of one's own Spirit. In this Lower Self state of being, there are many sheaths that shut out the light of the Divine Spark (the Real Self or Ego as it is called in the East). This is like several lampshades placed over one's mind.

As you, the student of self-improvement, awaken (called the Buddha effect); then remove one lampshade after the other; and then unfold into the knowledge of your real nature, the Divine Spark begins to increasingly throw out its light. This is evident by beginning to see the world as it is; by spontaneously exhibiting traits of good character; and by automatically shedding aspects of the False Self –i.e. the "Not I" aspects. Gradually, you realize that the Real Self is the home of where you go when you are over-whelmed and do not know what to do.

Just as a seed has an urge to express itself, so does your Real Self have an urge to express its owner's naturalness, talents, and skills. Tremendous problems result when, for whatever reason, you are not able to express these three—and that may cause you to get going on the wrong road and create a problematic life while on that road. Those problems generate bad emotions which interfere with the "Pure" Feelings needed for surviving and thriving.

By contrast, the **False Self** is man-made out of ones ignorance. Its effect is like the fashioning of several suits of armor around the Real Self— one over the other. Hence, as soon as we remove one layer of armor, another is beneath it. Lazy workers who claim they are striving to improve try to substitute the complete stripping off of their armor by merely removing only a few layers. But the Real Self does not wear any armor at all and is actually spiritually naked in order to feel the texture of the "skin" of reality, of beauty, and of truth.

The armor represents primarily a False "I" and is evidenced by you being attached to "things". Each day it creates artificial wants which you must labor to meet. As a result, your mind "committee" invents new and subtle means and ways of gratifying your senses— and often making this pursuit of "sensuality appetites" like a religion. The pursuit itself generates Bad Emotions.

Because this False "I" emotional pursuit has no limits and no moral conscious, the typical course is for one to become arrogant, vain, conceited, and puffed up with a sense of pseudo-importance. This bad self-recreating process leads one into a **Brute** type being—a crude person whose brutish features are magnified by the power of a misapplied intellect—a bully "little god."

An alternate course is for the afflicted to become morbidly (unhealthy) introspective and spend time analyzing every little thing they think, feel, say, and do. Arising out of this course is the exhausting of one's capacity for pleasure and happiness, despite desperately seeking both. Like addicts, they look outside for a lessening of their emotional pains and mental conflicts.

By being unsuccessful, they experience the sense of boredom, weariness, and discontent from a lack of occupation or interest in anything. They appear blasé about life and become a self-destructive affliction to themselves—and a problem to others.

The main feature of the False Self is that afflicted individuals are scarcely conscious of the Real Self "I" and thereby are little above the animal point of consciousness. Ancient Africans said the **"I"** is the Master of the Mind. The Consciousness "I" companion of the "Me" is the full consciousness of real existence which enables one to know that one is a real entity having a life not depending upon the body—a life that will go on in spite of the destruction of the body.

What little of the "I" that filters through the False Self armor is focused on the wants of the body. To varying degrees this shows in pursuing satisfaction of the appetites; in gratification of the passions; in greedily securing personal comfort; in expressions of lust, savage power, cruelty, lack of compassion, flexible morals; and in the lacking of a sense of well-being.

The "how to" knowledge for shedding the False Self and returning to the Real Self is not reached purely through intellectual reasoning. Yet, such efforts of the mind are often necessary to help in the un-foldment into truth. Ancient Egyptians worked out a way to recognize that the highest level is in internalizing the Oneness of All—i.e. *Wholism.*

"Man, Know Thyself": Their start of the Process of Selfhood Re-Ordering is to know who you are, where your want to go, and how you want to get there. That is why Ancient Africans wrote (? 5500 BC) on every major temple: "Man, Know

Thyself"—the recovering of one's Real Self from the earth world cloud of ignorance and self-consciousness through special knowledge of Spiritual Truth.

The process entails undergoing a Mystical Death of one's False Self; Spiritual Transformation into knowing that all God's creatures and creations are spiritually related (i.e. Wholism); and a regenerative Rebirth into knowing what Love really is and how to spread it so that it does the most good—for the most people—over the longest period of time.

The pursuit of this course requires that one follow ones true nature; acquire a disciplined mind with focused energy; and possess self-love (which embraces self-respect and self-trust). These provide the **foundation for virtue** and generate the inner strength for good character and the inner peace from which Love flows.

Since **Inner Peace** is the mindset for— and the manifestation of— harmony and unity, it serves as an alarm system to indicate when something is anti-harmony. The same applies when one is operating out of "Pure" or Spiritual Feelings which connect ones Real Self to the Sublime.

The factors which create **Reality** in ones life are Truth (which automatically comes from "Knowing Thyself") and having a strong sense of responsibility (shouldering the consequences of what one thinks, feels, says, and does) as part of being accountable to a higher spiritual authority.

To "Know Thyself" is to reach the plane of ones spiritual light which, in turn, ought to inspire ones System of Values (i.e. things of intangible worth and things of material value) in type, degree, and method of attainment; to inspire ones motives and actions; to inspire goodness in ones relationships, and to inspire one to live a balanced life of truth.

When one "Knows Thyself" ones mind is free, as indicated by realizing Wholism and, within that context, cultivating the expansion of ones mind.

To "Know Thyself" is to be aware of one's own intrinsic dignity and thereby not having to rely on any external evaluation and acceptance or to accept and internalize what is disrespectful. This means you do what has to be done because it is the right thing to do—including never, never allowing anyone to define who you are and tell you your destination in life.

To "Know Thyself" is to recognize the dignity (God's image) within all beings and to have compassion for their pain and suffering, even if you detest what they do. Such harmonious balance constitutes the Inner Self Stability Platform from which all choices, decisions, creations, and solutions spring forth.

Nothing is more important in "Knowing Thyself" than to develop Wisdom (which Ancient African defined as intuiting the Will of God). "The Way" is to stay in harmony while engaged in Ma'at. **Wisdom is achieved by striving for Good Character—and Good Character is the display of Wisdom**.

To stay in harmony and balanced requires **Mental Toughness**—i.e. remaining unchanged in integrity and in excellent work production under any circumstance (Bailey, Selfhood Mastery).

To "Know Thyself" is to *realize your Purpose in Life*—your Secret Dream—your Legacy as well as your Talent which you are given to make your Mission happen. Then your Talent must be developed within the context of your Mission in life. By possessing a clear and free mind, consider all the options which will enable you to find exactly the right niche for you to selflessly share your work product.

Once you know who you are then what is next? In order to reach a Masterpiece Life requires that you achieve maturity in general and emotional maturity. Such maturity will make it an easy next step to discover your destination in life and figure out the best way to get there.

Emotional Maturity

To be mature equates to **SELF-FULFILLMENT** — the completion of your true self, including your self-esteem, so that you have a satisfactory sense of self-worth and self value. These are the spring-boards for a happy and successful life.

Self-Worth is the appreciation of your dignity and the esteeming of achieving Internal Success (e.g. being loving), People Success (e.g. giving and receiving love), and Nature Success (e.g. knowing where to go in nature to find peace and harmony).

Self-Value is having external success (e.g. skills valued in the market-place and having enough money and possessions to live a comfortable life).

From birth to death, life is like a river with countless rapids, eddies, loops, back waters (isolated and stagnant places), and tributaries (streams which flow into other bodies of water) extending over a vast portion of the universe. Encountered along the way are caring, loving, and helpful hands as well as their opposites—e.g. alligators, ghosts, monsters, and dragons.

To satisfactorily navigate down the river requires maturity in physical, social, business, intellectual, and emotional realms. The actions and reactions having the best chance of success are those based on perfect mental models of the world — i.e. Love, goodness, truth, reality, perfection, harmony, peace, and beauty. These are the factors which are at the core of maturity, good self-esteem, and fulfillment in life.

A realistic result from the pursuit and acquisition of these factors is a **Satisfying Life**. To strive for a Satisfactory Life is to fashion the frame for mature emotional expectations. Being satisfied means having a sense that things have gone about the way you wanted them to and/or that things have gone in a way that seems fun and fair, based on the way you handled them. Satisfaction is not about having everything you want, doing everything perfectly, or winning all the time.

At the opposite pole of the Maturity Scale, the emotionally immature include the childish (i.e. "*spoiled*") child and the childish adult. No childish child is as bad off as a childish adult. Many Childish adults experience **DESPAIR** — the sense that their life was wasted and that it is too late to make up for lost time. Despair and other bad emotions create under-currents in the rivers of their minds. Under-currents influence one adversely without our knowing why.

But what does emotional maturity look like? Within the world literature there are numerous mythological or creative imaginative stories about the word "*maturity.*" In the way that a cultivated apple seed eventually develops into a fruit tree with delicious apples, so it is that maturity ("*ripeness*") describes the fulfillment of a process of growth toward a goal.

Emotional maturity in the child or the adult is CHILD-LIKE. Features of child-like are displays of affections from the heart, appreciation of things of worth, seeing and speaking the truth, and bursting with fun, fancy, imagination, and creativity. However, young children cannot meet their own physical or self-protection requirements and are not prepared to deal with the frustrations and the dangers of their world. Their emotions are bundled together like a handful of melted jelly beans into what they either like or dislike.

Emotional maturity involves knowing what our emotions are; how they control us in good and bad ways; and what to do to keep discipline. This is a process of teasing apart the bundled "*melted jelly beans*" emotions so that the good ones can be cultivated and the bad ones replaced with the ideal.

What does Emotional Maturity mean to me personally? The answer is in achieving the "5Ss" (Table X, page 306).

These five allow for **Steadiness**—the showing of little variation of fluctuation; not easily moved or upset; not lowering your work product of excellence during hard times. It is most effectively accomplished by keeping one's childish traits and bad emotions under control; by self-discipline in keeping one's word; by having an organized plan that follows certain steps so that a good result is consistent.

Table X — **Five "S" Human Fundamentals**

I. **SAFETY** *is a sense of being protected by something strong enough to survive any opposing forces.*

II. **SECURITY** *is the actuality of all one's needs being cared for-whether to get what one desires or to not get what one does not desire.*

III. **SURENESS** *equates to a sense of confidence and confidence is empowering (e.g. gives a personal sense of control).*

IV. **STABILITY** *is just short of being permanently fixed, in the way a spinning top is tilted from being knocked off course but then returns to its normal upright position.*

V. **STRENGTH** *is a resistance to unwanted change or the ability to bring about desired change.*

Steadiness is not needed or even desirable in every area of life but rather just for matters of serious business. Impulsiveness, curiosity, and spontaneity makes for creativity, fun excitement, and enjoyment.

Of course, you can never reach the the Western version of "ideal" (in contrast to the type of African Tradition) but selecting them gives you something to strive for. We will be emotionally mature if we do not allow any emotions — good or bad-to slow, stop, or reverse our progress toward a worthwhile goal.

STEPS TO EMOTIONAL MATURITY: In medicine, before a patient can be properly treated, a good physician must know the patient's history and integrate that history with a physical examination and the appropriate tests. Ordering and gaining impressions about that information point the way to what needs to be further researched so as to arrive at an appropriate diagnoses and various treatment options.

Sometimes patients have multiple diagnoses and therefore the place to start is to list them all and then deal with the most important one first. The most important diagnosis is the one most likely to threaten life or limb or the one causing the most pain, suffering, impairment (organic losses), or disability (how the patient's medical problems first affect his/her environment and vice versa). Often, handling the most important problem will cause the other problems to self-correct.

These same principles apply to bad emotions. Many people with bad emotions are dissatisfied with them but are unaware of which is which or of what to do. Here is an approach.

STEP I defines the problem: *"I do not like feeling this way because. . ." "The way I would like to be* is...". Discover the common theme within all of the "*becauses*" — some loss, some lack, some obstruction, some fear.

STEP II is the gathering of personal information by way of taking a self-history and by interviewing friends and enemies alike. Make it safe for you and them to be truthful. "*Freeze*" your opinions and judgments about what bad things they say about you.

STEP III— assess the gathered information: "*is my problem in relation to myself or in relation to others?*" In other words, do I have the problem or, since I am okay, are they having a problem with me? "*Where on the scale between localized (i.e. specific) and generalized is my problem?*"

STEP IV is analysis of cause and effect. Am I fighting others so that I can carry out my own impulses and avoid following the rules? Do my rights supersede the rights of society? Do I believe that if others or society is frustrating me then they are evil? Do my self-esteem or religious beliefs cause me to believe that I have no right to pleasure or success? Are the causes of my bad beliefs the result of not getting the proper emotional nutrition from my parents, from society, or from self-help measures? What patterns are my choices forming? Do I believe people should do as I say—and, if so, Why?

STEP V is manipulating the analyzed information. By understanding what is behind what you think, feel, say, and do will give the clue to what emotional hungers you are trying to meet. For example, a child needy for love may express this through bad emotions. Impulsive behaviors may be the result of over-protectiveness on the part of the parents or the parents' inadequacy in evaluating the child's ability to assume responsibility or parents who need to keep the child helpless.

STEP VI is maneuvering creatively to get around the losses, lacks, or blocks that were discovered in Step V. How can I give myself the emotional nutrition I did not get when my character was developing? Which one — if I "*lose myself*" in helping others or in doing interesting work or hobbies, or being involved in worthwhile causes — will best create good emotions to replace my present bad ones? What is a practical way to change a bad situation?

STEP VII is synthesis: How can I put all of this personal information together in order to best enjoy a high degree of peace and harmony.

STEP VIII is judgment — the plans A, B, and C you decide on to acquire good emotions and avoid excessive bad emotions.

In the way that a baby must learn to stand before he/she can walk, the steps to emotional maturity starts with "baby steps" so as to gain easy victories before taking on bigger struggles.

HUMAN CENTERING IS THE BELIEF IN BEING STRONG, SAFE, SECURE, SURE, AND STABLE ENOUGH TO WITHSTAND TRIALS AND TRIBULATIONS — the marks of mature people.

GENERAL METHODS FOR MANAGING EMOTIONS

Approaches (the way a goal is reached*), Methods* (how to do the job—the choice of saying or doing something), *Techniques* (how tools are used in the approach and method—what was actually said or done), and *Manners* (different ways a technique can be handled—the way it was said or done) are what cause, what effect, and what can improve the managing of emotions. Each of these requires a congenial mindset and a plan.

Congenial Mindset

Self-Discipline organizes of your thoughts, feelings, and behaviors into a team. As a result, you willingly do the things you should do even though you would rather not do them. An example is that of Concentration whereby, when faced with tedious and boring tasks, your creativity finds something interesting that provides motivation. This and related subjects have been extensively discussed in my book on Selfhood Mastery.

Self-Control is self-command — having your feelings, energies, and mental and physical faculties under the control of your Will-power so that you can command circumstances instead of circumstances controlling you. It directs what is desirable (e.g. skillfully learning to avoid conflicts) and restrains what is undesirable (e.g. stop engaging in "*Win-lose*" — causing someone to lose so that you can gain).

The foundational principle of JUDO, the Japanese science of wrestling (which is based on Buddhism and therefore African philosophy), has been described as "*victory by giving way.*" The mind that can learn to avoid an evil thought has gained its end with far less effort than by fighting it.

Off-shoots of self-discipline and self-control include SELF-DETERMINATION (the setting of limits within which you must act) and DELAYING GRATIFICATIONS (not giving in to immediate small wants in order to gain larger rewards later).

REAL SELF orchestrates the Selfhood. Its HIGHER SELF aspect leads you to expand beyond your self-centeredness so that your heart goes out to others.

HUMOR ought to fill your life.

Courage

The Prophet, the Leader, and the individual engagaged in selfhood mastery must be of courage. Courage, the basic tool for managing any emotion in oneself or managing people on any level, serves as the frame in which choice, decision, dedication, commitment, loyalty, determination, persistence, and perseverance work.

Although the English word "courage" comes from the Latin "cor," meaning "heart," the heart's association with courage originated with the Ancient Egyptians. Their concepts of courage pertained to doing what it took to achieve Salvation and Redemption and thereby overcome evil and death – both deemed to be manifestations of chaos.

Recall that Ancient Africans considered "the heart" (said to be the center of thought, feelings, emotions, and memory) to be linked to and located in a human's Real Self (an extension of the Soul and one's Soul is the image of God). In other words, by operating in life through one's Real Self, all the powers and wisdom needed for Salvation were present in the heart. Together, they brought order to one's selfhood and paved the way for stepping into the spirits of fellow human beings so as to create a "unity of hearts."

Such Unity connectedness with God and fellow humans gave great strength to the courageous person to work for the accomplishing of high level deeds (even in the face of danger) and with a moral conviction to do so (Josh. 1:6, 26:6). Thus, those who acted with confidence to attack vigorously the challenges before them were said "to have heart" or "to have courage." Their display of courage derived from their Highest Self –their Loving Self.

According to the Bible, one's "heart" connections with people and with God naturally leads one to manifest "good cheer" (Acts 27:22, 25; Jas 5:13). Although in Europe this cheerful mindset (in a confident state of being) primarily referred to military exploits, it clearly had and continues to have application to many other circumstances in life.

Courage is carried out by the "Will To Do"–the concentration of mental forces on the task at hand (see Will Power). The Will then directs those forces in conjunction with your mind committee. Each member of your mind committee contributes something different. For example, your Rational Thinking member contributes thoughtfulness; the "Centered" inner-self contributes steadiness and stability; the Concentration member contributes persistence and perseverance; the Desire member contributes deliberateness.

Although fear pops up at some point, the "courage committee" elects to see beyond the fear to work on what is possible for a good result. Hence, the love based committee elects to engage in self-preservation for surviving; in doing the right and decent things; in pursuing truth, beauty, and goodness; in having compassion for others; in helping the truly needy; and in taking those calculated risks needed to thrive in an honorable way.

INDICATIONS FOR COURAGE: Courage comes from the mastery of fear, not the absence of fear. To not have fear when fear is indicated is a sign of serious psychological problems. So is having fear that interferes with daily living. To not have courage when indicated constitutes a *Coward*. To have an excess of courage is *Foolhardiness*.

During natural catastrophes (e.g. fire, earthquake) **Heroes** appear and shift into a Selfless Service state of having no regard for personal safety. Their courage extends to the point of putting aside their own lives to save others. By going against one's human nature, courageous actions reach the height of noble deeds.

In non-life threatening instances courage comes into play in the face of threats, disturbances, or destructions; in circumstances of losses, lacks, or obstructions; in situations where there is temptation, pain, and going against the crowd or public opinion; and in giving up an advantage or taking on a disadvantage to do what is right (because that is what you believe to be your duty). Other examples can be seen in surviving poverty, in challenging bullies, and in facing the hostility of the crowd for doing the right and decent thing.

As leaders in truth, only the courageous can lift up a standard for a people and point out their shortcomings. The very nature of the tasks renders this unpopular and unacceptable to the lazy and the evil doers for they prefer to be let alone so as to continue with the way things are. In other words, the more a nail sticks out, the more it is hammered down. This was true for the Old Testament prophets who showed stand-out courage and has continued to be true ever since. But the courageous must not allow unpopularity to silence their voice (Woodson, 321).

By contrast, **Weak People**— cowards who lack courage or who lose it–are indecisive, full of doubt and hesitancy, unsteady in their purpose, and look for reasons why something can not be done when a challenging situation arises. They stay "stuck" where they are and almost never achieve what they really, really want. By feeling weak, they are automatically unequal to the task; discouraged; frightened; and possess a dislike for themselves.

Steps for Building Courage:

Step I—Form the habit of never thinking of anything unfavorable about yourself or anyone else. In dealing with difficulties—whether new or old—hold tight to the thought: "I am courageous. Besides, I desire it; I need it; I use it; and I refuse to become a coward and a weakling; I can not afford to not have it and get what I want and stop getting what I do not want." Whenever a doubt enters your mind, banish it immediately.

Step II—Never allow another person's opinion to over-rule your well thought out decision. If you do allow it you immediately lose some of the self-confidence that inspires courage. You become the directed and not the director by carrying out another's plan instead of your own. Instead of becoming self-reliant you become timid and this attracts what it takes to fail. Also, you are unable to judge each step as you should. For me, I want to pilot my own ship, even if it is sinking. My motto is to "do it my way!"

Consider what other's say; extract what seems right for you; and let the rest go. Make your own decisions and be responsible for the outcome. Others do not know what you can do when times are really tough—how much heart you have; how you are able to manipulate your inner forces. Actually, you do not know yourself until you are put to the test.

Step III—Learn to know what you can do. Keep trying new things that require "trial-and-error" so that you "stretch" your mental and physical skills and capabilities. Learn from every mistake. Sometimes all will be destroyed but that is merely an opportunity to rebuild something better. Most people fail because they doubt their own capacity and lack the freedom of mind to be able to draw on creativity to overcome potential or actual problems.

You have never come anywhere close to reaching your potential and therefore do not know how much you can accomplish. Even the most brilliant people only use 10% of their brains. When you believe with all your mind and heart and soul that you can get the job done, then you thereby develop the courage to steadily and confidently live up to that belief—and despite the set-backs.

Step IV—do not rely on other people's evaluation of how well you have done. Only you know that—the losses, lacks, and obstacles you faced; the time, energy and effort it took; and the creativity it required to get it as good as it is. Besides, they have no way of knowing how good a job you did—assuming you did your best. It is only their opinion. Others are simply looking at the results compared with some personal opinion or compared with some man-made standard or compared with how someone else did it. Success is not solely judged on the outcome but rather on the problems you had to overcome. They do what they do and you do what you do. Your job is to appreciate both for what they are.

Courage is yours for the asking—for the believing you possess it—for the claiming of it—and for the using of it. Difficulties soon melt away in the face of courage. But foolishness is not the same as courage. It is foolish to do something that will risk your limbs, life, or reputation. Discretion is the better part of valor." If you are in a permanent losing situation, then run away!

"Ships are safe in harbor but that is not what ships are for" (J. Shedd). Ships with courage eagerly look forward to leaving the harbor's gentle tide ebb and flow to venture out onto the high seas—with its huge waves caused by violent winds–to do their "destination thing." This scenario serves as a metaphor for human courage.

METHODS FOR TOOL USAGE

The six Emotional Management methods discussed here are the Check Method, the Bridge Method, the Court Room Method, Desensitization, Cognitive Therapy, and Philosophical Psychology. Part of the process of dealing with each method is to handle certain components that are related to bad emotions—components which are present in unique combinations for each individual.

Nevertheless, devise a Solution Plan for the problem at hand. For example, Selfhood ordering utilizes the Bridge Method of self-improvement and Selfhood Re-Ordering uses both the Bridge Method (fig. 11) and the Check Method (fig. 10). However, every thing inside the issue at hand is the Experience and to be able to know where to focus requires knowing the parts of an Experience.

CHECK METHOD

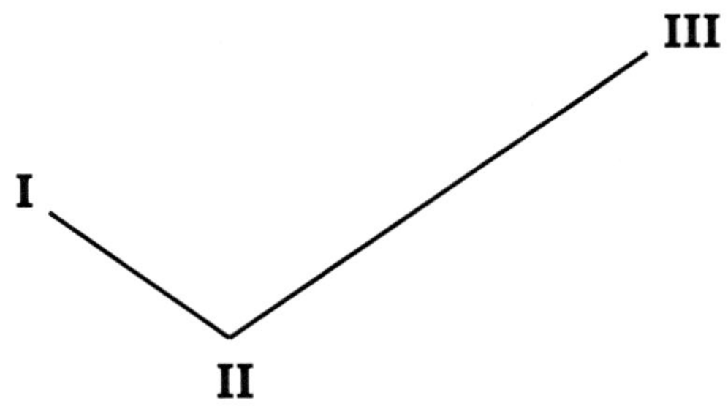

Figure 10
(Reprinted from Bailey, "Freeing Enslaved Minds")

BRIDGE METHOD

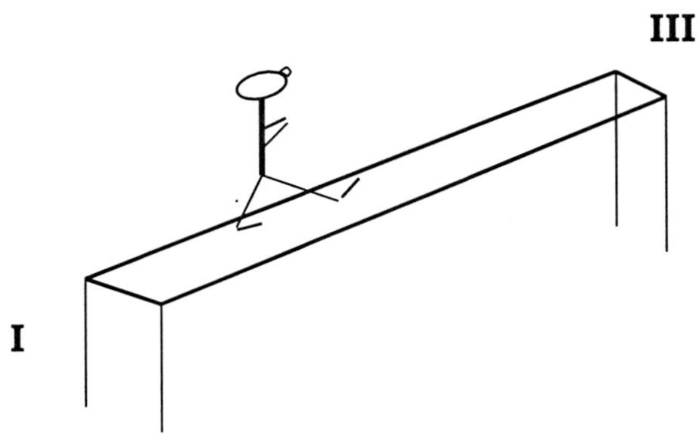

Figure 11
(Reprinted from Bailey, "Freeing Enslaved Minds")

The "SOBMER" Process

The "**SOBMER**" method — an acronym for Source, Origin, Beginning, Middle, End, and Result—elaborates on the parts of any Experience (Table XI). Most of its varied patterns concern fundamental aspects of dealing with emotions. Examples: Beginning is to End as Cause is to Effect. Motives are to Action as Reasons are to Conclusions.

The **Source** is that which furnishes a first and continuous supply; that which flows forth freely or may be readily recurred (returned to for a new supply) to—as the source of a river. The Source of any thing is that which first produces a range of essentials and then ensures a free flowing continuous supply of whatever the thing is about. For example, the brain/mind is the source of emotions.

Table XI – **An Experience**

I. Source
  A. Creator
  B. Matrix

II. Cause
  A. Predisposing
  B. Precipitating
  C. Immediate

III. Process
  A. Beginning
  B. Middle
  C. End (Ending)

IV. Effect on
  A. The Individual
    1. Human Nature
    2. Second Nature
    3. Tertiary Nature
  B. The Group or Society
    1. Group Mind
    2. Group Spirit
    3. Group Behaviors
  C. Activities of Daily Living

ORIGIN

Although Source is said by some authorities to mean Origin, a Source is that which furnishes a first and continuous supply. By contrast, an Origin is the point or place from which something starts or sets out from the Source. That Source may be spiritual (e.g. God) or material.

CAUSES

A Non-First Cause (i.e. not directly caused by God) is any event, circumstance, or force which produces or contributes to an effect or result. The Origin and non-First Causes arising from a non-spiritual Source refer to the initiator or motivating principle of something related to action. Motives are like the "why" of a behavior while Motivating Power is like interest, attention, and concentration.

Motives refer to why a motor is set in motion to start or move things. **Motivating Power** is a form of energy under tension that stimulates and energizes something to start the movement of action, or enhances an existing action, or maintains the momentum of an action. Within the mind, Motivating Power initiates, focuses, and sustains mental activities that either remains inside the mind and/or those carried through to completion in the outside world.

What originates or is caused by the Source seems to follow naturally. But common usage says that what is caused gives birth to or contributes to or ends in a result. Hence, the term "Cause"—more easily than "Origin"--allows for the placement inside of it such things as Reasons that give birth to Conclusions or Motives that give birth to Action. Motives have a goal they aim for and to achieve that goal is one's **Intention**.

As introduced in the discussion of Sources, within the mental structure of the *Medical Generic "Skeleton" Approach*, the Cause of a disease is often used as a synonym for Origin and this serves as a great source of confusion for Precision Thinkers (like me). These synonyms are so established by custom that it is too late to try to separate them for public usage. Hence, **in the SOBMER acronym, the "O" stands for Causes** and those Causes have three subdivisions.

PREDISPOSING CAUSES trigger the initial reaction—the Motivating Power--that starts the mind-**SET** (the mind's leaning or predisposition) to respond in a given way. In medicine the Predisposing Cause(s) is/are the first disease risk factors -- those paving the way for a disease to occur. An example would be a weakened immune system.

Mentally, Predisposing Cause(s) are like a shovel used to form a channel in your mind. Whereas the very first channel is shallow, each similar episode between your very first reaction and your present reaction makes the channel a little deeper each time. This illustrates the process used for developing a habit. This channel paves the way for, say, a frustration/anger reaction to occur.

PRECIPITATING CAUSE(S) are those bundles of energy which take advantage of the conditions created by the predisposing cause(s), and then accentuate those conditions. For example, bacteria upon finding an existing matrix (e.g. a wound) will grow rapidly. Mentally, Precipitation Cause(s) are all the situations that arise and lead to, say, frustration/anger.

Some are so mild as to accumulate at the starting gate while those expressed prior continue to leave their energy at the starting gate. Both are ready to take advantage of the channel formed by the Predisposing Cause. Then there are those situations that cause a band big enough to shatter the starting gate.

The **IMMEDIATE CAUSE** is that which opens the starting gate, combines with those Predisposing and Precipitating factors that have been waiting at the starting gate, and proceeds to step on to the race track,. If the situation pertains to a disease, out of what has been accumulated by the predisposing and precipitating causes the Immediate Cause is that which triggers clinical manifestations on the race track. When bacteria start producing their toxins, it is like lighting the fuse of a stick of dynamite. This shows as fever and other signs and symptoms of a disease process.

If the situation pertains to a mental state, the Immediate Cause generates intensity sufficient to trigger a frustration/anger reaction. For example, as a young child, if you responded to frustrating circumstances by having a "*temper tantrum*," all of the thoughts and feelings contained in that anger tantrum—whether clear to you or not-- will be present in your next response to a similar type of frustrating circumstance. All of the frustrations which have produced anger in similar situations are Precipitating Causes that act like a nourishing placenta to the developing frustration/anger response pattern.

If the Immediate Cause is simply like one of several "straws" of frustration tossed at the starting gate in rapid succession, then the nearest, most direct, and immediate "straw" (event) is called the **PROXIMATE CAUSE** of the anger. This Proximate Cause (which is part of the Immediate Cause) is "*the straw which breaks the camel's back.*" It generates the force needed to cause a mental state of chaos or at least disharmony. That force is added to the "forces-in-waiting" located at the starting gate of the previously made mental channel.

The same principles of Immediate or Proximate Causes apply in disease states. A person with allergies may need only to enter an area where there is a field on fire to trigger an allergic reaction. The first burnt weed that triggers an allergic reaction is the Proximate Cause, even though the person may then breathe in a thousand other weeds after that first weed.

If the Predisposing, the Precipitating and the Immediate causes are creations, then the human body or the mind constitutes a matrix. When a creation meets a matrix (a womb which nourishes a creation), a PROCESS begins. A process is like the spiral of a notebook—a series of gradual changes that go from one level to the next. To deal with this mentally, we crudely make estimates of portions of the process and call the parts "Beginning" and "Middle" and "End" as progression proceeds.

The **Beginning** is the first part, point, degree, or start of a process. It is the first step on to the race track. The letter A is at the beginning of the alphabet. When one strikes a match, the collective causes of the fire are oxygen, sulphur, dryness, and friction. When they meet at one point, a fire starts. The fire itself is the "Beginning"—i.e. the first part of action.

The Beginning of the disease is the point where the predisposing, the precipitating and the immediate causes meet. This is the moment some part of the body stops being normal and becomes abnormal. From a pathological lesion "leaping forward" into action, the first part of the disease manifestation process occurs. This process may either be subclinical or explode into clinical manifestations (e.g. fever, sweating). What the physician wants to know here is:

I—Who is the patient (e.g. strong/weak, stoic/complainer)?

II—What is the lesion (e.g. a virus, cancer)?

III—What does the patient do with his energy (e.g. work and daily activities)?

The **Middle** takes whatever conditions of the Beginning bring and enhance them. By the factors present in the Beginning now being more obvious, the Middle contains the best clues to the Cause(s) of a disease. It consists of all the things happening in the situation (see An Experience). For example, in medicine such things as muscle aches or vomiting are matured.

Besides, those contents involved in the Cause usually have measurable quantities (e.g. in degrees, numbers, and amounts) and recognizable qualities (e.g. characteristics, kinds) sufficient to constitute a syndrome. A "**Syndrome**" is a group of related signs and symptoms in an unhealthy person and some aspect of it shows where there is a need for treatment. Things to look for in the Middle Process are similar in any thoughtful problem solving. For example, in medicine the questions include:

1) How true are the presenting signs and symptoms"
2) How bad is it" (We call this "grade" in cancer, as malignant tumors may be high-grade or low-grade)
3) What is the extent of where the lesion has gone? (We call this "Stage I-

IV" in corresponding to degrees of local, regional, and distant spread of cancer).

4) How is the lesion moving on course"? Is it Continuous, Intermittent, Periodic, etc.?

5) What does the pattern of the lesion look like? Is it up/down, regular/irregular, wide/narrow, and/or large/small?

6) What is its progress? Is it getting better, getting worse, or staying the same?

The **End** is when the explosion present in the Middle activity has stopped; or whenever you decide to stop, even if the process is continuing in an active or chronic state or in a chronic but inactive state; or the lesion is no longer a threat; or the patient is getting better, getting worse, or staying the same; or the patient dies; and/or a cure has occurred.

The **Result** or the **Effect** –roughly the same—is the benefit, the impairment, or the disability that displays immediately, later, or ultimately. In medicine, it is the damage caused by the explosion of the disease (or the benefits present now and for the future). The Result (the Effect) embraces what remains related to you or others, or on a place, or on the environment from the time activity stops to the present and what can you can project for the future.

In summary, since nothing would happen if nothing moved, causes are about motion that gives rise to activity. Effects are what that activity did. Cause gives rise to an action; Beginning starts an action; end stops an action; and Effect (or Result) is the outcome of that action. The Beginning to End analysis finds causes; allows for better understanding of Effects; and opens opportunities for reasonable predictions.

The **BRIDGE METHOD** (fig 11): This is the direct way of going from where you are to where you desire to be. For example, in those instances in which structuring, and not restructuring, is in your best interest (as is true of small children), the process is to go from where you are (point A) directly toward where you desire to be (point C).Whereas it is the deliberate and natural mental movement from one plane of existence to another plane without the aid of any thing unnatural, the Check Approach is usually better for all the rest.

The essence of how the Bridge Method comes into play is that you are going along a certain path until something happens (e.g. a bad happening or a maturity insight). When that something happens, you are at a cross-road (point A). If you are sufficiently affected to either stop getting what you do not want or to start getting what you do want, then you will choose "ideal" goals (point C) and start working to achieve them. The big decision is to decide what constitutes the "ideal" goal (point C). A way to do this is by the Retrospectoscope Method, as discussed elsewhere.

The **CHECK METHOD** (fig 10): Surely you have made a grocery list of items and then, at the grocery store, picked up each item; placed it in your shopping basket; and made a check mark to indicate that part was done. Your "check mark" (fig. 15) started at point A; went straight down to end at point B; and then moved up and out in a slanting position toward point C.

Suppose a troubled boy, needing to restructure his life, is standing at point A. He is filled with all types of mental conflicts; overwhelming and confusing things; and an assortment of bad emotions (i.e. those which slow, stop, or reverse one's wholesome progress toward a destination). Thus, before he can move toward a custom tailored ideal manhood role, he needs to move to point B where he can clear up the ignorance, bad attitudes, and bad consequences of his bad choices and decisions which caused him to be at point A.

Next, the boy must decide on a custom tailored ideal manhood role and those goals which will allow him to reach his potential and express them for the benefit of the universe. This is point C.

Finally, he must connect where he is at point B to where he desires to go at point C and develop the habits to make happen the point C goals. These point A to B to C steps are called the **Check Method**.

The problems Black boys have at point A are tremendous—things like being burdened with enslaved minds and/or being victims of it. Although each Black male, and his experiences, and his interpretations of his experiences are unique and the way he should be managed is unique, there are things all Black males have in common.

One is the manner in which each has been and their continuing to be badly treated by every European society, with the worse being the USA. Another is much of their success or failure is based upon the child-rearing techniques applied to them. Still another, for the benefit of the Black community and for the world, is to see to it that they reach and serve their purpose in life. The only way this will happen is for guidance and help to come out of the Black community because no other group cares about them. Yet, the potential these Black boys have to make the world a better place is unlimited.

At point B, the idea is to clear up all bad thoughts, emotions, expressions, and behaviors which interfere with one's own and others' wholesome progress. All blame must be eliminated because it takes away your power of control.

Preparation for this very difficult task is to achieve a mental state of calmness and a spiritual state of basic goodness. A state of calm and peace comes from getting "centered" whereby one's physical, emotional, thoughtful, and spiritual energies best work by doing what they do as a harmonious team. This is cultivated by getting into the flow while at one of nature's beautiful locations, as in working in a garden, taking care of farm animals, or simply listening to a waterfall. Any of these allow one to experience basic goodness and that spark can be cultivated by developing good character (Bailey, Good Character, Trafford.com).

Basic goodness and calmness are parts of the platform of one's inner stability. They are used for figuring out how to handle crisis and emergencies properly because they allow one to correctly assess and decide what to do within a split second. This is not true in those who have trained themselves to scream and holler as a result of watching violence on television or in playing video games. Those activities are counter-productive to getting centered in a calm state. Here is the process used for:

The Check Approach Preparation Steps

Step I — Self-Inventory. At this point it would be helpful to review the "Tough Questions" that have already been mentioned. For example: "What do you think happens to you when you die (e.g. reincarnation or not)?" Or, "What do you believe you are here to do in this life?" Or, "How successful do you want to be and in what areas?"

Come up with similar life-shaping and life-changing questions to ask yourself, and list them as part of developing a "Self-Check" outline. "How do I feel?" "Why am I feeling like this?" "What am I thinking about?" — Am I thinking "how bad I am?"; "what don't I have?"; "Do I feel like a winner?"; "Do I believe I can do X?" "What do I wish I had done but have not?"

Design a picture of the little piece of the world you are in and then the piece you own and control. Next, consider how you can create success for yourself. Knowing the answers to your "Self-Check" outline puts you in control of yourself; generates power over choices within your own mental environment; gives you power over your responses; and fashions the power to deflate a terrible self-destructive bomb and even to disarm it.

Step II — Since your emotions have a great deal of power over you, they are a good place to start your self-mastery and Selfhood Ordering and Selfhood Re-Ordering program. Ways of doing this have been mentioned.

Step III—determine your standard, cherished values, and power approach which make up your main Philosophy of Life and your Functional Philosophy. Some people's top three selections relate to sticking with friends through thick and thin; some, to pleasure; some to simply dealing with everyday problems; some to achieving for themselves or others to the exclusion of all else.

The Court Room Method

The situation is a case concerning Atlas, a middle aged self-centered adult whereby the Court Room Method is illustrated. It was developed for patients too poor to afford, or not serious enough psychologically, for care by mental health specialist. At age five, Atlas had the perception that his mother did not love him. His *"I'll show you"* declaration rather quickly led to an inferiority complex.

At our first meeting, he related the feeling of *"floating"* around in the world—with no sense of attachment to anybody or anything and with the feeling of being isolated, insecure, inadequate, alone, and *"no good" in* coping with life's more difficult requirements. He had no direction or purpose in life and was totally unpredictable. In taking a work history, he mentioned that after dropping out of professional school he felt unable to achieve anything, had no marketplace value, and lacked a sense of self-worth.

On evaluation, it was obvious his life was a mess and that many of his adult problems were of a vicious cycle nature. Besides, after attacking people for *"no reason,"* he was both unaware of it and denied whatever he had just said. He absolutely refused advice because it implied that he was somehow defective. He was clueless about a self-improvement plan and immediately blocked any start-up suggestions because of thinking his problems were too numerous and too overwhelming to even begin. Furthermore, despite disliking himself, he feared any change would make him into another person. Many of his statements were exaggerations or of an *"all-or-none"* nature.

On one visit, when his defenses were down, he asked for my help (for reasons he refused to say). I simply guided him, as an outsider, toward solving his own problems. We started with him re-enacting, similar to a court room-like atmosphere, the age five predisposing, precipitating, and immediate causes related to his "I'll show you" situation.

The re-enactment, carried out in his head, was for the purpose of *"rewriting"* the age five story of pain into at a non-painful present mental state — similar to the freedom one gets from true forgiveness. In the hypothetical *"court room"* there were three participants — his mother; himself as a five year old client; and himself as an adult attorney.

Of course, as the adult attorney, and compared to himself as his five-year-old client, he had much greater character strength, more rational thinking skills, and better ways of handling interpersonal relationship conflicts. The steps were as follows.

Step I— the adult *"attorney"*— mentally back at the trigger happening and confronting his client's mother face-to-face— now does whatever it takes to discover, experience, and feel what the mother did to his *"client."*

Step II— the *"attorney"* reacts to the mother with retaliatory methods in a way that satisfies the client—even if this involves mentally attacking the mother violently. Once the client feels his mother has been punished sufficiently and agrees that all of his lifetime emotional pains have been absolutely released (as indicated by a sense of great relief), the punishment stops and negotiations begin.

Step III— the attorney explains to the child that the mother was having many emotional problems of her own and was therefore not mentally well. By lacking mental good health, she was not able to show love to the child.

Step IV— the attorney reasons with the child to forgive his mother. The importance he says is only for his client's benefit since, by forgiving, the child releases himself from the emotionally painful jail he has been in since the trigger event. This allows the child to *"unstick"* his mental faculties that had been "glued" together by loyalty to the stubbornness/hostility complex so they can resume the process of maturing into an adult state.

Step V— the attorney points out to the child that what originally got the five year old *"stuck"* was his own stubbornness and then loyalty to that stubbornness. He wants his client to see the part he played in creating his present problems. The attorney is quick to suggest his client forgive himself because he did the best he knew how to do at the time of the trigger event and therefore should carry no guilt or shame.

At this point, Atlas stated that he felt as if a weight had been lifted off him. He had never really connected his present problems with what happened at age five. Wanting to know where to go from here, he was guided into figuring out how to replace the fundamental bad habit of stubbornness and loyalty to stubbornness before trying to correct all the bad habits resulting from stubbornness.

A key to releasing his *stubbornness* was the use of understanding, a new way of thinking, and mental discipline to stop allowing emotions to enslave his mind. Some beginning corrective measures included no longer trying to control everything; letting some things evolve; and perfecting the skills of rational thinking.

Over time, we discussed other areas to work on—how to give himself the love he wished someone would give him; how to stop frightening himself with exaggerated self-destructive self-talk; how to empower his selfhood in order to build self-confidence; and how to learn to work independently and with people in order to get what he wanted.

Although Atlas' course was periodically *"two steps forward and one back"*, there was progress. His on-going home assignment has been to allow his adult *"attorney"* to take over each time he slips back into a client status. Three years later he was remarkably improved and with set backs occurring about once a year.

Desensitization

At a Middle School career day I was telling students about how to be an orthopaedic surgeon. One eighth-grader asked if I wasn't scared to touch dead bodies and see blood. I explained: "In medical school I could work on dead bodies because my focus was on learning to be a better doctor. In the operating room, I looked past the blood so as to find and fix the patient's problem."

Then, to demonstrate the answer, I asked the class to put both hands in front of their faces and say what they saw. A girl said: "I see me" (implying that she saw nothing outside herself). Me: "remove your hands and tell me what you see." In chorus, they said: "I see you." Me: "This is exactly what you have to do," I said, "to better yourself – see past your fears and feelings in order to help somebody else or to do what you have to do. In applying this to your life, to rise above poverty you must look pass your fears in order to develop and follow a plan." Me: To do this well is an exercise in COURAGE!

Developing a resistance to fear first starts by knowing when fear is proper, improper, or proper but is to be put aside. To be fearful of danger is proper; either "fight or take flight!" To be fearful of things unable to or not likely to hurt you is improper—and such fear comes from ignorance. Fears that are proper to be put aside pertain to those situations not involving risk to "life or limb" to oneself and to others (e.g. your children, mate, family). Resort to common sense to distinquish these.

An example of putting appropriate fear aside is in situations where substantial gains can be had by taking **Calculated Risks**, assuming the risks do not cause problems with "life or limb." Those calculated risks ought not to involve the possibility of hurting others (e.g. your children, mate, family). After you have done sound planning, preparation, practice and are ready to take the first step, then if any fear-producing thoughts come to you, cast them off as you would the deadly rattlesnake. If that does not work, then simply look past them.

Another boundary to consider before developing a resistance to fear is to avoid an inadequate amount of courage and to avoid an excess of courage. Courage is the mean or middle ground between two extremes. To not have fear when fear is indicated is a sign of serious psychological problems. So is having fear that interferes with daily living. To not have courage when indicated constitutes a COWARD. To have an excess of courage is FOOLHARDINESS.

Develop a Resistance to Fear: A way of building resistance to "the proper fear needing to be put aside" follows the same principles as those used to acquire "IMMUNITY" by artificial means — a process called Desensitization.

When we are vaccinated, a small amount of a weakened or killed disease-causing organism, or an extract from it, is introduced into the body. In response to the invasion of antigens, the body immediately begins producing antibodies. This constitutes the first exposure.

Thus, when we subsequently contact the "real thing" — i.e. the natural, virulent disease organism — the antibody response is ones pre-made ability—i.e. a "power-in-waiting" designed for defending the body. Because of this second exposure, the disease signs and symptoms either do not develop or they appear in a mild form.

Similarly, in dealing with proper fear, expose yourself a little at a time. This form of desensitization of fear is about taking "baby steps" in going from one stepping stone to the next.

To repeat an example already given, one approach is to expose patients to a tiny bit of the very thing that causes them their problem which, say, is anxiety. Over a number of sessions, the dosage of the anxiety trigger is gradually increased. A patient suffering from a phobia to dogs might be shown a picture of a dog at the first session; a dog's collar at the next session; and so on until a dog can not only be brought into the same room but the patient gives him a back rub. Relief can come in as little as two or three sessions.

Problems can arise if these procedures are tried by those who are not professionals. Or, problems may occur if treatment is cut short — i.e. before the patient has become inured (i.e. habituated) to the anxiety triggers. Under either situation the anxiousness may be *exacerbated* (i.e. usually temporarily increased manifestations) (Bailey, Medical-Legal Dictionary, p. 172).

Cognitive Psychology

The Cognitive System in an individual is formed by ones attention, perception, learning, memory, language, thinking, and problem solving. **Cognitive Behavior Therapy** emphasizes producing constructive changes in patient's cognitive systems, and particularly those with mood-disorders (e.g. anxiety and depression) who possess unduly negative and self-defeating thoughts about themselves and their circumstances (Eysenck p71). It is more like the Art of Medicine (caring for the well-being of the entire patient) than the Science of Medicine (caring for the organic problems of a patient).

Although the Western world claims Cognitive techniques (meant to help people recognize Bad habits and provide tools to break them) as its own invention, it dates back to Very Ancient Africans who laid the foundation for it as well as medicine, psychiatry, and surgery as we know them to be today. Here are a few stepping stone from the beginning to the present.

First, the African story starts 30,000 years ago when masks were fashioned for sacred purposes; for a conveyor of some deep symbolic meaning; and for teaching certain life-shaping concepts. Their colorful designs supposedly possessed magical powers to protect from evil spirits.

To frighten evil spirits out of a patient's body or mind, the earliest African psychotherapist dressed in skins of animals and equipped themselves with large grotesque masks as well as implements like rattles or drums capable of creating an annoying noise. Furthermore, these practices— in association with wild dance and mystical speech— were all intended to impress the patient and the people with the mysteries of healing. Something similar has been carried over into modern medicine, as in the form of using the mysterious Latin prescriptions and medical terms.

Second, for treating patients with "psychological" problems, masks were worn by a "ritual specialist" to **Personify** (to see something specific) that which African patients otherwise could not imagine. As a result, hidden fears located in the deep recesses of their psyche could be brought to light through discussion or other means and handled. Both practices were picked up by Western psychiatrist (e.g. the Rorschach tests).

Third, Ritual specialists allowed themselves to become possessed by the spirit in the mask (or the spirit represented by the mask) so as to invoke the powers of that spirit. Such "**Invoking**" worked as a result of Africans believing it was based on "the LAW OF SYMPATHY" (things act on one another at a distance from being secretly linked together by invisible bonds).

Again, although wrongly credited to Carl Jung, the Western world borrowed this "invoking" concept as a means of "act as if" self-improvement—"acting as if" the spirit of right is already within you. In other words, Ancient Africans taught that by wearing the "act as if" mask of assuming to already be successful, one would become possessed by the spirit of success until one actually acquired those powers.

Fourth, when Indigenous interior Ancient Africans conceived of the **Collective Unconsciousness** of humanity. They recognized that each member of the village had an individualized memory and a collective (or "group mind") memory (Somé African Healing p. 245). Whereas the individualized memory consisted of a collection of all of one's entire experiences, the collective memory represented a receptacle for the experiences of the entire living and dead community — the latter dating to the earliest or archetype ancestors.

Hence, Villagers urged its youth to master the ability to remember the knowledge "living in their bones" in order to carry out a personal life's purpose for the health and wholeness of both the individual and the community—a **"We/I"** society concept (meaning "**all for one and one for all**).

Apparently, Ancient Egyptians incorporated these interior African Collective Unconscious concepts into their works on the Dynamic Unconscious. They recognized that separation from the entity of Wholism was the result of ignorance and was the cause **Spiritual Pain and the need for Reincarnation.** Their teachings, discussions, and practices focused on doing what it takes to switch from such duality (e.g. "me vs. them") over to the harmony and unity experiences which characterize spiritual archetypal humans.

Eventually, the combination of indigenous African and Egyptian Collective Unconscious and Wholism (among others) concepts found their way into the Corpus Hermeticum and writings of the African scholar Saint Augustine (354-430 AD). His writings on "Principles" formed the foundation for, among others, the Western "archetype" and Collective Unconscious (King, African Origins p15).

As a result Western medicine beginning to realize the very high percentage of "sicknesses" that are due to psychological causes, they "re-discovered" management approaches for psychosomatic illnesses through psychotherapeutic maneuvers that originated in Ancient Africa. In the 1920s Freud and the Swiss psychoanalysis Carl Jung applied modified (from that of a spiritual into a more material world orientation) African concepts in their works and practices (Bynum, African Unconscious, p125; King, p16, 22). Those modifications have shaped the thinking of all Western mental health specialists up to the present.

One of those subspeciality fields is Cognitive Psychology which developed in the 1960s out of its parent, Behaviorism, as an open rejection of psychoanalysis. Whereas Freud probed the depths of the unconscious to explain behavior and mental illness, Cognitive Behavior Therapy stayed out of the mental recesses under the belief that mood disorders resulted from being off track as a result of trivial ignorant assumptions and thinking. The idea is that ones pattern of self-critical, perssimistic, and self-defeating thought are the disease and not merely the manifestations of a mental disease.

Cognitive Behavior Therapy in its simplest form is a short-term talking process designed to help people make small, seemingly mundane changes in the way they think (the cognitive) and act (the behavioral). It came of age in the 1980s as a treatment for depression (with a 55% success rate which is at least as good as drug therapy). It has since proven effective against more than a dozen illnesses in which mental distress plays some part.

Hypochondriacs often suffer under the mistaken assumption as those of Self-

Deceivers—e.g. a bodily symptom is always a sign of serious disease and demanding a 100% reassurance of not being ill. Yet, they and those with *chronic fatigue syndrome* show significant improvement with Cognitive Behavior Therapy.

More formally, the steps in Cognitive Behavior Therapy designed to help patients recognize bad habits (those which slow, stop, or reverse ones progress toward a wholesome goal) include things like identifying and self-correcting painful, depressing thoughts. This alone may provide a means for at least partially resolving induced and other transient depression states.

Up to half of people find Cognitive Behavior Therapy to be too disruptive and takes too much time and effort. Hence, these people prefer drugs but have no idea of the subtle side-effects of the drug. However, most depressed Black and Latino patients prefer talk therapy to anti-depressive drugs. Those patients who have foresight will realize that the cost of medicines over the long haul will be more expensive than paying for the Cognitive Behavior Therapy.

Since my only training in the mental health field was one semester (psychology in industry) at the University of Michigan as a freshman student and one semester of psychiatry at Meharry Medical School in Nashville, Tennessee, I had no idea of the existence of Cognitive Behavior Therapy. Nevertheless, I devised perhaps the simplest form of Cognitive Behavior Therapy while stationed in the Philippines as a USAF military general practioner in 1962.

We physicians were only suppose to see 20 patients a day but I would see 80—many of whom were "going crazy" for one reason or another. My approach was to give each emotionally disturbed patient one sleeping pill and tell each to get a good nights rest. Then each was scheduled to return as the last patient for the next day.

Most who returned said that a good night's sleep cured them. The rest would come in talking in machine gun like fashion. After they had "emptied" their minds by means of talking they would get up, shake my hand, and tell me what a good doctor I was because they felt so much better. All I did was say "hello" and "goodbye." They need to be with someone who is breathing that will listen and allow them to ramble.

Similarly, in my orthopaedic surgical practice many patients would enter who were overwhelmed with emotional problems. It was obvious that the vast majority had never been "heard"— and their minds were boiling over with chaotic conflicts to the point of them being "mad with the world."

This time, my approach was to assign to them a medical historian who took notes on everything they had to say. They were allowed to talk until they were on "empty"—and this could take up to 8 hours or more. Then I would come in and go over the pertinent aspects of their orthopaedic history, often within an hour. Simply talking to the historian and me cleared up most of their orthopaedic symptoms.

The same thing happened when patients would come to my office for a second opinion regarding the cause of their low back (or any other type) pain. After giving them a thorough evaluation, doing the required testing, and researching any questionable aspect of their case, on the next visit I would do nothing more than explain to them my findings and the results of pertinent research I did on their case.

Even though they were told elsewhere that surgery was indicated, I simply told them what to expect with surgical and non-surgical management and left the decision up to them. An amazing number thanked me for my efforts and for giving them a complete picture of where they stood at that moment. Many said: "now that I know what the situation is, I can tolerate the pain and will therefore elect not to have surgery."

The Philosophical Psychology Method

The background related to the Philosophical Psychology Method starts with the fact that psychology arose out of philosophy. When one gets a high academic degree such as a PhD, one has become a "doctor of philosophy." Based upon this, it would seem that philosophy is a forerunner of psychology. An analogy is that if ones philosophy of life is likened to the sun, ones psychology is like the light of the moon reflecting the light of the sun.

What I learned from my unsophisticated methods of Cognitive techniques just discussed expanded into an awareness of most psychological problems being reflections of a flawed philosophy of life—hence the name Philosophical Psychology. What led to the awareness that most psychological problems could be handled through a Philosophical Ordering approach came from an assortment of discussions with friends I had known for years.

It was evident that they, when unhappy about something significant, had a hazy or confused or bad philosophy of life. Or, their philosophy of life was alright but they were in conflict from not being able to figure out, say the Western philosophy of life as written on paper as opposed to what they saw in practice.

If they were really bogged down and receptive to another point of view, my approach has been to help them learn about putting their mental chaos in order before trying to solve any of their problems. It is explained that more indepth insight could be gained by studing Ancient Africans' philosophy of life.

Usually I pause to briefly summarize it by saying: a philosophy of life is broken into three parts—a standard; the cherished values arising out of that standard; and a power approach. For Ancient Africans the standard was God; the cherished values were the Ma'at principle (i.e. love in action); and the power approach was nonaggression.

The reason for selecting Ancient Africans' philosophy of life is that I had been terribly confused by Western Philosophy in college and needed to get some relief. To this end, I studied the world's major religions and philosophies but still did not feel that they "scratched the bump that itched." Then my sister Joselyn introduced me to Ancient African philosophy and was immediately struck by it being far and away the most sound I had ever known about.

It answered all my unresolved questions and gave me a direction for living up to my best self. It has visible brilliant achievements over several thousands of years old and has been the foundation for the best of what is in the world today—even though credit is not given to Africans. I conclude the discussion by saying that by acquiring a sound philosophy of life will put what one thinks, feels, says, and does in order and that will automatically correct ones mood or other psychological problems.

Philosophical Psychology is not designed to be a competitor in the realm of managing emotions. It can either be used as a supplement or as a replacement. Personally, I prefer that which is natural over anything man-made—and correcting a flawed philosophy of life by thinking and talk is natural. Besides handling your philosophy of life as discussed above, here are some useful tools to break "bad" thinking.

Step I—Monitor what you think and do. Learn to identify self-talk thought patterns that are self-defeating and which lead to self-fulling prophacies. Examples: "I'm no good at anything!"; "I always lose"; "I am not a likeable person." Avoid self-blame but accurately assess where you got off track.

Step II—present counter-arguments by disputing this bad self-talk using common sense, Rational Thinking, and facts. Make a list of your blessings and things you are good at and of the times you have won and the people who really like you. This provides a realistic inner platform to which you can return when you start getting illogical and irrational.

Step III—learn to handle setbacks and defeats by realizing they are a normal part of life and that they are what enable you to enjoy the victories and the beauty. People are annoying and mean and petty at times—and some will betray and humiliate you. That is simply the way it is! **There is nothing you can do to change people and therefore learn to accept them the way they are**. Do not take it personally if you have not said or done something to anger them. There is no point in brooding over this because the problem is within them, not you.

Step IV—when your selfhood is in chaos, go out into nature and get in tune with its rhythm. When you bathe in beauty, whatever is wrong becomes less bad and may even evaporate for a while. Seeking out beauty and peace is a good addiction.

Step V—self-praise is indicated as each stepping stone is reached or for doing things right.

Step VI—Be specific. Name one true friend who ignored you and how you know that to be true. The point is to re-evaluate all of your assumptions.

Step VII—After engaging in the Check or the Bridge Method, decide the ideal place of where you want to go and then proceed to take the first step. Make your goals realistic with your talents, skills, time restraints, and obligations to loved ones. The mere act of taking the first step on going toward where you want to go or toward handling what you want to get behind you can quickly increase your aliveness and blank out your dread of failure. To interrupt harmful self-talk and bad behaviors, replace them with constructive and harmonious thoughts and feelings that complement each other. This alone will put you on the right path.

XI

MANAGING EMOTIONAL FLAWS

STRENGTH is shown
By Admitting your
Weakness, *Flaws*, Limitations, and *Wrongs*

The 14th century European word "flaw" referred to a crack or blemish in a slab of stone. Thereafter, the sense spread to include a basic defect in substance or structure or continuity—as in a diamond or in a habit or in ones character or in reasoning. An emotional flaw is a lack in something that prevents it from being complete, wholly effective, or desirable. Or, it may be the presence of something that spoils what is otherwise okay.

Each of us has flaws in the emotions of our everyday lives. Some are of no consequence. Some are not in our best interest and can be shed. Some need channeling, modifying, replacement, or at least managing—and hence are deemed the Bad Emotions.

As mentioned, **Bad Emotions** include the outright Destructive Emotions (e.g. Chronic Anger or Chronic Fear); the destructive forms of "Negative" Emotions (e.g. excessive acute anger); and the Intemperance of Good Emotions.

Whether managing Bad Emotions by changing ones entire Philosophy of Life components or by changing some of those components or by changing the wayward emotions coming out of satisfactory Philosophy of Life, the process starts by taking charge, taking control, and proceeding toward an essentially ideal state.

A feature common to each of the categories in which managing is indicated is to find the trigger flaw—the one flaw from which others are generated and manifested (see discussion in Chapter I).

Something more like the "top dog flaw" is seen in individuals with an Inferiority Complex. The trigger flaw word "failure," defined as "emptied of power," is the judgment of having given up. To GIVE UP is a trigger flaw (see discussion in Chapter I). Never, never give up on something you know is the right and descent thing or the necessary destination.

The principle is to reverse the process that led to the trigger flaw or tear it down and rebuilt in the manner of the African Phoenix (Bailey, Creativity), or to over-compensate or to go around it or over it or under it or through it or take a different route or, if it is not worth it or is not in your best interest, then let it go.

Successful management of emotions is present when individuals, without necessarily being cured, no longer allow their emotional reactions to slow, stop, or reverse their "*good works*" progress. Of course, this includes the stoppage of doing harm to themselves and to others. The objective is to establish a habit of success along stepping stones present on the right path and to make it so attractive as to kill one's bad emotions from a lack of desire to use them.

But any time you change for the better there will be people working against you. That's the way it is! This is especially true if they perceive you as now having more than they have. As a result, what those people do will cause you to have an assortment of **"Withdrawal Emotions."**

These are emotions of confusion and the confusion generates questions: "Why do these people dislike me since I have said nor done anything to cause it?" "I helped them all I could and why are they upset that I did not give them more?" Why should they be complaining about my gifts to them when they gave me nothing but a hard time?"

Sometimes these personal attacks are too much for a person and they may react or experience things in one or more of the following. Their symptoms and emotions may be mild (vague, uneasiness, headaches); slight (early forms of depression); moderate (insomnia, nausea, restlessness); or severe (mental confusion, hallucinations, excruciating abdominal pain, delirium, and convulsion). Different degrees for the same attack will vary, depending upon how vulnerable you are or depending upon the nature of different attacks.

MANAGEMENT OVERVIEW OF EMOTIONS

Just as in medicine where it is essential for a physician to establish a diagnosis before instituting treatment, it is also essential to adequately deal with your own bad emotions or to help others handle their bad emotions. After identifying the specific bad emotion(s) involved, learn what it all about, what it does, and how it appears so that you can lay out a specific thought, feeling, and behavioral pattern from that information. Much of this information will come from simply knowing the historical story of the emotion involved and discovering its exact meaning. Once the pattern has been put into a clear form, the next step is to search inside the pattern in order to find any and all foundational principles and triggers which are shaping that pattern.

So how do you find foundational principles inside the pattern structure of an emotion? The answer starts by understanding that such principles are like the underground foundation which supports a skyscraper building and the pattern of the emotion is like the underground base on which the principles rest. The "triggers" are its basic materials.

To elaborate, recall that certain franchise food chains, restaurants, gasoline stations, or tract homes have used basically the same blueprint to build their housing structure, including the foundation, the framing, and the exterior appearance. Thus, to enter one tract house, for example, is like entering all of them because each house in the same area looks alike. In other words, what you are therefore trying to find in each emotion is that emotion's blueprint.

Examples of "*blueprints*" include: (1) the anger pattern that has as its foundation the violation of our well-being; (2) the fear pattern, the violation of our sense of security; (3) the emotional pain pattern, the wounding of our self-concept; (4) the depression pattern (which, incidentally has a great inner dynamic activity, as was present in the Great economic Depression of the 1930's), a "*sunk down*" sense of emotions which took away our aliveness; and (5) the spiritual pain pattern, an interference in the flow of love.

When you recognize a basic principle, say, to the world of fear, you will come to realize that this principle of a violation of your sense of security has been present in everything you have ever been afraid of, even though the nature and appearance of the thing you feared, including its contents, were different each time. Furthermore, the same is true if you feared one thing over and over, as when, starting in early childhood, you continually feared an abusive parent. Both of these foundational principles apply to everyone else who has been fearful at anytime in his/her life, including right now.

Understanding this violation of a sense of security gives you a place to start looking for cause and effect inside the structure of the emotion of fear. The "*cause*" is what started the problem in the first place and the "*effect*" is how your life has been changed as a result of the pattern formed by the cause (see prior discussion).

From studying such cause(s) and effects located inside your world of fear, clues will pop up on how to handle a particular type of fear.

For example, a boy might stop going to class (an effect) because he does not like mathematics (a cause). But testing shows that he does not understand fractions (a clue to management) and all that it takes to manage the cause is to get the boy a tutor who can teach him fractions.

Similarly, by discovering the basic principles making up the world of any emotion allows us to find the cause and the effect(s). Further investigation of cause and effect gives clues to management. Studying our own prior pertinent bad emotions and the pertinent ones of others helps us tailor-make a solution for handling our specific foundational bad emotion.

The degree of ones mental peace or mental conflict depends upon the kind and intensity of thoughts and feeling tone one has. This is a foundational concept for any selfhood mastery (Bailey, Selfhood Mastery). With respect to Inner Strength, Inner Harmony, and Inner Peace, the objective is to "make excellence routine."

Flaws in Good Emotions

It seems strange to think that too much of a good thing can be a problem. Yet, this is true about everything except the Sublime type of good emotions—and actually those are good feelings rather than strictly emotions. Thus, to speak of flaws in good emotions is to refer to those pleasures which are in the partially unbounded and the concrete (i.e. completely bounded) range (Table I). Within that range the mean between pleasure and pain is the virtue of Temperance.

The philosophy of Ancient Africans was that an essential part of character building is the development of a sense of *Self-Restraint* — the idea of reasonableness needing to be in charge of moderating passions and limiting the pursuit of pleasures.Those engaging in excessive pleasures are self-indulgent. Those deficient in pleasures may use temperance as an excuse for not enjoying life. Since it is so fundamental to flaws in Good Emotions, let us look at temperance more closely.

TEMPERANCE: As a little boy I thought everyone should eat candy all the time and for every meal. But now I know better because beyond the pleasures of taste is the gigantically bigger issue of my health. In other words, better knowledge has caused a shift from intemperance (the candy phase) to temperance (the vegetable and only a little candy phase).

To be temperant or intemperant—to do what we ought to do as opposed to excessively doing what we would like or want to do—is a major question each youth must face. This age old question continues to be debated between the public and moral philosophers. "Why not indulge myself?" the public says. Answer: there is nothing wrong with self-indulgence as long as it is done in moderation (i.e. with temperance).

In serious business temperance ought to discipline desires and keep to a minimum sensuality, self-indulgence, unchecked appetites, or passions running wild. In other words, it is reason that needs to be in charge of moderating passions and limiting the pursuit of pleasures.

Spiritual understanding, Ancient Africans said, is a clear, living, and inner knowing of the truth of God. Temperance depends on spiritual understanding. Without understanding, people seek satisfaction in material things. This "looking to the outer" throws the faculties of mind, body, and spirit out of balance and out of harmony and unity.

People then become deluded with the idea that there is satisfaction mainly outside of themselves. Therefore, they give in to the gratification of the senses so that every form of sensation is intoxicating. Only through inner vision done in order to become attached to ones Real Self is there any relief from wanting more and more excitement. To be able to reach fulfillment requires the great power contained in thoughts of harmony and unity.

A hard but necessary lesson for children and adults alike is learning to go without immediate satisfactions, to postpone gratifications, and to practice tolerance. In addition, we should completely renounce all forms of "sick pleasures" since they are totally personal, selfish, and destructive.

In short, we become reasonable by replacing the "pleasure-principle" with the "reality-principle." To cultivate an awareness of the demands of reality, to adapt to those demands, and to overcome mere appearances is not nearly as exciting as focusing on self-pleasure. However, the hard won success is far more meaningful in the long run than the temporary pleasure.

The essence of both "Temperance" and "selfhood-mastery" is the rule of the better part over the worse." Time honored Selfhood-mastery has been taught through martial arts and meditation. Nevertheless, the start of self-discipline (training the mind for strength and toughness) and self-control (restraining or regulating one's impulsive actions) is best done through the teachings of parents. Even little proverbs are meaningful as, for example, when Smitty, my step-dad, would say: "be not the first on who the new is tried nor the last to lay the old aside" or, when Mother would advise: "be not the spendthrift nor the miser."

However, over indulgence may be noble when applied to helping others who truly need help, as long as one can afford to do so. Another is enjoying the beauties of nature.

Flaws Leading to Bad Emotions

What everyone desires throughout life is having a sense of the *The "5Ss"* — safe, secure, sure, stable, and strong. These ideal concepts are never to be reached. Failure to achieve *The "5Ss"* (Table X) *or* the circumstances which cause a loss in one or more of The "5Ss" are major causes of Bad Emotions. Still, all of our choices head toward these ideals.

To this end, some pursue *The "5Ss" by* attaching themselves to a higher power or to a group or to a special person. Some focus upon their appearance in order to attract support. Some depend upon their acquisitions or make the most of whatever is available. Some resort to working and saving for a "*rainy day.*" Some rely upon their own inner powers.

The causes of flawed emotions are innumerable. Perhaps the most common is the presence of in an individual of an undisciplined Right brain. Such a "wild" mental state generates impulsiveness and is totally inadequate to handle matters of serious business. Out of the resultant continual state of frustration caused by an undisciplined Right brain comes every conceivable Bad Emotion.

For one to be controlled by ones emotions is an indication of immaturity. In ancient times this control of one's mind and the resultant bad actions was thought due to the presence in an individual of an evil spirit.

The Story of Morals and Ethics: A place to start an answer is to distinguish morals and ethics. Originally, both were synonymous, being concerned with human conduct about whether one should curb one's natural desires or seek their fulfillment or something in between or use some other alternative. Whereas the sciences of psychology, sociology, and anthropology serve the function of describing and explaining how humans act and why they act as they do (i.e. the laws governing these actions), *morals and ethics are about elevating human conduct.*

In a European setting, when morals and ethics began to separate, the Latin concept for **morals** was "customs" and the Greek word for **ethics** was "personal disposition." However, to try to put both concepts in their proper settings led to a variety of confusing and conflicting ideas and meanings.

One reason was their definitions were typically based on opinions related to oneself, one's subculture, and one's society at large. In essence, definitions boiled down to "whatever benefits me." Obviously this flexibility fashioned a double-standard of: "don't do as I do, do as I say."

To rise above such hypocrisy, attempts were made to steer "morals" in the direction of "sort of religious" and "ethics" as "sort of legal" or socially appropriate because religion affects the basic direction of the group's living while ethics affects the group's orientation to the "here and now."

Factors considered in the distinction concerned the nature of the problem; whether it was voluntary or not; if the action was intentional; and who was affected — oneself, others, or an institution of society (e.g. church, government). On each of these points, there have been limitless debates. In the end, the final definition decision was made by the person, group, or institution having the most power to enforce its will.

From a practical perspective, it is important to have a stable standard for deciding what to do in situations where you are confused about what to do. My approach is to distinguish morals as a society's **mores** — i.e. a society's common sense rules about right and wrong. By contrast, ethics are about **folkways** — a society's non-moral rules about what is proper and improper.

<u>A stable standard for determining morals is that which Sages (i.e. wise people) of all cultures and throughout all time periods have agreed to in characterizing what is right and what is wrong</u>.

Examples of what is **Right** is doing those things which create, enhance, and maintain the greatest harmony, for the most people, over the longest period of time. "**Wrong**" is of an anti-harmony, anti-unity, and anti-Love nature — killing, raping, robbing, stealing, cheating, and the like.

Ethical rules focus on ways of thinking, feeling, expressing, and/or behaving concerning what is customary regarding things proper/improper or appropriate/ inappropriate. This takes on great significance in realms of professionalism in one's career and in the rules of having good relations with and behaviors toward others. The rules of both may be written or unwritten but are peculiar to the group involved.

Morals and Ethics are to be distinquished from what is Legal/Illegal—that which is determined by local groups for a variety of personal reasons. For example, most state and local governments declare gambling illegal until they are running short of money. Then they legalize things like the lottery.

Determining Right and Wrong: To return to the specific issue of tolerance, the question at this point is how much do you permit others to stray from your stable standards for morals and ethics? When you have a choice to accept or not accept deviations, it is your decision as to how much this should be and how you will react once someone is deemed by you to be a violator.

Again, my approach is to draw a line as mentioned above. It is done as an aid in separating my concepts of what is right and wrong. When others do **dishonorable things** (e.g. cheat and steal), they are standing on the line. That means they have a chance to make things right by means of Retribution. Meanwhile, such actions generate very disturbing emotions within me that takes at least six weeks for me push out of my awareness.

When people do **evil things** by my standards and by the world's standards, I will fight it, leave it, or avoid it and them. I simply can not understand or relate to hate and evil.

On the "normal" (i.e. non-evil) side of the line, tolerance comes into play. This means considering what to do when things I dislike are of a nature not suitable to my taste or sense of fair play — and such happens a great deal.

Within this context, experience has taught me to investigate what all the facts are because many times I have a misperception from not knowing the truth or the complete truth. One of the benefits of having breakfast as the time for our **Family Talks** was that waiting over night until breakfast gave me time to cool off from something irritating about what my kids did. Then I could more calmly gather their excuses or reasons. This investigation will clear up many problems.

Experience has also taught me that *the more I understand, the more is my tendency to be tolerant.* The aim is to try to understand the situation from the perpetrator's point of view. Were their actions intentional and voluntary? Were they aware of the consequences of their actions?

If what they do seems unfair, then I try to rise above the unfairness in order to see a bigger picture. A common example is friends who charge me full price for some service they have rendered and then expect me to give them free medical advice. However, the bigger picture says it is far more important to maintain a harmonious relationship than lose the friendship over having to pay them money.

Besides, if I am true to my purpose in life of helping people to be a bit better, then I will give helpful advice unconditionally. By doing so, I am being true to my concept of who I am and this is not about what I get in return.

Repeatedly I have discovered that trying to live by a 50-50 "give and take" position of fair play is not sufficient because **EPs (emotional people) do not live by the rules of fair play**. Hence, to give people more than my share pays off in the long run. Whereas I give 100% today and get 0% in return, perhaps tomorrow the situation will be reversed, maybe from someone else. In the end, it all balances out. To re-emphasize: **do what is natural and true for your real self and do not allow any cause you to become who you are not.**

People Types Who Cause Flaws

Immature people—also known as *"the Childish"*— are those who lack Rational Thinking and Common Sense skills; have unpredictable outbursts of anger and periods of disagreeableness; are full of poorly thought out opinions and jump to conclusions; and do impulsive and often foolish things. To use an emotion at the right time, with the right intensity, and fashioning the right tone is Emotional Maturity. Anything short of that is Emotional Immaturity.

Immaturity is compounded when stubbornness and/or an **Obsession** occur. Obsessions are the full and persistent concentration on an irresistible idea, urge, emotion, or thought which, in turn, directs its activities. The obsessive thought tends to fill up the "space" in the mind that could be better used for something else. It is like an addiction to which one becomes a slave to that activity.

When an activity is done irresistibly and contrary to the inclination or will of the performer, such actions are called **Compulsions**. They are associated with a sense of powerlessness and inevitability. Obsessions and Compulsions generate Bad Emotions.

Short of obsessions, sometimes you are unable to get anything out of your mind—as happens with a catchy tune. When this causes you problems it becomes as unwholesome as any thought held continuously to the exclusion of goodness. This means the thought is ruling you instead of you ruling it. To not rule yourself and to not be in control of your mind is to doom yourself to an unsuccessful or "good" life.

Similarly, to be controlled by Bad Emotions (those which slow, stop, or reverse your progress toward a wholesome destination) means you are unhappy. So the control of your emotions requires that you mature and raise your functioning mindset to a level that is far above unhappy.

But sometimes the display of negative emotions is justified. Everybody does things which irritate somebody else and these are of two broad types. If you can imagine drawing a line and calling the side you are on as "normal" and the other side as "dishonorable," then the questions arise as to:

HOW MUCH SHOULD I TOLERATE?: Picky People are fussy over the "small stuff" of life to the point that people around them feel they cannot do anything right: "Your food is too greasy," "I don't like the way you wash dishes." Also, picky people are very hard to please: "It's too cold or too hot in your home," "Why don't you clean up while you are cooking?"

Another form of pickiness is not what you do but what people think you are thinking about what they do. Whereas the former type of Pickiness is an issue of intolerance, the latter type is not. Otherwise, Pickiness is to be distinguished from proper guidance, as in rearing children and sharing the benefit of your experience.

Being too picky is the process of designing a path leading to loneliness and unhappiness. So is not being able to accept criticism without reacting badly. So is failing to admit when you are wrong—and emotionally weak people can not make such an admission. So is denying your misdeeds and instead blaming others for the problems you help to cause.

But, on the other hand, you are entitled to be assertive in speaking up for your rights. Also, you are entitled to do what is ethically correct to stop or prevent being abused. Thus, much thought and research are needed to answer the question: “How much should I tolerate?”

Angry People: To become angry because someone is angry with you takes away the possibility of wholesome progress between the two of you and instead puts you on a downward course—and that makes no sense because you lose time, energy, and a time to be happy.With my angry patients, while listening quietly, I allowed them to say whatever they had to say so as to get all of the anger out of their system before trying to proceed.

Many EPs have a tendency to get angry for life and their minds are closed to making a change. In talking to them I mention that the concept of African Tradition is to seek harmony and unity but that I do not know how to make this happen with them. Perhaps they could explain why they are angry when I have done nothing and said nothing to justify that reaction. In appealing to their reason, I say we can get much better and much faster if we work together—the 1 + 1= 3 concept. If there is no benefit to being angry then why do it.

Some people are angry with you because they are envious of you. This is especially true of those you help. Their anger is because you have things they want and because they are not satisfied with what they have.

Some are suspicious of you because you are “different.” Some feel inferior to you: “You think you are better than me!” Some feel “you don’t need me.” Some feel “you haven’t done enough for me.” Some feel “you have not lived up to my expectations.” Some like you and feel you don’t like them.

Ask them to tell you what they think is the problem. If they get angry, chances are that the problem is within them and those inner emotions have to be projected on to you in order for them to have something they can react to by showing anger.

It has taken me until recently that some people who appear to not like me have no such thoughts. In fact, I do not cross their minds. Their seemingly angry or disinterest vibrations are simply a reflection of the way they are—a way that is part of their subculture with people that are not part of their in-group.

There are some people you can not interact with—like oil and water. Let them go. There will be others you meet and with whom you feel like you have known them forever. When both of you are the way you seem to be, you have a chance of having a good relationship. Regardless of the problem, the single most important place to start to solve it is to ask.

Problems with Being Liked

In Greek mythology, the mother asked a seer if her infant son would live a long life. The seer answered: "He will, if he never knows himself." But no one knew what that meant. Narcissus grew up to be so beautifully handsome that he attracted many would-be lovers but rejecting them all. One of these rejected lovers, Nemesis, the goddess of retribution, prayed that Narcissus would indeed "know himself." She had him catch sight of his own reflection in a pool on Mount Helicon.

Narcissus became entranced with his own beauty. The more he looked, the deeper he fell in love with what he saw and therefore could not bear to tear himself away from looking at himself. Held in the grip of passion for himself, he lay beside the pool day after day until he physically wasted away and finally died — all because of his exaggerated concern with himself.

The myth of Narcissus served as a source of inspiration to modern psychologists at the turn of the 20th century. They incorporated it into their new science related to the study of individuals morbidly (unhealthily) interested in themselves. They went on to say that an early stage in human development is characterized by extreme concern for the self and lack of concern for others. But what does all this have to do with you?

Let us assume, although it may not be completely true, that you do not like yourself. Does this mean that you do not like what you think, feel, say, or do? Does it mean you do not like who are are, the way you do things, or how you appear? If any of these are the answer, what in particular do you dislike? Write everything you dislike about yourself on paper and put a number from 1 to 10 to indicate how much you dislike each aspect — with 10 being extreme dislike (i.e. "I hate it!").

Now think about what you are thinking. Are you not thinking too much about yourself? Is it possible that you have too much attachment to yourself and that you are cherishing yourself too much? If so, why are you like the mirror image of Narcissus — having the same result from excessively looking at yourself but from the opposite position of disliking yourself?

Narcissus did not come to know his true and real self but instead came to know his appearance and therefore fashioned his life around that. What he thought was pleasurable and a true source of happiness — his handsomeness — was actually the source of dissatisfaction, suffering, and wasting away. Are you similarly engaged in disliking aspects of your appearance to yourself or your supposed appearance to others? If so, you have become a slave to appearances.

Being controlled by the master (i.e. appearances)—which is tremendously advocated by advertisements— you must understand what the master is about and what the master intends. The master is about concern for itself and absolutely lacks concern for you. What the master intends is for it to define who you are, what you do, how you appear, and to do what it takes for you to be a perfect slave to it. Once you become a perfect slave, you will realize that the master is not real and therefore you are choosing to serve an invisible shadow.

Now look at the things which are real about you — your thoughts and emotions and behaviors. Separate those which are about destructive selfishness — those that cause you to be concerned only about yourself as they bring harm to others; and those that show your lack of concern for others. What you have left are the constructively selfish aspects of yourself — those things that you think, feel, say, and do which are reflections or are seeking to reflect the fulfillment of your higher self.

The higher self is composed of your good character traits that includes compassion for the suffering of yourself and others as well as the caring to such an extent that you strongly desire and work toward a "win-win" success. The more you strive to reach your highest self the more you will like who you are.

HOW TO BE LIKED: Defense mechanisms may take the form of self-deception or the deception of others. To deceive others—"OTHER DECEPTION**"—** works on the principle that resembles those used in sports or war — "a good defense may include going on the offense." There is a real place for doing what it takes to keep people from disliking you because once their dislike is ingrained, you are always defending yourself — and generally unsuccessfully. For example, how do you stop the damage done by rumors about you? No one has yet come up with a successful way.

"*Taking the offense*" is done in various ways — having a suitable reputation that precedes you as you are entering a new situation; having important people in high places that can steer you through the maze of possible hostile reactions from others; being strong enough to challenge and beat the leader of the opposition; or resorting to the time-tested ways of causing strangers and leaders of potentially hostile groups to like you through the means of bearing gifts and ingratiation.

Historically, strangers entering foreign lands have brought rich **gifts** to the king, emperor, or one in charge. Sometimes these gifts have been better ways than fighting for the leader to better defend him/herself and/or his/her nation; sometimes, simply to make the leader richer — both methods being designed to boost the leaders self-esteem on a superficial level.

Invariably associated has been various pertinent INGRATIATIONS — a conscious effort to solicit someone's liking by using a variety of self-presentation strategies. Five commonly used techniques used in shrewd efforts to pursue others' attentions and possibly caring type affections are the following:

First is that of FLATTERY (an insincere compliment). When royal courts began to get started in the European Middle Ages, parties desiring the king's favor during sessions when disputed court cases were tried would begin by trying to "butter up" or flatter the courtesans (court mistresses). Some of the methods of "puffery" (i.e. flattery) that were perfected for controlling and manipulating people were stated as: (1) be specific in flattering the beautiful for their intelligence and the intelligent for their beauty; (2) flatter people who already get enough flatter; and (3) flatter people behind their back so that they will "find out."

Second is PRAISE. Since every member of the court, and in fact, the majority of people, are always hungry for recognition, they are quite susceptible to Praise (a sincere compliment for a genuine accomplishment). To be a really effective manipulative tool, compliments should appear spontaneous and believable.

Third, CONFORMITY — the going along with others' opinions and what they do and how they do it (e.g. breathing at the same rate they are breathing) tends to promote liking. As with compliments, timing, rhythm, and sincere tone — in the ways comedians practice their joke telling — are required to maintain credibility.

Fourth: DO SOMETHING SPECIAL to make them feel special. One form this can take is to do some extraordinary favor, with the idea that they are in your debt. But beware that some spectacular forms may leave the receiver irritated from being undebted to you. Work on the approach that is in your favor a little bit at a time — perhaps with a little teasing or with painting a picture of how their self-esteem can be boosted by the power or prestige or possessions or money or sexual conquest they could gain: the "picture this . . ." type approach.

Fifth, IMPRESSION MANAGEMENT focuses on learning how to portray yourself as likable. Find out what others like and want and give it to them if for no other reason than that is what they expect of you. Most people are controlled by their emotions and that implies they want to stay with the familiar and hear and see more of the same — in the way a child enjoys hearing the same story told over and over. But to maintain your good self-esteem, never violate the morals and principles that are part of your highest self — the good character part.

Switching To Good Emotions

Making the life-shaping change from bad emotions over to good emotions is simple to state but very hard to do. The principle either for staying the same or for change is that YOU BECOME WHAT YOU THINK ABOUT. Because thoughts are powerful, putting your thoughts on what you really, really want activates your mind committee and Will-power to alter the course of your life so that you will get what you want. Or, if you think about nothing in particular or have scattered thoughts, you will go nowhere in particular. Or, if you are curious about something evil you will head in that direction, even if you do not want to go there.

On the other hand, the ATROPHY METHOD is to completely stop your thinking about something bad. What this does is to withdraw all of the energy from that thought atmosphere. As a result, all bad thoughts and all bad emotions will eventnally collapse and die. But even from a peek revisit on rare occasions, you breathe new life into your old bad thoughts and bad emotions which are gasping for life. That peek will pump life back into them.

Let us use an example of hatred, a vice, to show how three methods — avoidance, replacement, and sublimation work. However, any vice can be used, whether similar to hate, like DESPISE (to look down on with contempt).

Hate is an enduring inner force that, by way of thought, pushes to activate evil behaviors. That force contains all sorts of destructive thinking and feelings related to hostility, malice, pride, envy, anger, fear, animosity, and disgust. If the hated person becomes injured or has a misfortune, "*sick*" pleasure is typically added. The hate force may be excessive, focused, widespread, and/or be misdirected on to the wrong person.

Whichever of these is within your hate force, list them on paper and examine each one in great detail. Analyze its cause, its nature and its effects, and face the fact that you are allowing it to dominate your mind. Then handle each one by whatever method is most appropriate. If the following suggestions do not work, search for the one that will —because there is a solution for every vice.

The method of AVOIDANCE is to give up thinking about the vice at all, and to keep your mind so filled with nobler thoughts that the undesirable quality, like a deflated balloon, fizzles out. Carefully avoid those things and persons and places which tend to stimulate your mind into the wrong way of thought. The gambler should stay away from casinos and the conceited should quash flatterers before they get started.

Avoiding temptation is not a sign of weakness. Why make getting better more difficult than it needs to be? Yet, avoid the trap of believing that a vice can be overcome by letting it have its way. You cannot kill lust if you keep lusting more and more, for then it gets worse.

The method of REPLACEMENT is the shedding of faults by substituting in the mind the opposite quality whenever the vice raises its unwanted head. A famous Buddhist stanza says: "*Hatred ceases not by hatred, hatred ceases but by love.*" For example, when a hateful thought about a person arises, make a concentrated effort to replace it with a pure affection and direct this force towards him/her — either at definite intervals or when the hateful thought pops up. Gradually your hate will weaken until a vanishing point is reached. In the process, you will start seeing "*the enemy*" in a better light because you are opening the flow of love.

Remember that the mind can only hold one of two opposite forces at a time. If constructive thoughts become a habit, they will automatically get rid of its opposite destructive ones. It helps to carry around notes containing uplifting thoughts as well as reading comedy or watching it, instead of violence, on television.

The method of SUBLIMATION is the redirecting of your energy, as characterized by the words of the song: "*if you can't be with the one you love, love the one you're with.*" This is the most mature of the defense mechanisms because, instead of being a love substitute, it is an expansion of your love. By contrast, some men with hostile impulses sublimate them by becoming a soldier or policeman.

It is useless to attempt to resist an energy which we cannot control. If the accumulating energy is not led into other channels, it will grow until it becomes stronger than both your Will-power and your reason. To control it, you must lead it into a higher and loving channel. Thus a passion for something hateful, when sublimated, is redirected into a passion for something constructive. Any vice may be changed into virtue by changing its aim — by choosing the higher self channel through which the mounting "*lower self*" energy force will flow.

For example, in medical school, there was an instructor who was really boring and whom my classmates "*hated.*" The method I used for redirecting any unpleasant feelings about him was by sitting in the middle of the first row — a short distance from where he stood. My objective was to write down every word he said — which, of course, increased my concentration and note taking skills.

Any of the numerous vices, faults, and failings will benefit from one or more of these three methods. Therefore choose the one most suitable and for reinforcement, when appropriate, use more than one. For example, anger can be sublimated and any hateful thoughts and emotions contained in anger are best avoided. Instead, replaced and Bad Emotion with love.

Replace Flawed Mindsets

FEAR MINDSETS: If there is a couple which produces the vast majority of Bad emotions it is Anger and Fear. Anger is more specific (e.g. hurt feelings) while Fear gives its "genes" to the more complex emotions ("What is going to happen to me?" "What is happening to me?" What will happen to me?"

Fear is called for when self-preservation is at stake. Overcoming Fear is called for when it is wise to take Calculated Risks—those risks where the reward is greater than the chance of losing—those risks which do not involve "life or limb" unless there is no alternative—those risks which do not put any one else at risk.

Calculated risk taking needs to partner with Courage. The process of forming Courage instantly and appropriately involves drawing on all of your moral qualities, self-confidence, self-efficacy aspects of self-esteem, boldness, and Ch'i forces within your selfhood structure. These are what characterize **Inner Strength**.

To tap into the sources of Courage and Inner Strength one needs to be clear that there is a good reason to do so and that there is no good reason not to do so. Good reasons for not doing so include situations that are not in your best interest and situations that are not worth it and situations that are too dangerous in case of loss.

Danger is measured in numbers of times it is likely to occur and in magnitude regardless of the number of times. The magnitude of the personal injury from motorcycle riding (e.g. paraplegia or quadriplegia) outweighs the rare chance that it could happen.

It is foolish to take unnecessary risks. Those who do are probably addicted to Fear. Some people are quite vulnerable to Fear. After analyzing the sensitivity to bad reactions and frustrating situations and then putting the pieces back into some order that makes sense, here are some suggestions to

Raise Frustration Tolerance:

Step I— after having sprung out of the mental chaos caused by your frustration, notice which emotion (e.g. anger or fear) is predominant. The reason the focus is on the emerging emotion (of anger or fear) and not the behavior caused by anger or fear is because the behavior of attack, for example, could be the result of anger or fear. Decide which is which.

Step II—If experience or observation has taught you that "*out of control*" anger does not work, then rearrange your view of the problem situation so as to correct your established bad response pattern to situations which cause anger. Hence, for improving your mind strength, much time should be spent clearing up old mental wounds which gave rise to the Predisposing Cause.

Step III—For improving your behaviors, replace your old socially and personally immature ones by means of the Bridge Method. Both corrections weaken your established frustration-prone mind set and if you fail to go back to the old ways then those old ways will die from lack of use.

From this point on you are better able to see that your next frustrating situations are sufficiently different from preceding ones. Therefore a fresh approach can be chosen to eliminate or bypass the proximate, precipitating, and predisposing causes.

HELPLESSNESS MINDSETS

Take a moment to feel the difference between Helpless and Hopeless. All of us have experienced that behind both, the feeling is much bigger and wider and deeper than those words imply. These are important considerations in practicing to develop or enlarge empathy for the most unlovable of troubled youth. Whereas HELP carries a strong sense of "advance toward an end," HELPLESS is a lack of advance, power, or strength — like in Uncle Remus' folktale whereby Brer Rabbit became completely stuck to the tar baby.

To feel helpless is to have paralysis of the Will so that we cannot move and have no idea what to do. Then, left on our own, we believe there is no escape. What happened was that we actually lost control in the process of getting into our helpless position. Now, we believe we have no control where we are, nor any control over how to get out of it.

When such helplessness becomes chronic — enduring as a way of life — certain terrible things happen. One consists of "ADD-ON" MENTAL STATES — like apathy, depression, and/or hopelessness. They come from prior bad experiences and the distorted ways those experiences were interpreted.

Another disaster is that most youth conclude they exercise LITTLE CONTROL OVER THEIR LIVES. It is true that significant controlling forces over them, especially if they are part of "the Poor," are within their political-economic-social situations which are dominated by others. As a result of reality and distorted beliefs, "the Poor" have many fewer options than others in their society as to how and where they will live, work, and play.

Inferior education is at the core which, in turn, leads to low income and an inability to secure financial improvement. Poverty makes education a luxury. But without education, accompanied by its associated skills and "certifications," the poor — even on lousy jobs — are the last to be hired and the first to be fired.

Still another barrier is that the poor have a strong feeling of NOT BELONGING IN MAINSTREAM USA. This makes for alienation, especially among Black youth. Resultant destructiveness may either be against others or may be slow or instant suicide.

People with moderate and extreme chronic helplessness reach the stage of no longer trying to avoid bad things. Such Learned Helplessness can progress into apathy to depression to hopelessness and to suicide. The term "learned helplessness" was coined when tests showed that dogs previously exposed to painful and unavoidable shocks eventually stopped trying to escape, even when it was possible to do so.

Apathy is a feeling akin to an unsmiling demoralization that is characterized by reduced motivation and work productivity. This is to be contrasted with LA BELLE

INDIFFERENCE (a hysterical conversion reaction whereby one even smiles in the face of reported disability).

Learned helplessness can come about for many reasons. One is when someone fails repeatedly on an important task, particularly if self-blame is choosen as the reason. Another is that something about the task has been deemed "impossible" – as when kids believe and say math, a foreign language, and physics are "too hard to learn." Still another is that there may be some uncontrollable outside interference to starting or to completing the task.

A prominent belief of helpless people is that: "nobody cares, nothing can be done, and no one can make a difference." They see no light at the end of the tunnel; but if they do they believe it to be a train!

Managing Helplessness: A valuable lesson in compassion, tolerance, and patience I recently learned is to substitute understanding for being so opinionated. Because of massive soil erosion following each heavy rain, the safety of my home demanded the necessity of expert landscaping. Eager to get the job done fast and right, I hired a landscaper with an excellent reputation for doing good work. Of those interviewed, he was the only one with a plan for solving the erosion problem.

Then I discovered that he would work for only a few days before stopping for months. His unreliability was extremely frustrating but since no one else could do the job, I felt helpless. Oddly, despite working only a few days a year, the erosion problem was handled early on and the landscaping looked increasingly beautiful.

Five years later, as he was finishing one of several ongoing jobs, he said "it was good to have done the work slowly because it gave me an opportunity to see how to overcome erosion problems with the change of seasons as well as what plants the rabbits and gophers would not destroy." What I learned is that things do not have to be done my way and at my speed—a realization that has eliminated many feelings of helplessness.

The point is that sometimes A CURE FOR HELPLESSNESS IS SIMPLY TO CHANGE A POINT OF VIEW. Had I merely focused on the benefits of doing the landscaping slowly instead of how much the landscaper was not working, I would have eliminated the feeling of helplessness.

Learned Helplessness happens with many poor people who have experienced such extensive failures and "shocks" that they no longer try to escape. They design causes to believe that no matter what they do, their fate is determined. They need to shed these distorted and fantasy beliefs as part of getting back to reality.

Once in reality, they are in a better position to assess their "failures" and become better educated about their options. Maybe with a shift in perspective, their "failures" can instead be assessed as "setbacks." Troubleshooting might show places where there is improper preparation; bad choices; where they "bit" off more than they could chew; or that they "bit" into the "wrong" thing and now need to find something else.

Similarly, many troubled youth have a tendency to wrongly believe that their lives are uncontrollable. By shifting their perspective, they can see that most of those obstacles are either controllable though using their creative problem-solving, or are in their best interest (as in my case with the landscaper). Those not in their best interest and/or not worth it can be bypassed. Looking at problems differently can make the barrier seem relatively unimportant and therefore easier to adjust to or let go.

Otherwise, teachers might consider doing what it takes to provide evidence to each student that he/she has the capacity and ability to succeed; that setbacks are always part of the climb to the goal; and that on the way to realistic goals failure will not occur unless one gives up.

The concept of SELF-RELIANCE needs to be explained. It carries a strong implication of independence and trust in one's own abilities, resources, judgments, and efforts. Self-reliance gets one out of seemingly helpless situations and prevents them from occurring or recurring.

HOPELESSNESS MINDSETS

Hopelessness is not quite the opposite of Hope because it is definite while Hope is not. To explain, Desperate is not to be confused with Hopeless. Although DESPERATE means the state of having given up hope, in common usage it is not quite as dark as hopeless. Rather, Desperate conveys a sense of recklessness resulting from a decrease in but not complete loss of hope.

By contrast, HOPE is a special type of expectation of something desired — an active way of coping with threatening situations by focusing on the positive or the attitude of looking forward to something that is to occur in the future.

Perhaps the word Hope originated from Low German in Medieval times in relation to "hop"— the notion of "jumping to safety." By having available the possibility and expectation of reaching a place of refuge while in a situation of desperation would give one hope. Today, hope may be well-founded in probability or completely beyond the pale of the possible.

The Story of Hopelessness: Pandora, in Greek Mythology, was the first woman on earth. Prior to her arrival and soon after the world had been created, the gods Zeus and Prometheus had a quarrel. Zeus did not want men to have fire on earth and so he hid it. However, Prometheus found it and brought it back again. Zeus was so angry that he decided to send the first woman down to men to cause men trouble — an evil thing—Pandora— that all men would desire.

The goddess Athena gave Pandora knowledge of the Arts; Aphrodite made her beautiful; Hermes provided her with cunning and flattery; and the Graces clothed her. Zeus named her Pandora, or all-gifted. Mercury took her to Epimetheus, the brother of Prometheus, who gladly received her into his house in spite of the warning from Prometheus. Mercury gave Pandora a box but with strict instructions not to open it.

Originally intended for Prometheus, the box from Zeus was filled with unconquerable evils. It was fastened, not by a lock, but by a magical gold cord. Its knot, having no beginning and no end, so fascinated the curious Pandora that she opened the box.

Upon lifting the lid, all the vices and sins, diseases and troubles in the world — like envy, evil passions, anger, and revenge — at once flew out, scattered abroad and forever thereafter tormented mankind. Pandora shut the lid quickly and thereby prevented Hope, which lay at the bottom, from escaping.

Hope had been packed into the box to make amends for that swarm of ugly troubles. Eventually, Hope was let out of the box in order to fly around the world and spring eternal from as many human breasts as possible.

So what we have in this story of Pandora's Box is a way of looking at hope and hopelessness. HOPELESS means giving up — the stopping of mental and physical effort. It refers either to emotions or a situation. The mental state associated with hopeless may be that of depression, acceptance, or resignation. Hopeless is closely associated with Apathy.

On the scale of hopelessness, there are degrees of fear and rage greater than doubt — fear and rage produced by external circumstances plus imagination. People experiencing hopelessness are marked by violent and impatient feelings from seeing but believing themselves to be unable to reach their dream.

In short, HOPELESSNESS IMPLIES ABANDONMENT TO FATE— AND YET THERE REMAINS AN EMBER OF HOPE.

Managing Hopelessness: Some say the process of hopelessness starts when the tendency to belong is denied — either from parental neglect or society neglect. Once denied, youth get stuck and stop their process of maturity. Their attitude becomes one of hostility toward others and with a preparedness to fight for anything they want.

"Herd" hopelessness is the process of "sort of" giving up. Members have negative expectations about the success of any attempts to obtain their dream or major personal goals. This is a direct result of feeling like an outcast in their own homeland

— not feeling that they belong — not having any stake in their own country. Such an estrangement from society says to them that life is not worth living. They may evolve into the mental states of despair, desperation, and despondency.

The fact that the herd members (see discussion on Belonging) have not given up completely—because they create their own world— means that they have a spark of hope. Focusing and enlarging upon this spark with love, compassion, tolerance, and patience are levers to opening the tightly closed clam shells in which these youth live. As important as anything in this regard is for youth to get involved with helping others.

Being in nature — doing things like working in the garden, hiking, canoeing — all while remaining quiet — is an excellent way to fan the embers of hope. This is particularly true if the afflicted have an animal (e.g. such as a horse on a farm) or pet to take of (e.g. a dog).

Next comes paving the way for youth to have a firm trust in Providence; cultivating each one's talent and creativity; and providing them with the education they need for their personal, social, economic, school, and career life.

Since hope is one of the creative properties of a mature mind, the emergence in troubled youth of a flame of hope for future success is an important sign of healing.

STUBBORNNESS MINDSET

The ancients considered stubbornness to be about that which is the strongest and the most ruthless mindset except for evil mindsets. Later, ideas inside the concept of stubbornness softened to concern those who were unforgiving, relentless, not easily pacified, and not even influenced by prayers. Still later, the word "stubborn" (or stubble) was applied to children who were perverse, wicked, obstinate, disobedient to parents, and wayward by associating with known criminals or other immoral persons.

At first, *"stubble"* referred to what was left when a tree was cut down and against which one might stub one's toe. When stubble started referring to half of the stem, the fact that it remained firm after cutting or harvesting stalks of grain (Exod. 5:10-14) gave rise to the word "stubborn"—applied in both a good connotation (as was the thought in Ancient Egypt) and a bad connotation (as was the thought in Europe).

In Egypt, those *"stubborn"* stalks had been used as brick straw because, when mixed with mud, the resultant interaction released chemicals which made the bricks harder. It was probably in this context that a stubborn person was viewed, despite the pressures applied, as sticking to his/her course for good or idealistic reasons.

In Europe, *"stubborn"* retained during and after Biblical times the ideas of a hard, obstinate attitude—and even that of rebelliousness. Both ideas, and especially those of a firm nature following an evil course, were thought of as beliefs antagonistic to God. When *"stubborn"* came into Middle English, as basically present in Chaucer's Canterbury Tales (1395), it carried the concept of being *"un-tameable," "unyielding,"* and *"obstinate."*

Next, whereas OBSTINATE was about acquiring unyieldingness, mulishness, and staying fixed, *"stubborn"* took on the meaning of an unborn tendency. For example, a stubborn child was one who would not do what another desired or required so as to proceed with what was in that child's best interest. Thereafter, "stubbornness" has meant an UNREASONABLE DETERMINATION NOT TO CHANGE. A way one might decide unreasonableness is that stubbornness creates, enhances, or maintains disharmony while PERSISTENCE, the constructive form of stubbornness, generates harmony in the long run.

Features of the Stubborn Childish Person:

(1) The stubborn individual is either mentally and/or physically fixed or not moving fast enough in a desired direction;

(2) Contains bad aspects that have a range of undesirable or bad effects;

(3) Persists in being *"un-tameable";* and

(4) Stays filled with a mindset consisting of more Negative and Bad Emotional energy forces than with reason (ability to think and act by truth). However, these features may not be all due to a choice made by the child.

Socialization Stubbornness is a common among Black Americans and it started during slavery. Any anti-work measures the slaves could fashion were considered avengements. Whereas "revenge" is payback for selfish reasons, to "avenge" is the act of righting wrongs in order to achieve at least some degree of justice.

Although revenge was no doubt a part of Slave Resistance, avengements were something to which all field slaves could agree and participate in. Despite revenge being thought of as the main cause of stubbornness, avengements had the same effect even though it arose out of a different type of intention.

Both revenge and avenge became a way of life for the field slaves; both took on the technical definition of stubbornness; and both were culturally transmitted through the "pipeline" connecting slavery with today's struggling Black community.

Because the slaves and ex-slaves were "herded" together and thereby these individuals were engaged in cross-fertilization of think, feel, say, and do ways of "Being", common patterns were formed as customs that spread nation-wide. Still, there are subtypes of stubbornness showing a different presentation and each requiring being distinquished from their look-alikes.

Forms of Stubbornness

MULISH stubbornness shows as ornery — difficult, aggressive, and intractable—as were a few of my elderly hospitalized patients. However, they have had a great deal of personal experience or information pertaining to incompetent treatment. As a result, appearing "stubborn" is a way of getting the staff's attention.

PIGHEADED stubbornness—stupidity (having eyes but can not see) is prominent. Some normal people's stupidity is due to fear. These individuals refuse to accept facts and this prevents having a reasonable discussion with them.

ARROGANT HEADSTRONG stubbornness has impulsiveness as its driving force—the type of impulsiveness that shows as recklessness or hot-headedness. Refusing to be held back by wise advice or argument, such people rush into things without forethought or foresight. Thus, from lack of predicting what will be faced, there is no planning. With no planning there is no taking of precautions and no preparing for what might happen and no readiness for consequences likely to happen).

UN-TAMEABLE stubbornness is characterized by a lack self-discipline and self-control.

The World of Stubbornness: When I began my orthopaedic surgical practice I wrongly assumed that anyone not following my orders was stubborn. But this belief changed with experience and with being more complete in gathering more information, and with putting myself in their position to see things from their point of view.

Reasonable patients *"delay getting started" in* or *"delay completion" of treatment* for a variety of sound reasons. Some wait for home chaos or physical pains to settle so as to gain a better view of a proposed treatment plan before deciding what to do. Others fail to medically comply because of treatment problems (e.g. bad side effects), the expense of treatment, difficulties in transportation, or from conflicting beliefs (as when Jehovah's Witness patients refuse blood transfusions).

Sometimes their decisions are proper and sometimes they are not. Yet, their intentions are good. The same applies to me. The point is that <u>the more I understood the less I was willing to blame, criticize, or label people</u>.

The ***Spinning Top Concept***: As a boy I had a great deal of fun spinning a top by repeatedly pushing down a lever attached to a wheel. The faster I pushed, the faster the top would spin. Then I would hit the lever with a side blow in order to see how far over on the side the spinning top would go before actually falling or toppling over. Invariably, if it was spinning in any position between upright and "topple over" it would eventually return to its original upright position.

Something similar has occurred in the Black youth I have mentored over the years. For example, for 15 years I worked hard on getting one boy to stop saying "Axed" when he meant "ask". When he would forget and say: "I axed him...." I would even symbolically demonstrate "chopping him up" with my hands. Yet, he still occasionally says it.

This is a reflection of socialization that is reinforced by "*the subcultural atmosphere*" in which the boy lives. There is some sort of mysterious force present in the atmosphere which causes certain things to happen to individuals or to groups. In sports, when things are going unbelievable well in the last half of the game whereas most members of that same team were terrible in the first half, it is said that "momentum" is on their side.

I am able to think better when at my desk than when in any other "atmosphere." The Yogi believe this atmosphere is the result of a "**Thought Cloud**" (Ramacharaka, Fourteen Lessons p77). Could a "Thought Cloud" be the explanation of "momentum"? Or, explain why the entire team played lousy? Does this also apply to two people who meet and immediately recognize they have "chemistry" or are "soul mates" which accounts for their relationship harmony? At least something is happening which is beyond human awareness.

Together, ones socialization and living in the atmosphere of the people populating that atmosphere represent a great counter-acting force to trying to change their belief system and behaviors designed to get Black youth back on the right road. I have seen inner city kids absorb out of "the atmosphere" certain characteristics of right or wrong that I am practically sure they were never taught or exposed to in their Black community.

Furthermore, this "atmosphere" seems to have an enchanting magical influence that amounts to a kind of spell or arrest of will power in those under its magnetic attraction. Instead of stubbornness, this overwhelming tendency to maintain or return to the status quo is a Spinning Top look-alike of stubbornness. The only thing I tried that worked a little was to get these individuals out of their atmosphere and have their peers work to help each other improve. But that is hard to do.

Management of Stubbornness

Just as there are different forms of stubbornness, there are different approaches to shedding them. The first shedding process is one of Rational Thinking. But let us start with some background.

If you were to draw two mountain tops on one sheet of paper, the one on the left could be labeled the mountain of "Being" and the other the mountain of "Doing". In African Tradition "**Being**" centers on fellowship and having good relations with and behaviors toward fellow humans. During African American slavery "Being" was the result of forced "herding" of the slaves in the African barracoons (slave holding areas), on board ship, at auction blocks, and on plantations.

Following slavery, forced "Being" of the ex-slaves occurred in the "Black Belts" of the South and later the North because there were no alternatives. This lasted in full force up to World War II and then those Black Americans who became successful in "**Doing**" (i.e. engaging in activities that brought thriving to them) began peeling off from the Black ghettos.

Meanwhile, during slavery there were several forms of Slave Resistances (Bailey, Freeing Enslaved Minds of Black Americans p112 to 123) of an anti-work nature which were designed by the slaves—Passive-Aggressive acts like procrastination, selective forgetting, inattention, failing to show "know-how", and carelessness "on purpose". After all, the slaves had no incentive to work except to avoid punishment. Work would not give them a better tomorrow or even a better today. Work would only increase the riches of the captors they hated.

Because this scenario of "caging work" became a way of life and was culturally transmitted into today's America, stubbornness ways of "Being" are considered acceptable—except for those which are obviously disrespectful— and, in fact, "normal" in most Black communities. This is comparable to Europeans accepting crime, wars, and evilness as normal (for everyone but them).

Nevertheless, when an ambitious Black youth reared in one of these struggling Black communities is "called" to enter the world of "Doing" in order to reach his/her potential then big problems arise. It is sort of like leaving the world of "Manners" (i.e. caring about the feelings of others—an African Tradition "We" society trait) and entering the world of Etiquette (i.e. dealing with social codes regardless of right or wrong—an "I" or individualism American society way of living).

The point is that the ways of doing things in the "Being" type of Black community will absolutely not work in the American marketplace of "Doing"—and it has nothing to do with "good" or "bad." Rather, it is a mis-match of the prevailing system of values between White and Black Americans.

Examples: Non-aggression is a feature of the Black community despite the contrary comments of Europeans. Yet, non-aggression does not work as well as non-hostile aggression in the American marketplace. This means it is necessary for every Black youth to do a great deal of learning the strange "table manners"—the code of etiquettes—and the unwritten rules of the marketplace.

Of equal importance is to do a great deal of appropriate reading as part of a great deal of planning and preparation and then get up early to go to the proper place where you do what it takes to "elbow your way" up to the head of the line.

Upon entering the USA medical training arena it was essential for me to break my tremendous stubbornness. One obvious reason is that it was not in my best interest to continue to do so. Another was the dumbness in denying myself something or in assuming a bad attitude simply to prove a point. Besides, trying to prove a point did not make any difference to the people it was aimed at and certainly I was no better off.

In fact, stubbornness wasted much of my valuable time—and more importantly my energy—time and energy much better used to do whatever was necessary to survive and thrive in any number of arenas. Instead, I took responsibility for whatever problems I faced and then handled each with eagerness. These aspects were behind **Thinking Ones Way Out of Stubbornness**.

Stubbornness Directional Shifts

The process starts by deciding on a proper definition. Although stubbornness is generally defined in dictionaries as an unreasonable, illogical, or irrational DETERMINATION NOT TO CHANGE, I prefer to substitute immature for unreasonable, illogical, or irrational because only the immature consistently creates, enhances, or maintains disharmony. "Immature" embraces the following terms:

Unreasonable implies a bias or intent to go wrong.

Foolish is that which is contrary to practical good Common Sense.

Silly means petty and contemptible in its folly

Irrational is a term with contrasting meanings. On the one hand, there is a *mature* type which consists of facts outside the realm of reason—e.g. the greatest density of water is found at 4.0 centigrade. Sensation and intuition are irrational because they "just are—and that's the way it is!"

On the other hand, *immature* irrationality suggests an uncontrollable lack of understanding: "it is irrational to expect people with different systems of values to reach the same end point. Immature irrationality consists of emotionally flawed beliefs which control behavior—beliefs which can not be justified—beliefs which are contrary to the evidence—beliefs which work to ones disadvantage in the long run. Delusions are examples of that which is outside the realm of reason and not established by reason.

Illogical is also a term with contrasting meanings. On the one hand, the *mature* type is that which violates the rules of man-made patterns of Logical thinking in such a manner as to not make sense or so as to not conform to concepts of fair-play. Yet, this does not necessarily make it wrong if the approach used consistently eventuates in good Common Sense. In this context, by being non-reproducible thought it is simply different than that of logic. On the other hand, the *immature* type gives flawed thinking; is not fair-minded; and does not make sense using any system of assessment.

The inconsistency and instability of emotions generate mental chaos, contradictory beliefs, and self-defeating behaviors. Thus, the combative emotions contained in the "I'll show you" syndrome are ineffective decision- makers in matters of serious business. Rational thinking development inside the frame of good character will automatically convert a "false" integrity to a "true" or "real" one (Bailey, Manhood, p. 176).

The objective of management is to shift the wrong direction of Immature Stubbornness to its opposite and proper direction called Persistence. The reason is that persistence generates harmony in the long run. The process involves Rational Thinking Maturity whereby mature thoughts replace the immature ones. One method has been discussed above—the method of "Thinking Ones Way Out of Stubbornness**."** A technique is to challenge the stubborn to change: "I'll bet you can't do the opposite of what you have been doing!"

Methods and techniques are best worked out according to the situation at hand. This requires understanding the parts. For example, stubbornness is bathed by the emotion of anger; has a power struggle at its core; carries the silent declaration of: "I'll show you"; and features the negative side of integrity.

When one has Good Character INTEGRITY one has the sense of being a complete and healthy person and that gives a sense of well-being. Whereas positive or constructive integrity is maintaining the correct nature of something in a complete and uninjured state, stubbornness is doing the same but in an incorrect direction. A "negative integrity" is a façade for a "whole well person" in that one's irrational beliefs lead to foolish behaviors.

The attitude of stubbornness is childish: —"My willpower is stronger than yours"— and the principle of the behavior of stubbornness is to "do the opposite of whatever you want me to do." The "I'll show you" reaction has been extensively discussed in my book on Self-Esteem (p. 114).

One form of Childish Stubbornness is the intent to "get back at" someone for some deep-felt psychological hurt—a "tit-for-tat". Another form, especially seen in Childish Aduts is about a competition over personal power: "I'll show you whose boss."

By understanding that the "glue" which holds together the anger, the power struggle, the negative integrity, the competitive attitude, and the oppositional behavior is **"Un-Noble" Loyalty** (Bailey, Self-Esteem), one has an approach to correcting Childish Stubbornness. This combination of components form a vicious circle and the method is to break the circle by correcting any one of its parts by any of the means mentioned in this book which might work for the individual involved.

VULNERABLE MINDSETS

Some people's emotional states are like a crisp potato chip in that the slightest touch causes them to crumble. These are people "who live lives of quiet desperation" (Thoreau). For some this is the nature of their selfhood make-up. For some, they do not know how to think so as to be able to solve their problems in life—and the answer is to learn how to think rationally. Some are full of fears and anxieties and worries. But what does it mean to be vulnerable?

The Story of Vulnerability: The European Valkyries were immortal women and the Norse (ancient Scandinavia) counterparts of the funerary vulture-priestesses of Egypt. Apparantly having been Amazonian priestesses who ruled the gates of death, they brought the souls of the heroes killed in battle to Valhalla (the Hall of the Slain). Then they feasted and afterwards, for amusement, fought one another with savage fervor. Yet, their wounds were immediately healed. From the act of bloody wounding — the result of being struck or attacked and defeated — came the word VULNERABLE.

This sense was carried over to ones experiences of emotional pain. "Big Bang" episodes or cumulative small episodes of emotional pain make one vulnerable—a vulnerability from having been "struck" in ones psyche to the point of causing a bloody wound in his/her self-concept. Of course, this vulnerability means the wounded person is more susceptible to lesser external injuries.

This idea was illustrated in Homer's (10th century B.C. Greek poet) Iliad. The mythological tale explains that Achilles' body was invulnerable because his mother dipped him in the holy river Styx when he was an infant. However, the spot on his heel, where her fingers held him, was not exposed to the magical waters. It was the vulnerability of this heel which cost him his life.

In the 1300s AD the expression: *"people who live in glass houses should not throw stones"* arose because glass houses are vulnerable to people seeking revenge. Such a desire for revenge was from those who criticized other and yet were open to criticism themselves. The expression: "the pot calling the kettle black" carried the same idea.

The World of Vulnerability: Medically we know that all wounds *(abrasions, incisions, punctures, lacerations, burns*) are potentially dangerous because of the possibility of infection that may lead to blood poisoning. In large wounds there is also the danger of shock, even death, through excessive loss of blood. The thickness of the healing scar depends upon the size of the gap needing to be filled. Infection results in the larger scars.

The same principles apply emotionally. But, in addition, cracks occurring in the eggshell-like armour of one's self-concept come from repetitive or ongoing stresses and strains. Those cracks cause emotional and sometimes physical pain. Just as there are many types of wounds, there are corresponding mild, slight, moderate, and extreme degrees of emotional pain. Just as different types of tissue heal at different rates (e.g. injured nerves do not heal quickly), the nature of emotional pains will result in various degrees of scar healing at various speeds.

Although, with physical wounds, little children tend to heal faster than the aged, the reverse is true regarding emotional pain. The infantile mind, equating words with things, regards unkind words as unkind acts. Even a certain tone of voice that utters a harmless set of words has the power of injury. The effects of the injury, often lasting "*forever,*" spread into all areas of the child's life instead of being compartmentalized as they might be in an adult (see discussion on Trigger Flaws in Chapter I).

The customs of a culture carry much weight in the degree, direction, and effects of emotional pain. For example, so called "*gentlemen*" throughout the ages would dignify resented insults into "*codes of honor.*" By "*honor*" they meant extreme readiness to duel — to pull out swords and pistols at even a hint of being insulted. Also throughout the ages, hurt feelings have greatly increased the killing rate.

Managing Vulnerability: So what can be done? As mentioned above, in each of us there are natural emotions and natural pains that are essential for self-protection and self-expression. Also in each of us there are acquired emotions stemming from real, distorted, and unreal (fantasy) interpretations. <u>The distortions and the fantasies within our emotions and within our pains are what extend the boundaries of realistic emotional pain</u> and, in fact, may eliminate the boundaries so that there is no limit to the emotional pain experienced.

To believe in these distortions and fantasies is a *delusion* (believing what is not real and not believing what is real). Thus, the essential first aspect in handling emotional pain is to shed the involved distortions and fantasies. Both are discussed elsewhere.

Certain people, particularly those who are full of worry and anxiety, can be managed by desensitization or by reducing sensitivity. This is discussed in prior Chapter.

MOVING ON WITH YOUR LIFE

If your life is full of needless conflicts and problems and trials and tribulations then that is either okay with you or it is not. If it is not, you will either do something about it or you will not. If you will not then you must like it (and that indicates you are a masochist) or are too lazy (and thus undisciplined) or too much of a coward to face your fears and thereby change for the better. If you have inner strength and desire to have inner peace, then you will do the hard things that will unlock or uncage you from where you are so that you can proceed toward your destination in life. There are three parts—letting go; forgiving; and the very hardest thing to do, Loving your enemies.

LETTING GO

There is a world of difference between making things happen and letting them happen. Both have their place. However, it you are "stuck" by choosing to be attached to the wrong people or to the wrong things, make your freedom happen by letting them go. To do so requires paying a high price which I call "Buying Your Peace."

To "*buy my peace*" has been and remains a frequent occurrence. I face all sorts of people who create problems for me by lying, cheating, stealing, looking for a verbal or legal fight, trying to show their superiority and power, and the like. One option, which I choose not to take, is to get myself locked up with them in some mental cage. For me, it is worth doing what it takes to let them have their way (within reasonable limits) so that they will go away.

My approach to any other type of problem is to be refreshed (perhaps from sleep) and alert and quiet. Sometimes this mental state of readiness comes from gathering all the important information I can find the night before and putting that information in its best order. Upon going to bed, I give Jann—my spiritual genie— specific instructions on what questions to answer, and then go to sleep. Immediately upon awakening, I am either flooded with meaningful, if not insightful, ideas or see the answer flashing in my mind.

FORGIVENESS

There are five forms of forgiveness (Bailey, Special Somebody, p142-151).

First is an **insincere forgiveness**.

Second is **conditional forgiveness,** an incomplete (a "yeah, but . . .) one whereby it is dependent upon something else.

Third is **conditional forgiveness for the offender but unconditional for**

yourself — meaning you release yourself from the offender for the sole purpose of moving on toward your life's destination.

Fourth is **unconditional forgiveness** for the offender but conditional for yourself — "I will forgive myself only if I do X, Y, Z."

Fifth **unconditional forgiveness for yourself and for the offender** is done at a level above a thought process. This is an automatic display of love whereby you absorb the evil done by the offender and thereby "wipe the slate clean." The result is the opening of the door to personal benefits of such high quality as to be beyond your ability to imagine. Since these five have been extensively discuss in my book (Special Somebody), only some addition comments will be made here.

A Story of Forgiveness: For Ancient Africans, forgiveness, one aspect of Ma'at's non-violence, was called for when someone did an evil deed. They ascribed Evil and suffering to disruptive spirits (called Seban by Egyptians) and unrighteous living. In addition, the character Set in Ancient Egyptian religion, a symbol of the lower self, represented the energy of uncontrolled egoism and brute force.

The Yoruban trickster messenger god, Exu, was said to cause strife by distorting messages between the human realm (prayers) and the Spirit realm — due to a dislike of an orderly world. The purpose of myths about Exu was to help the people develop discernment—either for making choices between the righteousness and the unrighteousness (the source of the experience of evil and suffering) or for outcomes leading to harmony and peace as opposed to adversity and disturbance.

Although never considered as a devil by Africans, outsiders (e.g. European missionaries) declared Exu, Set, and their equivalents to be devils. Whereas African tradition related adversity to passions and a movement away from virtue, Western religion attributed the devil to getting people off virtuous tracks. Thus, African concepts retain human responsibility for hate and evilness while Westerners assign blame to an outside force (Ashby, African Origins, p. 196).

A HUMAN'S RESPONSIBILTY, said Africans, is to overcome inner ignorance of one's higher spiritual reality and thereby shed egoism, anger, hatred, greed, lust, envy, jealousy, and frustration. SIN was understood as a separation between oneself and God. To reverse sin required using Ma'at principles to strive toward bringing into existence a sense of Divine Presence within oneself. Not to know and to practice this is ignorance. <u>Rising above ignorance (i.e. evil, egoism) has always been and remains the true goal of African religion</u>.

Along the path toward mysticism, humans always have a choice to follow or not to follow hate (i.e. destructive thoughts and actions) and evil (destructive deeds). By understanding all God's creations to be part of oneself, the practice of relating to others was based upon love, compassion, magnanimity, and forgiveness — much like when you immediately forgive your teeth when they bite your tongue (Ashby).

Ma'at principles dictate forgiveness of those who, out of ignorance, instantly chose hatred and evilness. Such forgiveness is to be done eagerly, reflexly, and wholeheartedly — even before offenders acknowledge their guilt and responsibility by apologizing to the victim. That this practice of renouncing personal moral anger persists as a survival in the Afrocentric diaspora is seen by Mandela in Africa and by certain Black Americans — both of whom readily forgave their jailers for false imprisonment (Wiredu, African Philosophy, p. 212).

Meanwhile, in the Western world the word "*forgive*" came from the Indo-European root meaning "*to give or to receive*," as in giving forgiveness and receiving the apology of forgiveness from others.

Its early use in the Old Testament was associated with pardoning an offense or with the remittance of a debt, as stated by Jesus (Matt. 6:12) in the Lord's Prayer. One African form of unconditional forgiveness finding its way into the Bible was the restoration of fellowship whenever sin caused an estrangement (i.e. Gen. 50:17; Ex 32:32). It was seen as an obligation in the relationship between people (Eph. 4:32).

Incidentally, the fact that this belief of unconditional forgiveness persisted among many slaves brought to the Americas from Africa and among many ex-slaves and among many of today's Black Americans has been largely responsible for Europeans being able to freely inflict such pain and suffering on them. This would suggest that there is an additional and better way to look at unconditional forgiveness that ought to be explored by religious leaders.

Forgiveness was frequently voiced by Christian missionaries during the Dark Ages. In the 16th century, its meaning was extended to include "*give and take.*" Later, it came to be associated with *Indentured Servants* who came to the American colonies after having exchanged some years of work for their passage, their upkeep, and their freedom.

To start the process, the servant would make a duplicate of his/her master's agreement. To prevent trickery, the two copies were dented or were simply written on one sheet and torn in half. At the proper time, the torn pieces were matched to seal the concept of forgiveness. Finally, the servant was free — i.e. given away to himself.

The World of Forgiveness: Emotions are powerful enough to influence your mental, physical, and spiritual health. The cornerstone to creating, enhancing, and maintaining emotional health as well as reversing a diseased emotional mindset is to forgive others, forgive yourself, and to accept the offer of forgiveness from others.

Unconditional Forgiveness is itself a triumph over evil and is brought about by the power of self-love. The injured party, by absorbing the evil done to him/her, releasing the offender, and converting the bitter energy directed toward the offender to produce good works is displaying the greatest amount of personal power and strength a human being can exhibit.

Management of Forgiveness: Your value judgment is best wiped out since to hold on to that judgment is to keep you in a vicious cycle. Stop judging and you are free to be open to other points of view. But do not mistake openness to being gullible. Something ought to be better than you already possess before considering accepting it into your belief system.

The application of compassion to forgiveness is the way to the cultivation of forgiveness as well as the cultivation of self-love — both being essential for truly declaring yourself as a "*good person with good character.*"

SELF-FORGIVENESS

The popular maxim: "*Forgive and Forget*" is misunderstood by most people. Its true meaning is: "*forgive and don't seek revenge*" — i.e. let go of both the resentment for a wrong and the destructive urge to return the harm. This applies to others as well as to oneself.

Not only is it impossible to completely forget a moderate or severe degree of offense leading to wounded feelings, but it is not wise to do so. Remember the lessons—e.g. the flaws leading up to what caused the hurt and the conclusion as to what to do about avoiding them in future situations. Meanwhile, forget the details associated with the hurt.

Of equal importance is to avoid SELF-CONDEMNATION. Besides being the opposite of self-forgiveness, it prevents self-forgiveness from happening. Self-Condemnation, one of the worse mindsets an individual can have, pertains to thoughts and emotions designed to either attack who one is as a person (i.e. of an inferiority complex nature) or attack what one has done (i.e. of a low self-esteem nature). Both can cause depression, apathy, or a superiority complex. An ultimate result may be slow suicide (e.g. drug abuse) or a "*big bang*" suicide.

Otherwise, bad label self-attacks become a self-fulfilling prophecy whereby one "*lives down*" to the label of an enduring inferiority complex or low self-esteem. The resultant self-talk is "*Bad*" (i.e. self-destructive), as if a tape recorder is playing these destructive messages inside one's head. It does not take long before these messages about "*who I am as a person — what I do — what I have — what I cannot do — and how I appear*" — become exaggerated and distorted. To this mix is added anger, fear, and guilt. So what can be done?

<u>Step I</u>— realize that during self-attacks concerning regrets, you either did your

best at the time or you did not. If you did your best then given the same mindset, the same circumstances, and the same choices, you would still do now what you did then. Hence, there is no just cause for self-condemnation. Disregard the fact of you having more knowledge and experiences today that would cause you to handle things differently. Here, self-forgiveness is not needed, regardless of how others might judge you.

Step II: Suppose you deliberately did things out of meanness or because of laziness in planning, preparation, or practice. Then there are two areas to address — the damage done and the self-forgiveness. For the damage done, the approach is to do whatever you can — no matter how inconvenient — to make things as close as possible to "*right*" (i.e. by restoring things). After retributions, do something "*extra*" to make up for the victim's inconveniences, losses, pain, and suffering. This is sort of like pay the penalty with interest.

Step III is self-forgiveness. One approach is to get professional help. A second is to engage in the spiritual form of meditation. Proper meditation causes one to lose attachments to the material world, including undesirable traits such as selfishness, hatred, fear, anger, and guilt (Harper's Encyc. Of Mystical and Paranormal Experience, p. 357).

A third approach is to combine Rational Thinking with some creative problem-solving. The rational part starts by analyzing why you caused harm — and a "*I don't know*" is unacceptable. This begins the restoration of self-harmony and self-trust. Possible other areas to investigate include ignorance, impulsiveness, having a lapse of morals, and being influenced or led by others. The idea is to find the weakness or flaw in what led you to cause harm, determine why, and make corrections.

The following is an example of a creative solution. Suppose you separate your selfhood into two people but who remain partnered. One partner—the victim—has deeply wounded feelings. The other partner—the preditor—has inflicted the wounded feelings on the rest of your selfhood.

The inflicter preditor feels sorry for the pain and suffering caused to its victim partner and so indicates this, but from a distance. This distance indicates that although the inflicter and the victim are partners, there are still gaps between them. These gaps prevent the deed and the consequences of the deed from merging—from being "*blotted out*," "*cleansed*," and "*let go*." As a result, at an emotional (i.e. psychical feeling) level both the victim and the preditor periodically feel bad. The gaps ensure there can be no self-forgiveness.

By contrast, self-forgiveness at a spiritual feeling level is the exercise of compassion. In other words, the inflicter partner has such remorse (i.e. moral anguish and bitter regret) that its spiritual nature causes it to become one with the pain and suffering of its victim partner.

By manifestating compassion, the inflicter is compelled to immediately do something to cure, relieve, or release the victim's pain and suffering. The victim permits the cleaning and then lets go of the pain in order to reestablish trust with the inflicter. Now self-forgiveness is complete.

SELF-LOVE

Ancient Africans considered God to be a Big Mind or Love—both concepts being above the ability of the human mind to conceive. This was an attempt to reduce the Infinite, the Unknowable, and the All into the human experience. Yet, there was nothing to which a "Big Mind" or Love could be compared and thus to even refer to this Immaterial aspect it was reduced to the Intangible and termed "the Ether" (or "Ch'I" by the Chinese). All children and many adults have had contact with the effects of this Intangible Love by bathing in Absolute Beauty, Perfection, Health, Goodness, Truth, and Wonderfulness and could therefore relate more intimately.

Peoples' experience of the Ether they are bathing involves them being completely surrounded by it as well as it flowing into and inside and out of them. Although "the Ether" is everywhere in the Cosmos, the portion which completely surrounds them as well as flows into and inside and out of them is the condition of Self-Love. Yet, it is the same condition experienced by all of God's creatures and creations.

In other words, there is no distinction between the experience of Self-Love and Love for other creatures and creations because all God's creatures and creations stand inside the same realm of love; because all of God's creatures and creations are spiritually related; and because the same Ether (or Love) that flows into, inside, and out of me is the same as that which flows into, inside, and out of you and you and you. This is like the air we breathe in and out being the same air all of God's creatures breathe in and out.

Ancient Africans believed that since humans share the same Spirit and Love—and these are the best things in life— then humans need to provide Love to each other and to themselves so as to qualify to enter the Heaven Afterlife.

Examples of such **displays of Humanity** are Truth, Balance (or Temperance), Order, Harmony, Peace and Tranquility, Fellowship, Justice, Righteousness, and Straightness. When humans try to reproduce these aspects of the effects of Love in fellow humans and in showing respect to animals, and nature, the Ancient African term **Ma'at** applies. This has nothing to do with Western concepts of love, which consists of degrees of love. Ancient African Love has no degrees because it is either present or it is not—like flipping a light switch on and off, as determined by the free will choice of the individual.

Displays of Ma'at are to be given to myself as I try to make them happen for you—

a "Win-Win" situation. For example, Love will not allow me to harm you and Self-Love will not allow me to hurt myself. Love means I will let you be free and Self-Love means I will stay mentally free. Love means I will show you compassion for your pain and suffering and Self-Love means I will show myself compassion for things I am not proud of and that I truly regret and am in the process of changing.

Self-Love means that since I can not tell where my Love for me ends and where my Love for you begins, then I must take care of you and what belongs to you as well as I would take care of me and what belongs to me. Love of others will cause you to do for yourself what you do for them. For example, you will treat yourself as nicely as you treat your baby.

SPIRITUAL PAIN

Problems occur in you if you choose to stop the flow of Love coming into you or stop it inside of you or stop it from flowing out of you. Problems also occur when you intensely desire to have your Love flow into another but that other will not receive it. Such an instance occurs when I want something good for someone more than that someone wants for him/herself. My Dad did loving things for the faceless people but those things were not of interest to them. This blocked the flow of his Love.

Whatever the cause, Spiritual Pain causes the worse selfhood misery known to man. That misery makes one hypersensitive, apprehensive, and self-absorbed.

Anytime the flow of Love is stopped coming into you, inside of you, or going out of you, the effect is that of Spiritual Pain. It happens when one is engaged in Hate. This is a pain that totally shifts your focus from doing beneficial things in the outside world over to trying to get some degree of relief. Those attempts are either of a superficial and non-constructive nature (e.g. excessive "partying") or they are "Sick Pleasures" (e.g. sadistic behaviors). These things, at best, give a momentary lessening of the Spiritual Pain. Nothing will bring permanent relief except the re-establishment of the flow of Love. This is sort of like what acupuncturists do to restore good health to those who have a blockage of their Chi.

A different type of Spiritual pain occurs when others will not accept your Love. It is like the pain one feels when one is inside a compassionate experience. This happens when children reject the Love of a parent. Some little relief can come from helping neighborhood needy children (e.g. mentoring, being involved in Boy Scouts or Girl Scouts) as a substitute for not being able to connect with the one you love.

A Case Example: Titan was taught as a child that he was not as good as People X. Although he had to cater to People X, he felt that was not fair to such an extent that he rebelled against any member of People X. That combination of the unfairness of having to show love to People X more than to himself—a Love Imbalance—and resenting and rebelling against it silently meant that his thoughts and emotions generated a new inner world that was filled with delusions. That inner world was contributed to by those who socialized him. Thoughts and emotions inside that world of delusions included: "I'm not good enough" and "I'll show you."

Once in a new society that was characterized by a fair system of values, Titan still maintained the old society generated mindset. So, in a relationship with a new society mate, Titan chose to create a situation which would allow him to re-enact his bad thoughts and emotions. He kept a score-card on how much he did for Landa. His score was greatly exaggerated in his favor regarding what was done in quantity and frequency for her and also in making comparisons with what Landa did for him. The essence was that Titan felt he did much more for Landa than she did for him.

To begin to recover from these delusions and get back to reality, Titan brought his distorted thoughts and emotions under control. One way was realizing that even though Landa did not do the same things for him as he did for her, what she did was equally as important—the Complementary Equal Concept. A second way was rising above the competitive "score-card" mentality and letting his Love for Landa make him eager to do things to please her and make her life easier.

Afterall, Love is not about 50-50 give and take but rather it is 100-100 give and take. Even if he did 100% of the work, she is more important as a person and to him than what she did not do. At some point she will do 100% of the work. In the long run all will be equal.

What Landa did was to act like water—showing power by not resisting and by giving way to flow in the goodness direction of her choosing. By not reacting to Titan's rebelling actions against her caused Titan's bad reactions to atrophy (waste away) simply because they were not staying strong by means of resistance. As a result of losing strength from the peace Landa provided, Titan's Real Self slowly began to show through his manufactured False Self—a Real Self which is about Love for self and for others. Hence, after a few years it dawned upon Titan that Landa is not a member of People X. That freed him to start voluntarily doing loving things for Landa.

Yet, the old society practices which generated Titan's bad thoughts and emotions were like a volcano. Early in the relationship it erupted several times a month. Despite less frequent eruptions as Titan improved in Self-Love, that volcano continued to erupt about twice a year once Titan had returned to reality. Landa knew that the eruption had nothing to do with her, even thought Titan directed it at her. Again, Landa did not react with meanness against the eruption. Of course, Titan was not aware of what he was doing because he was too self-absorbed and therefore could not stand back and observe himself.

Nevertheless, Titan did do things to help himself handle his bad thoughts and emotions and self-talk by taking workshops. Meanwhile, Landa kept giving him the big picture of what Self-Love is; what is Love; and where and how Love can be blocked. She showed him by her example that she loved him beyond his flaws. Whereas in Titan's old society the focus had been to try to make Titan better by people finding flaws in him in order for him to correct them, Landa did the opposite. She contributed to his self-esteem by daily complementing him on the good things he did. She helped him search for things that would give him a sense of accomplishment and taught him how to find good things in him to which he can give self-praise and self-love.

LOVE YOUR ENEMIES

"Ye have heard that it hath been said, Thou shalt love thy neighbor, and hate thine enemy. But I say unto you, , bless them that curse you, do good to them that hate you, and pray for them which despitefully use you, and persecute you" (Matthew 5:43-44).

To get to this elevated state of spiritual evolution is the result of a prolonged process of spiritual cultivation. Amen (Maat, p78) says "It is criminally irresponsibe to tell the spiritually, and intellectually, and morally immature person to love his enemies. This is a principle that requires 10 others to be awakened in the spirit of the person in order to safely and effectively put it into play."

The point is to keep in mind that all real creatures and creations are spiritual products of one Love. Yet, the form each real creature and creation takes is different. Inside that form is individual uniqueness and the display of certain aspects of that individuality may be destructive to the person, to other people, and to nature. Ancient Africans did not believe that one ought to love the destruction from any source. Rather, it is the spiritual Love aspect that one esteems in another. To be able to do this constitutes a "Loving person" with a "heart" filled with Love for all. Amen (Maat, p78) says that "since oneness encompasses those who will try to act against you, so must your all encompassing love."

CONCLUSIONS

Emotions many be inborn/acquired, acute/chronic, or positive, negative, or bad. "Negative" and "Bad" emotions are not necessarily the same. Whereas "negative" is the complement of positive (as occurs in electricity), "bad" emotions are typically self-defeating and are best shed. Three aspects of Emotions have been discussed—in dealing with oneself, in helping others, and in interacting with others. For each of these the focus is on the differentiation and understanding of numerous emotions for the purpose of getting started on a management program.

The anchor around which proper emotional management spins is a sound philosophy of life and strongly recommended here is the philosophy of Ancient Africans. It is built on God/Love as their Standard; Ma'at (the virtues springing out of Love) as their Cherished Values; and Nonaggression (the natural behaviors relating to having good relationships with and good behavior toward Human beings and Nature) as their Power Approach.

The next step is to gain experience in differentiating, in understanding, and in properly managing the numerous emotions. The only way this can be done is to interact with people. In the process, one customizes ones personality to fit in with the outside world. This occurs by paying close attention to the details deriving from the interaction of ones character as well as the proper use of the monitored feedback from one's interpreted experiences with other people.

Once inside this process, the single most important first questions for *self-improvement* are: "What part did I play and am I playing in contributing to problems related to my emotions? Honestly answering these questions and taking appropriate corrective measures puts one on the journey to self-improvement.

But note, that as you improve, people may not react well to the "new and improved you." The reason is that people do not like change and with you changing they will no longer "know" you. Some may even say and do bad things that cause hurt feelings. What bad things they do to you is normal and your hurt feelings are normal. Both problems will eventually fade away.

With respect to the *emotional problems of others*, the single most important first step into a management program is to hear everything they have to say about their problem. Once they get that boiling tension out of their system, many will be able to figure out solutions without any advice. Otherwise, they may need to be referred to a mental health specialist.

In *people's emotional interactions*, the single most important first step is to determine the primary cause of the emotional reactions of the people involved. This has two parts—spotlighting their trigger emotion (the "top dog" cause) and then determining the source giving rise to that trigger emotion.

For example, let us suppose the trigger emotion of Black Americans is Anger and its source is that of the dominant society disrespecting their dignity. Let us also suppose that the trigger emotion of Euro-Americans is Fear and its source stems from a philosophy of life based upon things of Value (material treasures) which leads to means of acquisition that disregard the rights of other people. Fear comes from a sense of scarcity; an intense concern about losses, lacks, or obstructions; and from the possibility of retaliation from victims.

If personally involved in a difficult situation with others, the point is to understand the principles of a workable approach. Once you determine the trigger emotion and its source, you can consider doing one of the following:

Adaptation (make changes);

Accommodate (give in);

Compromise (accept less);

Relocate (go to a new setting);

Adjustments (rearranging);

Replacement (restoring or returning);

Substitution (using something different);

Passive acceptance ("make do");

Aggression (go after something overt);

Passive-Aggression (go after in a masked way);

Self-Assertive (insist on what is proper).

Whether for good or bad, there is no limit to the power one can have from mastering ones own emotions as well as managing the emotions of others.

REFERENCES

Amen RUN. MAAT, Brooklyn: Khamit Media Trans Visions, Inc. 2003

Amen RUN. *Metu Neter, -vol. 1.* Bronx, NY: Khamit Corp, 1990:

Amen RUN. *Metu Neter* vol. 2, Brooklyn: Khamit Media Trans Visions, Inc., 1994.

Anderson E. *The Code of the Streets,* In: Ault A. Race and Ethnicity, St. Paul: Coursewise Publishing, Inc., 2000: 203.

Ani, M: *Yurugu.* Trenton, NJ: Africa World Press, Inc., 1994.

Asante MK. *The Egyptian Philosophers.* Chicago: African American Images, 2000.

Ashby MA. *The African Origins of Civilization, Religion, Yoga, Mystical Spirituality and Ethics Philosophy.* Miami: Cruzian Mystic Books, 2002.

Ashby MA. *Egyptian Yoga,* Miami: Cruzian Mystic Books, 1995.

Ashby MA. The Egyptian Book of the Dead. Miami: Cruzian Mystic Books, 2006.

Bailey II JA. Echoes of Ancient African Values, Bloomington, Indiana: Authorhouse, 2005.

Bailey II JA. Good Character, Canada: Trafford, 2004 (1-888-232-4444).

Bailey II JA. The Handbook for Worker's Compensation Doctors. California: I.C.E. Publishers, 1994.

Bailey II, JA. Afrocentric English and Critical Thinking, Livermore, California: Wing Span Press, 2006.

Bailey II, JA. American Crime From A Black American Perspective, Livermore, CA: Wing Span Press, 2006.

Bailey II, JA. Anger In Black Americans. Livermore, California: Wing Span Press, 2006.

Bailey II, JA. Becoming a Champion Somebody, Livermore, CA: Wing Span Press, 2006. (Wingspanpress.com)

Bailey II, JA. Black Voice News, Riverside, California: (blackvoicenews.com).

Bailey II, JA. Common Sense Inside African Tradition, Livermore, California: Wing Span Press, 2006. (Wingspanpress.com)

Bailey II, JA. Creativity, Invention & Discovery, Livermore, California: Wingspanpress.com, 2007. (Wingspanpress.com)

Bailey II, JA. Deceptive Orthopaedic Patients. Unpublished, 1995.

Bailey II, JA. Disproportionate Short Stature — Diagnosis and Management, Philadelphia: W.B. Sanders Co., 1973.

Bailey II, JA. I Am A Special Somebody, California: wingspanpress.com, 2005.

Bailey II, JA. Manhood in Black Americans; Livermore, CA: Wing Span Press, 2006. (Wingspanpress.com)

Bailey II, JA. Preparing to Prepare, Teacher's Guide, Lincoln, NE: iUniverse (www.iuniverse.com; 1-800-288-4677), 2005.

Bailey II, JA. Rising Above Poverty. Livermore, CA: Wing Span Press, 2007

Bailey II, JA. Selfhood Mastery. Livermore, CA: Wing Span Press, 2007

Bailey II, JA. Self-Esteem in Black Americans, Livermore, CA: Wing Span Press, 2005. (Wingspanpress.com)

Bailey II, JA. The Foundation Of Self-Esteem. J. Natl. Med. Assoc. 2003; 95: 388-393.

Bailey II, JA. A Classification of Black-American Self-Esteem; J. Natl. Med. Assoc. 2004; 96: 23-28.

Bailey II, JA. Freeing Enslaved Minds in Black Americans, Livermore, California: Wing Span Press, 2006. (Wingspanpress.com)

Bailey II, JA. Self-Esteem Masqueraders in Struggling Black Americans; Accepted for publication in the Journal of Black Studies in the Fall of 2005.

Bailey II, JA. Self-Image, Self Concept, and Self-Identity Revisited. J. Natl. Med. Assoc. 2003; 95: 383-386.

Bailey II, JA. The Concise Dictionary of Medical-Legal Terms; London: The Parthenon Publishing Group, 1998, 60, Preface.

Brewer's Dictionary of Phase and Fable; New York: Harper& Row, 1970

Bynum EB. *The African Unconscious*, New York: Teachers College Press, 1999: 125.

Campbell J. *Primitive Mythology*, New York: Penguin Books, 1969.

Campbell J. *An Introduction*, New York: Penguin Books, 1990.

Choisy M. Psychoanalysis of the Prostitute New York: Philosophical Library 1961

Coetzee PH, Roux APJ. *The African Philosophy Reader.* London: Routledge, 1998

Eze C. *African Philosophy,* Malden, MA: Blackwell Publishing, Ltd., 1998.

Eysenck MW. The Blackwell Dictionary of Cognitive Psyschology Oxford: Blackwell Publishers 1994

Gregory I. Fundamentals of Psychiatry Philadelphia: W.B. Saunders Company 1968

Guiley RE. Harper's Encyclopedia of Mystical & Paranormal Experience. Edison, NJ: Castle Books 1991

Harrison RK. *Encyclopedia of Biblical and Christian Ethics*, Nashville; Thomas Nelson Publishers: 1992, 40.

James GGM. *Stolen Legacy.* Trenton NJ: Africa World Press, Inc., 1954: 88.

Karenga M. MAAT. Los Angeles: University of Sankore Press, 2006

Kenyatta J. *Facing Mount Kenya*, New York: Vintage Books, 1965: 301.

King R. *African Origin of Biological Psychiatry*, Hampton, Virginia: U.B. and U.S. Communications Systems, Inc., 1984.

London P. Beginning Psychology, Homewood, Illinois: The Dorsey Press 1975

Myers DG. Social Psychology 5th ed. New York: Mc Graw-Hill, Inc. 1996

Nelson RS, Shiff R. *Critical Term for Art History.* Chicago: The University of Chicago Press, 1996.

Some` MP. *The Healing Wisdom of Africa.* New York: Penguin Putnam, Inc., 1998: 245.

Ramacharaka Y. *Fourteen Lessons in Yogi Philosophy*, Chicago: The Yogi Publication Society, 1904: 77.

Ramacharaka Y. *Lessons in Guani Yoga*, Chicago: The Yogi Publication Society, 1934.

Runes DD. *Spinoza Dictionary*, Westport, Connecticut, Greenwood Press Publishers, 1951.

Tavis C. Anger; New York: Simon & Schuster 1989

Thorpe LP. The Psychology of Mental Health, New York: The Ronald Press Company 1950

Three Initiates. *The Kybalion.* Chicago: The Yogi Publishing Society, 1940.

Wade C, Tavris C. *Psychology.* New York: Harper Collins College Publishers, 1993, p. 437.

Wiredu K. *A Companion to African Philosophy.* Malden MA: Blackwell Publishing, Ltd., 2004.

Woodson CG. The Works of Francis J. Grimke; Vol. II. Washington, D.C.: The Associated Publishers, Inc. 1942

Index

A

abandonment 50, 51, 267
ability 1, 8, 12, 13, 34, 36, 40, 41, 42, 46, 48, 51, 59, 63, 85, 95, 96, 102, 111, 112, 116, 117, 124, 142, 146, 159, 216, 228, 233, 234, 242, 245, 249, 258, 285, 298, 305, 306, 322, 323, 347, 350, 359, 363
abuse 12, 15, 50, 53, 74, 76, 80, 82, 113, 159, 200, 201, 248, 286, 287, 361
acrobatic maneuvering 4
addiction 82, 83, 87, 98, 99, 133, 141, 200, 201, 214, 327, 337
adversion 278
affections 15, 63, 170, 187, 304, 340
age-grade 192
aggression 8, 59, 69, 75, 112, 131, 184, 187, 210, 215, 219, 221, 222, 224, 263, 265, 270, 284, 288, 289, 353
agitation 2, 3, 72
aliveness 105, 117, 118, 119, 132, 146, 265, 328, 331
alpha 35
amnesia 251
amygdala 12, 35, 37, 137, 157, 159
analysis 63, 85, 98, 251, 306, 316
ancient brain 33, 157
anger 3, 4, 10, 11, 12, 16, 28, 31, 37, 46, 47, 48, 49, 52, 53, 57, 59, 66, 71, 72, 73, 74, 75, 76, 77, 78, 79, 80, 81, 82, 83, 84, 85, 86, 87, 88, 89, 90, 93, 94, 109, 112, 120, 132, 133, 149, 150, 151, 169, 173, 174, 186, 187, 200, 201, 207, 209, 210, 214, 218, 236, 243, 251, 262, 264, 266, 272, 278, 280, 286, 288, 290, 291, 293, 313, 314, 327, 329, 331, 336, 338, 342, 343, 344, 348, 355, 356, 359, 360, 361, 362, 385, 387
anxiety 12, 35, 36, 41, 53, 59, 64, 66, 69, 72, 91, 92, 93, 98, 123, 149, 150, 151, 152, 153, 154, 155, 156, 157, 158, 159, 160, 161, 162, 163, 164, 167, 168, 180, 198, 208, 216, 219, 224, 232, 233, 234, 235, 240, 243, 246, 247, 249, 250, 251, 266, 274, 322, 357
apathy 27, 81, 83, 93, 104, 109, 111, 130, 200, 202, 203, 204, 236, 241, 265, 266, 345, 361
appearances x, 143, 148, 184, 190, 208, 211, 259, 280, 333, 339
appreciate 5, 29, 48, 65, 82, 184, 194, 209, 226, 310
approaches xi, xii, 29, 78, 89, 100, 117, 119, 129, 155, 222, 224, 226, 228, 230, 246, 324, 352, 386, 387
Aristotle 2, 121, 202
arrogance 109, 127, 177, 189, 205, 210
Aryan 1, 2
Athena 348
attacks 28, 51, 63, 65, 159, 209, 211, 224, 282, 330, 361, 385
Aunt Cherry 78, 134
Aunt Julia 78
autonomic nervous system 31, 71, 125, 149, 153
avenge 274, 350
aversion 62, 63, 278
avoidance 133, 138, 154, 160, 248, 291, 342

B

baby blues 111
bad emotion x, 13, 49, 90, 201, 250, 331, 332
baffled 215, 233, 234
bargaining 277
barnyard courts 260
beginning 12, 19, 20, 30, 39, 87, 88, 113, 145, 157, 165, 175, 199, 205, 207, 209, 223, 230, 234, 254, 260, 269, 274, 282, 283, 287, 295, 300, 314, 320, 322, 324, 348
behaviors 3, 8, 13, 15, 16, 25, 27, 32, 33, 34, 38, 40, 46, 47, 50, 51, 54, 57, 59, 66, 72, 74, 81, 93, 94, 105, 115, 117, 143, 145, 150, 153, 155, 162, 165, 166, 168, 180, 181, 185, 188, 213, 215, 221, 240, 249, 250, 258, 259, 261, 262, 266, 274, 276, 277, 286, 289, 298, 306, 307, 317, 328, 335, 340, 342, 344, 352, 353, 355, 364, 367
Being 17, 45, 50, 63, 71, 80, 95, 110, 117, 121, 134,

216, 225, 230, 233, 255, 267, 269, 276, 289, 298, 304, 337, 339, 349, 351, 353
Bellona 187
belong 60, 67, 69, 84, 134, 145, 164, 261, 271, 348, 349
Beowuef 91
beta 18
bias 20, 154, 354
bile 186
black 62, 186, 356
blame 15, 19, 42, 52, 79, 110, 130, 131, 179, 193, 206, 232, 255–259, 262, 317, 327, 346, 351, 359
bliss 132–134, 145
boredom 203, 301
brain/mind 11, 22, 44, 300, 312
brain anatomy 69
brain waves 35
brutes 27, 199
bullies 76, 210, 309
burnout 203
buy your peace 101

C

calculated risks 42, 308, 321
camouflage 4, 254
capacity 8, 31, 40, 48, 95, 125, 127, 139, 141, 198, 206, 301, 310, 347
caste 1
Ch'i 344
chaos 27, 45, 68, 101, 102, 165, 214, 215, 223, 308, 314, 326, 327, 344, 351, 355
child abuse 53
childish 80, 206, 304, 355
choking 151, 159, 232, 288
chronic anger 49, 74, 77, 83, 84, 85, 86, 90, 93, 200, 201, 210, 272, 293, 387
civility 166, 167, 195, 215, 255, 260
clarity 66, 72
classification 68, 78, 152
clinical depression 111
codes of honor 357
commissions 11, 129, 179, 180, 182, 278
compassion 19, 25, 27, 36, 72, 73, 82, 100, 128, 133, 169, 176, 182, 190, 206, 207, 209, 210, 240, 270, 275, 276, 277, 278, 283, 301, 302, 308, 340, 346, 349, 360, 361, 362, 363, 364
competent 162
complementary equals 36, 47
complex 11, 12, 15, 17, 18, 25, 27, 58, 66, 69, 76, 80, 110, 116, 124, 141, 148, 150, 155, 188, 189, 206–209, 215, 217, 229, 230, 244, 254, 263, 266, 272, 282, 291, 319, 320, 343, 361
complex emotions 272, 282, 343
compromise 197, 247, 277
concealed 4, 71, 74, 76, 79, 106, 122, 132, 149, 170, 210, 276
concrete 154, 161, 217, 332
conduct 28, 56, 155, 180, 181, 191, 192, 243, 247, 260, 268, 270, 280, 281, 290, 334
confession 178, 180
conformity 25, 191
confusion 16, 45, 84, 112, 166, 175, 223, 248, 330
conscience 178, 179, 191
constant 12, 21, 54, 79, 80, 126, 210, 215, 224, 233, 273
contemplation 133, 145, 180
contempt 53, 189, 192, 205, 289, 342
contentment 101, 132, 134, 144, 177, 178
control 5, 7, 12, 13, 14, 18, 25, 31, 35, 37, 44, 50, 53, 65, 72, 73, 81, 83, 85, 86, 87, 90, 95, 97, 99, 100, 105, 110, 124, 126, 134, 136, 144, 157– 167, 180, 187, 200, 205, 212, 213, 214, 216, 230, 232, 242, 246, 249, 250, 257, 258, 259, 263, 266, 268, 275, 277, 284, 292, 293, 304, 305, 307, 317, 318, 320, 329, 333, 334, 337, 343, 344, 345, 351, 354, 365, 387
coping mechanisms 8, 196
cortisol 36, 53, 108
courage 29, 71, 93, 95, 96, 99, 154, 156, 201, 241, 246, 307, 308, 309, 310, 321
courteous 255
covetousness 174, 280, 290, 291
crisis 12, 13, 14, 26, 37, 240, 258, 318
criticize 351
crowding 59
cruelty 54, 207, 275, 285, 288, 301
cues 220
curiosity 9, 40, 96, 120, 132, 204, 223, 225, 305
cursing 48, 222
Cybele 185

D

dainty 56
deceit 46, 214, 280
defense mechanisms 20, 50, 131, 152, 154, 161, 196, 197, 198, 213, 218, 226, 235, 236, 238, 250, 278, 343
deflection 255, 262
dejection 105, 119, 204
delusions 87, 112, 120, 142, 168, 177, 189, 200, 211, 212, 213, 214, 238, 243, 268, 279, 365
denial 19, 27, 50, 110, 168, 170, 181, 198, 213, 240, 280, 285
depression 15, 36, 38, 41, 47, 53, 66, 104–120, 146, 149, 150, 155, 158, 169, 170, 173, 175, 180, 193, 203, 204, 209, 215, 218, 219, 224, 236, 257, 265, 286, 291, 322, 324, 325, 330, 331, 345, 348, 361
deprivation 41, 108, 114, 218
desensitization 322, 357
desires 8, 20, 72, 78, 93, 95, 99, 132, 141, 146, 152, 155, 164, 175, 176, 181, 196, 203, 216, 217, 218, 221, 222, 225, 240, 242, 251, 252, 263, 288, 305, 317, 333, 334
despair 37, 71, 106, 111, 118, 203, 204, 349
desperation 141, 203, 204, 347, 349, 356
despise 208, 210
despondency 12, 125, 204, 349
dignified 56, 190
dignity 54, 55, 56, 57, 58, 82, 183, 276, 279, 302, 303, 368
disability 218, 305, 315, 346
disappointments 85, 125, 130, 165, 222, 247
disguise 68, 198, 238
dishonorable 28, 87, 129, 156, 166, 173, 182, 183, 193, 335, 337
dislikes 125, 262, 296
disorder 53, 80, 82, 106, 162, 163, 223, 243
disposition 39, 124, 146, 334
disrespect 54, 57
dissociations 241, 242, 262
distinct 178, 223
distortion 14, 31, 73, 94, 148, 237, 242, 243, 246, 272
dopamine 111
doublet 56
Dr. Jekyll 242
duty 73, 133, 181, 182, 271, 282, 309

E

effectively 172, 177, 215, 247, 304, 366
efficiency 159, 162, 172, 224
egoism 173, 176, 359
embarrassment 165, 166, 167, 168, 192, 198, 240, 248, 272
emergency 12, 34, 37, 49, 87, 101, 131, 159, 198, 229
emotional experience 6, 14
emotional insulation 203
emotional maturity 226, 303, 304, 306
emotional pain 12, 47, 64, 112, 115, 120, 123–131, 146, 150, 165, 170, 173, 185, 187, 191, 193, 201, 209, 218, 224, 231, 236, 271, 283, 291, 331, 356, 357
emotional vocabulary 10
emotive 3
end 5, 21, 25, 26, 28, 31, 33, 35, 84, 117, 129, 141, 145, 181, 190, 209, 216, 226, 228, 230, 241, 243, 260, 269, 273, 278, 279, 285, 292, 307, 316, 317, 327, 334, 335, 336, 345, 346, 348, 354, 385
enemy 7, 8, 10, 18, 55, 91, 100, 254, 275, 276, 277, 284, 298, 343, 366
energy 2, 3, 29, 32, 34, 41, 43, 71, 73, 93, 98–101, 105, 107, 116, 123, 126, 132, 154, 160, 162, 172, 204, 214, 222–224, 227, 235, 238, 248, 251, 265, 266, 267, 270, 271, 277, 302, 310, 313, 314, 338, 342, 343, 350, 354, 359, 361
entitlement 80, 141, 205, 206, 210
envy 5, 19, 28, 46, 52, 63, 170, 171, 172, 173, 174, 185, 186, 187, 210, 224, 269, 271, 272, 280, 281, 282, 283, 284, 289, 342, 348, 359
erosion 64, 346
escape 8, 11, 20, 44, 88, 91, 92, 96, 153, 206, 209, 214, 235, 237, 238, 239, 251, 252, 254, 283, 345, 346
essence 61, 141, 145, 176, 232, 272, 284, 316, 333, 334, 365
esteem 8, 12, 17, 18, 25, 56, 63, 64, 66, 75, 95, 109, 116, 123, 125, 131, 155, 166, 173, 174, 184, 187, 190, 197, 198, 208, 209, 224, 235, 240,

241, 249, 256, 258, 259, 261, 282, 293, 299, 303, 306, 340, 341, 344, 361, 366
ether 43
ethics 84, 334, 335
etiquette 167, 243
euphemistic 259
evil 2, 4, 15, 27, 45, 54, 63, 75, 84, 89, 91, 104, 105, 121, 137, 143, 160, 173, 174, 175, 176, 205, 207, 211, 253, 254, 255, 258, 269, 272, 273, 274, 278, 280, 282, 284, 289, 290, 291, 306, 307, 308, 309, 323, 334, 336, 342, 348, 349, 350, 359, 360, 361
evil eye 273
excuse 28, 76, 175, 272, 332
extreme 11, 17, 25, 26, 27, 46, 65, 67, 71, 72, 77, 93, 94, 106, 112, 128, 152, 160, 175, 183, 187, 188, 193, 203, 214, 217, 218, 234, 238, 248, 251, 263, 276, 280, 282, 283, 287, 289, 339, 345, 357
Exu 359
eye of a needle 177, 211

F

façade x, 173, 190, 211, 355
faculty 137, 143, 221, 245, 276
fancy 244, 245, 246, 304
fantasy 4, 6, 9, 14, 15, 73, 92, 94, 124, 126, 131, 135, 148, 149, 153, 187, 188, 196, 211, 214, 236, 237, 238, 239, 244, 245, 246, 252, 264, 272, 279, 346, 357
fatigue 59, 74, 79, 108, 154, 158, 222, 324
fault 20, 123, 130, 178, 256
fear 3, 4, 10, 11, 12, 16, 20, 21, 28, 37, 47, 60, 64, 66, 69, 70, 71, 72, 77, 80, 81, 91–101, 104, 107, 113, 120, 121, 123, 146, 149, 150, 151, 156, 157, 159, 160, 161, 168, 171, 177, 181, 186, 187, 193, 201, 209, 210, 218, 219, 221, 222, 224, 233, 235, 236, 241, 243, 246, 248, 251, 266, 268, 269, 271, 273, 274, 278, 289, 291, 305, 308, 309, 321, 322, 331, 332, 342, 344, 348, 351, 361, 362
fear of failure 94, 248
feud 49, 102, 274
flatter 341
flaw 17, 18, 19, 52, 184, 197, 293, 329, 330, 362
flexible morals 182, 301
flight 4, 12, 27, 32, 49, 59, 70, 71, 74, 91, 93, 94, 107, 159, 160, 163, 219, 233, 254, 321
folkways 46, 222, 335
fools 189
foresight 34, 96, 112, 141, 212, 239, 325, 351
forethought 34, 112, 141, 239, 257, 351
forgiveness 176, 202, 252, 319, 358, 359, 360, 361, 362, 363
forms 8, 9, 25, 46, 48, 71, 75, 77, 81, 95, 102, 106, 107, 112, 115, 116, 119, 125, 128, 132, 133, 135, 140, 143–146, 154, 157, 171, 173, 174, 201, 206, 209, 233, 238, 254, 255, 259, 276, 281, 282, 285, 286, 293, 329, 330, 333, 341, 352, 353, 358, 385
fraud 46, 165
frequency 26, 70, 106, 173, 217, 221, 365
frontal lobes 12, 34
frustration 15, 49, 50, 52, 59, 64, 69, 78, 84, 93, 130, 150, 165, 167, 181, 187, 198, 203, 209, 210, 214–226, 236, 248, 266, 313, 314, 334, 344, 359, 385

G

gap xi, 9, 94, 272, 357
gentleness 207
gifts 65, 118, 222, 330, 340
glob 4, 70, 118, 200, 213, 214
gluttony 174, 281
grace 58, 179, 202, 224
greed 28, 66, 75, 80, 114, 143, 173, 174, 175, 176, 177, 190, 205, 206, 207, 221, 256, 271, 272, 280, 281, 359
grief 3, 69, 110, 121, 168, 169
group mind 323
grudge 49, 89
guilt 16, 19, 47, 108, 111, 120, 121, 122, 143, 150, 178,–184, 192, 193, 198, 201, 224, 240, 251, 255, 272, 284–286, 289, 320, 360, 361, 362
gun 14, 110, 156, 205, 233, 325

H

habit 65, 66, 72, 83, 96, 98, 124, 146, 151, 167, 177, 183, 200, 201, 209, 225, 236, 239, 260, 266, 275, 277, 294, 309, 313, 320, 329, 330, 343

hallucinations 112, 120, 142, 238, 330
hate 15, 27, 46, 48, 50, 63, 64, 71, 72, 76, 77, 79, 80, 120, 143, 144, 150, 170, 171, 172, 173, 180, 185, 186, 201, 218, 221, 243, 248, 250, 261, 263, 268, 269, 270, 271, 273, 275, 276, 278–284, 290, 291, 336, 339, 342, 359, 366
heart 7, 24, 32, 37, 73, 79, 81, 83, 88, 107, 108, 121, 139, 142, 158, 161, 174, 176, 178, 225, 232, 280, 298, 304, 307, 308, 310, 366
helplessness 37, 64, 83, 110, 112, 200, 203, 209, 257, 258, 287, 345, 346
herd 164, 349
heroes 30, 356
Hetep 132, 139
hippocampus 35, 36, 159
histrionics x, 79, 128
Homo Erectus 242
hopelessness 81, 83, 84, 106, 107, 108, 110, 111, 112, 193, 200, 204, 256, 287, 345, 348
horror 190
hostility 46, 62, 63, 71, 79, 82, 86, 114, 115, 130, 187, 193, 210, 217, 222, 239, 246, 263, 280, 288, 309, 320, 342, 348
humanity 24, 323
human nature 9, 25, 28, 70, 100, 181, 240, 282, 300, 309
humility 58, 190, 214
humors 105
Humpty Dumpty 18, 121
hurt feelings 12, 21, 86, 162, 169, 343, 357, 367
hypersensitivity 125, 232
hypocrisy 261, 334
hypocrites 76, 261
hypothalamus 31, 34, 35, 125, 137
hysteria 127

I

I'll show you 15, 319, 355, 365
ignorance 8, 50, 100, 130, 131, 141, 142, 176, 196, 243, 268, 272, 273, 290, 300, 302, 317, 321, 324, 359, 360, 362
ignored 50, 57, 64, 128, 213, 252, 328
illogical 126, 279, 327, 354
illusions 142, 211
imagination 8, 32, 45, 64, 72, 92, 135, 138, 152, 153, 154, 170, 234, 244, 245, 304, 348
immaterial 143
immediate cause 115, 314, 316
immune system 158, 313
impairment 305, 315
inclination 160, 337
indifference 27, 28, 162, 202, 203, 217, 247, 265, 273, 278, 283
individualism 5, 177, 180, 181, 190, 204, 272, 273, 353
inferior 208, 213, 217, 256, 338
inferiority complex 15, 17, 18, 58, 80, 116, 189, 208, 209, 254, 263, 282, 319, 361
ingratiation 340
inhibition 249, 263
iniquity 178
insecurity 15, 18, 63, 65, 66, 93, 94, 102, 154, 155, 173, 208, 210
instructions 295, 348, 358
insults 76, 81, 123, 218, 220, 222, 357
integrity 49, 101, 112, 146, 183, 194, 261, 303, 355, 356
intemperance 332
intention 161, 178, 232, 350
invertebrates 32
invisible man 267
irrational 91, 94, 102, 126, 150, 154, 160, 167, 187, 188, 250, 279, 327, 354, 355
isolation 15, 59, 60, 155, 204, 222

J

Jann 118, 358
jealousy 4, 46, 170, 171, 172, 173, 185, 186, 187, 188, 238, 271, 272, 281–284, 290, 359

K

karma 176
King, Jr 55

L

left brain 36, 51, 115–117, 283
likes 125, 149, 296
limbic 32, 33, 35, 125, 157
lip service 172
little gods 76, 80, 81, 141, 189, 205, 206, 210, 218, 288

lofty 42, 44, 132, 135, 139, 143
loneliness 128, 222, 337
lower self 75, 208, 343, 359
lucky star 138

M

Ma'at 8, 44, 54, 57, 58, 117, 139, 146, 173, 177, 296, 298, 303, 326, 359, 360, 363, 367
magical minds 123, 146
making do 209
male stoicism 109
malice 174, 275, 280, 281, 282, 283, 342
Mama Clara 78
manage 1, 155, 224, 235, 291, 292, 332
manipulation 100
manners 129, 166, 167, 215, 260, 354
masked 4, 71, 74, 76, 106, 122, 148, 210, 259, 276, 368
masks 76, 110, 177, 201, 253, 254, 323
masochists 285
masquerades 1, 76, 253, 254
master/slave 126, 275
matrix 23, 39, 313, 314
mature 9, 26, 48, 71, 116, 134, 188, 197, 210, 226, 303, 304, 305, 306, 337, 343, 349, 354, 355
melancholic 105, 119
mentally caged 214
mercy 280
methods 1, 13, 55, 65, 66, 81, 105, 118, 120, 124, 129, 133, 171, 174, 175, 176, 180, 193, 201, 207, 209, 259, 274, 283, 294, 311, 319, 326, 340–343, 386
middle 8, 12, 26, 113, 209, 216, 227, 230, 269, 318, 321, 343
Middle Ages 7, 91, 105, 133, 170, 174, 181, 184, 185, 190, 200, 281, 340
Middle Passage 58, 59, 241
Midus touch 176
mild 11, 17, 25, 26, 46, 65, 67, 71, 72, 73, 77, 90, 92, 94, 105, 106, 107, 108, 116, 127, 128, 129, 157, 160, 164, 172, 184, 189, 217, 218, 234, 264, 276, 282, 313, 322, 330, 357
mimicry 4, 76, 254
mind's castle 8
mindset 27, 28, 69, 70, 88, 94, 109, 115, 127, 129, 139, 140, 142, 151, 155, 164, 197, 200, 205, 210, 217, 233– 236, 262, 267, 282, 283, 302, 307, 308, 337, 349, 350, 360, 362, 365
misperceptions 27
moderate 11, 17, 25, 26, 46, 65, 71, 72, 74, 77, 85, 93, 94, 105, 106, 116, 123, 128, 160, 172, 183, 188, 193, 218, 243, 267, 276, 282, 330, 345, 357, 361
Monera 3, 120
morals 46, 180, 181, 182, 183, 289, 301, 334, 335, 341, 362
mores 335
motives 208, 249, 302
mourning 110, 169, 170
mystics 138

N

Narcissus 339
natural emotions 70, 124, 130, 357
Near East 45
negative emotion 271
neglect 28, 50, 182, 348
non-hateful envy 172
normal depression 120
numbness 110, 170, 217, 241

O

obligation 21, 52, 58, 181, 182, 271, 360
OBMER method 231
obscenities 3
obsessions 83, 337
obstinate 349, 350
occasional 225
offensive language 3, 58, 74, 90
Olympus 255
omissions 129, 179, 180, 182, 278
origin 21, 23, 39, 45, 138
ostrich 239
overnight specialist 131
overt 4, 74, 75, 90, 106, 112, 122, 210, 276, 278, 368
overwhelmed 6, 14, 100, 107, 109, 113, 115, 209, 223, 226, 227, 230, 231, 235, 241, 283, 325
oxytocin 38

P

pain 3, 12, 16, 25, 26, 28, 47, 53, 63, 64, 66, 68, 73, 74, 76, 82, 87, 89, 93, 94, 111, 112, 115, 116, 117, 120–134, 142, 143, 144, 146, 150, 158, 159, 165, 169, 170, 173, 185, 187, 191, 193, 195, 200, 201, 207, 209, 213, 214, 218, 224, 231, 232, 236, 240, 242, 246, 249, 251, 271, 275, 280, 283–288, 291, 302, 305, 309, 319, 325, 326, 330, 331, 332, 356, 357, 360–364
Pandora 223, 347, 348
panic disorder 163
passive 48, 66, 76, 81, 83, 131, 202, 220, 282
passive-aggressive 76, 81, 83, 282
patience 4, 85, 86, 89, 182, 204, 270, 276, 277, 346, 349
peace 1, 9, 27, 28, 31, 36, 55, 58, 79, 81, 88, 101, 102, 112, 132, 134, 136, 139, 144, 145, 153, 190, 208, 209, 261, 276, 289, 298, 302, 303, 306, 317, 327, 332, 358, 359, 365
penalty 121, 122, 178, 186, 255, 285, 362
periodic 41, 230
persona 167, 184, 198
personality 16, 102, 130, 165, 218, 254, 259, 367
pettiness 275
phantom 245
philosophy of life 8, 12, 47, 50, 54, 74, 81, 196, 206, 240, 272, 294, 295, 298, 326, 327, 367, 368
phobias 163
Phoenix 101, 330
physical feelings 33, 141
picky people 337
picnics 254
planes of existence 5, 29, 36, 42, 69, 124, 133, 137, 138, 190, 243
planets 43, 104, 138
please 133, 247, 259, 261, 275, 337, 365
pleasure 3, 4, 6, 25, 26, 32, 38, 42, 44, 47, 56, 68, 69, 93, 108, 109, 121, 124, 125, 130, 133–146, 149, 174, 187, 188, 240, 242, 245, 251, 281, 283, 285, 286, 288, 301, 306, 318, 332, 333, 342
poker face 98, 254, 264
polite 164
power approach 318, 326
praise 56, 189, 262, 327, 366
pre-colonial Africans 117
precipitating causes 115
precision 25
predisposing causes 344
prefrontal cortex 34, 35, 157, 159
prejudice 20, 217, 256
pride 1, 60, 174, 183, 189, 190, 191, 192, 205, 212, 272, 280, 342
primary emotions 69, 70, 147
private self 167, 193, 197
problem 13, 14, 20, 21, 23, 31, 34, 35, 42, 51, 52, 65, 80–84, 91, 96, 97, 99, 100, 106, 107, 127, 129, 130, 131, 141, 143, 146, 155, 159, 161, 162, 166, 167, 181, 183, 194, 201, 210, 211, 221, 224, 225, 226, 232, 235, 236, 238, 241, 242, 246, 248, 251, 257, 258, 263, 271, 275, 277, 283, 290, 301, 305, 306, 311, 315, 321, 322, 327, 331, 332, 335, 338, 344, 346, 347, 358, 362, 367
profanity 50
projection 221, 235, 261, 262
prolonged 27, 41, 58, 71, 74, 83, 151, 152, 155, 256, 284, 366
Prometheus 347, 348
psychical feelings 3, 33
psychosomatic 115, 120, 125, 127, 324
psychotherapy 105, 112, 118, 127
psychotics 154, 155, 189
purpose 4, 7, 9, 53, 56, 71, 100, 101, 121, 128, 134, 135, 138, 144, 145, 152, 157, 178, 200, 204, 210, 212, 215, 231, 243, 250, 254, 255, 265, 274, 275, 278, 288, 290, 300, 309, 317, 319, 323, 336, 353, 359, 367

R

racism 62, 77, 112, 113, 115, 128, 242, 258, 261, 279
rage 15, 46, 53, 71, 72, 85, 120, 137, 146, 203, 204, 222, 271, 275, 278, 348
rationalization 235, 262
rational thinking 14, 23, 162, 270, 319, 320
re-enactment 54, 319
reaction-formation 289
real self 115, 116, 336, 339
recurring 83, 155, 225, 347
regrouping 215

rejection 50, 61, 62, 63, 64, 65, 66, 67, 85, 189, 218, 225, 248, 286, 324
Renaissance mind 190
replacement 110, 169, 170, 291, 327, 329, 342
repression 50, 116, 182, 213, 249, 250, 251, 264
reputation 55, 75, 192, 221, 255, 275, 278, 310, 340, 346
resentment 81, 108, 170, 186, 188, 208, 210, 277, 281, 361
reserves 74, 161
resignation 77, 298, 348
respect 19, 54, 55, 56, 57, 58, 67, 70, 102, 106, 123, 131, 137, 139, 143, 155, 184, 190, 196, 198, 208, 226, 231, 248, 279, 302, 332, 363, 367
respectful 57, 164
responsibility 20, 132, 163, 176, 178, 180, 181, 182, 192, 201, 206, 224, 255, 257, 258, 271, 287, 302, 306, 354, 359, 360

retaliation 273, 274, 368
revenge 4, 15, 27, 46, 48, 49, 53, 54, 72, 76, 77, 80, 142, 186, 188, 198, 218, 243, 247, 274, 275, 276, 277, 348, 350, 356, 361
rhythm 44, 144, 327, 341
ridicule 76, 173, 191, 193
right 8, 9, 13, 19, 20, 23, 25, 26, 29, 35, 36, 37, 40, 41, 44, 47, 51, 52, 57, 58, 62, 72, 79, 88, 95, 115–117, 127, 131, 136, 140, 143–145, 151, 152, 161, 162, 166, 167, 175, 180, 182, 183, 184, 188, 191, 213, 218, 228, 232, 240, 244, 249, 256–258, 271, 273, 277, 285, 290, 294, 302, 303, 306, 308, 309, 310, 323, 327, 328, 330, 331, 335, 337, 346, 352, 353, 362
right brain 36, 51, 115, 116, 117
righteous indignation 278
road rage 222
royal courts 259, 340

S

sacrifice 137, 174, 178, 286
sadist 63
sadness 36, 104, 107, 108, 110, 112, 121, 149, 150, 168, 231
safety 26, 48, 53, 59, 91, 94, 101, 112, 139, 146, 150, 152, 209, 234, 239, 309, 346, 347
saving face 167
scapegoats 76, 80, 210, 255, 256
scarcity 175, 177, 243, 368
scars 15, 18, 50, 53, 83, 85, 126, 232, 357
second nature 9, 207, 267
security 27, 53, 92, 93, 101, 113, 139, 146, 150, 151, 152, 153, 188, 209, 224, 234, 239, 331
self-awareness 181
self-concept 17, 18, 50, 122, 123, 125, 130, 167, 183, 184, 195, 197, 238, 240, 250, 266, 331, 356, 357
self-condemnation 362
self-confidence 18, 64, 95, 109, 155, 188, 197, 208, 224, 248, 249, 258, 309, 320, 344
self-control 81, 85, 86, 97, 200, 250, 277, 307, 333, 351
self-correction 67, 87, 180, 226
self-discipline 9, 46, 81, 86, 277, 304, 307, 333, 351
self-disgust 285
self-efficacy 344
self-esteem 8, 12, 17, 18, 25, 63, 64, 66, 75, 109, 116, 123, 125, 131, 155, 173, 184, 187, 190, 197, 198, 209, 224, 235, 240, 241, 249, 256, 258, 259, 261, 282, 293, 299, 303, 306, 340, 341, 344, 361, 366
self-forgiveness 202, 361, 362, 363
self-fulfilling prophecy 123, 361
self-fulfillment 182, 271
self-knowledge 44
self-love 41, 126, 209, 302, 361, 366
self-pity 15, 130, 165, 185
self-preservation 3, 4, 24, 25, 26, 33, 69, 70, 255, 282, 300, 308, 343
self-protection 8, 36, 70, 71, 73, 124, 131, 196, 254, 264, 267, 288, 304, 357
self-respect 184, 190, 198, 302
self-responsibility 180
self-talk 52, 60, 61, 64, 320, 327, 328, 361, 366
self-trust 18, 151, 183, 302, 362
selfish 21, 22, 24, 25, 26, 28, 29, 53, 85, 92, 132, 135, 170, 171, 187, 278, 281, 283, 333, 340, 350
selfless service 144
sentiments 43, 104, 116, 117, 119
serotonin 12, 38, 109, 111, 159, 163, 169
Set 45, 359

sets 18, 101, 106, 179, 238, 313
seven moral virtues 290
shame 5, 16, 47, 155, 165, 166, 180, 181, 183, 184, 189, 191, 192, 193, 195, 198, 224, 240, 251, 272, 285, 320
shell-protection 254
shutting down 278
shy 160, 181
sick pleasures 143, 333
sin 121, 176, 178–181, 189, 191, 231, 238, 291, 359, 360
slight 11, 17, 25, 26, 46, 65, 67, 71, 72, 73, 74, 77, 90, 92, 94, 105, 106, 116, 123, 128, 129, 160, 164, 172, 184, 218, 220, 264, 267, 276, 282, 283, 330, 357
smiling 76, 86, 89, 173
social anxiety 167, 168
socialization 134, 171, 190, 215, 218, 276, 286, 289, 295, 296, 352
soul 44, 104, 133, 204, 259, 280, 310, 352
source 3, 21, 22, 23, 24, 43, 45, 67, 76, 79, 85, 119, 120, 130, 142, 165, 174, 175, 178, 181, 186, 207, 217, 230, 242, 244, 268, 277, 300, 312, 339, 359, 366, 367, 368
spider web 123, 152, 153
spinning top 305, 352
spiritual pain 16, 28, 53, 63, 64, 82, 94, 115, 116, 120, 143, 170, 191, 195, 200, 201, 214, 236, 249, 271, 275, 283, 284, 287, 331
standards 57, 59, 64, 80, 142, 179, 180, 181, 290, 294, 335, 336
star 104, 138, 142, 183, 262
steadiness 308
stress curve 157, 158
stubbornness 80, 82, 210, 287, 320, 337, 349, 350, 351, 352, 353, 354, 355
subjective 104, 230, 244, 268
sublimation 291, 342
Sublime 3, 5, 6, 31, 34, 42, 43, 44, 55, 69, 96, 133, 136, 137, 138, 143, 269, 300, 302, 332
substance 61, 82, 113, 159, 200, 214, 329
suffering 28, 53, 68, 73, 100, 110, 120, 121, 127, 128, 163, 166, 173, 201, 206, 207, 209, 231, 232, 240, 271, 273, 283, 285, 287, 288, 302, 305, 322, 339, 340, 359, 360, 362, 363, 364
suppress 263, 264
surprise 3, 79, 137, 149, 150
suspicion 93, 186, 187
swearing 3, 183
sympathetic nervous system 34, 73, 74
sympathy 21, 76, 202
syndrome 107, 157, 208, 324, 355
system 8, 13, 15, 29–34, 37, 52, 59, 62, 64, 71, 73, 74, 76, 84, 87, 104, 108, 116, 121, 124, 125, 133, 143, 149, 150, 153, 155, 157, 158, 159, 172, 179, 197, 200, 215, 241, 251, 254, 256, 259, 266, 268, 269, 270, 274, 278, 279, 281, 289, 293, 296, 302, 313, 338, 352, 353, 355, 361, 365, 367, 385, 386, 387

T

tarda 296
target emotions 17
techniques 14, 34, 81, 129, 186, 194, 198, 236, 249, 259, 289, 317, 322, 326, 340, 355
temperament 35, 39, 107
temperance 53, 332, 333
tempered 4, 71, 74, 75, 90, 106, 122, 148, 149, 210, 276
temper tantrum 78, 314
temporal lobe 71
terror 91, 94, 288
tertiary emotions 149
Thanatos 290
the projects 48
therapy 105, 110, 119, 120, 159, 160, 161, 163, 324, 325
theta 36
third candle 88
Titan 16, 20, 21, 51, 52, 104, 257, 290, 316, 364, 365, 366
tolerance 4, 85, 86, 89, 182, 200, 204, 216, 217, 220–226, 270, 276, 277, 333, 335, 336, 346, 349
tools 1, 1, 21, 54, 119, 216, 233, 292, 307, 322, 327
tragedy 12, 231, 241
trained right brain 115, 116, 117
transition 43, 121
treatment 53, 78, 109, 110, 111, 113, 118, 119, 120, 155, 160, 161, 163, 164, 176, 201, 217, 232, 233, 287, 288, 289, 292, 293, 305, 315, 322,

324, 331, 351
trickery 360
trigger 12, 14–18, 27, 38, 49, 51, 63, 66, 67, 70, 72, 73, 76, 80, 81, 85, 88, 125, 126, 156, 157, 159, 163, 168, 201, 202, 221, 223, 233, 252, 262, 265, 313, 314, 319, 320, 322, 330, 367, 368
trigger emotion 16, 49, 51, 63, 66, 67, 367, 368
trigger flaws 18
turf 59, 274, 275

U

unnoble loyalty 80, 82
untrained right brain 116, 117

V

value 20, 27, 49, 55, 56, 61, 66, 67, 81, 95, 102, 105, 106, 125, 135, 136, 139, 142, 143, 146, 172, 173, 179, 184, 190, 194, 197, 198, 208, 209, 210, 216, 217, 223, 265, 266, 282, 285, 289, 296, 302, 303, 319, 361
values 8, 9, 20, 26, 29, 48, 49, 58, 64, 77, 100, 105, 124, 125, 139, 146, 155, 177, 192, 197, 198, 216, 218, 221, 222, 256, 262, 270, 284, 289, 293, 296, 298, 318, 326, 353, 354, 365
vanity 189, 214
vengeance 53, 274
vices 174, 181, 190, 291, 343, 348
vindictiveness 275
violence 9, 50, 66, 74, 75, 91, 203, 220, 227, 254, 285, 287, 288, 318, 343, 359
vulnerable 11, 89, 208, 241, 282, 330, 344, 356

W

"WE" 26
weak people 63, 337
Wholism 90, 101, 298, 301, 302, 324
wickedness 54, 178
win-win 4, 29, 35, 48, 164, 206, 340
winner 29, 130, 160, 206, 318
wishes 20, 238, 246, 252, 264
withdrawal 98, 109, 111, 202, 215, 219, 248, 254, 265, 266, 267
word infusions 233
worldview 84, 112
worry 91, 107, 151, 152, 158, 163, 210, 232, 233, 234, 235, 243, 357
worth 20, 27, 41, 55, 56, 61, 66, 67, 81, 89, 95, 102, 105, 139, 143, 145, 161, 162, 173, 184, 194, 197, 198, 208, 209, 210, 211, 212, 215, 223, 225, 256, 285, 289, 296, 302, 303, 304, 319, 330, 344, 347, 349, 358
wounds 50, 53, 86, 123, 126, 130, 165, 218, 344, 356, 357
wrong 8, 16, 18–21, 26, 41, 42, 63, 64, 72, 79, 80, 88, 102, 121, 123, 127, 128, 131, 142, 165, 166, 167, 179–184, 191, 192, 193, 194, 206, 212, 213, 215, 231, 249, 255, 258, 274, 277, 300, 327, 333, 335, 337, 342, 347, 352–355, 358, 361

Y

Yin/Yang 23, 143, 144

Z

zeal 185, 186, 187, 188
Zeus 71, 347, 348

ABOUT DR. BAILEY

Born 70 years following the end of African American slavery and living in the USA South, Dr. Bailey grew up among wonderful people in all-Black communities. His "thinker and Doer" mind was fashioned by constantly being in nature (gardening, the Boy Scouts), by reading, by humor, and by an absence of anger, fear, or hatred. But this pleasant atmosphere profoundly changed to a hostile atmosphere once he left the South to pursue his education and training as a physician inside a Euro-American setting.

Besides newly developing bad emotions induced from racism, there were frustrations related to career pursuits. He creatively handled and channelled those emotions and frustrations in socially acceptable ways. This was necessary in order to stay focused during medical emergencies; during times of demanding work while overwhelmingly fatigued; during depositions and court room scenes run by arrogant aggressive attorneys; and during times of tremendous personal problems. These controlled reactions to personal attacks and his refusal to be baited off the path of his goal constructively expanded Dr. Bailey's character. Success in these areas meant that he could better understand the emotions of those struggling people who were inclined to "give up" on life.

Compassion for the truly needy has motivated Dr. Bailey to devise many forms. One form is the mentoring and holding of work shops for struggling youth over the last 25 years. A second form is setting up "all for one and one for all" programs as, for example, Cub and Boy Scout troops. A third is as an educator of youth, parents, and youth leaders in churches, Boys and Girls Clubs, in the University system, and individually. Particular attention is paid to shedding self-defeating emotions and returning to Ancient African Values.

Fourth is published writings—in medical journals of a non-orthopaedic (on Self-Esteem) and an orthopaedic nature (e.g. numerous orthopaedic articles; in inventions of appliances and operations; in medical textbooks as a world authority on Disproportionate Short Stature and a Medical-Legal Dictionary); in 17 published books directed toward struggling Black Americans; in weekly "Family Talks" as a columnist in Black newspapers for over 13 years; and in his popular website: jablifeskills.com.

Fifth is Dr. Bailey's donation of a building to house a Black American Museum in honor of his Dad—Joseph A. Bailey, Sr. Sixth was funding a Los Angeles Accelerated School for elementary minorities as well as a Charter College of Education project to develop educational materials for inner city youth. Seventh was establishing an endowed chair pertaining to the American Communities Program and also to the African American Experience—both at California State University Los Angeles.

Other Books by Dr. Bailey

I Am a Special Somebody is for anyone having strayed away from his/her destination in life and yet still possesses the intense desire to get back on the path and then head toward happiness.

Self-Esteem in Black Americans presented from a historical perspective, is extensively discussed from the dawn of mankind to the present. Nine major syndromes prominently found in Black people are featured—and with suggestions on how to improve each.

Echoes of Ancient African Values discusses who Ancient Africans were as a people; their genius and creative ways of thinking; their philosophical and spiritual foundations; their world shaping achievements; and how these echo into today's Black Americans.

Preparing to Prepare (iUniverse.com) is about implanting seed ideas of a good character nature. Lesson plans are plentiful to serve as a guideline for stimulating ideas and methods to help youth achieve their dreams and talents for a balanced, mature, and wealthy life.

Good Character (trafford.com) explains the history of 50 traits and discusses in practical terms the skills needed to instill or develop good character. These traits are fundamental for achieving a successful and happy life.

Becoming a Champion Somebody provides the "nuts & bolts" of choosing ones legacy dream, discovering ones talent, and becoming a successful person. The approach a systematic 9 step process— called the 9Ps—is based on practical experiences of many people. It is designed to help youth in identifying and pursing their goal in a way that applies to any career or for adults keen on achieving even greater success.

American Crime From A Black American Perspective points out the USA conspiracy against Black males; exposes who the real (non- Black) criminals are; and explores in detail the course of Black males likely to be pushed into and then be destroyed as they go through the unfair prison system.

Manhood in Black Americans classifies the nine broad types of manhood and gives approaches and methods to structuring male children and restructuring the orientation of youth who are off the path that is best for them. Both are mainly directed toward single mothers.

Afrocentric English and Critical Thinking is a book designed for making these subjects more interesting for Black youth from a Yin/Yang perspective. This traces the history of African languages through Europe and on into the Americas up to the present. A full discussion is given on Black English, Ebonics, and the special ways

Black Americans use both. The stories of 25 key words required for formal English are given.

Enslaved Minds in Black Americans starts with their origin in slavery and with contributions from "bad" African retentions. Numerous patterns of enslaved minds are then given (e.g. procrastination), with extensive comments on their diagnoses and management.

Common Sense inside African Tradition centers on how it developed and was used by Ancient Africans and how it can be developed and used in Black American children. For this to happen requires the cultivation of pure feelings and poetic thinking of African Tradition. The approaches for teaching are out of mathematics, art, literature, and games.

Anger in Black Americans is the primary emotion related to racism. Though entirely justified, it is self-destructive for daily living. This book points out why and offers a variety of detailed management approaches for a variety of chronic anger types—approach which have a track record of effectiveness.

Creativity, Invention, and Discoveries emphasizes ways to cultivate each in children, reactivate them in those who have fallen into a rigid predictable pattern of living, and remove limitations on those desiring to explore new worlds. Methods are presented for practical application on how to see the uncommon in the common and the common in the uncommon.

Rising Above Poverty is about changing the belief system of those who chronically struggle in life. For Black Americans this means switching from an Enslaved Mind belief system to that laid out in African Tradition because its brilliance has stood the test of time. This switch is followed by correcting self-defeating bad habits which are spin-offs from bad beliefs.

Selfhood Mastery Inside African Tradition is a guide for creating, enhancing, and maintaining the Inner Strength and Inner Peace that leads to contentment and happiness. It emphasizes stabilizing your inner self and maintaining it by Mental Toughness in order to remain in control and be alert while dealing with life's most difficult problems.

ORDER FORM

Title	Publisher	Quantity	Unit Price (USD)	Sub-total
Preparing to Prepare	iUniverse 1-800-288-4677		$27.95	
Echoes of Ancient African Values	Authorhouse 1-888-280-7715 x 5216		$24.95	
Good Character	Trafford 1-888-232-4444		$25.50	
Self-Esteem in Black Americans	WingSpanPress WingSpanBooks.com		$19.95	
I Am a Special Somebody	WingSpanPress WingSpanBooks.com		$19.95	
Becoming A Champion Somebody	WingSpanPress WingSpanBooks.com		$19.95	
American Crime	WingSpanPress WingSpanBooks.com		$19.95	
Manhood in Black Americans	WingSpanPress WingSpanBooks.com		$19.95	
Afrocentric English and Critical Thinking	WingSpanPress WingSpanBooks.com		$19.95	
Freeing Enslaved Minds of Black Americans	WingSpanPress WingSpanBooks.com		$19.95	
Common Sense Inside African Tradition	WingSpanPress WingSpanBooks.com		$19.95	
Anger in Black Americans	WingSpanPress WingSpanBooks.com		$19.95	
Creativity, Invention & Discovery	WingSpanPress WingSpanBooks.com		$19.95	
Rising Above Poverty	WingSpanPress WingSpanBooks.com		$19.95	
Selfhood Mastery Inside African Tradition	WingSpanPress WingSpanBooks.com		$19.95	
			S&H	
			Total	

*** * Books can be reviewed on www.jablifeskills.com**

1) From the author: jab2md@yahoo.com
   - Discount offered for bulk sales.
   - Shipping and Handling determined by quantity of sales

2) From the publisher (see above)
3) From Amazon.com

Printed in the United States
104081LV00004B/15/P